KNOWLEDGE MANAGEMENT SYSTEMS FOR BUSINESS

Robert J. Thierauf

Q

QUORUM BOOKS
WESTPORT, CONNECTICUT • LONDON

Library of Congress Cataloging-in-Publication Data

Thierauf, Robert J.
Knowledge management systems for business / Robert J. Thierauf.
p. cm.
Includes bibliographical references and index.
ISBN 1–56720–218–7 (alk. paper)
1. Management information systems. I. Title.
T58.6.T475 1999
658.4'038—dc21 99–10405

British Library Cataloguing in Publication Data is available.

Library of Congress Catalog Card Number: 99–10405
ISBN: 1–56720–218–7

First published in 1999

Quorum Books, 88 Post Road West, Westport, CT 06881
An imprint of Greenwood Publishing Group, Inc.
www.quorumbooks.com

Printed in the United States of America

The paper used in this book complies with the Permanent Paper Standard issued by the National Information Standards Organization (Z39.48–1984).

10 9 8 7 6 5 4 3 2 1

Contents

Figures

Preface

To face the continuing challenges placed on business organizations in these fast-changing times, decision makers are utilizing a wide range of information systems to improve their decisions. On-line analytical processing (OLAP) systems, for example, enable them to build and work with analytical models easily and view the output in multiple dimensions. Although OLAP tools allow decision makers to see new relationships in a way that was not possible previously, the focus is on showing them what has happened in their business. What is needed are systems that go beyond relationships found in information and allow decision makers to extract patterns, trends, and correlations that underlie the interworkings of a company. As such, these systems should be able to tap into the collective knowledge of the company's employees. This is the approach found in a *knowledge management system* (KMS), where information is the raw material of knowledge. Information over time can be turned into important knowledge for decision makers.

In the past, systems for business have focused on selected *data* within a certain *context* to produce *information*. A better approach is to take *information* accompanied by *experience* over time to generate important *knowledge*. In addition, knowledge that is renewed and enhanced can be a creative source to outmaneuver competition.

Knowledge management systems center on a structure that effectively leverages a company's knowledge capital. These systems are capable of managing knowledge assets to optimize their value and provide a good return on investment. Even though knowledge management systems may sound like "the new kid on the block," their underlying concepts date back at least a decade. Search-and-retrieval software, data warehousing, and the proliferations of intranets, to name a few, have revolutionized the ability of organizations to find, accumulate, organize, and access information as well as knowledge. The bottom line is that effective knowledge management, like effective management of any kind, starts with a strategy. The focus of that strategy is on making knowledge available to company employees in the right format and at the right time and place to make even better decisions than was possible in the past.

An important theme of knowledge management systems found in this text is that *knowledge is power*. This translates into satisfied customers, improved marketing efforts, effective production methods, just-in-time inventory control, and more profitable operations. Knowledge that is developed constantly, renewed where necessary, and applied where applicable is an important source of competitive advantage. The more a company's employees use knowledge, the more they contribute to a company's overall well-being. Companies that really succeed have greater expertise than their competition. Utilizing some form of internal and external computer networks, a company can enhance the knowledge of its personnel and support them with software that encapsulates knowledge. Thus, for knowledge management systems to be successful, there is a need to create an infrastructure to capture and create knowledge, store it, improve it, clarify it, disseminate it to all employees, and put it to use on a daily basis.

Not only is this book designed for company managers, it is also written for information systems professionals and end users. Company managers (i.e., decision makers) will be particularly interested in installing their own systems or assisting in their installation somewhere in their companies. End users in the various functional areas of a typical company can also benefit from the text. Information systems professionals will find the text helpful for understanding one of the most important developments in systems for decision makers and how to build knowledge management systems. Furthermore, it should be noted that the book is quite suitable in an academic environment—that is, an undergraduate or graduate-level course covering the fundamentals of knowledge management systems.

The structure of this text follows a logical order for a complete treatment of knowledge management systems. The topical areas that are illustrated by real-world applications where appropriate are as follows:

Part I: Knowledge Management Systems for Business in the 21st Century. In Chapter 1, the emergence of knowledge management systems, which are an outgrowth of data processing and management information systems, is explored in some depth. In addition, the utilization of knowledge to help gain competitive advantage for a typical company is discussed. Chapter 2 sets forth a framework that underlies knowledge management systems found in business. The tie-in of knowledge with problem finding (which includes uncovering future opportunities) along with a company's critical success factors is also covered.

Part II: The Essentials of Knowledge Management Systems for Business. The types of databases, along with data marts and data warehouses, are explored in Chapter 3, with emphasis on building an effective data warehouse. This material is complemented by the use of data mining to discover new knowledge about a company's operations. Chapter 4 centers on sharing knowledge in a typical company through the use of its own network communications infrastructure (i.e., intranets and extranets) as well as the Internet. In Chapter 5, software found in knowledge management systems is the subject matter of the chapter's first half. In the second half, key steps in implementing successful knowledge management systems are detailed along with their continuing support.

Part III: Typical Knowledge Management Systems Found for Functional Areas in Business. In Chapter 6, important strategic planning principles that underlie knowledge in this functional area are explored, followed by important factors that are useful in discovering strategic planning knowledge. Strategic planning areas that lend themselves to discovering knowledge are set forth along with typical applications. The remaining chapters follow a similar format. That is, Chapters 7, 8, 9, and 10 explore underlying principles and factors that are related to knowledge management systems for marketing, manufacturing, finance, and human resources, respectively. In turn, representative applications of these systems are presented to demonstrate their usage on a continuing basis.

For a project of this magnitude, I wish to thank the many professionals who have assisted me. First, I would like to thank the many vendors who have supplied materials that have been included throughout the text, especially Angoss Software International Limited. Second, my graduate students at Xavier University who have expressed a need for a book of this type are to be commended for their helpful suggestions. For the most part, these students who are employed full time by a wide range of organizations in various industries throughout the Midwest are computer professionals. Third, I am especially thankful to Mr. Larry Schwalbach of R&L Management, Inc. for assisting me in getting a handle on knowledge discovery (i.e., data mining) software. Fourth, but not least, a special note of appreciation is in order to Mr. Eric Valentine, publisher of Quorum Books, for his encouragement and suggestions in this project that impacts the 21st century.

Abbreviations

ABC	activity-based costing
AI	artificial intelligence
AID	Automatic Interaction Detector
ASRS	automated storage and retrieval system
ATM	asynchronous transfer mode
BASIS	Battelle's Automated Search Information System
BISDN	broadband integrated services digital network
BLOBS	binary large objects
BP	British Petroleum
CAD	computer-aided design
CAM	computer-aided manufacturing
CAMS	Computer Aided Maintenance System
CART	classification and regression trees
CASE	computer-aided software engineering
CBT	computer-based training
CCITT	Consultative Committee of International Telegraph and Telephone
CD-ROM	compact disk–read-only memory
CEO	chief executive officer
CGI	Common Gateway Interface
CIM	computer integrated manufacturing
CIO	chief information officer
CKO	chief knowledge officer

COMMS	customer-oriented manufacturing management software
CPA	certified public accountant
CRT	cathode ray terminal
CSF	critical success factor
CSO	Computer Systems Organization
DBMS	database management system
DDP	distributed data processing
DES	Data Encryption Standard
DOS	disk operating system
DP	data processing
DSS	decision support system
EDI	electronic data interchange
EEO	Equal Employment Opportunity
EIS	executive information system
EOQ	economic ordering quantity
ERP	enterprise resource planning
FAQ	Frequently Asked Question
4GL	fourth-generation language
GB	gigabyte
GBP	Global Best Practices
GDP	gross domestic product
GDSS	group decision support system
GIF	Graphical Interchange Format
GUI	graphical user interface
HBO	Home Box Office
HD	hard-disk drive
HDTV	high-definition television
HP	Hewlett Packard
HR	human resources
HRMS	human resource management system
HTML	Hypertext Markup Language
HTTP	Hypertext Transport Protocol
IDS	Information Discovery System
IP	Internet Protocol
IPS	idea processing system
IS	information system
ISDN	integrated services digital network

ISV	integrated software vendor
IT	information technology
JAD	joint application development
JIT	just-in-time
KB	kilobytes
KISS	keep it simple, stupid
KMS	knowledge management system
KPI	key performance indicator
L&D	logistics and distribution
LAN	local area network
LP	linear programming
MAN	metropolitan area network
MB	megabytes
Mbps	megabits per second
MDD	multidimensional database
MES	manufacturing execution system
MIS	management information system
MOLAP	multidimensional on-line analytical processing
MPP	massive parallel processing
MRP	material requirements planning
MRP-II	manufacturing resource planning
NC	network computer
NCA	network computing architecture
NCOS	network computer operating system
NCRP	Network Computer Reference Profile
ODBC	open database connectivity
OLAP	on-line analytical processing
OLTP	on-line transaction processing
ONA	open network architecture
OO	object oriented
OOAD	object-oriented analysis and design
OODBMS	object-oriented database management system
OOP	object-oriented programming
ORB	Object Request Broker
OSI	open systems interconnection
PAN	Practice Area Network
Pawws	Portfolio Accounting World-Wide Service

PC	personal computer or microcomputer
PIMS	Profit Impact of Marketing Strategies
POS	point-of-sales
PPI	purchase performance index
PQL	Pattern Query Language
RAD	rapid application development
RAID	Redundant Array of Independent/Inexpensive Disks
RAS	reliable, available, and scalable
RDBMS	relational database management system
ROI	return on investment
ROK	return on knowledge
ROLAP	relational on-line analytical processing
ROM	read-only memory
SAM	Strategic Analysis Model
SAS	Statistical Analysis System
SCM	supply chain management
SMP	symmetric multiprocessing
SPIN	Supply Partner Information Network
SQL	structured query language
TCP/IP	transmission control protocol/Internet protocol
3-D	three-dimensional
TQM	total quality management
VAN	value added network
VAR	value added reseller
VB	Visual Basic
VLAN	virtual local area network
VLDB	very large database
VR	virtual reality
VRML	Virtual Reality Modeling Language
WAN	wide area network
WBT	web-based training
WMS	wisdom management system

PART I

Knowledge Management Systems for Business in the 21st Century

1

Introduction to Leveraging Knowledge in Business

Issues Explored:

- Why do changing times demand more innovative approaches to business systems, such as knowledge management systems?
- What is the rationale for including knowledge as a major resource of a typical company?
- What is the relationship between learning organizations and leveraging knowledge?
- How are knowledge management systems tied in to past and current information systems?
- What is the relationship between knowledge management systems and OLAP systems, expert systems, and neural networks?

Outline:

Changing Times Necessitate More Innovative Approaches to Business Systems

  A Broad-Based Approach Using Knowledge Management Systems

Relationship Among Data, Information, and Knowledge

  Shifting Paradigm to Knowledge

  Broad-Based View of Knowledge

  Beyond Knowledge

Employment of a Learning Organization to Leverage a Company's Knowledge

  Creating a Knowledge Infrastructure

  Need for a Chief Knowledge Officer (CKO) to Oversee a Company's Knowledge Infrastructure

Utilization of Knowledge to Leverage a Company's Position

  Gaining Competitive Advantage

CHANGING TIMES NECESSITATE MORE INNOVATIVE APPROACHES TO BUSINESS SYSTEMS

For all sized organizations, change will be a constant in the next millennium. Technological advances, including non-technical ones, are coming more quickly than ever before, thereby affecting all aspects of a typical company. As network computing technology progresses, there are increasing pressures to create a new type of workplace. The current workplace will experience a transition that will fragment it into myriad on-site and off-site offices. Not only will the work environment change dramatically in the 21st century, but there will also be a need for business systems to support the new work environments.

More specifically, there will be a need for new types of systems that focus on discovering knowledge that responds to the changing environment. Although past and current information systems have served the needs of management and operating personnel, newer types of business systems, such as those stressed in this text (i.e., *knowledge management systems* [KMSs]), will be at the forefront of these newer types of systems found in a typical company. An important goal of knowledge management systems is to provide competitive advantage by giving decision makers (from the highest level to the lowest level) the necessary insight into patterns and trends that affect their domain. In effect, a broad-based KMS environment challenges decision makers to evaluate changing times more thoroughly. Such an environment allows decision makers to tailor their information and related knowledge requirements by discriminating according to user-defined criteria.

Essentially, a knowledge management system is capable of making comparisons, analyzing trends, and presenting historical and current knowledge. But more importantly, such a system enables decision makers to analyze and understand the patterns quickly and identify the most significant trends. As such, it is an accurate predictive method for decision makers. In addition, a knowledge management system can track and evaluate key critical success factors for decision makers, which is valuable in assessing whether or not the organization is meeting its corporate objectives and goals. Overall, a knowledge management system can assist decision makers in making better informed decisions that affect all aspects of a company's operations.

As will be seen in this chapter and future ones, past management information systems basically used the computer as a means of providing information to solve recurring operational problems. A better approach today, however, is the utilization of knowledge management systems to position decision makers at the center of the decision-making process. By increasing the capabilities of decision makers, a KMS environment improves the chances that an organization will achieve its goals of increased sales, higher profits, and so forth by placing knowledge and related information in the hands of decision makers at the proper time and place and by providing flexibility in their choice and sequence of analysis and in the final presentation of results. From this enlarged perspective, knowledge management systems provide essential knowledge and related information to decision makers so that they can better cope with changing times. This chapter gives not only a background on the essentials of knowledge, but it also highlights the important features of knowledge management systems that will be examined in more detail in Chapter 2. Additionally, there is a tie-in between knowledge management systems and past and current management information systems, with emphasis on OLAP (on-line analytical processing) systems, expert systems, neural networks, and virtual reality systems.

A Broad-Based Approach Using Knowledge Management Systems

Fueling the interest in knowledge management systems is the prospect of going beyond the traditional approach to actually finding out what went wrong. In the past, a management information system told the decision maker *what had happened, but not why and what should be done*. The focus, then, has shifted to finding out why and what can be done to meet and possibly beat competition.

Figure 1-1
Relationship of Data to Higher Levels of Summarization

Level of Summarization	Definition	Problem Importance	Decision Approach	Nature of Problem
Truth	Conformance to fact or reality	Critical	Consensus	Structured to unstructured
Wisdom	Ability to judge soundly	Critical	Consensus	Unstructured
Knowledge	Obtained from experts based on actual experience	Major	Advisory Group	Semistructured
Information	Structured data useful for analysis	Major to minor	Advisors	Structured and semistructured
Data	Unstructured facts	Minor to trivial	Individual	Structured

In a few words, "what" is not satisfying—that is, it only provides the decision maker with an opportunity to solve today's superficial problems—whereas "why" and "what should be done" help the decision maker get to the root of the problem in order to prevent future occurrences.

To place a knowledge management system in its proper perspective, consider an investment bank. In the world of investment banking, there are many sources of power, such as a large amount of available investment capital or the ability to be all things to all people. Another important source of power is knowledge. By focusing on its substantial resources in a number of rapidly changing industry sectors—for example, computer technology, health care, financial services, and transportation—the investment bank strives to maintain an in-depth industry knowledge that gives it a competitive advantage. From this perspective (whether individual, institutional, corporate, or municipal), this superior knowledge from a knowledge management system is helpful in understanding a customer's needs and in providing creative ideas and effective solutions to the problems at hand.

RELATIONSHIP AMONG DATA, INFORMATION, AND KNOWLEDGE

To show the relationship among data, information, and knowledge, reference can be made to Figure 1-1, which shows important factors about each of these levels. *Data* represents the unstructured facts and figures, which have the least impact for the typical manager. It is the "data soup" of information processing at the lowest level. Due to the proliferation of data, it is sometimes referred to as "dataglut." Many decry the dataglut as distracting, confusing, and not helping the typical manager. Generally, the ability to prioritize and rank data decreases in direct relationship to the amount of data being used. While there is still some work to be done at the data level, the typical manager has moved well beyond data tabulation to the information level.

At this next level, *information* is structured data that is useful to the manager in analyzing and resolving critical problems. In the past, a typical company is said to have had *five* major resources: men (i.e., people), machines, money, materials, and management (the five Ms). More recently, information has been added as the *sixth* resource. However, within the context of information technology, many companies regard such technology as an overhead expense, not as a valued asset. It is time that these misconceptions be turned around and that organizations can actually lower their costs, increase profits, or enhance their market image through the latest information technology (IT) advancements.

Today, it is recognized that *quality and timely business information* is among a manager's most important resources. This vital business asset has been generally undervalued, underestimated, and underused. A major problem facing a typical manager is the volume of information crossing his or her desk. It can be so voluminous that it becomes almost unmanageable; yet good planning and control over operations via effective decisions must be based on a steady flow of good-quality, up-to-date information. Given these conditions and the accelerating pace of business changes, there arises a definite need to change the working habits of managers. A human-computer dialogue should not impede their thought processes, but rather it should augment their capabilities and become an extension of their minds. From this view, the computer is an important means of providing essential information to the manager. It should be noted that the wealth of information available today can, at times, impede a manager's decision-making capabilities rather than simplify them. From this broadened perspective, there may be a need to move on to the next level.

At the next level, there is *knowledge*, which is obtained from experts based upon actual experience. In order to see patterns and trends that enable a manager to make the transition to insight and prediction, there is a need to integrate a range of information. Essentially, this is the function of broad-based knowledge management systems that go beyond expert systems as found in the past. For an example of this type of system, reference can be made to a consulting firm or a CPA firm where knowledge can be gathered and disseminated to clients.

Basically, information can become knowledge in the hands of an expert. A body of information organized into a coherent framework forms the basis for the creation of knowledge. For example, an annual report forms the body of knowledge for financial accounting. Typically, knowledge about a company's financial position is impossible without a framework to organize ratios derived from accounting data and information in the balance sheet, income statement, and cash-flow statement. Knowledge comes from insight and understanding of the underlying structure of financial information. It requires expertise to interpret financial results in a creative way. Overall, while information is data about the data, knowledge is basically information about information.

Shifting Paradigm to Knowledge

In a typical organization, there is valuable information out there just waiting to be tapped: information about what customers like about a company's goods and services, what non-buyers do not like, and how customers view a company's competitors. Today, this goes beyond just information. This represents a shifting paradigm to knowledge, which goes much deeper into the distilled essence of customers' and employees' personal experiences. Such ingrained smarts can benefit an organization vastly more than just information by itself. Yet this kind of knowledge is rarely shared, even among peers. Also, such knowledge typically never reaches top executives. However, a few companies are involved in the full utilization of knowledge in terms of their everyday operations. For example, the mission of DataTimes Corporation (Oklahoma City) is to deliver business information services to business professionals through a variety of distribution channels. DataTimes's EyeQ on-line network is one of America's top electronic networks for businesses, with more than 5,000 sources (real-time news wires, newspapers, magazines, broadcast transcripts, financial and company reports, regulatory filings, and much more) available for searching and retrieval.

Broad-Based View of Knowledge

Before knowledge can be developed and harnessed as a competitive tool and an important business resource, it must be extracted from the great assimilation of daily activities and data and turned into useful information. Information needs to be related to business needs and then distributed to appropriate executives and managers who will act on it. In turn, translating information into knowledge means more than summarizing information on a periodic basis—daily, weekly, or monthly. It centers on detecting important trends and patterns that are relevant to the organization. In some cases, this means identifying important milestones that affect the direction an organization should take today and tomorrow. From this broad perspective, knowledge centers not only on identifying important changes that are related to important opportunities facing a typical organization, but also on helping the organization's executives identify important problems (i.e., trouble spots) that need to be addressed immediately for solution. As will be seen in the next chapter and future ones, this takes the direction of *problem finding* (forward looking) as opposed only to *problem solving* (backward looking).

To illustrate this broad-based view of knowledge, reference can be made to Hewlett-Packard (HP). This company has always been a knowledge-based organization. The company's mission statement centers on creating information products that accelerate the advancement of knowledge and improving the effectiveness of people and organizations. Because of its ability to deliver on that promise, Hewlett Packard has been and continues to be a leading global manufacturer of computing, communications, and measurement products and services. Also, it has earned wide recognition for excellence in quality and support. In all HP product areas the goal is the same: to provide people with the tools they need to convert information into knowledge. HP's Computer Systems Organization (CSO), which focuses on systems solutions, software platforms, and consulting and integration services, is a good example of the company's leadership position in delivering high-end knowledge solutions. In essence, Hewlett-Packard has maintained strong momentum and growth over the years, and part of that success is due to its accumulated knowledge, which has given the company the ability to anticipate market trends and customer needs and develop solutions that deliver improved performance.

Beyond Knowledge

At the second highest level in Figure 1-1 is *wisdom,* which is the ability to judge soundly. This high level of understanding involves such philosophical attributes as the awareness that the models constructed will not always hold true. Wisdom requires the intuitive ability, born of experience, to look beyond the apparent situation to recognize exceptional factors and anticipate unusual outcomes. Largely untapped today, wisdom is a vital organizational resource, accumulated through experience and applied in everyday learning at work. Essentially, wisdom is a personal capacity acquired through experience and thinking. As such, wisdom can be used as an organizational strategy to develop human potential in organizations. There is a tendency to replace past hierarchical and functional roles with learning relationships that focus on wisdom as the foundation of the new organization. Typically, a wise manager knows what knowledge or know-how is needed in a given situation and knows how to renew that knowledge by working with others to solve a problem or achieve a goal.

Truth, the highest level in Figure 1-1, is conformance to fact or reality and represents the lofty pinnacle of understanding. Although its place in the typical organization is being debated at this time, it is safe to say that certain truths centering on ethical and environmental issues are always useful to the typical manager and help guide a company at all times. A violation of basic truths held by the general public can only jeopardize a company's standing in the community. Going beyond the truth found in the business community, one enters the realm of truth found in the religious community. To the ultimate degree, truth is equivalent to God.

Basically, an analysis of Figure 1-1 emphasizes that generally decisions with the most significant ramifications for the operations of a company tend to have characteristics that are most suited to a participatory decision-making process. The decisions that are best made by an individual manager do not appear, in general, to have as wide-ranging or overall an organizational impact. Hence, the implications of this figure is that group decision making is the way to promote quality decision making in many business situations. As the environment becomes more complex, the typical decision makers will have to call upon more resources if effective decision making is to prevail. Studies have shown a relationship between characteristics of decisions and the nature of the decision-making process. Decisions have been found to be more participatory when decision quality and user acceptance are important. Participation is also preferable when the problem is complex or unstructured. Studies have shown that decisions are found to be less participatory when the manager has all the necessary information, the problem is routine or structured, or time is limited and immediate action is required.

EMPLOYMENT OF A LEARNING ORGANIZATION TO LEVERAGE A COMPANY'S KNOWLEDGE

Currently, many experts believe that failing to make use of knowledge can have harmful long-term effects on corporate health. The basis of a new and often revolutionary model for organizational growth and survival is one that seeks to gain competitive advantage from intellectual capital the way earlier models drew profit from investment capital, and later from information technology. Whatever it is called, the *learning organization* promises to sweep away structures and assumptions long ingrained within the top-down, bottom-line driven organizations of the 20th century. This newer direction of the learning organization—to leverage knowledge for gaining competitive advantage—will be a major driving force of the 21st century.

Although there is disagreement among the experts concerning its various aspects, most view a learning organization as one that develops over time and is linked with knowledge. In addition, its performance improves over time, which can be linked to improved financial performance. In terms of knowledge acquisition and use, a learning organization is skilled at acquiring and utilizing knowledge and, at the same time, at modifying its operations to reflect new knowledge and insights. Peter Senge, who popularized learning organizations in his book, *The Fifth Discipline*, described them as places "where people continually expand their capacity to create the results they truly desire, where new and expansive patterns of thinking are nurtured, where collective aspiration is set free, and where people are continually learning how to learn together."[1]

Today, a typical company uses approximately 20 percent of its intellectual capital. If, through a learning organization approach, a company could raise that to 30 percent, that would represent a 50 percent gain in some of the company's assets, such as knowledge experts. For example, the Corporate Strategy & Alliance Group of Digital Equipment uses a team learning process called "deep diving" that leverages from Digital employees knowledge they have had for years but never truly shared. In effect, the power of knowledge in the organization is now being more effectively realized than in the past.

Another example is the Polaroid Corporation where teams are asked to pretend to be working for competing firms in order to reveal Polaroid's own potential weaknesses. Outside dealers, customers, and industry friends are also invited into some of the exercises. People became so involved in this process that they are asked to enact what they know and feel. In other words, they are told not just to give suggestions, as, for example, a chief executive officer would. Needless to say, this process demands openness. If people are brought together to share what they know and describe what should change, they have to feel comfortable throughout the process.[2]

While learning organization advocates leave no doubt about the importance of the free expression of ideas, organization experts note that the exchange must be tempered for maximum efficiency. The value of knowledge is in its use and not in its collection per se. That is, it is important not to collect and save every bit of information but to relate what is known and not known to *what needs to be known* to fulfill organization objectives and goals. Thus, organizational knowledge of relevant information that is known by individuals needs to be shared to make decisions. In this manner, knowledge can be leveraged by a learning organization for best results.

Creating a Knowledge Infrastructure

Creating a knowledge infrastructure for a learning organization or otherwise does not happen overnight for a typical organization. It requires time and an organizational plan. Because large amounts of knowledge can come from learning groups once the participants are comfortable, there is need to get the commitment of senior management. Without it, it will be very difficult to tackle the massive cultural changes that are required to get an organization to embrace the idea of sharing and reusing knowledge.

Building incentives for adding to a company's knowledge base is one way to gain commitment from organizational personnel. Another important item is to demonstrate to the ''feeders''—the organizational experts who will actually capture the knowledge for the infrastructure—that they, too, will benefit from contributing their know-how. If the feeders make their expertise more accessible in a central, organized repository, they can spend less time helping people and more time on their own work. They may also be able to extend their own skills by tapping into the knowledge infrastructure.

Frequently overlooked are the people who are critical of creating a knowledge infrastructure. It is highly recommended that they be involved from the start in building the infrastructure itself. It is helpful to advertise early successes. In that way, everyone will be more likely to support continued work on the knowledge infrastructure when the benefits of sharing expertise start to crop up. Due to the importance of building an effective knowledge infrastructure, it is tied in with an organization's data warehousing operations, which are discussed in Chapter 3. The subject of sharing knowledge through network computing is covered in Chapter 4. Additionally, the knowledge infrastructure is discussed further in Chapter 5.

Need for a Chief Knowledge Officer (CKO) to Oversee a Company's Knowledge Infrastructure

To assist in building and maintaining a knowledge infrastructure in a typical company, there is a need for a chief knowledge officer (CKO) who has the power and clout to develop and place knowledge at every worker's fingertips. Corporate titles such as chief knowledge officer, chief learning officer, and even chief transformation officer are multiplying as fast as the books that push strategies for success in the information age. Among the corporate giants that have named chief knowledge officers or their equivalents are Coca-Cola, Monsanto, and IBM.

The premise behind the boom in harnessing knowledge is this: employees possess a wealth of knowledge and experience about their company, from its products, customers, and competitors to its production processes and internal technology. But much of that knowledge is held in bits and pieces by various individuals or sections of a company. If these bits and pieces could be gathered and distributed throughout the entire company, this shared knowledge would be a powerful force. Workers can use the pool of information to create competitive advantages and thereby increase revenue. A company, for example, might discover that a process used in one sector can have applications in another. Or a company representative, using all of the company's knowledge about its customers, could make a superior presentation to the client, helping to secure a contract.

Among the first companies to assign top-level managers to address knowledge management directly were professional services firms such as Ernst & Young, Coopers & Lybrand, and Andersen Consulting. After programs were developed for the consulting firms themselves, the firms then found a lucrative business in helping other companies that wanted to leverage their knowledge but did not have the in-house expertise. Continuing advances in databases and computer networks are making such knowledge projects possible. As will be seen starting in the next chapter and throughout the text, computer networking technologies are providing the basis for the creation of ''knowledge bases,'' ''knowledge webs,'' and ''knowledge exchanges.'' Although it takes more than just sophisticated technology to make such systems work, sifting, editing, and updating knowledge turns out to be a management rather than a technology challenge. And, more important, it takes a manager to ensure that workers are inspired to contribute to the knowledge base and share it.[3]

UTILIZATION OF KNOWLEDGE TO LEVERAGE A COMPANY'S POSITION

If a company truly leverages its knowledge, it should be able to accomplish three goals. *First*, knowledge should make the organization more responsive to rapidly changing competitive conditions. In this way, new opportunities can be more quickly exploited and competitive vulnerabilities can be reduced. *Second*, knowledge allows managers and their staffs to evaluate a company's critical success factors more thoroughly. These factors are the ones that can make or break any company. *Third*, knowledge should enhance the internal efficiency and productivity of the organization, with emphasis on managerial productivity. This includes better coordination of the organization's functional components such as sales and marketing, manufacturing and production, distribution support and service, finance and accounting, and personnel and administration.

Gaining Competitive Advantage

From past surveys of American competitiveness, the consensus is that U.S. competitiveness has deteriorated and that diminished competitiveness will hurt America's economic performance for the foreseeable future. The net result is that the current situation represents a threat to the company's standard of living and economic power. In light of these comments, there is a need for organizations "to shift gears" by employing knowledge technology to gain a competitive advantage. It is the job of information systems management, working with top management, to bring about the needed change in the *competitive landscape* by employing the proper approach to organization-wide computing activities.

Essentially, an important thrust of this text is on the latest direction in information systems (i.e., knowledge management systems) to gain competitive advantage. Knowledge that is constantly renewed and enhanced can be looked upon as an important source of competitive advantage. Similarly, network computing is changing the parameters of competition in every industry whether it is manufacturing or service oriented. Formerly, information technology was directed toward being a "storekeeper" of data and information. In today's fast-changing world, knowledge technology has the capability to facilitate change so that the organization remains competitive. The importance of knowledge technology (including its related information technology) as a competitive weapon for furthering the organization's objectives, goals, and strategies is equally applicable to the small, medium and large company.

Currently, many companies do not view information or knowledge technology investments as creating a competitive advantage. In any industry, competitors have access to the same technology and can make investments at the same relative level. The difference in performance lies in the way the technology is used to enable and support competitive advantage. Additionally, many companies believe that the period of cost advantage as the basis for competitive advantage has passed. Companies now must look at core competencies and use technologies to get a hold on their knowledge assets and make use of them. For example, because Wal-Mart can squeeze many dollars out of its distribution costs, it can sell products at a lower price than Sears. In a similar manner, if the Japanese can make their manufacturing even more efficient, they can get the edge on the Americans and Europeans. On the other hand, if the Americans and

Europeans can out-innovate the Japanese and add some interesting and needed new features, consumers around the world will buy American and European. The bottom line is that a typical company needs to capture and deploy its knowledge assets to gain competitive advantage.

Evaluating a Company's Critical Success Factors Thoroughly

Although the typical manager undertakes a number of roles, the accent in this text is on relating decision making to *problem finding* in order to expand the manager's view of how problems can be solved and how new opportunities can be identified for implementation. In the process of making a wide range of decisions, there is need for the manager to take into account the organization's critical success factors (CSFs)—that is, those factors that are critical in making or breaking the organization. The process of identifying CSFs was originally defined by John Rockart of MIT in the late 1970s. (A rich discussion of these CSFs will be given in Chapter 6.) At this point, it is sufficient to say that there are a specific and limited number of areas in which satisfactory results will dramatically affect the competitive performance of an organization. Typically, these areas are the ones to be measured and evaluated. As the old saying goes, ''If you can't measure, you can't manage.'' Similarly, ''What you measure wrong, you manage wrong.'' Establishing the wrong measures will lead to far worse results than establishing no measures at all.

Depending on the strategic direction of an industry and the specific organization, there are different ways of managing change and reshaping a business. The CSF process identifies what these specific needs are. In turn, various types of information processing systems can be used to monitor these CSFs. Within the context of a knowledge management system, CSFs can be evaluated more thoroughly over time such that their analysis leads to new and different ways of exploring opportunities for a company. This enlightened approach can result in leveraging a company's CSFs for its betterment. Thus, by using a CSF process, a knowledge management system can provide access to broad-based views of knowledge that allow company managers and their staffs to direct present and future operations in a more effective manner.

Improving Managerial Productivity

Improving managerial productivity relates to gaining competitive advantage and evaluating a company's critical success factors thoroughly. Discussions have generally ignored productivity of managers at the top. Attention has focused on assembly-line robots or the implementation of the paperless office, whereby the productivity of individual workers at the lower levels of an organization is increased. However, when viewed from a strictly financial perspective, the productivity of labor and clerical workers is only one element in achieving organization productivity. The financial community measures productivity in terms of return on stockholders' equity, return on capital, and other financial tests. If the management of an organization decides to launch a new product which the customer will not buy, it is irrelevant whether the workers actually assemblying the product are performing their jobs efficiently. Having the right product at the right time, however, has a much greater impact on organizational productivity than gaining an incremental improvement in labor or clerical productivity.

Because a manager makes decisions and not products per se, his or her productivity is measured by the quality and timeliness of those decisions. Accepting the fact that management decisions are generally more important to organizational productivity than the automation of lower-level work leads to the conclusion that managerial productivity is worthy of a great deal of time, attention, and money. As will be seen later in the chapter, the problem with past information systems was that there was plenty of data, but the data became information only when it was gainfully employed in supporting decision making. However, when information is broadened over time to become useful knowledge, managerial productivity can receive an important boost.

ESSENTIALS OF KNOWLEDGE MANAGEMENT SYSTEMS

An underlying framework for knowledge management systems consists of: (1) the use of problem finding and its related techniques to get a handle on present and future problems as well as to identify future opportunities; (2) a knowledge infrastructure that is related to very large databases, data warehouses, and data mining; (3) network computing that ties in with a company's intranets and extranets as well as the Internet; and (4) a wide range of appropriate software that is quantitatively and statistically oriented. All of these essential elements of knowledge management systems are noted below.

In terms of the *first element*—the use of problem finding and its related techniques—the focus is on determining present and future problems along with identifying future opportunities that come from uncovering problems. In the next chapter, not only are the types of problems identified, but also specific problem-finding techniques are set forth. In turn, the two approaches to the problem-finding process (i.e., the problem-centered approach and the opportunity-centered approach) are given. These two approaches precede the traditional problem-solving process for solving structured, semistructured, and unstructured problems. All aspects of problem finding and its tie-in with knowledge and critical success factors are found in Chapter 2. The *second element*—an introduction to building a knowledge infrastructure—was covered in a separate section above, with further elaboration to come in the next several chapters.

The *third element*—the use of network computing that ties in with a company's intranets, extranets, and the Internet—has the capability of changing the workplace; that is, changing the way companies deal with their customers, suppliers, and employees. If applied properly, sophisticated network computing can help companies make their operations a lot simpler. In effect, network computing provides a road to the future by allowing companies' information systems to talk to one another. Electronic data interchanges enable businesses to streamline support operations or hand them off to outsiders. This is transforming how companies define themselves and how they deal with their customers and suppliers. At the same time, network computing is allowing the dissemination of important knowledge to the appropriate parties whether they are within or outside the organization. This important area of network computing and its integration with knowledge is also discussed in Chapters 2 and 4.

The *fourth element* of knowledge management systems focuses on the use of appropriate software to collect data, information, and knowledge; the search for knowledge that is needed; and the sharing of results with other people. This topic is covered in some depth in Chapter 5. It is sufficient to say here that there is a wide range of software packages today to meet most users' needs.

An overview of knowledge discovery within a KMS environment is found in Figure 1-2. Essentially, the *first phase* centers on the preprocessing of data and information—that is, the selection of appropriate data and information along with its necessary cleaning. In the *second phase*, there is the processing of data and information using appropriate tools to find useful trends, patterns, rules, etc. This phase goes by the name of knowledge discovery or data mining. A wide range of software is typically employed that includes knowledge extraction tools, knowledge management software, knowledge management–intranet search engines, knowledge discovery or data mining software, on-line analytical processing software, and statistical analysis tools. As will be illustrated in several future chapters, KnowledgeSEEKER enables users to analyze knowledge quickly and understand the patterns and important relationships. It is also useful as an accurate predictive tool. Essentially, KnowledgeSEEKER allows the user to look at all of the information and tells the user what the most significant trends and patterns are. In the *third* phase, there is the interpretation and dissemination of knowledge to the proper parties.

Based on the foregoing elements, a knowledge management system centers on the organization, codification, and dissemination of knowledge in an organization. As such, it represents a collaborative work environment in which organizational knowledge is collected, structured, and made accessible organization-wide to facilitate better and faster decision making. Basically, a knowledge management system is designed to capture appropriate knowledge in order to manage a company more effectively. Because a knowledge management system takes a longer time frame into consideration, it provides a broader view of the organization than was possible with past information systems. The end result is that there is a focus on knowledge that can be used to improve the effectiveness of a company's decision makers.

Figure 1-2
Overview of Knowledge Discovery Within a KMS Environment

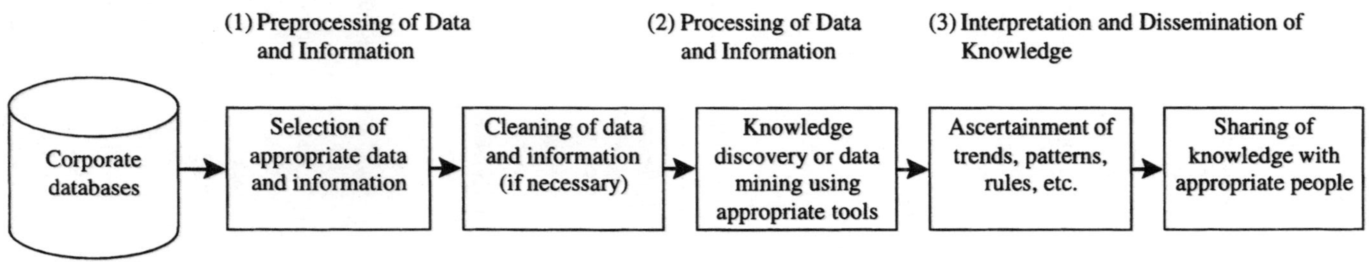

A TYPICAL APPLICATION OF KNOWLEDGE MANAGEMENT SYSTEMS

Dow Chemical serves as a good example of a typical KMS application. The company wanted to see if it could earn additional money from its tens of thousands of patents. The company's chief knowledge officer got each of Dow's 15 major businesses to catalog their patent holdings in a standard format. He then cross referenced them. The result was more licensing deals with other companies and new revenue as the company identified new markets for products it had already developed. When Dow's epoxy business in Freeport, Texas, cataloged its 3,500 patents, for example, it realized that its production process for bisphenol (a material used in resin) could be marketed to other companies. Dow is now licensing the process through a partner.

Typically, patents, trademarks, and copyrights are easy compared to the intangible know-how that makes a company competitive. In a pilot project involving three of Dow's businesses, the chief knowledge officer brought together heads of the units, along with research engineers, manufacturing managers, patent attorneys, and marketing teams to identify the 200 to 300 most important technical processes at Dow. To document these processes, the teams used a template similar to the one used in the application process for patents. The result provided important know-how that company professionals needed to have (i.e., the four to five keys to their business). In many cases, that key know-how is the reason why Dow is in that business. This represents not an end point, but provides a springboard to capture Dow's marketing, sales, and customer knowledge. In the end, all of this key know-how gives Dow a competitive advantage articulated and databased. Once this knowledge is measured and visualized, it can form the basis for improvement.[4]

PAST AND CURRENT MANAGEMENT INFORMATION SYSTEMS

Having set forth an overview of broad-based knowledge management systems, it would be helpful to look at the development of management information systems over the years. Past and current management information systems (MISs) that influenced today's knowledge management systems indirectly are integrated management information systems,[5] real-time management information systems,[6] and distributed management information systems.[7] Continuing developments in MISs will be explored in the next sections of this chapter. For the most part, these systems center on processing a company's mission-critical applications. The term *critical* generally refers to applications without which the business could not continue to operate. Essentially, integrated, real-time, and distributed MISs center on producing periodic reports designed not only to recap past operations with an accent on exception items but also to pinpoint possible control problems about current and upcoming operations for lower and middle management. Although these factors represent improvements over prior information systems, they can be viewed from a *two-dimensional framework*—that is, the computer gives a periodic answer that is indicative of what should have been done or what should be done to control operations. However, in this fast-changing world, there is need to bring in a *third-dimensional* viewpoint—namely, that of the decision maker, who brings personal judgment, expertise, and the like to bear on the whole process. From this broadened perspective, the manager is able to get a macroview of the problem.

CONTINUING DEVELOPMENTS IN MANAGEMENT INFORMATION SYSTEMS

Because the preceding systems are rather narrow in their perspective (two-dimensional framework), a much broader perspective (three-dimensional framework) is found in such systems as decision support systems (DSSs). A DSS allows managers and their staffs to be at the center of the decision-making process as changes occur through the use of computer-query capabilities to obtain requested information. This is in contrast to relying on periodic control reports, for the most part, as found in previous management information systems. In the discussion that follows, decision support systems are viewed from an individual and a group perspective, and their tie-in with executive information systems (EISs) is also addressed. Additionally, idea processing systems (IPSs) and on-line analytical processing (OLAP) systems are considered to be an extension of DSS and EIS. Often these systems are publicized as the DSS/EIS/OLAP continuum that is related to idea processing systems. This tie-in should be obvious in the discussion that follows. However, the utilization of an underlying framework—namely, electronic data interchange (EDI) systems and image processing systems—is presented first.

It should be noted that many other types of information systems could have been included below. These could have included multimedia systems, voice recognition systems, visual information retrieval systems, geographic information systems, fuzzy systems, and choatic systems. Space limitations narrow the range of information systems presented below. However, knowledge-based systems, commonly known as expert systems, neural systems, and virtual reality systems, are discussed later in the chapter as is their tie-in with a KMS environment.

Electronic Data Interchange Systems

Electronic data interchange systems represent the exchange of documents and transactions by a computer in one company with the computer(s) of one or more other companies in an open-system environment. Prior to EDI, the data flow focused on paper documents. The paper documents, for example, were mailed by the buyer to the seller, and the seller moved the paper documents to the proper departments for appropriate processing. In turn, the buyer undertook the necessary processing as well as the receipt of the goods. In contrast, the application of EDI involves the conversion of a written document into a machine readable form so that a computer in one company can communicate directly with the computer of the other company. Generally, the bulk of these documents relate to events that would generate input transactions for accounting systems to be processed into information.

EDI transmissions go from application to application between buyers and sellers without human intervention. An EDI system is involved in electronically exchanging purchase orders, invoices, payments, shipping notices, and similar transactions. In the process, staffing needs are cut by reducing paper handling, reducing errors and eliminating the need to rekey data, and improving transaction turnaround time. The net result of utilizing an EDI system is a computerized exchange of business documents in a specific format between companies. Fundamentally, an EDI system can be defined as a computer-to-computer exchange of routine paper documents, such as purchase orders, material releases, or receipt advices, by one company with other companies. This computerized information is transmitted in a standard format between a company and other companies. In an EDI system, electronically transmitted data replaces paper documents throughout a company's transaction cycle.[8]

Today, models for business-to-business communications encompass much more than traditional EDI. Through intranets and extranets, companies are automating the entire supply chain, such as business to supplier, business to consumer, and business to payment system. The focus is on reducing costs found in complex processes and sharing information across systems. Extranets encompass any area where companies open up their intranets or create encrypted secure 'tunnels' on the Internet to conduct business. Basically, tunnels are secure pathways that use two-key encryption systems to protect sensitive information. Going beyond intranets and extranets, companies are using the Internet to allow trading partners direct connections to their internal networks, eliminating the need for a value added network (VAN). This approach represents a fast-growing form of EDI since it allows trading partners to avoid VAN transmission charges and monthly maintenance fees. As companies move more into the 21st century, the focus of EDI will be on electronic systems that support interentity computing within and outside a company.

Image Processing Systems

From another perspective, electronic processing can be viewed only from within the organization—called *image processing systems*—whereby electronic imaging is used to replace paper-intensive information systems. From an overall standpoint, there is an advantage to automating existing business processes with image processing systems. The present method of paper processing is replaced by capturing all data initially in an electronic form. All subsequent processing refers to the same electronic images. But there is a need to go a step further. There is need to find applications for image processing that transform the business.

Organizations that have faced up to the issue of their survival can be very innovative in changing their business culture. For example, the Xerox Corporation revolutionized its own methods of designing and manufacturing copiers when extreme competitive pressures came from Canon. Companywide integration and systems coordination is another key to improving customer service and guaranteeing success. Procter & Gamble pulled together under the umbrella of ''product delivery'' three separate functions that covered suppliers, manufacturers, and finished goods delivery. In effect, image processing systems can offer a competitive edge while also making employees more productive.[9]

Decision Support Systems

Essentially, an individually oriented *decision support system* is designed to satisfy the needs of a manager at any level in a distributed data processing environment. The system is designed to support the problem-finding (future problems related to the present) and problem-solving decisions of the manager. It incorporates features found in management information systems and in quantitative models of management science. Such a system emphasizes direct support for the manager in order to enhance the professional judgment required to make decisions, especially when the problem structures tend to be semistructured and unstructured. The use of interactive systems and CRT displays in a decision support system are examples of this point. Emphasis is placed on helping the manager to make decisions by being at the center of the decision-making process rather than on actually making decisions for the manager. This interplay results in a total effort that is greater than the manager or computer operating independently (as in traditional MIS), thereby providing *synergistic decision making*. Also, information is presented in a useful form rather than as a mass of all information that might be useful. From this perspective, an individually oriented decision support system builds on present management information systems as well as complements them.[10]

Since there is a move toward *group decision support systems* (GDSSs), there is a need to define such an approach. Fundamentally, group decision support systems combine computers, data communications, and decision technologies to support problem finding and problem solving for managers and their staffs, which may also include operating personnel in the newer work environments. Technological advancements, such as groupware electronic boardrooms, local area networks, teleconferencing, and decision support software have spurred an interest in this area. In addition, fundamental changes in the external environment of organizations are encouraging organizations to head in this direction. Typically, organizations are currently experiencing the emergence of a postindustrial environment characterized by greater knowledge, complexity, and turbulence. One important effect of this trend is that decision-related meetings are becoming more frequent and more important. At the same time, the decisions confronting groups are becoming more complex and must be made more quickly and with greater participation than in the past. As part of the transition into this new environment, organizations are exploring advanced information technologies that might be employed in group meetings. Overall, group DSS has the capability to allow marketing executives, for example, to outmaneuver their competition and assist in resolving issues that center on making employees more productive.[11]

Executive Information Systems

To a degree, *executive information systems* (EISs) are an extension of DSS. EIS is used mostly for highly structured reporting, sometimes referred to as status access. DSS has become almost synonymous with modeling and unstructured, ad hoc querying. Executive information systems are aimed at senior executives who currently have few, if any, computer-based systems to assist them in their day-to-day responsibilities. EIS brings together relevant data from various internal and external sources, delivering important information quickly and in a useful way. More important, it filters, compresses, and tracks critical data as determined by each executive end user. EIS performs the conceptually simple task of informing senior executives on matters relevant to their organizational responsibilities. Unlike traditional MIS functions that focus on the storage of large amounts of information, EIS focuses on the retrieval of specific information and on status access. The emphasis is on reducing the time and effort that the executive user must expend to obtain useful information for making the organization more competitive and its employees more productive.

An executive information system can be defined in its broadest sense as one that deals with all of the information that helps an executive make strategic and competitive decisions, keeps track of the overall business and its functional units, and cuts down on the time spent on routine tasks performed by an executive. As such, an EIS is capable of providing an executive with the right information in the right format, fast enough to enable the individual to make the right decisions.[12]

Idea Processing Systems

Generally, *idea processing systems* (IPSs) are considered to be related to decision support systems. Some in the field consider them a subset of group DSS. No matter how idea processing systems are looked upon, they are essentially systems designed to capture, evaluate, and synthesize individual ideas into a large context that has real meaning for decision makers. From this perspective, idea generators are generally used to assist in the idea formulation stage. To better understand this type of system, it would be helpful to examine initially the meaning of ideas. An *idea* can be thought of as a formulated thought or opinion. Ideas spring from knowledge that is essentially derived from observation of the environment in which one lives as well as from an awareness of one's internal emotions and feelings about these observations. Knowledge implies more than observations of past experience. It also includes some form of interpretation of past experience. Ideas can be thought of as the conscious expression of these interpretations.

The basic stages of an idea processing system center on *inputs* in the form of a problem statement and an observation about the problem. *Processing* involves idea generation and evaluation of ideas for solving the problem. The end result is *outputs* (i.e., report preparation and dissemination of information about specific ideas to solve the problem). Regarding idea generation, the behavioral sciences have not been able to explain how a person's mental process operates nor how a person's knowledge is organized. However, there is ongoing research by behavioral psychologists as well as by computer scientists who are attempting to imitate such functions by a computer. Needless to say, idea processing systems are a natural for helping management and their staffs in gaining competitive advantage and improving employee productivity.[13]

On-Line Analytical Processing (OLAP) Systems

Related to decision support systems, executive information systems and idea processing systems are on-line analytical processing (OLAP) systems. These systems focus on asking and answering "what happened" to operations. Multidimensional analysis capabilities are a most important part of OLAP systems. Multidimensional analysis goes beyond the traditional two-dimensional analysis. Essentially, it represents an important method for leveraging the contents of an organization's production data and other data stored in company databases and data warehouses because it allows users to look at different dimensions of the same data—for example, by business unit, geographical area, product level, market segment, and distribution channel. As such, OLAP makes it easier to do analyses that cross departmental and even corporate boundaries. Another way of viewing OLAP is getting a typical company out of the custom report writing business and into the data cube server building business. An OLAP data structure can be thought of as a Rubik's Cube of data that users can twist and twirl in different ways to work through "what happened" scenarios to get at the real issues of the situation.[14]

RELATIONSHIP OF OLAP SYSTEMS TO A KMS ENVIRONMENT

Current OLAP tools have proven their value in providing a multidimensional view of summarized data. This will be evident in Part III of the text (Chapters 6–10) where multidimensional analysis will provide a starting point for knowledge discovery within a KMS operating mode. Although OLAP tools meet many needs, they do not allow for the analysis and understanding of individual customer behavior at the transaction level. The reason is that OLAP tools, both those implemented on top of relational databases (ROLAP) and those implemented on the top of multidimensional databases (MOLAP), center on aggregating and summarizing data. Although aggregated data can provide trend analysis information, it is not actionable at an individual level. For example, knowing that 5,000 products were sold does not help a company's decision makers to focus on individual customers. It is knowing who those 5,000 customers are that can help decision makers to get at the underlying profiles and possible motivation for buying a company's products or services. From this broader view, knowledge discovery is needed to complement the information found within an OLAP system that decision makers have discovered by ''slicing and dicing'' through reams of data rapidly.

Comparison of OLAP Tools to Knowledge Discovery or Data Mining Tools

Because knowledge discovery or data mining tools are complex and sophisticated mathematical and statistical methods, they complement but are different from existing OLAP software which tells decision makers what happened in their business. On the other hand, knowledge discovery focuses on telling them why. With knowledge discovery tools, new patterns, trends, and correlations are uncovered by sifting through a large store of detailed data. Guided by the way the problem is set up, the software discovers significant relationships that often let decision makers get a better understanding of business results by examining the *why* of the problem under study.

In the past with most decision support systems, the software did not do the discovering, the user did. The user posed a hypothesis about the business, created a set of complex queries to test the hypothesis, and saw if the data supported it. This was a highly interactive and uncertain process that required a highly knowledgeable person. In addition, it could only answer the questions one knew enough to ask. In contrast, a knowledge discovery approach answers questions the individual did not know enough to ask. It identifies new categories of customers for targeted marketing or customer retention programs, discovers questionable billing practices and credit card frauds, and defines a profile of high-performing stocks, among other tasks.

Overall, OLAP tools are capable of assisting decision makers in answering specific questions under study while knowledge discovery or data mining tools are capable of uncovering patterns that can lead to discovering new knowledge. Typically, knowledge discovery tools can be looked upon as the next step beyond on-line analytical processing for querying data warehouses. Rather than seek out known relationships, they sift through data for unknown relationships. Using knowledge discovery tools, the decision maker can, for example, come up with a model to find who are the most profitable customers. In turn, more traditional OLAP analysis of that subset of data can be used to see what the impact would be if those customers were lost and how it would affect the bottom line. Although OLAP tools are used in this situation after the fact, they are also useful before the fact as will be seen in Part III of the text.

APPROACHES TO KNOWLEDGE ACQUISITION AND USAGE HAVE CENTERED ON EXPERT OR KNOWLEDGE-BASED SYSTEMS

In the recent past, knowledge acquisition and usage have typically centered on expert systems (i.e., knowledge-based systems). Essentially, an *expert system* arrives at intelligent solutions to user queries by using the rules contained in the system's knowledge base. A *knowledge base* consists of "If-Then" rules, mathematical formulas, or some other knowledge representation structure to represent the knowledge of experts in a certain domain. An expert system scans through its knowledge base to find the appropriate rules, formulas, or some other knowledge structure to apply. Knowledge for such a system is extracted from human experts (i.e., domain experts) on the subject in which the expert system is expected to specialize. The knowledge in the form of rules is then stored in the expert system's knowledge base for use when needed.

Knowledge engineers who have been trained in the techniques of obtaining knowledge from domain experts procure the knowledge necessary to develop rules, formulas, or some other knowledge structure for the problem under study. In effect, knowledge engineers develop the expert system that is designed to parallel decisions made by recognized experts in a field by acquiring knowledge about the particular problem and applying appropriate rules. Once the rules are captured and programmed, a panel of domain experts reviews the program's recommendations in a series of test cases to verify the newly designed expert system.

For typical business applications, most often the knowledge is stored in the form of "If-Then" statements known as rules. This collection of rules is interpreted by an *inference engine*. Fundamentally, an inference engine navigates through the knowledge base much like a human would reason through a problem. Each rule can have one or more statements in its *If* and *Then* parts. If all the premises of the *If* part hold *true*, the conclusions reached by the expert system in the *Then* part are also *true* and the rule is said to "fire." Furthermore, the conclusion of a certain rule may exist as a premise of another rule that may itself "fire" and "ignite" other rules in succession, until a final conclusion is reached.

Basically, expert systems are designed to mimic the problem-solving abilities of experts in a particular domain. Expert systems can be thought of as knowledge transfer agents. Because an expert system works roughly the way human experts do, it combines factual knowledge with rules that experience teaches (i.e., heuristics) and then makes inferences about the situation at hand, whether it is diagnosing the financial portfolio of a client or the cost of a new product. In light of these facts, an expert system can be defined as a computer program that embodies the expertise in a specific domain that would otherwise be available only from a human expert. It represents a codification of the knowledge and reasoning used by human experts. Once operational, it can be copied and distributed at marginal cost to assist users, whether they are experts or inexperienced personnel. From this perspective, experts systems can help company employees become more productive when assisting users inside or outside the organization.

Although expert systems have found their rightful place in many companies, they do have their caveats. Among these are the use of dedicated platforms, maintainability, and implementation. From the standpoint of dedicated platforms, most expert systems require a dedicated one, at least for initial implementation. Users have found that it is difficult to justify. Some expert systems were ported to mainstream platforms but had performance problems. In terms of maintainability, several thousands of rules may require several people to maintain the expert system. A rule-based structure can prove to be unwieldly. Lastly, implementing expert systems also requires more organizational change than most companies can manage successfully. Several major insurance companies wanted agents to use expert systems for financial planning with customers. Since this required a new sales process, a broad knowledge of industry offerings, and several calls before making a sale, most companies have not been able to pull off the changes that were required to use the system effectively.[15]

Neural Networks Augment Expert or Knowledge-Based Systems

Since an expert system contains expertise in the form of a knowledge base, the system goes through its knowledge base and picks out the most appropriate response. The real problem is that if a person queries the expert system about something outside of its knowledge domain, it cannot respond. This is where *neural networks* come into play. The key distinction between expert systems and neural networks is that neural nets do not involve specific recordings or transcriptions of someone else's thinking. Neural networks can learn from experience; they can be used in medical testing and financial applications.

Because a neural network does not require a complete series of rules and extensive programs to interpret them, it learns the human decision-making process by example. By exposing a network repeatedly to the problems that must be solved, the system internally develops the proper algorithms for problem solving on its own. In a neural network, each input signal is directed by the weighting factor that determines the extent of its influence on the output. The weighting factors are adjusted by the processing nodes as data is processed. Hence, there is no need for information to be stored as a set of values in specific memory locations. On the other hand, expert systems require that large amounts of memory be used to store the knowledge base to be interpreted and processed according to rigidly specified sets of "If-Then-Else" instructions. They depend on accurate and complete data to check against hundreds and even thousands of stored rules. Typically, a neural network provides a limited explanation about how it arrived at a decision, while an expert system offers a great deal of explanation to justify the decisions it makes.

Neural networks are very effective in handling fuzzy, incomplete, and distorted data, thereby making them suitable for supporting decision making under conditions of uncertainty. This feature makes them an excellent candidate for financial applications, like stock market analysis, economic forecasting, and insurance underwriting, but not for standard transaction processing applications, like accounts receivable and payable, payroll, and inventory updating. In summary, neural networks are not good alternatives to traditional information processing or to expert systems. Rather, they provide many of the missing pieces of the overall corporate information systems environment. As their applications become more common, it may be necessary to create an appropriate neurocomputing environment to support an overall corporate strategy. As will be seen in Chapter 3, neural networks are extremely useful in data mining and other database specialized tasks.

VIRTUAL REALITY (VR) SYSTEMS COMPLEMENT KNOWLEDGE MANAGEMENT SYSTEMS

Although knowledge management systems have their roots in prior information systems, this does not mean that the capability of KMS technology need end at this point. Rather, there is a migration to something that makes the output from broad-based knowledge management systems more meaningful and interesting to its users—namely, virtual reality (VR). The transition to a combined KMS/VR environment must be carefully managed if it is to benefit the typical company. This combination will bring new levels of involvement by users, increased flexibility in their analyses, and unprecedented amounts of knowledge to users. If the transition is not properly managed, this new era will result in a widening gap between those empowered with newer technology and those without. The integration of knowledge management systems with virtual reality has the capability to help users, particularly decision makers, think from a different perspective to enhance their skills.

In order to ensure the success of virtual reality that is truly complementary to knowledge management systems, several market forces are now converging. First, three-dimensional applications have need of high-powered PC graphics accelerator cards that are more widely available for business use after their success with computer gamers. Second, a group of suppliers—the VRML (Virtual Reality Modeling Language) Consortium—has gained strength as the standard bearer for the technology. Formed in 1996 to create a common language in order to specify 3-D scene descriptions on the web, the group has received ratification of its VRML 2.0 standard by the International Standards Organization. Third, there is a stable platform for developers that has been endorsed by Microsoft's and Netscape's agreement to support the VRML 2.0 standard. Fourth, browsers from both Microsoft and Netscape come prepackaged with a ''universal'' VRML client to view the VRML. Thus, an underlying structure for virtual reality is now in place that is useful in a KMS environment.

Experience Via VR What Knowledge Management Systems Display

One way to experience what knowledge management systems display is to enter virtual worlds. In a VR experience, sophisticated interactive computer programs put a person inside a world of computer graphics. This allows the person to treat system-generated objects almost as if they were real things. The person interacts with the environment using special clothing and fiber optic sensors, if deemed necessary, that interpret body positions as computer commands. In theory, the person can create a world limited only by his or her imagination and programming capabilities.

Computer scientists are looking into ways to use what they call ''augmented'' or ''see through'' reality. On the shop floor, workers would wear clear goggles with 3-D images reflected onto the lenses. The goggles would superimpose a virtual image of the desired result on a real object, so that workers would know what to do with the object without consulting manuals or blueprints. For example, an assembler inside a fuselage would see the real operations for hydraulic ducts or communications cables with a virtual image of the installed ducts or cables superimposed on them. The goggles could also reflect schematic and wiring diagrams, location of drill holes, and other information. Similarly, in a manager's world, virtual reality provides the capability to experience what a knowledge management system displays. For example, a sales manager could fly over a simulated landscape of sales by specific areas in terms of sales dollars and time periods (past four quarters versus budgeted four quarters). The color *red* could be used to indicate where sales efforts have been and will be lagging and the color *green* could indicate increased sales. The color *yellow* could be used to indicate when sales have changed less than 5 percent from their budgeted amounts. The end result is better quality analysis in less time. Some virtual-reality experts predict that VR will eventually have an impact as great as the invention of writing. If they are wrong, it will not be for any want of ambition or confidence among pioneers in the field. The major drawbacks are the ability to write complex software programs and the speed of light—that is, the limitations of the physical world.[16]

What Lies Beyond Knowledge Management Systems

Related to knowledge management systems are the forthcoming knowledge-based businesses. Knowledge-based or ''smart'' products filter and interpret information that enables the user to act more effectively. For example, a coat that heats or cools in response to temperature changes or a tire that tells the driver its air pressure are early versions of smart products. These products can be identified by such characteristics as being interactive and smarter the more they are used. Also, they are capable of being customized to fit a customer's changing needs and can be tied in with the capability of preventive maintenance where deemed appropriate. The bottom line is that a person's use of knowledge-based products may be critical to their everyday operation and economic success. From this perspective, companies that know how to convert information into knowledge will be more successful than those that do not.[17]

Despite the coming advancements in knowledge-based products and services that can be tied in with improvements to knowledge management systems, these forthcoming changes are not the "end game." The rationale for a KMS environment not being the end point is that an upgraded computer infrastructure will eventually bring global computing and information along with resulting knowledge to most businesses, homes, and schools via the Internet and the World Wide Web as a normal way of life. Just as people in the past have picked up the telephone expecting a certain level of service, the same will be said for a combined digital, voice, and video infrastrasture of the future where people will expect a computer service utility that is available, ready, and waiting. The consequences of such a pervasive computer infrastructure are enormous for business as well as society. It could well be that many industries will change dramatically or possibly will be eliminated. For example, the present *print-and-distribute* approach to information and knowledge found in business organizations may be replaced by a *distribute-and-print* approach. That is, the focus is first on the *distribution* of information and knowledge under the guidance of wisdom that brings everything together for a company to meet even faster changing times. Second, new company policies and procedures that are guided by a company's wisdom emanating from its management can be *printed* as guidelines for organizational personnel to follow. Thus, underlying this much broader view of knowledge management systems are *wisdom management systems*.

Essentially, wisdom management systems (WMSs) are enhanced knowledge management systems that inspire greater loyalty and trust from a company's employees, including its customers. A comment from Aristotle—one of the great masters of the past—is relevant here: "Action without knowledge is folly. Knowledge without wisdom is perilous." Company managers operating within a WMS environment will encourage their employees (and customers) to generate ideas for new products and services. Similarly, wise managers will assist their employees (and customers) to anticipate problems and solve them before they happen as well as help employees achieve their objectives and goals so that there is a "win-win" situation for both the company and the employee. Wise managers will also help their employees identify opportunities that come out of problem finding (which is covered in the next chapter). At this point, the question can be asked: Why should this text concentrate on knowledge management systems when what is really needed today is greater wisdom in running a typical business organization? The answer lies in the fact that wisdom management systems are just a concept today. In the 21st century, it may well be that these systems will be taken very seriously and the appropriate computing infrastructure to implement these type systems will become a reality. Needless to say, time will be the real judge of this new approach to assisting organizational personnel to meet the challenges of today and tomorrow.

SUMMARY

Initially, the chapter focused on the need for broad-based knowledge systems, (i.e., knowledge management systems) in an ever-changing business environment, followed by a discussion showing the relationship among data, information, and knowledge. Next, the employment of a learning organization to leverage a company's knowledge was discussed. The utilization of knowledge to leverage a company's assets was also explored at some length. The second half of the chapter focused on different approaches for processing mission-critical applications that have preceded knowledge management systems. For the most part, previous information systems assisted managers first and provided accounting results second. Although the development of information systems is still continuing, it should be recognized that knowledge management systems are not the end state, but rather another stage in the ever-evolving state of computing technology.

NOTES

1. Peter Senge, *The Fifth Discipline* (New York: Doubleday, 1990), p. 1.

2. Walter A. Kleinschrod, "In Business, Knowledge Is Power," *Beyond Computing*, March–April 1995, pp. 36–38, 40.

3. David Bank, "Know-It-Alls," in *The Corporate Connection, Wall Street Journal*, November 18, 1996, p. R28.

4. Ibid.

5. Robert J. Thierauf, *Systems Analysis and Design of Real-Time Management Information Systems* (Englewood Cliffs, NJ: Prentice-Hall, 1975).

6. Ibid.

7. Robert J. Thierauf, *Distributed Processing Systems* (Englewood Cliffs, NJ: Prentice-Hall, 1978).

8. Robert J. Thierauf, *Electronic Data Interchange in Finance and Accounting* (Westport, CT: Quorum Books, 1990).

9. Robert J. Thierauf, *Image Processing Systems for Business: A Guide for MIS Professionals and End Users* (Westport, CT: Quorum Books, 1992).

10. Robert J. Thierauf, *Decision Support Systems for Effective Planning and Control, A Case Study Approach* (Englewood Cliffs, NJ: Prentice-Hall, 1982); and *User-Oriented Decision Support Systems, Accent on Problem Finding* (Englewood Cliffs, NJ: Prentice-Hall, 1988).

11. Robert J. Thierauf, *Group Decision Support Systems for Effective Decision Mak-*

ing: A Guide for MIS Professionals and End Users (Westport, CT: Quorum Books, 1989).

12. Robert J. Thierauf, *Executive Information Systems: A Guide for Senior Management and MIS Professionals* (Westport, CT: Quorum Books, 1991).

13. Robert J. Thierauf, *Creative Computer Software for Strategic Thinking and Decision Making: A Guide for Senior Management and MIS Professionals* (Westport, CT: Quorum Books, 1993).

14. Robert J. Thierauf, *On-Line Analytical Processing Systems for Business* (Westport, CT: Quorum Books, 1997).

15. Robert J. Thierauf, *Expert Systems in Finance and Accounting* (Westport, CT: Quorum Books, 1990).

16. Robert J. Thierauf, *Virtual Reality Systems for Business* (Westport, CT: Quorum Books, 1995).

17. Stan Davis and Jim Botkin, ''The Coming of Knowledge-Based Business,'' *Harvard Business Review*, September–October 1994, pp. 165–170.

2

A Framework for Knowledge Management Systems in Business

Issues Explored:

- Why is it necessary to rethink a company's operations as a way of capturing knowledge for decision makers?
- How useful is problem-finding within a KMS environment?
- Why is it necessary to integrate multiple databases and knowledge bases in the development of a company's knowledge infrastructure?
- How can a company's networking computing structure assist in accumulating and disseminating knowledge?
- What type of software is useful in the acquisition, storage, and usage of knowledge for decision makers?

Outline:

INTRODUCTION TO A FRAMEWORK FOR KNOWLEDGE MANAGEMENT SYSTEMS IN BUSINESS

Today, the success of a typical company, as noted in Chapter 1, depends on its ability to anticipate changes, reduce product life cycles, adjust to changing government regulations, compete with companies in every corner of the globe, and transform ever-increasing amounts of data into information and, in turn, into knowledge that can be acted upon. In addition, success depends on the ability of employees to learn to work in new and different ways, including acting on acquired knowledge that can change over time. All of these activities center around a company's declining profit margins.

In light of this changing business environment, it would be helpful initially to explore the need to rethink a company's operations as a way of capitalizing on knowledge. Similarly, the different levels of knowledge acquisition and usage, in knowledge management systems, need to be examined as they affect company personnel along with the types of problems that can use knowledge in their solutions. The central focus of the chapter is on the essentials of knowledge management systems (KMSs), which provide a basis for their underlying structure. They were noted briefly in the prior chapter and include:

1. the utilization of *problem finding* and its related techniques to get a grasp on present and anticipated problems and to identify future opportunities that are tied in with a company's critical success factors.
2. a *knowledge infrastructure* that is related to very large databases, data marts, data warehouses, and knowledge bases.
3. the employment of *network computing* that is linked with a company's intranets and extranets as well as the World Wide Web.
4. a wide range of *appropriate software* that includes knowledge extraction tools, knowledge management software, knowledge management intranet search engines, knowledge discovery or data mining software, and OLAP and statistical analysis software.

Each of these areas is covered in more detail in this chapter and subsequent chapters of the text.

Need to Rethink a Company's Operations as a Way of Capitalizing on Knowledge

Building upon the comments made in the prior chapter regarding the need to establish a chief knowledge officer (CKO), a typical company needs to rethink its operations as a way of capitalizing on its knowledge. Typically, companies are still staffed by people who believe knowledge is power, but they are not about to give it up to their co-workers. Additionally, employees recognize the value of shared knowledge but do not have the time, the tools, or the tangible incentives either to contribute to or take advantage of the process. Overcoming these obstacles, for example, is the job of John Peetz, chief knowledge officer at Ernst & Young for the firm's 20,000 U.S. employees, many of whom are already working long hours and are scattered around the country in airplanes, hotels, and client offices.[1]

To expand further upon this example, the plan is for each Ernst & Young auditor and consultant to utilize a laptop loaded with Lotus Notes, Microsoft Office software, and a browser for the World Wide Web. They are all expected to download to their laptop, and master the contents of, at least two of 80 available "power packs"—databases containing information on particular areas of the firm's practice, such as expatriate tax processing or changing regulations in the health industry. Each of the power packs has 42 specific entries, including contact information for the firm's network of "subject-matter experts" (senior consultants available to help a junior associate out of a jam), client information, industry background, and templates for presentations. For example, specific power packs might contain a basic diagram for planning supply-chain management, sample shop floor layouts, or a simulation of a pizza shop's production process.

The main thrust behind this rich knowledge is to help Ernst & Young consultants meet project deadlines and impress clients by having essential information organized efficiently and stored in their laptops. During a meeting, the consultant can quickly pull up the answers to, say, an arcane tax question. Or after the meeting, the consultant can create a claims form processing model for an insurance industry client based on a template in the power pack, something that would be time-consuming if the consultant had to start from scratch.

To establish a broad-based knowledge database, Mr. Peetz had to persuade the firm to change the way it thinks about knowledge. Many people feared that wide publishing of Ernst & Young's best ideas would inevitably lead to leaks to their competitors. In reality, a good idea by itself has relatively little value. However, the key is rapidity and execution. The risk of losing the firm's ideas is not as high as the risk of not capitalizing on them. Also, he had to overcome the functional divisions within Ernst & Young. The firm's tax people, for example, did not think they had any knowledge that the consultants needed to see. Consultants could not imagine that auditors would be interested in what they knew. Each group wanted a separate database. Finally, Peetz had to get people to contribute to the database, a process he initially dubbed ''dental extraction.'' The solution is linking participation to job evaluations. Now, at the end of the year, one-fourth of a person's annual performance review is based on his or her contribution to the knowledge process. Overall, the rethinking of Ernst & Young's operations has, to a degree, taken off in the direction of reengineering as way of capturing important knowledge about their client's operations. In turn, this knowledge has useful applications for consulting projects.[2]

BASIC TYPES OF KNOWLEDGE IN A KMS ENVIRONMENT

Before exploring the different levels of knowledge as found in a KMS operating mode, it would be helpful to explore the two basic types of knowledge (i.e., explicit and tacit). *Explicit knowledge* is clearly developed with all of its elements apparent. Such knowledge is documented and codified. Because it is distinctly stated, it is largely structured and has no disguised meaning. A good example of explicit knowledge is a development methodology that dictates an orderly approach to solving a problem and the roles and responsibilities for participants in the process. In contrast, *tacit knowledge* is implied or indicated but not always expressed. It is largely unstructured and is generally based on personal knowledge from personal experiences and capabilities. For example, handwritten and unsolicited comments regarding a new product are received periodically by a company's marketing department.

Currently, many companies are pursuing strategies to leverage tacit knowledge that is held by employees, customers, and others. Since tacit knowledge is not documented or stated explicitly, it is typically a high-value understanding that employees gain from experience on the job and learning from customers and others. With turnover that is caused by downsizing and an aging workforce, part of a company's "corporate memory" leaves with each employee departure. Hence, it is critical that companies capture tacit knowledge. Many times, tacit knowledge serves as a basis for explicit knowledge that needs to be managed over time for best results. The result is that, as tacit knowledge becomes explicit, the organization moves closer to achieving sustainable competitive advantage.

DIFFERENT LEVELS OF KNOWLEDGE IN A KMS ENVIRONMENT

Even though there are two basic types of knowledge, the focus of this text is on a much broader framework for acquiring, storing, disseminating, and, in general, managing knowledge. To assist operating managers and their support staffs at different levels of an organization during the coming days, weeks, and months, *operational knowledge* is employed. At the next level for lower- and middle-level managers and their staffs, *tactical knowledge* is useful for overseeing the overall performance of their functional areas during the coming year. At the highest level, *strategic knowledge* is useful for top-level managers and their staffs for combining pertinent external knowledge with internal knowledge for future periods, say from two to five years and beyond, for accomplishing an organization's strategic plans as they relate to its objectives and goals. For the most part, this breakdown is similar to that for information found in all types of management information systems, including decision support systems, executive information systems, and on-line analytical processing systems. Due to the importance of knowledge levels, which must be clearly understood by knowledge management systems developers, they are are discussed below.

Operational Knowledge

Since operational knowledge can be associated with expert systems, reference can be made to developing knowledge using one of the many expert system shells that are widely used today or minimizing a system's knowledge engineering efforts (i.e., minimizing the effort associated with knowledge acquisition). Such an approach is linked to *shallow knowledge* where the type of knowledge acquired is domain specific and ad hoc. Since the acquisition methods allow large amounts of knowledge to be collected with minimal effort, these systems exploit large amounts of shallow knowledge. From this perspective, the benefits of acquiring specific shallow knowledge typically exceed their costs. It should be noted that shallow knowledge is often criticized because it is not generally reusable in other systems and is useful only in the specific application for which it was created. However, as just noted, shallow knowledge may be so low in cost that it is cost-effective to treat it as a disposable artifact. If shallow knowledge proves to be adequate for the application at hand—even if only for a single domain, a single task, and a single system—shallow knowledge can be a cost-effective way to acquire and use operational knowledge.

Going beyond the acquisition of operational knowledge, the use of any approach to developing expert systems, knowledge extraction, and discovery (data mining) tools along with knowledge management and intranet search engines can be an important source of knowledge for operations managers and their support staffs, including technical workers at the different levels. In a similar manner, OLAP software, statistical analysis packages, business graphics packages, fourth generation languages, financial planning languages, and management software packages provide useful sources of operational knowledge. Most of these software packages are discussed later in the chapter and future chapters (especially in Chapter 5) along with the employment of groupware that is tied in with a company's intranets and the Internet.

Typically, operational knowledge is related to operational control of day-to-day operations in specific departments so that these can be controlled effectively. For example, a manufacturing supervisor has to know if material wastage is exceeding the standard, if costly overruns that exceed the standard are in the making, and if the standard time allocated to a specific job has been exceeded. All of these standards are based on knowledge of past operations. Similarly, local sales managers want to know, based on past knowledge of their type of sales operations, the number of customer calls that the sales staff needs to make everyday of the week. In these examples, accuracy of detailed past knowledge is particularly important at this level for managerial activities, since lower-level managers may find it necessary to take on-the-spot action to rectify upcoming unfavorable situations. Essentially, the time frame for operational control relates to daily operations but can also be related to weekly, monthly, or quarterly operations.

Tactical Knowledge

At the tactical knowledge level, there tends to be a mix of external sources and internal sources. Whereas the sources for operational knowledge are based on internal sources for an organization, tactical knowledge tends to be a blend of the two. Lower- and middle-level managers and their staffs use tactical knowledge to help these managers oversee their functional areas and use this knowledge to give direction to their operations in the near future. The time frame is generally confined to the coming year and slightly beyond. The software used can differ depending on the functional area under study. Essentially, the software is the same as that set forth above for developing operational knowledge. However, there may be more of a tendency toward knowledge management and knowledge discovery tools. In some cases, there will be more of an accent on employing groupware within the organization as well as outside it.

Because tactical knowledge can come from both external and internal sources, marketing managers, for example, are concerned about the overall sales performance of their regions versus competing firms. They therefore need internal information and knowledge on quarterly and yearly sales as well as information and knowledge about competitors. In a similar manner, other functional-level managers are concerned about current and future performance of their organization units. They need external information and knowledge on important matters that affect their units, such as problems with suppliers, sales declines, or increased demand for one or more products. In addition, these managers need to have internal knowledge (i.e., plant costs and the periodic performance of their units as well as anticipated performance) to take advantage of specific opportunities.

Strategic Knowledge

Strategic knowledge represents the highest level. It is oriented toward many sources that are based outside the organization. From this viewpoint, there is a relationship between a company's critical success factors, which are generally related to a specific industry, and being successful in that industry. In turn, these factors help top management and the corporate planning staff to determine the strategic direction the company should take today and, more importantly, tomorrow. Included in this future direction is the employment of problem finding that not only looks at future problems within the context of the current time period but also centers on developing important opportunities for the company immediately and within the next several years.

To help develop appropriate knowledge at this highest level, knowledge extraction tools, knowledge management software, intranet search engines, and knowledge discovery or data mining tools are extremely useful. They help top management and corporate planners get a handle on patterns of the immediate past. Analysis of data and related information allows these high-level professionals to spot significant trends that impact the total organization. Other software, such as OLAP and statistical analysis packages, can also be helpful. In addition, the dissemination of this knowledge can be made to members in a global organization through the company's intranets as well as the Internet's World Wide Web.

For strategic knowledge, the typical time frame goes beyond one year and up to five years or more. For top management and their staffs, the knowledge management system must provide specific knowledge upon which corporate strategic plans can be soundly based. For this task, external sources that center on economic conditions, technological developments, competitive reactions, and like matters assume paramount importance. Knowledge from these external sources does not have to possess the greatest accuracy since corporate strategic plans are broad rather than very detailed in nature and because they require approximate indications of future trends rather than exact statements about the past or present. However, when combined with internal knowledge, this provides a sound basis for developing broad-based strategic plans that are linked to a company's mission, specific organization objectives, and measurable goals.

Continuum of Knowledge Acquisition and Usage

A thorough analysis of these three levels of knowledge indicates that they overlap, thereby forming a continuum. That is, the sources that center on knowledge for *operational control* are based largely within the organization, whereas the sources that revolve around knowledge for *strategic planning* are based largely outside the organization. In the middle, sources for *tactical planning and control* are somewhat balanced between external and internal ones. The scope of knowledge is somewhat narrow and well defined for operational control, very wide for strategic planning, and in between for tactical planning and control. The level of aggregation is very detailed for operational control, moderately detailed and somewhat summarized for tactical planning and control, and very summarized for strategic planning. In terms of time horizon, operational control is historical in nature, including some projections; strategic planning relies heavily on futuristic patterns and trends; and the middle of the two makes use of both historical and futuristic projections. The other characteristics of knowledge, including accuracy, currency, and frequency of use, can be interpreted in a similar manner.

To utilize knowledge effectively within the above planning and analysis framework, a creative approach needs to be undertaken from the outset. New patterns and trends need to be uncovered, using the latest knowledge tools that allow decision makers to look at the results from new perspectives and to ask questions based on one or more previous analyses. This creative analysis may result in new perspectives or answers not envisioned through conventional problem solving or problem finding. Thus, decision makers should be able to select, analyze, and resolve difficult present and future problems facing them throughout the organization. Similarly, decision makers can explore many new opportunities. Whether problems or opportunities are the focus of attention, decision makers have a natural entrée using knowledge management systems to help them achieve desired objectives in their decisions.

TYPES OF PROBLEMS THAT CAN USE KNOWLEDGE IN THEIR SOLUTION

Within a KMS operating mode, well-structured, semistructured, and unstructured problems are capable of being solved. However, knowledge tends to be more useful with the second two problem types, while information is generally sufficient for well-structured problems. A problem is said to be *well-structured* if all of its elements can be identified and quantified in order to determine an answer. Typically, the time frame is short, say up to one year. For example, in a production allocation problem, the time available this month and next month on the first and second shifts as well as the costs to produce the products in the manufacturing departments can be identified. Also, the level of production is known based upon the forecasted sales for these months. Thus, the problem is well defined and can be solved within the information parameters set forth using a quantitative approach to decision making. Since the problem is fully structured, generally an appropriate mathematical or statistical model can be utilized to reach a good solution.

A problem is said to be *semistructured* if it contains both well-structured and unstructured elements. The time frame can range from the short run to the long run. For example, an investment problem that concerns determining a specific portfolio is considered to be semistructured. From one viewpoint, a systematic search through data and information on portfolios and securities is required; they can be effected through retrieval, reports, and display via a PC or workstation using mathemtical and statistical analytical models. At the same time, the criteria for making investments based upon past information and investment knowledge gained over time need to be left to the manager's judgment. Thus, output from the computer is combined with the portfolio manager's judgment to select appropriate securities to solve the investment problem.

If the significant parameters of the problem cannot be identified precisely, it is said to be *unstructured*. In this case, human intuition and judgment are generally needed to reach a decision. Typically, the rationale for the inability to identify specific parameters in the problem is that the time frame is too long—for example, beyond five years. Consider the problem of determining a company's personnel needs ten years hence. Because there are a large number of unknowns relating to sales and production, the net result is that the appropriate level of personnel to support these areas is also unknown. In effect, the parameters of the problem are too loosely defined to solve it with a high degree of accuracy. If the problem is unstructured from the user's perspective, computerized mathematical or statistical models are generally inappropriate. To reach a decision, there is a need for general knowledge as well as meaningful experience, know-how, intuition, judgment, and past experience. This may mean taking a qualitiative approach to decision making. However, *rules of thumb* (i.e., heuristic methods) may be appropriate to resolve unstructured uproblems. This may require resorting to trends, patterns, evaluations, educated guesses, hypotheses, and the like. Essentially, it is problem solving under conditions of uncertainty. The attendant circumstances must be surveyed to determine whether or not heuristic methods are appropriate for solving unstructured problems.

Typical examples of well-structured, semistructured, and unstructured problems found at various managerial levels that can employ knowledge in their solution are given in Figure 2-1. These examples take into account the time factor and the capability of defining the problem. Numerous other examples of these three problem types appear later in the text (i.e., Part III).

Figure 2-1
The Relationship of Top-, Middle-, and Lower-Level Managers to Well-Structured, Semistructured, and Unstructured Problems

Managerial Level	**Well-Structured Problems**
Top-level manager	Manufacturing facilities problems
Middle-level manager	Budget problems
Lower-level manager	Production problems
	Semistructured Problems
Top-level manager	Merger problems
Middle-level manager	Sales forecasting problems
Lower-level manager	Purchasing problems
	Unstructured Problems
Top-level manager	Future anticipated new product problems
Middle-level manager	Motivational problems
Lower-level manager	Group behavior problems

PROBLEM FINDING VERSUS PROBLEM SOLVING WITHIN A KMS ENVIRONMENT

An important *first* factor in an effective KMS environment is one that focuses on an overview of a company and its operations. Such an approach is found by using problem finding and its related techniques to get a handle on present and future problems along with identifying future opportunities. Although problems range from structured to unstructured, it is helpful for company managers to take a broader view by distinguishing between a reactive and a proactive approach to resolving problems. A survey of many companies today indicates that many managers spend more time putting out fires and less time helping their business grow. Typically, these companies have taken a *reactive approach* to problems—that is, as problems arise, they try to apply appropriate management techniques in order to resolve current problems. In reality, several more problems tend to crop up that require the attention of management. This never ending scenario of fighting problem fires never seems to get under control.

In contrast, it is better to take a *proactive, preventive approach* that keeps managers on top of the problems confronting them. Generally, these problems have always been there, but management has either ignored them hoping they would go away or assigned them to others who did not have the time or clout to get them resolved. Hence, the preferred approach today is to have managers get involved in *problem finding* versus just *problem solving*.

The problem-finding process not only includes anticipating future company problems and bringing them back to the present time for solution, but also looking for future opportunities that are related to these future problems. In marketing, for example, problem finding includes knowing what customers want

Figure 2-2
Management Effectiveness in a Proactive Mode versus a Reactive Mode as Related to a Basis for Decision Making Using Data, Information, and Knowledge

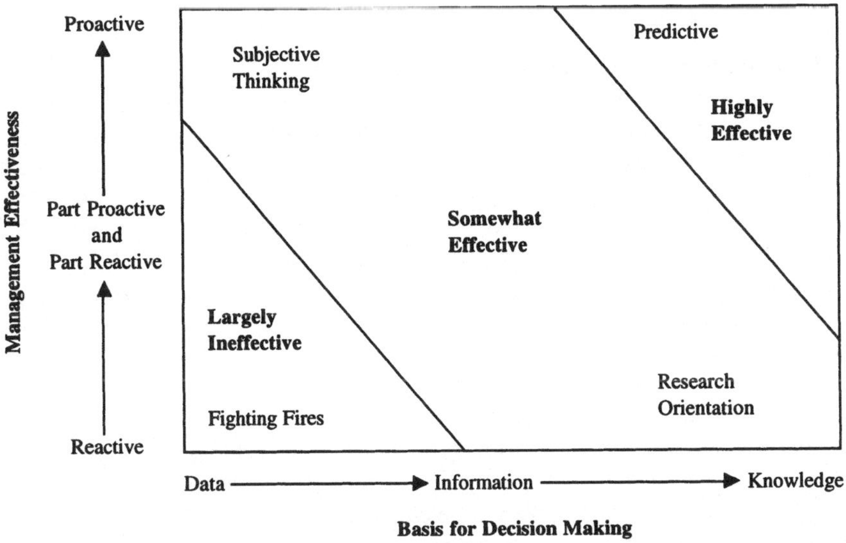

before they know themselves versus just meeting the competition. Similarly, in finance, this means that risks can be managed with foresight rather than damage being controlled through hindsight. This proactive management approach to a company's problems and its related opportunities is an important prerequisite for improving a company's competitiveness in today's fast-changing times. Also, the problem-finding approach can be tied in with a company's critical success factors—that is, upcoming problems and opportunities that impact a company can be related to those factors that are critical to a company's survival. Overall, a problem-finding approach is related to the old saying: "A danger foreseen is half avoided."

To relate problem finding to knowledge, reference can be made to Figure 2-2 where management effectiveness is shown as it ties in with a basis for decision making. As illustrated in the lower left-hand corner, management is ineffective where management spends its time putting out problem fires as they occur. In contrast, management is highly effective using knowledge in a proactive mode, as shown in the upper-right-hand corner. Right in the middle is a somewhat effective approach. Adopting a proactive management approach that operates on knowledge and ideas and creating an organization that encourages people to engage in problem finding represents an important challenge for the typical company. Hence, there is a need to change to a new type of management system and decision making protocol that values analysis and useful knowledge in anticipating and shaping future outcomes. Such systems are found within a KMS environment, which holds the promise of increasing organizational effectiveness to meet the challenge of changing times.

Creativity Underlies the Problem-Finding Process

In the problem-finding process described below, the focus is initially on information useful in getting at a company's future problems and opportunities. But more importantly, the focus then shifts to knowledge that is useful in exploring ideas to solve future problems studied as well as new ideas that can enhance further important opportunities for a company. This new point of view displaces the prior belief that more information will solve a company's problems. There was a time when information was indeed the limiting factor, and more information made for better decisions. Generally, this is no longer considered the case. Knowledge that underlies ideas is the limiting factor today since detailed analysis does not necessarily yield new ideas. The manager's mind can only see what it is prepared to see. The manager needs to start ideas on his or her own. The current emphasis on problem solving, then, needs to be changed to emphasize the manager's creativity in terms of developing new ideas based on knowledge of a company's overall operations. This is the approach found in the problem-centered and opportunity-centered approaches presented below. Initially, problem-finding techniques are set forth.

Useful Problem-Finding Techniques

To assist in problem finding, it is helpful to employ one or more techniques that can identify problems and/or opportunities. Among those useful in problem finding are: (1) creative process, (2) brainstorming, (3) synectics, (4) accurate problem definition, and (5) idea generators, which are noted below. Some of these techniques can assist managers and their support staffs in getting around the need to be right all of the time, which can be a significant barrier to developing new ideas. Thus, it is better to have some new ideas based on knowledge of a company that may prove to be wrong. Or to state it another way, managers and their support staffs will always be right without having any new ideas at all.

An early descriptive model of the *creative process* useful to an individual thinker was formulated by Graham Wallas in 1926. This process appeared in his book, *Art of Thought*.[3] He specified four phases of the creative process: (1) preparation, (2) incubation, (3) illumination, and (4) verification. Preparation consists of gathering facts, information, and knowledge that may be applicable to some problem under study. Typically, the second and third phases of this creative process involve respectively, initially a pause (incubation) in which some unconscious sifting, sorting, and/or relating of information gathered during the first phase takes place, followed by a sudden awareness or recognition of a new relationship that has importance to the decision maker (illumination). Essentially, incubation is related to the search for and identification of ideas and/or problem solution alternatives at a subconscious level. This stage can be seen as the actual creative process itself. The illumination stage involves the conscious awareness of new ideas and/or solutions to the problem under study by the decision maker. Finally, in the fourth stage the insight gained from the illumination is tested and seen to be viable and acceptable or not acceptable, in which case it is reworked until the insight becomes acceptable. The decision maker imposes closure—that is, accepting or rejecting the validity of the idea and/or solution for the problem under study.

Probably, the best-known creativity technique is *brainstorming*, which was developed by Alex F. Osborn (cofounder of BBD&O) to help solve advertising problems. It is used to improve problem analysis by providing more possible solutions and unusual approaches to the problem under study. Osborn suggests four rules necessary for the utilization of brainstorming: (1) Judgment is withheld; ideas may be criticized and evaluated later. (2) Wild ideas are encouraged; ideas are easier to modify than to originate. (3) Numerous ideas are desired; more ideas increase the possibility of obtaining an excellent idea. (4) The participants are encouraged to utilize the ideas of others to develop additional ideas. Other recommended procedures include: the sessions should be recorded because some ideas may be missed during a meeting; the problem must be manageable, even if it requires breaking large problems into smaller parts; and samples should be available if products are being discussed. After the brainstorming session, the group must set up the criteria for evaluation. Then, all the ideas are evaluated based upon the criteria and the best two or three possible solutions are chosen. In the end, there may be a need to modify an idea in order to make it meet the desired criteria more closely. In this way, a seemingly wild notion can be transformed into a workable solution. No brainstorming process is complete until the most promising solutions are placed into practice.

Although not as well known as brainstorming, *synectics* is based on the assumption that creativity can be described and taught. Its purpose is to improve the quality of creative output from those assigned to a synectics team. Essentially, the synectic process involves two steps: (1) making the strange familiar and (2) making the familiar strange. The first step requires that the problem be understood and that the ramifications be considered. The mind tends to emphasize its own experiences and to force strange ideas into an acceptable pattern. Thus, it is necessary to reorient these strange ideas into familiar ones. The second step, making the familiar strange, involves distorting, inverting, and transposing the problem in an attempt to view the problem from an unfamiliar perspective. For more detailed information on synectics, reference can be made to a book by William Gordon.[4]

Many problem-solving failures occur because efforts are directed at solving the wrong problem or only parts of it. An inability to identify accurately what is going on can lead to inaccurate problem identification. To assist in *accurate problem definition* (i.e., defining the real problem), a cause-and-effect diagram is recommended. Because problems cause other problems, a whole complex of symptoms and problems emerges in need of a solution. A problem-diagramming procedure can help to isolate root causes. First, list all the problems, symptoms, and related problems. Number each one. Next, write the numbers at random on a piece of paper and draw a circle around each. Then draw arrows to show what causes what. For example, if problem 1 causes problem 2, draw an arrow from circle 1 to circle 2. Consider each circled number, asking: "Which of the other problems causes or helps cause this one?" After all the arrows have been drawn, the root problems become clear. They are represented by the circles with arrows leading only away from them. The real root problem is the farthest one to the left.

Idea generators offer an important new direction in problem-finding techniques. When making business decisions, it is more difficult for decision makers to visualize all possible options than it is to select the most attractive choice from the list. Research shows that decision makers tend to anchor their thoughts early in the process, using their first ideas as a starting point from which other ideas arise. Hence, solutions are often variations on a central theme rather than genuinely different options. Although computers are unable to suggest new ideas on their own, they are free from a human's subjectivity and can aid the human decision maker in exploring a broader range of possibilities in a systematic manner. Even though these programs are easy to learn, each demands that decision makers adapt their work styles to fit the program's interpretation of the idea generation process. Idea generators can help organize random or related thoughts but cannot create new ideas per se. Typical packages include IdeaFisher and Idea Generator. IdeaFisher (from Fisher Idea Systems Inc.) helps the user develop new ideas by providing a linked idea database that fosters free association. For users who demand a more analytical or linear approach, the structured question-and-answer approach of Idea Generator (from Experience in Software Inc.) may be more productive. Idea Generator's more analytical approach presents a series of questions designed to cultivate new perspectives. The questions can help users explore problems from different points of view, but the program requires users to complete a problem analysis initially. Overall, decision makers must determine which software package meets their specific needs. For more information on idea generators, reference can be made to a publication by the author.[5]

TWO APPROACHES TO THE PROBLEM-FINDING PROCESS

In traditional approaches to the problem-solving process, the accent is on some type of analytical technique, which has been the main thrust of information systems. However, there is a need to go a step further by incorporating creativity in the form of "logical-analytical thinking." Logical-analytical thinking goes beyond the analysis of present problems in an organization that is typical of the problem-solving process. Its accent is on identifying *future problems* and their impact on the organization today and tomorrow. In addition, logical-analytical thinking is directed toward future problems that are actually *future opportunities* in disguise. In order to solve future problems and grasp opportunities, it is helpful to employ one or more of the creativity techniques set forth above. Generally, a manager who has identified future problems has also identified opportunities. This means that the problem-finding process within a KMS environment can be separated into a problem-centered approach and an opportunity-centered approach.

For the *problem-centered approach*, logical-analytical thinking centers on examining the environment with the idea of looking into the future and exploring problems that will have an impact on the organization now or at some time in the future. Essentially, the process is one of projecting into the future, determining important problems (i.e., problem finding), and bringing them back to the present time to examine their cause-and-effect relationships. Likewise, logical-analytical thinking is needed in the *opportunity-centered approach.* However, the perspective is somewhat different. The main focus is on identifying opportunities for the organization to pursue that generally come from problems uncovered. In effect, managers do need to change an organizational liability into an asset. They need to identify problems that can result in important opportunities for the organization. But the opportunity-centered approach need not always be related to future problems. It can center on current opportunities that are identified by top management and/or the corporate planning staff. Specific opportunities can be addressed directly by organization members at the higher levels of management. In addition to the following exposition on the problem-finding process, other information and examples will be found in Part III of the text.

Problem-Centered Approach

The problem-centered approach as set forth here is taken from one of the author's previous publications with modifications where appropriate to include the generation of new ideas using creative computer software.[6] As shown in Figure 2-3, it consists of four steps plus the solution and implementation phases from the problem-solving process. Essentially, these four steps precede the actual solution of the future problems under study.

1. *Generation.* This first step is the most important one in problem search because it focuses on a probe of potential problems that might have an impact on the company. Initially, the analysis is "forward-looking," because it is a search for future problems. Once these problems are identified, the analysis becomes "backward-looking," since there is a need to evaluate the cause-and-effect relationships of each problem and its possible effects on the organization currently. Accent is placed on each problem, from the short range to the long

Figure 2-3
A Comparison of Steps in the Problem-Finding Process: The Problem-Centered Approach and the Opportunity-Centered Approach

Basic Phases	Problem-Centered Approach	Opportunity-Centered Approach
Search	*Step 1. Generation*—Probe for potential problems that might exist in the future using a *brainstorming approach.* *Step 2. Evaluation*—Review problems uncovered for managerial concern, backed up by a *cost-benefit analysis*. If appropriate, use creative computer software to generate new ways to evaluate future problems.	*Step 1. Exploration*—Examine the environment for opportunities that come from problems uncovered using a *brainstorming approach*. If appropriate, use creative computer software to explore new ideas to exploit these opportunities.
Identification	*Step 3. Validation*—Select actual problems for managerial concern. If appropriate, relate to the company's *critical success factors*.	*Step 2. Selection*—Determine that one or more opportunities should be explored by management. If appropriate, relate to the company's *critical success factors*.
	Step 4. Establish Boundaries—Define each potential problem within its boundaries to cover the whole area encompassed by the problem.	*Step 3. Examine Boundaries*—Survey the environment for each opportunity and determine the proper boundaries.
Solution and Implementation	Use steps from the problem-solving process.	Use steps from the problem-solving process.

Note: There is *Feedback* from the Last Step of Both Approaches to the First Step.

range. It may also be necessary to look at each problem in different economic climates (good, average, and bad conditions).

To generate important problems, the best approach is to use *brainstorming*. Generally, top managers and their staffs, along with members from the corporate planning staff, meet periodically to brainstorm future organizational problems. In a typical session, all important problems uncovered are recorded; then analysis is performed to explore the important aspects of each problem. These steps are performed in a back-and-forth fashion—that is, the original question concerning the *problem as given* and the subsequent spontaneous ideas are all written down. When participants' minds have cleared, they concentrate on reformulations produced from the collected material, and a choice of one or more is made before continuing with questions in sequence concerning the *problem as understood*. (As noted, the initially forward-looking analysis becomes backward-looking.) This can be repeated until all aspects have been considered. Complex problems may require the application of other creativity techniques in order to uncover an unexpected new angle.

2. *Evaluation.* After the problem-generation phase, the second step centers on examining problems in terms of their being worthy of managerial concern. Because many of these problems are found in the future—the next two to five or possibly 10 years—the question can be asked, "Which problem or problems should be undertaken for solution?" To answer this question, it is necessary to evaluate the impact the solution to a problem has on the organization—for example, in terms of net profit and return on investment. In other cases, consideration might be given to other important areas of an organization, such as sales and customer service. Similarly, it may be necessary to relate the problem or problems back to the organization's critical success factors.

If deemed appropriate, creative computer software can be used to generate related new ways and ideas to help in the evaluation of future problems. In this manner, a broader approach can be used to evaluate the problems uncovered in the first step. In this evaluation process, it is possible that more problems may become apparent. If this happens, it may be necessary to add these problems to this evaluation step.

Generally, there is need to perform a *cost-benefit analysis* to determine the impact of the solution on the financial aspects of the organization today and tomorrow. This task, for example, can be relegated to managers at the appropriate levels and their staffs to determine which problems are of valid concern for managerial action. The problems generated, then, are evaluated in terms of benefits versus costs, thereby becoming the basis for validation in the next step.

3. *Validation.* Building on the prior step of problem evaluation, actual problems in this third step are selected as being worthy of managerial concern for today and tomorrow. The validation for solving these problems is generally backed up by a cost-benefit analysis and related to the company's *critical success factors* if appropriate. If such an analysis is not available or too difficult or costly to develop, it may be necessary to use alternative means, such as the consensus of the majority of this problem-finding group, to substantiate this selection as an important problem to be solved. For example, to determine what problems should be validated and solved, the problem-finding group meets again and reviews the recommendations of the managers and their staffs. For the most part, the staffs have prioritized the important problems to be solved. It is up to the problem-finding group to pass judgment on them. As noted, some of the problems cannot be resolved in terms of a cost-benefit analysis. Input from managers and their staffs is generally necessary to finalize the prioritized list for implementation.

4. *Establish Boundaries.* After the problems have been validated in step 3, it is necessary to describe (define) each problem within its boundaries in this fourth step. This ensures that areas that the problem might touch or come into contact with will be included in the problem-finding process. The net result is that there is a need for some fine tuning so that the appropriate boundaries of the problem will be considered in its solution. Typically, to establish realistic boundaries, the problem-finding group must have a rich knowledge of the future (good, average,

or poor economic conditions), a clear description of performance that a solution must fulfill, and a clear idea of what to expect from solving the problem. These areas must be as clear and as accurate as possible because if the problem is badly defined, the solution is generally of no value to management.

Solution. Solution to the problem-centered approach can take one of two directions. One is using appropriate steps for the quantitative-centered approach, which determines the best solution for well-structured problems. The other is selecting a good solution from a set of feasible ones using the decision-centered approach for solving semistructured problems. In either case, the solution centers on solving problems before they actually occur. The accent is on practicing "management by perception," rather than using the "management by exception" approach that is found in traditional problem solving.

Implementation. In this last part of the problem-centered approach, the implementation steps for the problem-solving process are usable. Fundamentally, these steps for the quantitative approach and the decision-centered approach are the same. In addition to implementation, it is necessary to establish control over the solution in order to detect how changing times are affecting it. It should be noted that there is need of *feedback* in the problem-centered approach from the last step back to the first one.

Opportunity-Centered Approach

This second approach to the problem-finding process is also taken from a prior publication by the author.[7] As illustrated in Figure 2-3, it consists of three steps plus the solution and implementation phases from the problem-solving process. Like the problem-centered approach, these three steps precede the actual solution to the future opportunity under study.

1. *Exploration.* This first step examines the internal and external environment for opportunities that come from problems uncovered. As in the problem-centered approach, *brainstorming* is generally used by managers and their staffs. The focus is directed away from the short range to the medium and long range where every effort is used to determine which opportunities are presented by the problems discovered in the future. As in the prior approach, the analysis is initially forward-looking in that there is a search for future problems. Once the problems have been identified, they are examined from the standpoint of identifying opportunities for improving the company's operations (from the standpoint of sales, profits, or whatever). From this perspective, the concept of opportunities has a "positive" connotation while the concept of problems has a "negative" meaning.

If deemed appropriate for the situation, creative computer software can be gainfully employed to assist managers and their staffs in developing new ideas that exploit appropriate opportunities for a company to pursue. Generally, creative computer software results in the exploration of more new ideas than if performed manually. This will be apparent in the various examples given in Part

III of this text. The selection of more opportunities helps to assure managers that this exploration step is performed in a most comprehensive manner.

2. *Selection.* Having identified appropriate opportunities, the second step is to determine what opportunities (one or more) should be explored by managers and their staffs. The selection process should focus on opportunities that can relate to a company's *critical success factors.* Typically, these factors include price, sales promotion, customer service, product mix, inventory turnover, cost control, and quality dealers. In turn, the interrelationships of the critical success factors and the company's goals and objectives are discussed for further clarification. But more important, this discussion determines which opportunities should be pursued by the company, thereby identifying them in a clear and meaningful way. Moreover, it takes into consideration all the important facts that bear on important company opportunities. Where deemed necessary, a *cost-benefit analysis* can be used to determine which opportunites are more important than others in terms of how they effect the company's future profits.

3. *Examine Boundaries.* The third step centers on surveying the environment for the opportunities identified before pursuing an opportunity solution. Due to the nature of some opportunities, the boundaries may be quite wide—that is, they may extend beyond the company and may be related to emerging and established organizations and industries. Generally, greater opportunities are found when boundaries are extended. Thus, top management and the corporate planning staffs need to examine the boundaries surrounding the opportunities from a narrow to a very wide perspective. The net result is that the proper boundaries are used in the solution and implementation of the opportunity.

Solution. As in the problem-centered approach, the solution to the opportunity-centered approach can take one of two directions—determination of the best solution using a quantitative-centered approach or the selection of a good solution from a set of feasible ones using the decision-centered approach. Current problem-solving approaches require that the decision maker pick an appropriate solution from the set of feasible ones. In a similar manner, an opportunity solution requires that the decision maker select the best opportunity from the set of feasible ones under study. As with the problem-centered approach, the main thrust is on practicing management by perception.

Implementation. In this last part of the opportunity-centered approach, the implementation steps for the problem-solving process are used. The opportunity must be monitored and implemented and the necessary adjustments must be made to accommodate changing times. This approach also provides for *feedback.*

DEVELOPMENT OF A KNOWLEDGE INFRASTRUCTURE

The *second* important factor in an effective KMS framework is the development of a knowledge infrastructure. Because the ability to get at vast amounts of information and, in turn, knowledge provides that all-important competitive edge, a company needs to share this information and knowledge across the organization. As a result layers of management can be eliminated and the organizational structure can be flattened. These flattened organizations can make and implement decisions quickly. Moreover, sharing information and knowledge with customers and suppliers helps break down the organizational boundaries. When people share information and knowledge and work together, teamwork is enhanced, and when employees are empowered to deal directly with their customers, the quality of service improves, thereby cementing relationships with the customers.

Capturing an organization's information and knowledge and making both accessible to users across the company requires an investment of time and money. Not only must the right systems be put in place and the right applications chosen for accessing the information and knowledge, but the company's employees must also learn to understand and use the appropriate knowledge tools. The issues involved in providing the right technology are complex. For example, in today's newer structures, information and resultant knowledge are closer to the individual. This means that the centralized information systems organizations are no longer the clearing houses, but rather provide guidance and standards while the line organizations of individual business units own the systems. Thus, the development of an appropriate knowledge infrastructure must take this important fact into account.

Essentially, the development of a knowledge infrastructure can reduce costs and increase profit margins. It enables the reorganization (i.e., reengineering) of business processes and functions. Moreover, the new knowledge infrastructure eases the development of strategic alliances, whereby companies and their suppliers form long-term relationships or companies join together to provide a wider range of services than any one of them can provide on its own. To assist in the development of an appropriate knowledge infrastructure, it may be necessary to develop very large databases, data marts, and data warehouses. In turn, these approaches can be related to an organization's knowledge bases. All of these important areas are discussed below from the viewpoint of the development of strategic alliances. A further elaboration of these topics can be found in Chapter 3.

Very Large Databases

As companies grow and their systems expand to meet this growth, they are coming up against the limits of their current system architectures—in particular, relational database management system (RDBMS) software, hardware platforms, and manageability. On-line transaction processing (OLTP) systems, which have historically been kept small to achieve maximum transaction rates, are raising their ceiling limits. On-line applications are becoming more complex. For example, automated teller machines today offer customers access not just to savings and checking accounts but also to a full array of financial services. The net result is that improved service requirements demand more knowledge about customers and products be placed on-line to assist sales and support personnel. And as users demand more from these kinds of systems, their demands are driving up the sizes of OLTP databases to what is currently called VLDBs (very large databases).

Currently, some experts define an OLTP VLDB as larger than 200 gigabytes and a VLDB data warehouse as anything bigger than 500 gigabytes. Managing a database becomes an issue for users when they go beyond the 100 gigabyte level for either an OLTP application or a data warehouse. When databases move into the hundreds of gigabytes, and even into the many terabytes, the management problem is compounded. Still, other experts state a database is a VLDB when it gets so large that it is difficult to manage. Although very large databases can be of great help to management in distilling the realities of their operations in terms of specific knowledge, there is first a need to manage the VLDBs properly.

It is expected that new VLDBs will differ from those of the past not only in their size and the platforms on which they run but also in the framework with which their developers undertake their construction. Some database developers are even beginning to plan for multipetabyte databases, driven by the incorporation of new information types, including audio/video, unstructured text, images, and spatial data, into traditional relational database frameworks. (A petabyte is 1,000 terabytes.) Some database developers predict that it will not take as long to go from terabytes to petabytes as it did from gigabytes to terabytes. Overall, VLDBs in this next generation are simply going to be quite larger than their predecessors for housing appropriate information and knowledge.

Data Marts and Data Warehouses

Typically, a *data mart* is a subset of an enterprisewide data warehouse. It performs the role of a departmental, regional, or functional data warehouse. As part of the iterative data warehouse process, the organization builds a series of data marts over time and eventually links them via an enterprisewide logical data warehouse. In contrast, a *logical data warehouse* contains all the metadata, business rules, and processing logic required to scrub, organize, package, and preprocess the data. In addition, it contains the information required to find and access the actual data, wherever it actually resides.

An important element in both is the level of complexity and size. The complexity of the data model for a data warehouse normally increases in accordance with the number of lines of business it serves. On the other hand, a data mart, regardless of size, requires a far simpler data model since it generally focuses on a single subject area. The subject of a data mart is generally determined by the department or line of business for which it is created. Typically, the first data marts that an organization develops are marketing and sales marts since the customer information they contain is essential to the welfare of the business.

Currently, data marts are subdivided into two varieties: independent and dependent. An *independent data mart* derives its data from a number of sources and operates autonomously. A *dependent data mart* is fed data from the enterprise data warehouse and is essentially a subset of the warehouse. The nature of the organization's business determines whether a data mart will be independent or dependent.

Companies are turning increasingly to data marts for the decision support needs for two principal reasons. They get simplicity and fast return on investment. Specifically, the data mart's focus on a particular line of business means the number of data sources tapped are fewer, which makes modeling the data mart a simpler process. The time and effort required to get the data mart up and running may be only a few months. In some cases, the cost is about a tenth or less than that of an enterprise warehouse. It is important to note that a company cannot indefinitely proliferate data marts because of the complexity of managing the data flows. This is one of the dangers of data mart operations. If an enterprise data warehouse structure is not built underneath, data marts grow into data warehouses on their own. The net result is that appropriate information and related knowledge cannot be garned from the data warehouse.

Knowledge Bases

Going beyond these database approaches in the development of a knowledge infrastructure, a company may have several expert systems or knowledge base systems. As discussed in the prior chapter, they use knowledge bases which consist of If-Then rules, mathematical formulas, heuristics, or some other knowledge representation structure to represent the knowledge of experts in a certain domain. Essentially, expert systems scan through their knowledge bases to find the appropriate rules, formulas, or some other knowledge structure to apply. The power of these systems derives from the knowledge they possess, rather than from the inference mechanism employed. To ensure the desired performance from expert systems, the acquisition of knowledge becomes a vital task in their development.

Typically, maintenance of knowledge bases is extremely important because knowledge is usually much more dynamic than data or information. In some cases, especially when knowledge can be derived from many sources, it changes on a daily basis. Human experts have trouble keeping up to date with all the changes in the knowledge domain with which they deal. Furthermore, some knowledge is not documented or well distributed. This can complicate matters. To assist in the maintenance of knowledge bases, it is essential to establish detailed plans. Generally, a methodology consists of planning, extraction, analysis, and verification. This orderly process can assist in assuring a company that its knowledge bases are current and relevant.

Broad-Based Approach to a Company's Knowledge Infrastructure

In the discussion above about very large databases, data marts, data warehouses, and knowledge bases, each area was treated as a separate entity. To better serve the interests of decision makers at all levels of the organization, there is a need for these multiple knowledge bases and databases to be integrated into a corporate-wide knowledge base. Although there is a distinction between knowledge bases and databases, their integration into a corporate-wide knowledge base is necessary in order to have a knowledge infrastructure that supports decision makers at all levels of the organization. More specifically, there is a need to integrate appropriate knowledge—no matter its source—for a company's functional areas (i.e., marketing, manufacturing, finance, and human resources) into this company-wide knowledge base so that decision makers can find desired knowledge in one place.

Object-oriented technology is an appropriate choice for designing a broad-based knowledge base that integrates a variety of distributed, hetergeneous knowledge bases and databases. An object-oriented design can be used to provide not only external views but also an internal representation of the broad-based knowledge base so that appropriate interpreters can be used for reasoning about the distributed knowledge. That is, by sharing a common protocol, the internal knowledge representation of the distributed objects may remain hidden from other objects. Object-oriented programming supports a powerful form of data abstraction in system design. Hence, object-oriented technology is useful as a framework for integrating the functional elements of a companywide knowledge base. Object-oriented design and programming supplies a helpful paradigm for modeling the separate knowledge-based agents of a company's functional elements. More information will be set forth in Chapters 3 and 5 on corporate knowledge bases and in Part III of the text.

DEVELOPMENT OF AN ORGANIZATION-WIDE COMPUTER NETWORK ARCHITECTURE

The *third* important factor in an effective KMS framework is the development of an organization-wide computer network architecture in order to take advantage of the information and its related knowledge that is typically widely dispersed in a company. As will be seen in the discussion to follow (and in Chapter 4), there are different approaches to getting at information and knowledge desired by decision makers. Advances, including enterprise network computers, groupware, intranets, and the Internet, are enabling decision makers "to draw a straight electronic line" bypassing much of the company's overlay of computer technology that has accumulated over the years. A most effective company network architecture is one in which decision makers can sit down and download what they need from the network. Although the decision makers may not be aware of what is happening, there is a lot of infrastructure for distributing, managing, and using that computer network. Overall, as computer technology for transferring information and knowledge grows more sophisticated, companies are using it to simplify their operations and, at the same time, better meet competitive challenges.

Employment of Groupware by Business Teams

Even though information and knowledge can be used on an individual or team basis, today there is increasing emphasis on a team approach, based on the old concept that several heads are better than one. Instead of spending money on problems or forming committees to talk about them, companies are sending out teams to find solutions. Generally, while self-directed work teams are getting things done on a day-to-day basis, cross-functional teams are reaching into all parts of an enterprise to address problems, implement plans, and make necessary changes.

Teams are currently the most rapidly expanding approach for involving employees in the effort to improve business results in situations where the use of information and knowledge is required. Where applicable, *groupware* such as Lotus Notes can be used to keep team members apprised of results when they are not physically present. It should be noted that newer groupware systems are entering the next generation with Internet features that free users from proprietary platforms and protocols.

A typical business team has six to 20 members. Successful ones have the right chemistry, a mix of problem-oriented, analytically oriented, and action-oriented individuals. Before seeking solutions, these teams first identify the problem, rigorously gathering the facts. This includes assessing pertinent information and knowledge using a type of groupware system commonly referred to as *collaboratory computing*. It also involves grasping the problem's dimensions. At times, this process dictates the solution, pinpointing obstacles that must be removed. Where improvements, changes, and breakthroughs are called for, the collective energy and creativity of team members come to the fore. Overall, enterprise network computing systems, as well as intranets and the Internet, can be of great assistance to business teams in accomplishing their assigned tasks.

Organization-Wide Network Computers to Accumulate and Disseminate Information and Knowledge

To assist decision makers in accumulating and disseminating information and knowledge, some companies are using enterprise network computers (NCs) to replace desktop computing. An NC, which is based on the concept of putting application computing on the network, includes a PC-compatible VGA display, keyboard, mouse, and a box with TCP/IP networking and PC-compatible serial ports. What differentiates the NCs are their operating system architectures and the type of remote application services they offer. Currently, there are several basic architectures for NC desktops, differing in how they support Java, Windows, and Unix applications. X-terminal vendors employ X Window desktops with some Java enhancements. Sun has licensed its JavaOS with Java Desktop. Microsoft and Intel are stressing Windows 95, 98, or Windows NT Workstation as the desktop for the NetPC. Network Computer Inc. (Oracle Computer's subsidiary) has licensed its NCOS to hardware vendors.

All NCs have TCP/IP for networking and offer, through application, the most common of the various protocols layered on top of TCP/IP. All these desktops adhere to one of the somewhat loosely defined NC reference standards. Each standard attempts to pin a least common denominator on what constitutes an NC in terms of network connectivity, network protocols, basic input/output hardware, and application support.

The concept of a low-maintenance desktop machine that gets most or all of its applications and storage from a network server is nothing really new. For example, in the past, a Sun 3/50 Unix workstation or a Network Computing Device X Window terminal had nearly all of what is now the network computer. What is new, however, is today's emphasis on LAN and Internet connectivity and the widespread use of the TCP/IP protocol as the fundamental transport for a wide variety of standardized service protocols, such as Post Office Protocol for E-mail, File Transfer Protocol for file transfers, and Hypertext Transfer Protocol for web browsing. Overall, network computers provide a low-maintenance and low-cost desktop for businesses and a robust upgrade path for sites using X Window applications and character terminals.[8]

Utilization of a Company's Intranets and Extranets

A company's intranets are related to enterprise network computing. In one sense, a company's intranets are simply a variation of the Internet and the World Wide Web. Unlike the normal use of the Internet (a public highway), a company's intranets are a private or semiprivate use of either the Internet or Internet-related technology for a particular organization. Intranets let companies exploit what they have learned from the Internet for the use of private, internally focused networking needs.

Many companies, for example, have volumes of policies and procedures of which they would like their employees to be aware and actually use when appropriate. Unfortunately, most of the time a set of policies and procedures sits on a shelf somewhere in a company and collects dust. Employees may not know that the specific policies and procedures exist or even how to locate a current version. Intranets allow companies to take their policies and procedures and put them on-line for ready access by internal employees. In the past, the effort to put such policies and procedures on-line might have been arduous and costly.

By using company intranets, employees are able to get at the policies and procedures quickly and relatively inexpensively.

Intranets are not just for company employees anymore. The phenomenion of ''outside intraneting'', or extranets, is widely used today as companies explore more creative uses for their intranets. Extranets give third parties such as trading partners and customers access to the corporate World Wide Web site. At their most powerful, intranets can be harnessed in this manner to create new types of organizations, such as virtual groups that convene for a specific purpose and time period and later disband once a project is complete. In essence, intranet innovators are marrying internal networks and extranets with the web technologies to create powerful collaborative capabilities for employees, business partners, and customers. The bottom line is that they see the potential to transform business into something that resembles electronic commerce.

In light of the current direction of intranets and extranets, innovators are changing the way companies think about information and knowledge access and distribution as well as transforming network infrastructures. The accounting and consulting firm of Coopers & Lybrand, for example, is developing an intranet called KnowledgeNet. This ''multidimensional map'' offers unprecedented access to the firm's institutional expertise. Although still in the first stages, planners foresee that users will be able to type in a description of a subject area and KnowledgeNet will refer them to the partners and staff members in the firm who are most knowledgeable about the subject. Hyperlinks will let users get the latest reports, articles, or materials from recent conferences on the subject. Coopers & Lybrand's intranet currently contains approximately 6,000 pages, less than 10 percent of the information and knowledge it eventually will contain. The project involves consolidating 2,500 existing databases. Overall, giving company employees access to the vast databases within an organization is a high-priority opportunity for many companies. Web browsers, HTML editors, and other intranet tools are the ideal front end to defuse the complexities of multiple incompatible business sources.[9]

Linkage with Outside Organizations Using the Internet to Share Knowledge

In the above exposition on the utilization of company intranets and extranets, reference was made to the Internet. The Internet has basically become the postal service, telephone system, and research library of the electronic age, thereby allowing millions of people to exchange information and knowledge virtually anywhere in the world and at any time, usually in a matter of minutes, using available data communications and networking technology. Its appeal is that anyone on the Internet can post and retrieve desired output. Thus, it behooves a company to plan Internet use with a clear focus on the customers who will be the most important to it in the future. Although most companies focus on building an informational web site, it is more important to provide a service defined by key customers.

Customers do not come to a company's web site because it runs secure web servers. They come if they are given value for their time—that is, it reduces their cost of doing business. In some cases, it is possible that customers will pay higher prices if their overall costs of identifying and acquiring the products or service are significantly reduced. Typically, a company's web site says more about the company than its logo, buildings, or annual report because it is where customers go first to find out about and gain access to a company's products and services. In turn, this input may help customers reduce the costs of their operations. Gaining a favorable presence on the Internet's World Wide Web, then, is the name of the game for the typical company today. Information about customers' responses can lay the foundation for future knowledge about customers' reaction to favorable web sites.

The ability of knowledge-based expert systems to answer specific well-defined problems makes them ideal web-resident technology for product selection, technical support, help desks, and regulations (i.e., any area that requires specific decision-making knowledge). Accessing an expert system on the web, as opposed to a Frequently Asked Question (FAQ) list, is like talking to an expert instead of reading a technical manual. If, for example, a customer has a problem with a PC printer, an expert does not tell the person all the things that can go wrong with the printer to see if any apply. He or she asks questions about the problem and its symptoms and, in turn, gives one or several recommendations. That is exactly what the expert system does. Rather than using a FAQ list, it presents questions for the user to answer, followed by a solution. This is not just a database search because the questions are focused. Subsequent questions depend on the answers to earlier ones and on the relevance to a possible solution. Essentially, straightforward development tools allow developers to build expert systems rapidly on PCs. In turn, they can move them to a web server and run them with the appropriate runtime engine.

On the other hand, when referencing problems that are much larger in context and way beyond the scope of expert systems (which is somewhat typical today), there is a need to make use of enterprise-wide knowledge. For example, when calling on large customers, sales representatives may lack the required knowledge about cost and quality issues needed to answer tough questions that go beyond the confines of the customer's organization and get into issues concerning the union, or governmental and financial institutions. To facilitate the flow of knowledge to the customer, it may be necessary to access appropriate knowledge sources about the area under study via the various web sites on the Internet. This knowledge can then be brought to bear on the selected areas under investigation. From this viewpoint, linkage with outside organizations via the Internet can bring appropriate knowledge to decision makers in order to resolve important issues.

UTILIZATION OF APPROPRIATE SOFTWARE WITHIN A KMS ENVIRONMENT

The *fourth* important factor in an effective KMS framework is the utilization of appropriate software. Before knowledge can be accessed by decision makers, it must available in a format that is easy to understand and use. Although the company may have in place an effective knowledge infrastructure, generally it is necessary to analyze appropriate information in order to get at the underlying knowledge to answer the question(s) under study as well as explore ''what-if'' situations. Hence, there is a need to employ the appropriate software for extracting, storing, and disseminating the desired knowledge. In addition, the software employed can be designed exclusively for discovering knowledge.

As will be seen in Chapter 5, not only will the essentials of knowledge extraction tools, knowledge management software, knowledge management intranet search engines, and knowledge discovery or data mining software be presented, but also some of the current popular packages that are found widely in a typical company will be examined. In certain situations, other types of software packages, such as OLAP software, statistical analysis software, and GUI/4GL software, can be useful in getting a handle on knowledge that is contained in multiple knowledge bases and databases found throughout an organization. Overall, the utilization of knowledge software of some type will be evident in the discussion that follows.

It should be noted at the outset that most companies are likely to end up with more than one software package because the situation dictates that knowledge software is judged best by its users. That is, the focus is *situational* to get at the appropriate knowledge, store it, and disseminate it. Typically, very large databases are used where there are larger volumes of data and information and detailed analysis is required to discover the knowledge to solve problems. When the queries are simpler and the data and information is smaller, simple and easy-to-use software will do the job to discover the knowledge needed to answer questions surrounding the problems. However, more and more companies today find themselves in situations where users demand a wider range of decision support, EIS, OLAP, and knowledge discovery software packages to solve a growing number of problems facing them.

Knowledge Extraction Tools

Within a KMS environment, there are often a number of off-the-shelf products that can be employed. In addition to groupware, E-mail, document management systems, object and relational databases, and workflow software, which are often an integral part of business process analyses and/or reengineering efforts, knowledge extraction tools are generally the first ones acquired to get a handle on a company's current knowledge. More specifically, knowledge management systems employ knowledge extraction tools to identify and extract important technical information from organization files, documents, etc., so that their contents can be turned into practical knowledge for a company's personnel. Thus, the important challenge of knowledge extraction tools centers on their ability to provide fast and accurate current knowledge about a company's current operations that can be used as is or analyzed further by a company's decision makers.

For many companies, knowledge extraction tools must not only deal with textual information to derive knowledge but also must be able to treat text in several languages. From this perspective, the extraction tools must be capable of meeting the varying needs of an organization within its KMS environment. For example, Inxight's LinguistX product line has multilingual natural language processing capability for extracting knowledge at a very high rate of speed. It is capable of supporting a number of functions, including automatic language identification, phrase extraction, and automatic summarization in several languages. Currently, LinguistX is an integral part of major applications from companies that market some type of knowledge discovery software.

Knowledge Management Software

Going beyond knowledge extraction tools, knowledge management software is useful to contain a massive amount of data and information, organize it logically, and make its resulting knowledge accessible to the right people at the proper time and place. It is certainly a challenge when considering the multitude of sources and a corporate culture that has typically thrived on hoarding rather than sharing knowledge. Companies have found that employing knowledge management software requires a good deal of hand-holding from vendors. It is also expensive and will not deliver without a research analyst or knowledge worker dedicated to the development efforts on a full-time basis.

Currently available knowledge management software views a KMS environment somewhat differently. For example, Wincite is a goal-oriented solution that organizes and distributes information related to a specific problem. On the other hand, grapeVine stores information on a variety of topics and distributes it to people based on their individual profiles. Still other KMS software is somewhat in between these two. The best advice for a company is to approach its KMS operating mode with eyes wide open. If a company already has a person or department committed to tracking information, these software packages can help them work more effectively to get a grasp on the company's knowledge.

Knowledge Management Intranet Search Engines

In response to the times, leading intranet search engine vendors have repositioned themselves as knowledge management companies. They offer strategic services and software tools that include intelligent agents, push technology, and database crawlers capable of searching across multiple platforms. Two typical software vendors are Fulcrum and Verity. Fulcrum states that intelligence is delivered in two phases. The first phase takes a logical view of the entire collection. In phase two, the view of the collection provides the foundation for intelligent analytical assistance for knowledge workers. Empowering knowledge workers with the ability to find, create, and share information is a major element in capturing the tacit knowledge that exists in an organization.

Verity, on the other hand, made a name for itself with its Topics, a knowledge categorization framework that is recognized as a direct precursor to today's push techniques. In recent years, they have licensed Search to over 300 ISVs (integrated software vendors), from Adobe to Xerox, who incorporate Verity software into widely distributed products. The new Search '97 family is the latest generation of products. The major challenger to these intranet search engine software vendors is the Microsoft Corporation, which offers customers its Index Server text retrieval software for free. But to date, Microsoft has not focused seriously on this market.

Knowledge Discovery or Data Mining Software

With the proliferation of data warehouses, many traditional report and query tools as well as statistical analysis systems are using the term data mining in their product descriptions. In addition, some AI-based (artificial intelligence) systems are being promoted as data mining tools. The main objective of data mining is *knowledge discovery*. The methodology of data mining involves the extraction of hidden predictive information and resulting knowledge from large databases. However, with such a broad definition, many OLAP products or statistical packages, such as SAS, can qualify as data mining tools. For true knowledge discovery to occur, a data mining tool should arrive at this hidden knowledge without too much trouble.

Essentially, data mining is the process of analyzing data and information within a multidimensional framework. Data mining allows different individuals to retrieve as much or as little data and information as they need. They can retrieve current detail data and information from within or outside the organization and summarize it by any desired category. Data mining products provide a basic analysis capability (minimum, maximum, and average) and the ability to drill down to obtain more detail and to summarize details as necessary. Additionally, some data mining products go beyond basic analysis capabilities by providing statistical and mathematical routines to calculate the coefficients and powers of prespecified independent variables. This is known as curve fitting or trend analysis. Trend analysis is used to determine patterns and relationships and to see if key measurements are still within their limits and expectations.

It is not difficult to determine patterns when the variables are known. Mathematical techniques are available to determine the relationship of one dependent variable (such as sales of a particular model) to several independent variables (such as the selling price, competition, number of sales channels, sales of complementary products, inflation rate, etc.). However, the difficulty is identifying key patterns and trends when the analyst does not know the independent variables or, for that matter, may not even know what dependent variable should be analyzed. This is where more sophisticated and powerful knowledge-based techniques can be useful.

A data mining product with knowledge-based capabilities can detect patterns in data and information that are not readily apparent. That is, it can indicate that there is a relationship between one dependent variable and one or more independent variables. Some data mining products utilize data visualization techniques to present these relationships graphically. The analyst can change the scale, display format, and present factors to represent the relationships better. The relationship need not be causal nor readily apparent. A typical knowledge discovery tool is KnowledgeSEEKER, which can analyze and understand patterns and relationships as well as serve as an accurate predictive tool.

OLAP and Statistical Analysis Software

Other useful software for uncovering hidden patterns and relationships includes OLAP software and statistical analysis software as well as GUI/4GL languages. Although the first two are treated below, all of these software approaches can be helpful to decision makers under varying circumstances. On-line analytical processing (OLAP) applications (which will also be found where appropriate in Part III of the text) are essentially focused on employing multidimensional analysis. Generally, this analysis centers on dividing data into the important dimensions that are useful for understanding and managing a company's operations. Multidimensional analysis provides for selection, analysis, summarization, and reporting by dimensions and attributes within dimensions.

Because multidimensionality is the core of on-line analytical processing, major vendors have developed specific software to focus on this feature. These vendors recognize that users need to look at different slices of data trending by time periods and by types of transactions. Their needs go beyond the traditional spreadsheets. Typically, users would enter numbers into spreadsheets and work them through until they thought they had it right. There was no inherent integrity to the results. However, with many OLAP products, users can perform such analyses quickly and simply since all the required calculations and aggregations have been already executed and validated. Typical successful OLAP vendors include Arbor Software, Inc's Essbase and Pilot Software Inc's LightShip Suite. Some of the software products currently offered can store up to six dimensions with relative ease, thereby making the job of multidimensional analysis much easier for users. For complete coverage of OLAP software, reference can be made to a recent text by the author.[10]

Today, there are a number of statistical software packages available from a wide range of vendors. Some are focused on different methods of forecasting. The Statistical Analysis System (SAS) from the SAS Institute is the most widely used software. This firm offers 70 to 80 statistical routines. Some other statistical analysis packages, like Forecast Pro, have the capability to analyze data and information statistically. The software conducts the analysis that will determine which method (i.e., simple methods, exponential smoothing, Box-Jenkins, and dynamic regression) will do the best forecasting based on data and information supplied. There are also business graphics software packages that complement statistical-analysis packages. Lastly, it should be noted that knowledge discovery or data mining tools have a statistical orientation since they help decision makers analyze patterns and trends and serve as relatively accurate predictive tools.

KNOWLEDGE MANAGEMENT SYSTEMS DEFINED

In the preceding discussion on the essentials of knowledge management systems, four factors were explored. *First*, knowledge serves as an underlying basis for decision makers to engage in problem finding (i.e., in finding and solving future problems and identifying opportunities for implementation as well as solving current problems). *Second*, the development of an appropriate knowledge infrastructure that complements the information infrastructure was explored. *Third*, as a way of gathering knowledge (including information) and disseminating it to organizational members, a companywide network architecture was discussed that included intranets and extranets as well as a tie-in with the Internet. *Fourth*, the utilization of appropriate software was discussed from the standpoint of developing knowledge about a company's functional parts as well as the total organization. In summary, the collective wisdom gained through the sharing of information and knowledge can make a significant difference in the company's profitability. Today that information and knowledge must be available in real-time because of the speed with which changes take place.

For most companies, information and its related knowledge that is analyzed, shared, and acted upon is what provides the competitive advantage organizations need. The tools an organization employs for the management of technology, for bringing the right resources to the right people, determines whether or not information and its related knowledge makes a difference of the order of magnitude companies are seeking. The development of knowledge management systems that fit organizational needs and can adapt to changes in the organization is a crucial issue. Selecting and implementing the right technology for the organization takes a thorough understanding of the nature of the business, its organizational structure, its culture, and the way management works. That is why those who assist organizations to choose their knowledge direction must look at the organization *holistically*. Optimizing functions and streamlining processes to develop appropriate company knowledge requires a thorough understanding of the processes, functions, and technology in place. This knowledge is then readily available for use by company decision makers. Today, this generally means extending knowledge to a company's trading partners (i.e., customers and suppliers). From this broad perspective, a KMS operating mode centers on managing internal and external information and resulting knowledge in a proactive manner to create a competitive advantage that is linked to a company's business objectives and its measurable goals.

Based on the essentials of knowledge management systems discussed so far in the text, they can be defined as enterprise-wide systems that employ a rapid retrieval capability using appropriate software from an organization-wide or global knowledge base, including data warehousing, for the purpose of providing decision makers with timely knowledge for problem solving and, in particular, problem finding. Knowledge management systems make use of an open system and client server architecture. Decision makers can deploy all types of knowledge and provide access outside their employee base to customers, partners, suppliers, and investors. Typically, the end result of this internal and external search is knowledge that is required by decision makers to understand the *whys* and *wherefores* versus the *whats* for the problem(s) under study. Overall, successful knowledge management systems depend on the capability of decision makers to employ readily accessible knowledge that can be acted upon in a timely manner.

REAL-WORLD EXAMPLES OF KNOWLEDGE MANAGEMENT SYSTEMS

To help its professionals work smarter, Coopers & Lybrand has given its chief knowledge officer (CKO), Ellen Knapp, the job of collecting and cataloging the expertise of its staff worldwide into a knowledge management system, sometimes referred to as the firm's intellectual assets. Basically, her job entails all aspects of knowledge generation, both among its professionals and between the firm and its clients. As CKO, she also facilitates knowledge sharing among the company's 73,000 professionals as well as between the firm and its client base. In addition to these duties, she is responsible for formulating a strategy with respect to new knowledge-based products and services. Overall, she makes sure that knowledge is available through the Internet and throughout electronic communities.

An integral part of generating and sharing knowledge for Coopers & Lybrand's professionals is the utilization of traditional groupware products, like Lotus Development Corporation's Notes. Groupware products are becoming more suited for a knowledge management system environment because they represent a move toward a nonproprietary software paradigm. The vendors are adopting the metaphor and presumed ubiquity of the World Wide Web as the fundamental communication environment. The part of groupware that is really interesting is found in companies that are building intelligent agents and knowledge agents. At this accounting and consulting firm, not only are news services used but a large amount of knowledge is also generated internally along with a lot of information that is embedded in legacy systems. With software agents, for example, information on three specific companies can be delivered to one's desk each morning if necessary. Other products that can help greatly are add-ons to groupware products. These create knowledge maps of all the information in the company. There are also products that function as yellow pages for all the corporate databases. Such technology makes it relatively easy to traverse a knowledge management system.[11]

At 3M, a company that prides itself not only on learning from its mistakes but also on turning them into profitable products, researchers do not need to go home to pursue a personal project. They are free to do research on the job, with full access to company equipment and facilities. This is the result of 3M's strong culture of knowledge management. 3M has a history of spinning off new businesses from its existing technical platforms and sharing technical knowledge to communicate about current project activities and status.

At London-based British Petroleum (BP), when a remote oil drilling rig needs repair, the company no longer has to fly in an expert, committing a large investment of time and money. Using desktop teleconferencing, repair specialists around the world can view, discuss, and assess a malfunctioning part and recommend a solution. The solution is then captured and stored for later analysis to guide future repairs, saving millions of dollars in travel costs and downtime each year. It is all part of an organized strategic intent. The company's vision can be summed up as follows: BP knows what it knows, learns what it needs to learn, and uses knowledge to deliver overwhelming sustainable competitive advantage.

Another example of a KMS environment can be found at Xerox where AmberWeb was established as an intranet-based virtual workspace that enables employees to share research and documents through bulletin boards and calendars. (AmberWeb is a collection of web-based CGI scripts written in Python object-oriented code that runs on both Sun UNIX and Compaq NT servers.) Teams can create their own settings and publish documents without going through the webmaster. At its Palo Alto Research Center, Xerox generates knowledge about collaborative and knowledge-sharing systems, visualization technologies, and virtual workspaces by bringing together anthropologists, artists, and computer scientists. Because each specialist asks different kinds of questions, the answers that emerge tend to be creative and wide ranging. The focus of knowledgement management systems is to create a learning environment in which knowledge can be more systematically created, accumulated, used, and reused—at both the individual and organizational levels.[12] In summary, the phenomenon at Coopers & Lybrand, 3M, BP, and Xerox—and a growing number of other firms—now has a recognized label: a KMS operating mode. A bottom-line strategy behind the rise of knowledge management systems is the recognition that capitalizing on a company's wealth creates competitive advantage and profitable outcomes.

SUMMARY

The initial focus of the chapter was to provide an overview of what constitutes a framework for knowledge management systems. Essentially, such systems focus on the capability of a KMS to improve decision makers' effectiveness, with an accent on "a knowledge focus" and "a syngeristic interaction" to share knowledge. The various levels of knowledge were then viewed in terms of their relevance to the various levels of management and support personnel. Next, the four factors that underlie knowledge management systems were presented. First, the type of problems that can be solved were discussed along with a tie-in of knowledge with problem finding. In the problem-finding process, the problem-centered approach pinpoints future problems that can be solved today to minimize their impact in the future. Related to this is the opportunity-centered approach, which searches the environment for opportunities that derive from problems uncovered. Second, the focus was on the development of a knowledge infrastructure. Third, the need for an overall company network architecture was explored. Fourth, the employment of appropriate software for developing knowledge that ties together the diverse elements found in a KMS environment was stressed. These four factors provided a basis for defining knowledge management systems that allow decision makers the capability of solving the simple to complex problems facing them.

NOTES

1. David Bank, "Know-It-Alls," in *The Corporate Connection, Wall Street Journal*, November 18, 1996, p. R28.

2. Ibid.

3. Graham Wallas, *Art of Thought* (New York: Harcout Brace, 1926).

4. William J. J. Gordon, *Synectics: The Development of Creative Capacity* (New York: Harper & Row, 1961).

5. Robert J. Thierauf, *Creative Computer Software for Strategic Thinking and Decision Making: A Guide for Senior Management and MIS Professionals* (Westport, CT: Quorum Books, 1993), chapter 6, pp. 131–173.

6. Robert J. Thierauf, *A Problem-Finding Approach to Effective Corporate Planning* (Westport, CT: Quorum Books, 1987), chapter 2, pp. 17–43.

7. Ibid.

8. Jason Levitt, "Shedding Some Light on NCs," *InformationWeek*, November 18, 1996, pp. 57–64.

9. Connie Winkler, "Opportunities Knock," *InformationWeek*, November 18, 1996, pp. 122–124.

10. Robert J. Thierauf, *On-Line Analytical Processing Systems for Business* (Westport, CT: Quorum Books, 1997), Chapter 4, pp. 101–129.

11. Barb Cole, "The Knowledge Chief Speaks," *Network World*, September 16, 1996, p. 127.

12. Dr. Edward Wakin, "Knowledge Management: Tapping Intellectual Capital," *Beyond Computing*, May 1998, pp. 37–41.

PART II

The Essentials of Knowledge Management Systems for Business

3

Data Storage Useful in Discovering Knowledge

Issues Explored:

- What is the basic framework that underlies storing and discovering knowledge?
- What are the current directions in corporate databases?
- What is a desirable approach to building an effective data warehouse to discover knowledge?
- What is the importance of data mining in discovering knowledge?
- What is a low-cost approach to securing a company's data and information?

Outline:

INTRODUCTION TO DATA STORAGE USEFUL IN DISCOVERING KNOWLEDGE

Currently, most successful companies are just beginning to leverage what is almost certainly their most valuable asset: knowledge. As noted previously in the text, the collective knowledge of an organization, its intellectual capital, is embedded in the personal skills, experience, and brainpower of its employees as well as in its processes, policies, databases, and other information repositories. It is from this perspective that storage useful in discovering knowledge is discussed in this chapter.

As will be seen, this includes first looking at an underlying framework for data storage, followed by current directions in corporate databases. An important part of discovering knowledge involves the use of data storage, such as data marts and data warehouses. Basically, data storage supports analytical processing by providing integrated and transformed enterprise-wide historical data from which to do appropriate analysis. A corporate-wide perspective of data warehousing allows for improved business processes, realization of new business opportunities, improved decision making, and improved comprehension of complex data and high-quality information that is the raw material of knowledge. This presentation will be followed by looking at data mining, which is the knowledge discovery process of extracting previously unknown, actionable facts from databases. The bottom line in this whole process of data analysis and mining is to provide the *right information and knowledge* to the *right people* at the *right time* so they can make the *right decisions*.

UNDERLYING FRAMEWORK FOR DISCOVERING KNOWLEDGE

In order to realize the full potential of knowledge management systems, it is helpful to look beyond their technology and requirements by establishing a fundamental framework that will facilitate their development. Such a framework is found in an *open systems environment*, which allows users to retrieve information locally that may be found halfway around the world. Complementary to this environment is *client/server technology*, which centers on the way computers and networking technologies are applied. Because both are important, they are discussed directly below. In addition, it should be noted that the current movement to *very large databases* is also set forth below. In all cases, consideration should be given to *scalability* (i.e., the ability to add processors and disk drives incrementally as system demand grows), and *high availability*, including on-line backup and recovery.

Open Systems Architecture

Because computer managers are being asked continually to manage more and more of the information technology (i.e., hardware, software, and networks in their organizations), they must develop the ability to reach beyond the mainframe-oriented data center, into an end user domain filled with a diversity of microcomputers, departmental systems, and networks as well as a melange of software tools and applications. And they must be prepared to make the elements of this mixture work together. No longer can computer managers think in terms of a single vendor or hardware or a single operating system. Currently, they need to find ways to integrate an expanding assortment of computing products and services to meet the demands of enterprise-wide and even inter-enterprise information in a competitive environment that has expanded to a global scale. Such an approach is found in an open systems environment.

Open systems implement specifications for interfaces, services, and supporting formats that enable properly engineered application software to be ported across systems, interoperate with other applications, and interact with users in a consistent manner. To place open systems in perspective, large retailers, such as Wal-Mart, Kmart, Dayton Hudson, and Sears, manage inventory by linking them to manufacturers as if in a single network. While this open systems approach eliminates the advantages of a supplier's proprietary network, it also gives manufacturers valuable information. These retailers provide manufacturers with updated sales and inventory information electronically so that manufacturers can plan production. With such data arriving in a standard format from so many customers, a manufacturer like Levi Strauss or Vanity Fair can easily estimate aggregate demand weeks in advance and produce sales forecasts to help plan production even further in advance. This capability can be very helpful to a company that wants to take the analysis one step further using knowledge management technology.

Client/Server Architecture

A client/server is a computer architecture in which any device in a network can request information or processing services from any other. When a device is asking for data or processing power, it is a *client*. When it is supplying information or services, it is a *server*. As such, client/server architectures provide users with transparent access to file servers, database servers, print servers, and other devices, thereby maximizing user options and network throughput while minimizing operating costs and response time over the network. The client/server model is a powerful method for writing applications that partition the program into pieces installed in two or more separate network stations. Tools built for implementing applications in this way allow program parts developed independently to interoperate over a network.

Client/server architecture improves the payoff from information and knowledge. It makes sense because it helps organizations maximize their extensive investments in processing power—from the desktop to the computer mainframe. But client/server architecture only makes sense if it is appropriate for all organizational applications. There are a number of factors required for the shift to client/server computing. Most important are networks, standards, and the tremendous power and versatility of today's desktop devices. Currently, no single vendor can supply all the pieces to make client/server computing a reality. A good test of how well a vendor is positioned to meet an organization's client/server needs is to examine how open the company's product line is. Open computing, software, and network tools are the plug-and-play components that are the foundation of client/server architecture.

Very Large Databases

Another important technology for discovering knowledge is the utilization of very large databases (VLDBs). Basically, there are two main categories of VLDBs: OLTP (on-line transaction processing) and data warehouses. OLTP systems are generally plain, simple, and to the point (i.e., functional and without artifice). On the other hand, data warehousing systems are large, complex, and varied.

Typically today, OLTP databases are at the vanguard of larger and broader use of transaction processing applications in the organization. Many companies are consolidating previously isolated, stand-alone, or single-product-line databases into VLDBs that provide a unified view of their business operations and customers. Hence, data warehouses are growing very large and very quickly. They are, after all, called *warehouses* for that reason. They are designed to store a company's inventory of corporate data for later retrieval in much the same way a manufacturer stores finished goods in a physical warehouse. To that can be added daily copies of transactions from a business's ongoing OLTP operational systems as well as outside data from historical archives, demographics, market research, and the like. In fact, an average data warehouse can grow up to sixfold within two years.

For some large companies, data warehouses have reached the terabyte level. This growth is experienced not only because more data is collected, but also because it is being kept longer to analyze trends. In addition, data that centers on discovering knowledge about the company and its customers is being opened up to more users, and indexes are being created to support their queries. As will be seen later in the chapter, very large databases are needed to assist companies in data mining, which is the use of knowledge discovery, pattern recognition, data analysis, and expert systems technology to automate the search for information locked up in (typically) very large databases. This is the cutting edge of decision support, already in use by large organizations for sales and inventory analysis, database marketing, fraud detection, financial prediction, and pharmaceutical development. Data mining algorithms and techniques have been and will be the focus of expert database research. Overall, very large databases have become the norm to help companies discover appropriate knowledge to meet their decision-making needs. It should be noted that NCR's Teradata has become the database of choice in more than 50 percent of the large data warehouses in production worldwide.[1]

CURRENT DIRECTIONS IN CORPORATE DATABASES

Because there is a need to provide on-line access to database elements for immediate processing using direct access file storage devices, one popular method of maintaining a database and managing relationships among the database elements is to employ a database management system (DBMS). Typically, the reach of a database management system extends beyond the individual file management systems, such as inventory files and accounts receivable files of the past, to an entire database (or databases), consisting of corporate planning, marketing, manufacturing, finance, human resources, and other data elements. Futhermore, a DBMS allows *procedure independence* of the database for a large number of data elements. This means that the programmer does not have to describe the data file in detail, as is the case with procedure-oriented languages like COBOL, but rather need only specify what is to be done in a *data management language*.

Currently, there are several directions in corporate databases that have and will continue to impact the typical company. They include relational databases, object-oriented databases, and multidimensional databases. Each of these types covered below should be an integral part of a company's total database infrastructure. Consideration should be given to consolidating storage management under an enterprise management platform that provides centralized access to the control mechanisms for managing not only storage but also data, systems, networks, security, and output. These mechanisms existed in the computer mainframe world and were largely overlooked as corporate computing moved out of the glasshouse. They need to be added to distributed computing environments.

Relational Databases

A *relational* database management system is simply a collection of two-dimensional tables (called relations) with no repeating group. In the tables, the rows constitute records and columns constitute fields. The term ''relational'' comes from the clearly defined relations among data within a field, relations that order the records in the database. For example, numeric fields can be ordered from least to greatest, alphabetic fields can be in alphabetical order, and so forth.

The relational model, which is found currently in DBMS models, offers many advantages over hierarchical and network models. It is based on a logical rather than a physical structure and shows the relationships among various items. Data are represented in tabular form and new relations can be created. Searching is generally faster than within the other schemes, modification is more straightforward, and the clarity and visibility of the database are improved. Because the relational database management system (RDBMS) is based on a flexible row-and-table format, this approach is appropriate for most business applications, from the simplest ones built by end users to high-volume applications involving millions of transactions per day built by computer personnel.

A RDBMS also processes records one set at a time. The computer will search for and identify all members of the sought-after set—for example, all past due accounts. By contrast, hierarchical DBMSs examine each record and identify whether it is past due. If it is not, the system goes to the next record. If overdue, the system sends out a notice. In addition to these time and money-saving attributes, the RDBMS has a formal theoretical foundation, which provides rules for structure, maintenance, and integrity (preserving the data against unauthorized changes). More important, organizations can add new data fields, build new access paths, and split tables without disturbing other programs or data stored in the database.

Object-Oriented Databases

Although relational DBMSs have been popular, they are being replaced or, in some cases, being supplemented by object-oriented technology. Now companies can take advantage of the structure, performance, and scalability of relational technology while adding object types and software modules. The simplicity of the relational model of data and the acceptance of the relational SQL (structured query language) as an industry standard have contributed to its popularity. Even as the acceptance of relational database management systems has spread, their limitations have been exposed by the emergence of various classes of new applications, including design, engineering, multimedia, geographic, scientific, and OLAP systems. These complex applications do not always lend themselves to relational DBMS. However, object-oriented database management systems (OODBMSs) provide a more universal approach to a multitude of applications that extend beyond the business community.

Today, object orientation is a term whose meaning changes in different situations. End users encounter *objects* in their graphical user interface in the form of icons or other graphical representations of parts of an application. Programmers use object-oriented programming (OOP) languages to write highly modular applications. In an object-oriented database management system, developers use *objects* to store complex data—for example, for CAD/CAM (computer-aided design/computer-aided manufacturing) or geographic information systems. Object-oriented analysis and design (OOAD) allows programmers to apply design methodologies and use CASE (computer-aided software engineering) tools to create object-oriented programs. In addition, Distributed Object Management provides a way for distributed, heterogenous applications spread across a wide area network to communicate and share data. Typically, OODBMSs are interwined with computing activities throughout the organization.

The first users of OODBMSs tended to be engineers who found that relational databases were unable to handle the storage requirements of complex scientific data or CAD drawings. While RDBMSs can store straightforward, predefined alphanumeric data types, a system for storing scientific data might require the use of a variable dimension array. A database for CAD drawings would need to preserve the relationships between the lines and angles of the vector graphics within each file.

In a somewhat similar manner, businesses have begun to consider OODBMS to centralize and simplify the storage of a wide range of complex data, such as text files and mapping data. Some of this information is stored in file systems with the applications that created them; much is still on paper. Business organizations are also expressing interest in OODBMS products for their capability to cut application development backlogs by reducing development time through the reuse of code. As organizations move more toward a unified, organization-wide system, they will be able to take a lot of disjointed systems that have been built on an application-by-application basis and create a single, local perspective on customers or products and services using object-oriented DBMS.

The leading OODBMS vendors include Object Design, Inc. (Burlington, Massachusetts), Gemstone Systems, Inc. (Beaverton, Oregon), 02 Technology, Inc.

(Palo Alto, California), Objectivity, Inc. (Mountain View, California), Versant Object Technology Corporation (Menlo Park, California) and Ontos, Inc. (Lowell, Massachusetts). Today, large relational database management systems vendors such as Informix Software, Inc. and the Oracle Corporation are getting into the act by adding object-oriented DBMS features to their relational products. This usually takes the form of support for undifferentiated binary large objects (BLOBS). BLOBS, however, do not provide the performance of a true object-oriented database. Also, a group of hybrid relational/object-oriented DBMSs has emerged to bridge the gap between the two database worlds. It should be noted that until recently, object-oriented DBMSs have lacked many of the basic features considered necessary for business production use. These includes locking (which prevents two users from changing the same data simultaneously) or rollback (which restores a database to its original state if a transaction is interrupted in midstream).

Multidimensional Databases

Going beyond the above models for database management systems, there is a more recent model that focuses on the use of *multidimensionality* in on-line analytical processing systems. Multidimensional databases (MDDs) logically store data in arrays rather than store information as keyed records in tables. Currently, there is no agreed upon multidimensional model—that is, MDDs have no standard data access method and range from narrow to broad in addressing user requirements for decision making. At the low end, there are single-user or small-scale, LAN-based tools for viewing multidimensional data. Although the functionality and usability of these tools are high, they are limited in scale and lack broad OLAP features. Tools in this category include PowerPlay from Cognos, PaBlo from Andyne, and Mercury from Business Objects. At the high end, tools such as Acumate ES from Kenan Technologies, Express from Oracle, Gentium from Planning Sciences, and Holos from Holistic Systems have such diverse functionality that each tool could define a separate category. The pure multidimensional database engines are Essbase from Arbor Software, LightShip Server from Pilot Software, and TM/1 from Sniper.

Basically, there are two approaches to multidimensionality: the hypercube and the multicube. The *hypercube*, exemplified by Essbase, is meant to describe a similar object of greater than three dimensions, with flat sides and each dimension at right angles to all of the others. Designing a hypercube model is a top-down process: (1) Start by selecting the aspect of the business to capture, such as sales activity or financial reporting. (2) Identify the values to be captured, such as sales or account balances. This information is almost always numeric. (3) Identify the dimensions or granularity of the data—the lowest level of detail at which analysis is feasible. Common dimensions are measure, time, scenario, geography, product, and customer. A single cell in a cube, for example, could store the sales in March in the Southeast of a specific product to a specific vendor.

Because MDDs store information in arrays, values in the arrays can be updated without affecting the index, which is the reason MDDs are so well suited for read-write applications. However, a drawback to this hypercube model is that even minor changes in the dimensional structure require a complete reorganization of the database. Another drawback is that every value shares the same dimensionality. For example, it is redundant to store customer discounts repeatedly by geography if the same discount is used throughout the organization. Although some hypercube products get around this problem, a better approach is to employ the *multicube*. Inasmuch as implementations vary, multicubes dimension each variable separately and deal internally with the consequences. The drawback is that this approach is less straightforward and carries steeper learning curves. Hence, if multidimensionality can be handled with a hypercube, it is a much simpler approach.[2]

DATA QUALITY REQUIREMENTS IN A KNOWLEDGE MANAGEMENT ENVIRONMENT

Related to the current directions in corporate databases (i.e., relational, object-oriented, and multidimensional) is the need to address the problem of data quality in a KMS environment. Since data is collected from multiple data sources and stored in various databases, data quality problems may arise anywhere in the process. More specifically, problems can arise in the following areas: (1) the generation of the data, (2) the storage and management of the data, and (3) the final use of data by an individual or a group of people that may involve data aggregation and integration. Each of these three roles is associated with a process or task that can involve data quality problems.

An excellent way to improve data quality and meet data quality requirements is preventing non-quality data from being entered into the database in the first place. An important benefit from eliminating the entry of incorrect data is the reduction in costs for fixing problems caused by non-quality data. Next, there is need to employ *data cleansing*, which is the process of extracting data from its most authoritative sources and conditioning or reconditioning it to a quality state. This includes analyzing data to discover its real meaning or use. To set up effective data cleansing and quality improvement processes, a well-defined plan needs to be developed that centers on an enterprise-focused data model that identifies authorized data sources. In turn, a schedule needs to be devised for propagating and transforming the data.

Currently, a number of automated tools are available for data cleansing and data quality improvements. These products perform one or more of the following functions: rule discovery, analysis/audit, and data cleansing/scrubbing. In terms of the *first* function, rule discovery products analyze data in databases to discover data relationships and rules describing how the data is used. These tools help analyze data that is not well documented or whose usage has evolved from the original documentation. For example, WizRule from WizSoft is a low-priced, easy-to-use rule discovery product that analyzes data from one or more files to discover both quantitative (formulas) and qualitative (relationships) rules. It also identifies exceptions that may be errors.

Related to the *second* function, data quality analysis and audit products analyze data against a set of business rules to discover inconsistencies. Reports from QDB Solutions' QDB/Analyze, for example, include exception reports and Pareto diagrams that graphically depict the number of violations by error type. A useful Metrics feature lets the user define a weight or cost for each error type so that Pareto diagrams show the financial impact of non-quality data. Statistical control charts illustrate the results of automated data audits over time. In terms of the *third* function, products that cleanse data and automate much of the tedious job of data cleanup are important when porting data from disparate databases and software into a single data architecture. They analyze and standardize data, identify duplicates, and transform data to correct or probably correct values.

Focus on Total Quality Management (TQM)

Underlying data quality requirements in a knowledge management environment is total quality management (TQM). Total quality management provides a useful definition of quality that centers on meeting customers' expectations. It is important to note that TQM means "meeting" customers' needs, not necessarily exceeding them. For example, the luxury automobile producer Rolls-Royce experienced financial difficulty in the early 1980s. Analysis revealed that Rolls-Royce was improving components that the luxury automobile customers felt were irrelevant. This drove the price beyond what the luxury automobile customer (like myself, a current owner of two Rolls-Royces) felt was value for money. Overall, quality means improving those items that customers care about and are worthwhile.

This statement regarding quality can be applied to data quality. To define data quality, one must identify the "customer" of data, the person who needs data to perform his or her job. Data quality centers on consistently meeting user's expectations through information and knowledge, thereby enabling the individual to perform his or her job effectively. Data quality exists when information and knowledge enables users to accomplish their desired objectives and goals. Data quality is measured not just by the immediate users, but also by users downstream. The bottom line is that total quality management focuses on customer needs that can impact a company's competitive advantage.

START WITH DATA MARTS TO DISCOVER KNOWLEDGE

To be successful when developing knowledge management systems for any functional area of a company, it may be necessary to start small. Vendors are therefore marketing products and services that make it easier and much cheaper to deploy scaled-down sources for generating knowledge, known as *data marts* or mini data warehouses. Their sales pitch suggests that data marts help put important business information and knowledge into the hands of more decision makers. From this view, data marts can be the key to enhancing strategic decisions in all functional areas of a company.

Essentially, data marts are subject-specific data warehouses, often departmental or a line-of-business, usually under 50–100GB. As such, data marts are database server systems that make important business information and knowledge easier for managers and their staffs to access, manipulate, and analyze. To do so, these systems must be able to extract operational data from transactional databases or other data sources on a regular basis, present the data for analytical processing, and deliver the converted information and knowledge to local servers for quick retrieval by decision makers. This process not only preserves the integrity of existing on-line transaction processing databases but also makes important business data available to a wider array of decision makers throughout the company. It is not surprising that data marts are widely used in highly competitive industries where accurate analysis of sales trends as well as customer preferences is essential to the business. For example, a retail chain could use a distributed set of local data marts to let regional store managers analyze sales figures on a daily basis. In turn, the store managers could use these figures to decide which items to mark up or down and which to relocate to the front of the store for faster turnover.

The essential difference between a data mart and a data warehouse (covered in the next part of the chapter) is scale. Data marts, which are typically smaller than data warehouses, comprise less than 100GB of data. They are usually optimized for a single subject, such as customer trends analysis or inventory management, and they reside on a server local to each work group. By providing dedicated performance for work groups, departments, and small business units, data marts are often faster and easier to install and manage than data warehouses. Because data marts contain a subset of data for a single aspect of a company's business, their focus is more on a functional approach to data warehousing.

A Low-Cost Approach Using Data Marts

Low cost and ease of development are the main attractions of data marts. For not much money, a pilot project can be put together so that the company can gain some experience. Vendors have descended upon the data mart market from every direction. The major vendors range from those who promote tools for specific functions to those who offer a data mart in a box. There are many new vendors—Informatica Corporation (Menlo Park, California), Intellidex Systems Inc. (Waltham, Massachusetts), and Sagent Technology Inc. (Menlo Park, California). Veteran vendors include IBM, Information Builders, NCR Corporation, Prism Solutions Inc., and SAS Institute Inc. As the market matures, vendors are moving toward turnkey solutions, and analysts agree that no one vendor provides all the pieces of the puzzle.

More recently, the World Wide Web has been used as a means to tap into data marts. This approach is helpful to fulfill the potential benefits of data marts by providing an access platform that is highly interoperable, accessible, and affordable and that eliminates the need to deploy business analysis software on each desktop through a company. As more data mart vendors support HyperText Markup Language (HTML), it becomes easier to share corporate information and knowledge and mix and match it with related information and knowledge residing elsewhere on the Internet. Typically, using the web as a data mart access vehicle provides an end-to-end solution. It allows a company to open up data marts to employees at no expense when an intranet is in place. Because of the web's unique technologies, such as HTML and Common Gateway Interface (CGI), certain issues and limitations demand attention. Data mart managers should evaluate tools with careful consideration about performance, ease of use, and security to maximize and protect this potential information and knowledge distribution.

Problems Facing Data Marts

Currently, there are several problems facing data mart systems. First among these is query performance. The data mart server may sit virtually idle while knowledge workers perform a variety of nonanalytical tasks, and then requests for information and knowledge may all come in at once, all calling for similar data sets. Users can submit queries that are relatively simple to run, requiring the extraction of a single easily defined data set, or they can submit highly complex, processing intensive queries. At this time, many data mart vendors have failed to take into account this broad range of query demands. A related problem is a lack of tightly integrated tools to perform initial and continuing data extraction, data mart loading and presentation to users, and similar items. Hence, it is necessary to put together an array of products from a variety of vendors. This exacerbates performance and administration difficulties, thereby making data marts nearly as complex and time consuming as many data warehouses.

None of the above problems are insurmountable, however. Using a multitiered, multithreaded architecture, data mart server software can speed query performance considerably. Within the multithreaded structure, the architecture can enable software agents to be dispatched to process users' queries simultaneously. Additionally, these agents can be leveraged across connected servers to deal with unexpected surges in queries and updates. For complex queries, such software agents can "wait in line" on behalf of users, thereby speeding perceived performance by enabling users to proceed with other tasks as their queries are being processed.

UTILIZATION OF DATA WAREHOUSING TO DISCOVER KNOWLEDGE

Data marts, as discussed above, can provide a starting point for decision makers to discover knowledge that they can use throughout an organization. In turn, knowledge about a company and its operations can be further expanded using an enterprise-wide approach that ties in to its widespread database. From this view, reference can be made to data warehousing, which serves as a delivery mechanism to provide integrated business information and knowledge to a company's decision makers. Although the data warehousing concept has been around for some time, only recently has its implementation become truly realistic. It is based on the use of specially designed electronic databases, (i.e., data warehouses) and a series of powerful tools to extract data from original sources and convert it into valuable information and knowledge for decision makers. In effect, decision makers who gather data from several sources in order to answer a critical business question or questions using information and knowledge about a company's operations are generally engaged in some form of data warehousing.

Because the data warehouse is designed to serve the information and knowledge needs of decision makers for an entire company, there is a need to store data at different levels of granularity—from current detail data to highly summarized reports. Generally, the more current the detail data is, the more immediate is its use. Current detail data supports day-to-day decisions while historical data supports trend analysis and long-term decisions. As such, a data warehouse combines various data sources into a single resource for user access. Users can perform ad hoc queries, short- to long-term analysis, and trend plotting against the warehoused information and knowledge. Typically, data warehousing involves combining products from a variety of technology vendors into an integrated solution.

One of the requirements in the design of a data warehouse is the ability to accumulate and manage large amounts of data. Thus, it is important to choose levels of granularity and summarization for the data in the warehouse. Other design considerations for managing large amounts of data in the warehouse are storing data on multiple storage media, summarizing data when detail becomes obsolete, encoding and referencing data where appropriate, and partitioning data for independent management and indexing.

Justifying the Data Warehouse

Since data in the warehouse is organized by subject rather than by application, the data warehouse contains only that which is necessary for decision support processing. The data is collected over time and used for comparisons, trends, and forecasting. Also, this data is not updated in real-time, but rather is refreshed from operational systems on a regular basis when the data transfer will not adversely affect the performance of operational systems. In light of these comments about the operational aspects of data warehouses, the issue of their justification comes into play. Basically, the justification process revolves around identifying key business objectives and goals the data warehouse will meet for a company's decision makers. These objectives and goals include increasing national and international sales, lowering the rate of accounts receivable charge-offs, and improving the impact of advertising expenditures. If the data warehouse, for example, can help the company generate more sales, then it can serve as a model for achieving other business objectives and goals as well.

Going beyond this initial reason for data warehousing, there are a number of other important reasons for developing a data warehouse. They include:

- allows a company to become more competitive
- improves the decision-making capabilities of company personnel at all levels
- helps company personnel to identify hidden business opportunities
- improves productivity through improved access to information and knowledge
- improves customer responsiveness to company promotions
- speeds retrieval of company information and knowledge
- lowers the cost of access to information and knowledge

It should be noted that the justification stage is generally the time when the seeds of most data warehousing failures are sown. When the project is driven by technologists who are not focusing on important, measurable business objectives and goals, the data warehouse team may be in jeopardy. Many other problems that may arise in the development of data warehouses is given in a subsequent section of the chapter.

Common Applications of Data Warehouses

Typically, data warehouses are updated on a daily, weekly, or biweekly basis. In this manner, the warehouse helps users make complex queries about a business without slowing the high input. Users (i.e., corporate executives, managers, and analysts) employ data warehouses to analyze historical and operational data. For example, a bank executive could use the data warehouse to interpret the profiles of credit card applicants over the past years. Or a sales manager might need a history of sales orders to help launch a new marketing program. Or a corporate planner could analyze strategic information that provides the foundation for the company's five-year strategic plan. The data warehouse has even helped some companies downsize.

According to a survey of 250 information systems professionals by the Meta Group, Inc. (Stamford, Connecticut), the most common applications of data warehouses were: (1) customer information systems—26%, (2) marketing—

24%, (3) finance—22%, (4) sales—12%, and (5) other—16%.[3] Some of the companies building and implementing data warehouses include insurance companies, telecommunications companies, financial services firms, pharmaceutical companies, and hospitals. Their common characteristic is the need to build better information systems about their customers to better track and direct their businesses.

Additionally, data warehousing has been helpful to companies that want to improve their customer response times. Saving time in this area may be an important key to controlling short- to long-range costs. To achieve lower costs, data warehouse architects should consider data warehouse tools that link operational databases with the warehouse. In addition, they should consider using tools that extract, update, and replicate information as well as help users query databases. In this manner, a number of useful data warehouse applications can be developed that do assist in making managers and their staffs more effective in their jobs.

Typical Companies Using Data Warehousing as a Strategic Weapon

To place the foregoing common applications of data warehousing into focus, reference can be made to any of the *Fortune* 500 companies that have launched some form of data warehousing initiative. For example, Wal-Mart has been using its data warehouse to determine what items need to be on the shelves, at what stores, and at what price. It is difficult to find a major player in the retail industry that is not attempting to emulate Wal-Mart's data warehousing successes. In a similar manner, it is difficult to find a federal agency or a state government that is not looking at data warehousing to play a major role in addressing many of its problems.

The impact of data warehousing has also been felt in most other industries. For telecommunications providers, MCI is leading in the transition from a product-driven company to a client-driven company through the analysis of customer preferences and needs. CVS delivers a global view of its pharmacy operations to all levels of the organization that have a need to know. MasterCard, using the World Wide Web, empowers its member banks to analyze credit card data for highly targeted one-on-one marketing. Bank of America accurately anticipates fraud and takes appropriate preventive action. R&V Insurance in Germany has found the key to integrating information about its lines of insurance into a common, accessible data warehouse. And Hughes Electronics has revolutionized its buying patterns and cut costs by aggregating all its purchases from individual vendors. All of these examples are focused on data warehousing in terms of the need for information and knowledge. In all of these examples, strategic thinking benefits from information and knowledge, but the more powerful strategic ideas are demanding it.

BUILDING AN EFFECTIVE DATA WAREHOUSE

Building an effective data warehouse means getting involved in identifying several different types of tools and related issues. A suggested list is given as follows: (1) data modeling tools; (2) a meta-data repository; (3) the core database; (4) data transport tools; (5) data extraction, scrubbing, and normalization tools; (6) middleware connectivity tools; and (7) end user data access tools.[4] In addition, there is a need for tools to manage the data warehouse along with the means to handle replication and synchronization of multiple data warehouses. Based upon the data warehouse built, warehouse developers need to develop applications that use the data warehouse effectively.

In general, building a data warehouse can be costly—in the millions for a very large one—and time consuming—for example, two years. This costly and time consuming undertaking shows that the value of information is a strategic asset to a typical company. Getting there, however, is not simple, since computer managers must wrestle with the problem of moving various forms of data from legacy and OLTP systems. It requires preparing, conditioning, and staging data so business users armed with appropriate data access tools can perform analyses that previously were either impossible, too expensive, or too time consuming.

Components of a Data Warehouse

Today, there are many different data warehouse architectures designed to meet the users' needs. Typically, data warehouses are composed of a distributed data architecture with the bulk transfers of data occurring during off hours and extensive interactive querying occurring at peak hours of the day. Thus, proper planning for warehouse operations is very important, especially a company's network infrastructure. To prevent performance disasters, networking professionals should be involved in each stage of warehouse planning and development, including implementation. Network analysis should consider a number of items, such as how often data updates should occur, how they should be scheduled, when they should occur, how much interactive querying to allow, how the front-end tools work, and what user query habits will be.

A typical data warehouse architecture is illustrated in Figure 3-1. Essentially, there is data extraction of operational production data that is passed on to the warehouse database. A specialized data warehouse server is used to host the warehouse databases and decision support tools, including OLAP and knowledge-based tools. This server is used to pass on extracted data to the warehouse database and is employed by users to extract data from the data warehouse using some type of software to answer users' questions and meet their information and knowledge processing requirements. Although not shown in Figure 3-1, operational production databases are updated continuously via OLTP applications. In turn, a warehouse database is "refreshed" from operational production systems on a periodic basis, usually during off hours when

Figure 3-1
The Basic Components of a Data Warehouse

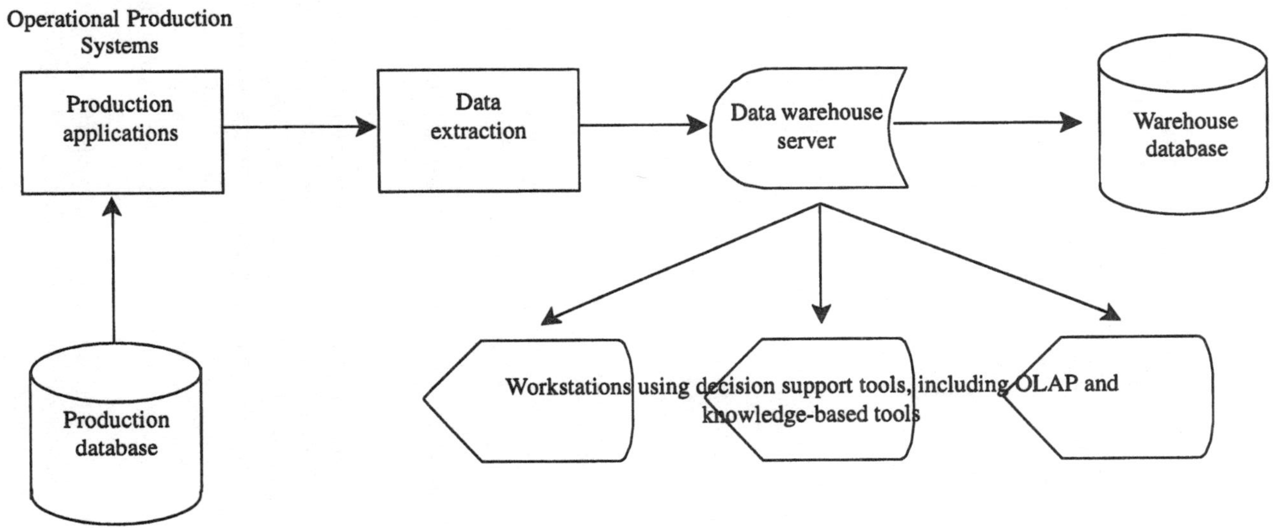

network and CPU utilization is low. Essentially, then, a data warehouse is a specialized database for supporting decision making. Data is taken from a variety of operational sources and then ''scrubbed'' to eliminate any inconsistencies or errors.

A common and simple type of data warehouse involves a *two-tiered, homogeneous architecture*. For example, the IBM DB2 data on a computer mainframe might be periodically extracted and copied to a DB/2 database on a Microsoft Windows NT server. Then a data access product, such as Information Builders Inc.'s FOCUS Reporter for Windows, can be used to read, analyze, and report on the warehouse data from a front-end graphical client on the Windows NT LAN. In contrast, more complex data warehouses are based on a *three-tiered architecture* that uses a separate middleware layer for data access and translation. The *first tier* is the host for production applications and is generally a mainframe computer or a midrange system, such as Digital Equipment Corporation's VAX or IBM's AS/400. The *second tier* is a departmental server, such as a Unix workstation or a Windows NT server, which resides in close proximity to warehouse users. The *third tier* is the desktop where IBM PCs, Apple Macintoshes, and X terminals are connected on a local area network (LAN). In this three-tiered architecture, the host (first level) is devoted to real-time, production-level data processing. The departmental server (second level) is optimized for query processing, analysis, and reporting. The desktop (third level) handles reporting, analysis, and the graphical presentation of data.

Populating a Data Warehouse

Once the data warehouse architecture has been established on the server, there are two primary methods for populating a data warehouse. The *first* method is called *change-based*. Here, only the changes or differences are copied from the production database to the warehouse databases. The *second* method is called *batch copy*, in which the entire warehouse is periodically refreshed in a bulk upload or download of production data. Typically, bulk downloads can tax the network. Although transmitting only the changes puts less stress on the network, it requires more complex programming and maintenance. Which architecture is selected depends largely on the size of the warehouse and available resources. If there is limited network capacity, the change-based method is generally the best. On the other hand, if the network can handle large data transfers, the batch-copy architecture will be simpler to set up and maintain.

Building an effective data warehouse, however, involves more than just copying data and letting users employ PC-based query and reporting tools. As the data warehouse is populated, it must be restructured—that is, tables must be denormalized, data must be cleansed of errors and redundancies, and new fields and keys must be added to reflect the needs of users for sorting, combining, and summarizing data. The more thought that is given to the design of the data model, the easier it will be to maintain, update, and retrieve warehouse data.

Overall, effective data modeling relieves network stress by rolling up or summarizing information into meaningful constructs so that users do not have to perform as many interactive queries to join tables in real time.[5]

Choosing a Proper Server Platform

A most important decision to be made when planning and constructing a data warehouse architecture is the choice of server platform. Small databases with local query activity can often be hosted by Pentium-based PCs or Unix workstations. However, for larger databases supporting a larger number of users, multiple network segments, and large queries, SMP (symmetric multiprocessing) computers are recommended. Where very large databases and very complex queries are required, companies usually use mainframe processors or sometimes turn to massive parallel database processors. In the final analysis, there is need for careful planning and involvement of the networking staff in order to ensure a successful implementation. Many companies have found that data warehouses tend to create a lot more demand than originally anticipated. It is essential that extensive predictive analysis be undertaken so that network demand is estimated realistically.

To assist in choosing the proper server platform, there is a need to assess the work to be done by the client and the server. For example, ''Give me the top 20 customers by sales volume for the month of March.'' To arrive at an answer, the system must add up all the business from all possible customers over that time period. Then there are two ways to determine the 20 customers. The *first* is to transfer all the customer and revenue data from that period across the network and process it on the *client*. The *second* is to place a query engine on the *server* to perform the query operation. In this second case, just the answer set—the information about the top 20 customers—gets sent back across the network to the client. The differences from the network perspective are quite substantial. The first scenario might involve a transmission of 200MB, while the second might involve only 200KB. Thus, depending upon the client/server situation, the demands on the company's networking can be quite different and must be considered by the networking staff.

Accessing Data Warehouses Using the Internet and Intranets

Today, accessing data warehouses has been made easier for a company's decision makers because of the pervasive influence of the Internet and the World Wide Web. The Internet has opened the door to a global business community where being able to make informed decisions and move quickly is important. Following on the heels of the Internet are intranets which are private networks that leverage the Internet's infrastructure to extend corporate client/server networks to users wherever they may be. Currently, companies are leveraging the Internet's infrastructure to extend their corporate networks. The reasons are clear: intranets are easy to use, rapidly implemented, cost-effective, and efficient for making information and knowledge available to the people who need it. The fact is that any authorized user can get to information on an intranet with nothing more than a standard web browser.

Essentially, the web offers a real information and knowledge highway to companies who want to extend data warehouse access to others in their supply chain (i.e., suppliers, distributors, and even customers). Web browsers are cheaper than most client tools. And maintenance releases are much simplier to administer since updating the client application on the web simply requires updating the server. The bottom line is that the web offers a compelling new way to deliver data warehousing applications that can broaden the reach and value of data warehousing investments.

Until recently, intranets were basically stores of large volumes of information, much of which was static corporate communications materials, such as telephone listings, internal memos, corporate communiques, and similar documents. Today, because intranets have become more pervasive, the kinds of information and knowledge on them has changed and expanded. Companies use their intranets to give users dynamic access to the information and knowledge in their databases and data warehouse that can help them improve the speed and quality of their decisions.

An important goal of a data warehousing strategy that includes the Internet and a company's intranets is to ensure that its information and the knowledge derived from it has value and that a company and its clients and suppliers can use it when and where it is needed. For the typical data warehousing manager, web-based distribution reduces the complexity and delay associated with supporting remote users. New web development tools automatically link web pages to databases or data warehouses. Among the key tools are those based on Sun Microsystems' JAVA language, which is embedded in the latest version of Netscape; Oracle's web-enabled tools; and web-enabled ROLAP (relational on-line analytical processing) tools from Dimensional Insight, Information Advantage, and MicroStrategy. Because both webs and data warehouses have a common goal of data access, newer releases of query tools will be web-enabled so that web-browser software is able to access data warehouses. In fact, innovative user companies like MasterCard are already building such interfaces between their applications. MasterCard now offers banks access to its customers' buying habits, for instance, based on their credit card transactions. Additional information will be given in the next chapter on the use of browsers for the Internet and a company's intranets.

Problems with Data Warehouses

Just as with data marts, there can be problems with data warehouses. For one, there needs to be support from top management that centers on an enterprise approach to data warehousing. If there is no all encompassing solution, but rather one that addresses only one part of the business, the data warehouse will never be fully embraced or utilized by the entire organization. From this view, the company has no clear vision of the end-state data warehouse. For real success, the goals of the data warehouse program must be aligned with the company's strategic goals. Although this may seem obvious to the reader, this may not be obvious in everyday corporate life.

Another typical problem that a company faces is a technology-based approach to data warehousing. There is a need to take a close look at users' fundamental needs to be sure they are seeking highly innovative and strategic capabilities. Such goals demand a basic change in design and development that, if ignored, is likely to result in less than optimum results. Other problems lie not in the technology but in the decision making that determines the uses, expectations, and means of data warehousing applications. More specifically, they include the lack of leadership to get the data warehouse up and running, poorly understood relationships between technical capabilities and business benefits, absence of executive input regarding data warehousing applications, poor strategic use of data and information to arrive at important knowledge about the company, and lack of up-front overall involvement by computer personnel in the computer department.

Still other problems with data warehousing center on data quality and performance. Many data warehouses had to be substantially redesigned due to data quality and performance issues. Generally, there is a need to assign several analysts and a manager who will maintain the warehouse's data integrity and performance over time. As data warehouses grow in number as well as in size, it is necessary to create and maintain a data repository road map for users. A data repository road map enables users who look at the data warehouse to track where the data and information originated. Additionally, data warehouse developers should provide the capability to maintain software and hardware independence. That is, there should be the ability to select from a variety of hardware and software programs to ensure that a company has the flexibility to switch to best-of-breed tools for data access and/or data mining.

TYPICAL DATA WAREHOUSING SOFTWARE

Before focusing on representative data warehousing products per se, it is wise to state that most data warehousing software products currently focus on one of these three areas: (1) acquisition, (2) storage, and (3) access. Most software vendors that provide these products have a proven track record for performing one of these functions well. Generally, most have simply retrofitted existing products to meet warehousing requirements. In the *first* category, there are a number of vendors who have products designed to manage and automate the acquisition process. Some of the data acquisition product vendors have begun to integrate several of their products into complete warehouse offerings. The largest vendors in this category include Prism Solutions Inc., Carleton Corporation, and Platinum Technology.

In the *second* category, there are a number of storage software products. A representative listing is found in Figure 3-2. Currently, firms like Oracle, Sybase, IBM, and Informix control the bulk of the market. When a typical Unix server or mainframe computer seems incapable of handling the envisioned workload, MIS executives look to SMP (symmetric multiprocessing) or MPP (massive parallel processing). For the truly large jobs, SMP may not be enough. In those cases, some companies are turning to MPP machines. Although SMP machines can handle up to 16 additional processors at a time, MPP systems incorporate the use of dozens or even hundreds of processors. The power of these machines cannot be approached by any other hardware on the market today.

In the *third* category, access software products include the following: First, unlike the overly simplistic report writers of the past, query facilities tools turn a large, complex data-warehouse environment into a friendly, well-managed workstation. Second, access software tools center on statistical analysis as found in products like SAS and SPSS. Third, a number of data discovery products are getting a lot of attention. These include decision support tools as well as artificial intelligence and expert systems. Using neural networks, fuzzy logic, decision trees, and other advanced mathematical and statistical tools, these products allow users to sift through massive amounts of raw data to discover new, insightful and, in many cases, useful things about the company, its operations, and its markets. These data discovery products are widely used in data mining as covered later in the chapter.

In addition to the three areas above, representative data warehouse software typically includes data visualization and on-line analytical processing. Data visualization represents a graphical rendering of information from data warehouses. As such, data visualization software products bring graphical representation to new heights. A popular visualization tool that falls under this group is geographical systems. Such systems turn data about stores, individuals, or anything else into easy-to-understand, dynamic maps.

On-line analytical processing (OLAP) centers on multidimensional analytical tools for accessing, storing, and manipulating decision support and EIS (executive information system) style information. These tools represent a whole new generation of high-powered, user-friendly data investigation systems that allow users to look at information from numerous different perspectives. OLAP software products provide the capability to slice and dice reports dynamically, and to look at the same kinds of information from different perspectives. For example, at the press of a button, a product manager is able to view sales figures for a given product at the national level, or view them broken down by division, or drill down to view figures by territories within a division, or check sales numbers for each store in a territory and then compare them against sales of stores from a different territory. This last category of data access products can

Figure 3-2
Popular Data Warehouses

Company	Product	Warehouse Management Features
Apertus Technologies Inc. New York, NY 800-310-4624 http://www.apertus.com	Enterprise/Integrator	Graphical administration manager for configuration management
Hewlett Packard Company Palo Alto, CA 800-637-7740 http://www.hp.com	Intelligent Warehouse	Summary management, usage reports, query blocking, partition management, security
IBM Corporation Armonk, NY 800-426-3333 http://www.ibm.com	Visual Warehouse	Access to heterogeneous data sources for population and updates, transformation and replication, management of technical and business data
Informatica Corporation Menlo Park, CA 800-653-3871 http://www.informatica.com	OpenBridge	Monitor and control of data transformation and loading, real-time reports
Information Builders Inc. New York, NY 800-969-4636 http://www.ibi.com	Enterprise Copy Manager	Management of queries, loading and updates, mapping and data transformation, log file and report generation
Intersolv Rockville, MD 800-547-4000 http://www.intersolv.com	DataDirect, SmartData	Meta-data management
Oracle Corporation Redwood Shores, CA 800-633-0596 http://www.oracle.com	Designer/2000, Open Gateways, Symmetric Replication, Parallel Loader	Automatic replication of operational data, flat-file population to warehouse
Prism Solutions Sunnyvale, CA 800-995-2928 http://www.prismsolutions.com	Prism Warehouse Manager, Prism Directory Manager	Changed Data Capture modules for current or near-current data, captures only delta changes to source files
Red Brick Systems, Inc. Los Gatos, CA 800-777-2585 http://www.redbrick.com	Red Brick Warehouse	Company has partnerships with third parties providing data extract tools
SAS Institute Inc. Cary, NC 919-677-8000 http://www.sas.com	SAS System for Data Warehousing	Menu-driven interface for managing building process, data extraction, transformation, scheduling of updates
Software AG Reston, VA 800-843-9534 http://www.sagus.com	SourcePoint	Automated extraction, transport, and population of a warehouse

enrich a decision maker's capability to ask and answer important questions facing him or her on a daily basis.

UTILIZATION OF DATA REPLICATION IN DATA WAREHOUSING

In the past, multiple corporate databases were consistently synchronized and were, in essence, clones of one another. This task, frequently called "nightly refresh," has been practiced for years in the world of computer mainframes. When a few PCs were added, the job progressed into downloading and uploading data between the PCs and the mainframe. The situation was quite controllable. However, when there is a network, servers, users spead across multiple time zones, groupware applications, and reliance by users on real-time information, this chore grows into a network manager's nightmare, better known as *replication.* Essentially, replication copies information from one database to another so that the contents of both databases are consistent. That can mean transferring data from a central mainframe to branch servers and then down to local workstations, from news feeds to reporting and analysis applications, between networked servers, or within almost any architecture. Data movement can be one-way or bidirectional. It can be event driven (triggered by data value changes) or time dependent (performed at regular intervals or nightly).

Typically, there are many benefits to replication. It is often implemented to offload processing onto a single server. Copies of corporate data are downloaded to branch offices where departmental users can access the local data more efficiently. Replication can also be an important part of a data warehouse strategy—that is, consolidating data from multiple operational databases to a single data store for analysis. Having multiple copies of data also sets the stage for quick disaster recovery and cost-efficient load balancing on busy networks.

Replicated DBMSs are recommended for applications such as backup as well as knowledge management, OLAP, and DSS systems that do not require up-to-the-minute information and knowledge. Most managers who use these systems do not require up-to-the-minute facts. Most companies doing backup do not require the up-to-date capabilities of two-phase commit. That is, many users would probably prefer working with a backup system that was slightly out of sync to waiting for the main database management system to be restored. Replication also allows companies to divide up a database and ship information and knowledge closer to those users who work with it the most. Response time improves because the information and knowledge is stored locally rather than at a central site. Wide area network costs fall because users no longer need to access the network to work with what they need.

VIRTUAL DATA WAREHOUSING

From a different perspective, companies may find that building a data warehouse may be more than they are able to undertake at the present time. A vendor such as INTERSOLV allows companies to migrate to storage-focused and subject-area databases as needed. The end product is just-in-time data warehousing that is a rapid approach to providing infrastructure transparency for companies while enabling immediate end user access to enterprise information and knowledge. Overall, a virtual data warehouse allows a company to operate a data storage facility that can be implemented at a fraction of the time and expense required for a data warehouse.

INTERSOLV's Virtual Data Warehouse looks like its Q+E end user, data access tool, somewhat enhanced and renamed Explorer. There is no distinct physical data warehouse since the data resides in the production systems. The virtual warehouse organizes and smooths out access to the data for users. This approach is similar to those taken by end user access tools such as Business Objects' Business Objects and Dimensional Insight CrossTarget. Basically, INTERSOLV is providing an open semantic mapping layer. It is this mapping layer, which INTERSOLV calls SmartData, that disguises the complexity of the multiple back-end data sources and allows users to access, for example, ''Sales'' without knowing from where the sales data is actually coming. Other products also provide a semantic mapping layer, but they are proprietary. INTERSOLV, a developer of open database connectivity (ODBC) drivers, employs industry standard ODBC as the access method.

INTERSOLV's Virtual Data Warehouse establishes access to the data first, without requiring heavy analysis and infrastructure. Decision makers can access information and knowledge from any data source in everyday business terms, working with the presentation tools of their choice. Typically, virtual data warehousing is most useful in small-scale situations, since it allows users to get up and run quickly with data access as an interim step to building a real data warehouse. Most of the experts concede that the virtual data warehouse will not replace the real data warehouse.

DATA MINING OR KNOWLEDGE DISCOVERY

Data mining, also known as knowledge discovery, explores the knowledge held within a company's database by revealing patterns and trends that can suggest improved performance in terms of greater customer satisfaction, higher quality products, savings, and profits. In effect, data mining uncovers *hidden patterns* and provides *predictive trends* which can be easily applied to benefit the business. Since the raw materials for data mining are abundant, data contains records that could potentially reveal hidden patterns and predictive trends that could further a company's mission, its objectives, and its measurable goals. Sales records, for example, could reveal highly profitable retail sales patterns. In turn, financial analysts could find future trends that are highly profitable. As another example, an engineering firm could determine the combination of data conditions (e.g. manufacturing time, lot size, assembly parameters, operator number, reject rate, etc.) that determine the quality of the products being produced. In the final analysis, the key to successful data mining is to employ those tools that result in real knowledge discovery.

To discover meaningful patterns in a data set, consider, for example, gross margins that are stored in a retail sales database. Gross margins fluctuate over the course of a year with a 10 percent increase between summer and autumn. A company executive might be tempted to conclude that sales margins generally increase from summer to autumn and that the increase in gross margin depends upon the season. In reality, there are many other potential variables housed in the database that could influence gross margin. These might include quantity sold, discount rate, commission paid, customer location, other purchases made, and length of time as a customer. If the discount rate is greater in the summer than in the autumn, the increase in gross margin could simply be a result of a lower discount rate and have nothing to do with a change in season. By removing the effect of discount rates on gross margins, gross margins might be found to be higher in the summer. In the final analysis, data mining examines all potential explanatory factors and associated data elements to ensure that the best pattern is retrieved from the data and that no potentially misleading effects are introduced into the chosen patterns. Going one step further, in place of showing the effect of only one condition, such as season, on gross margin, data mining can show the combined effect of a pattern, such as a particular time, location, and discount rate, that produces the maximum gross margin. By replicating that pattern, a longer-term strategy that will systematically increase gross margin and associated profitability can be established. That optimal pattern becomes a basis for predicting future trends.

Tie-In of Data Mining with Data Warehousing and OLAP Systems

Today, data mining is considered to be a direct outgrowth of the data warehouse concept. It allows data access and analysis that gives users unparalleled capabilities to extract hard-to-get-at data, spot trends, and recognize patterns in corporate databases. While many companies have built data warehouses to consolidate data located in disparate databases, they are implementing data mining to learn more about the data. Although data warehouses are a part of the technology mainstream, available data mining tools now allow companies to improve their knowledge of their customers and markets. For example, retailers want to use data mining to target customers for sales promotions better or to manage inventory across various geographic locations. Similarly, telecommunications companies want to use it to forecast demand patterns, profile and segment customer groups, customize billing, and analyze profitability. In addition, financial services companies are employing data mining to consolidate information from multiple sources, analyze customers' business patterns, and sell them more services.

Today, data warehousing and data mining have the following requirements in common: They need very large databases and highly scrubbed and integrated data sources, along with facts that provide insight and new directions for further analysis. Even though these items are complementary, data warehousing is a prerequisite for data mining. Typically, the business objective is to extract patterns, trends, and rules that are implicit within data warehouses to evaluate proposed business strategies. In turn, a company can improve its competitiveness, return on investment, and business processes. Data mining utilizes a number of traditional technologies, such as RDBMS, massively parallel processing (MPP), symmetric mutliprocessing (SMP), and statistics as well as newer technologies, to provide pattern recognition and analysis, including neural networks, inductive reasoning/decision trees, and advanced data visualization. Essentially, data mining is built on the foundation laid by a successful data warehouse. Most decision support solutions require an effective data warehouse in combination with multiple data mining and OLAP tools, in addition to high-end systems integration assistance to pull it all together for decision makers.

As just noted, most data analysis is done with data mining and OLAP tools. Data mining tools help users find answers to questions that they never thought to ask. They do this by characterizing the patterns inherent in the data, developing a hypothesis from these patterns, and using the hypothesis to predict future behavior. In contrast, OLAP allows users to explore corporate data from a number of different perspectives. Using drill-down analysis, users can discover the facts and implications of a high-level trend, or discover individual implications.

OLAP servers and clients provide an easy-to-use multidimensional interface for drilling down from high-level to low-level summary data and for slicing and dicing data. They can also provide support for complex derived functions that are common in financial reporting and consolidation. Some of these tools are based on a multidimensional database (MDD) while others impose a multidimensional model directly on relational data. OLAP tools have powerful analytic capabilities and are well suited for fast response time, complex calculations, and budgeting/forecasting "what-if" analysis.

Inasmuch as on-line analytical processing provides top-down, query driven data analysis, data mining provides bottom-up, discovery driven analysis. Data mining identifies facts or conclusions based on patterns discovered. OLAP, and in particular data mining, are two emerging data analysis tools that impact the typical organization's use of corporate knowledge assets. In essence, these tools are reinventing the way companies think about business capabilities, customer satisfaction, and strategic goal-setting for the future.

Types of Data Mining Information

Because data mining reaches much deeper into databases, its tools provide users with the capability to find patterns in data and infer rules from them. Those patterns and rules can be used to guide decision making and forecast the effect of those decisions. In addition, data mining can speed analysis by focusing attention on the most important variables. Although users might find these patterns with a series of queries against the data, data mining lets the users explore a much wider range of possibilities than even the most sophisticated set of queries.

Typical types of information that can be obtained by data mining include forecasting, associations, sequences, classifications, and clusters. Essentially, all of these may involve predictions.[6] However, the *first* type (forecasting) is a different form of prediction in that it estimates the future value of continuous variables—like sales figures—based on patterns within the data. The *second* type of information centers on associations that happen when occurrences are linked in a single event. For example, a study of supermarket baskets might reveal that when potato chips are purchased, 60 percent of the time some type of cola is also purchased—unless there is a promotion, in which case cola is purchased 80 percent of the time. Knowing this fact, managers can evaluate the profitability of a promotion.

In the *third* type of information or sequences, events are linked over time. For example, if a house is bought, then 60 percent of the time a new oven will be bought within one month and 65 percent of the time a new refrigerator will be bought within three weeks. For the *fourth* type, or classifications, patterns are recognized that describe the group to which an item belongs. It does this by examining existing items that already have been classified and inferring a set of rules. Because a common problem for many companies is the loss of steady customers, classification can help discover the characteristics of customers who are likely to leave and provide a model that can be used to predict who they are. It can also help a company determine what kinds of promotions have been effective in keeping which types of customers. The *fifth* and last type of information is clustering. It is related to classification, but differs in that no groups have yet been defined. Using clustering, the data mining tool discovers different groupings within the data. This can be applied to problems as diverse as detecting defects in manufacturing or finding affinity groups for bank cards.

Past Approaches to Multidimensional Knowledge Discovery

Several approaches over the years have been utilized in multidimensional knowledge discovery. Essentially, all try to use the information contained in many fields in the data store to explain variations in the outcome field (i.e., the field in question, such as profit, defects, interest rate, and so forth). One of the earliest methods used is *multiple regression*, which is a standard statistical technique that uncovers the pattern of dependencies between multiple predictor fields and the outcome. Another method is *decision tree analysis*, which was developed to compensate for some problems that had arisen from using multiple regression as a data mining tool. Decision trees show the combined dependencies between multiple predictors and the outcome as a number of decision branches.

The user is able to see how the outcome changes with different values in the predictors. More recently, *neural networks* have been used. They resemble multiple regression in many ways, except that rather than using statistical theory as the basis of the technique, they imitate the information processing methods of the human brain.

In reference to decision trees, J. N. Morgan and J. A. Sonquist were interested in developing a statistical analysis technique that would more accurately depict "real world" social and economic events than was possible using standard statistical regression techniques. They proposed an "automatic interaction detector," which is an idea based on earlier notions of designing a data discovery tool that was modeled on the techniques used by humans to solve problems. They suggested a mechanical or automatic system that would mimic the steps taken by an experienced data analyst to determine any strong data interaction effects. An interaction is the kind of effect that was observed above among discount rate, season, and gross margin. The automatic interaction detector technique involves an exhaustive examination of all possible relationships between predictor fields and the outcome field to determine the strongest, or best, prediction. When found, the data is divided into two groups that are determined by the predictor field, and the process is repeated for the descendent groups that are formed by the selection of the strongest predictor. The result is a series of splits, or branches, in the data. Each split produces a new data set that is in turn split. The final result is a series of branches that resemble a decision tree.

When the Morgan and Sonquist procedure was implemented as a company program called AID (Automatic Interaction Detector) at the University of Michigan in the early 1970s, it was enthusiastically received by many researchers, statisticians, and data analysts. The beauty of decision trees and of the original AID program is that they address the problem of hidden dependencies and spurious relationships. Decision trees provide models that are easier to interpret than those produced by the mathematically intense regression and neural network techniques. Furthermore, given the way a decision tree is built, the analyst can more easily control the model's construction and can assemble a more valid and reliable final result.

In reality, observers found some problems with AID. For one, AID was overly aggressive in identifying relationships and dependencies in the data. Furthermore it could not discriminate meaningful relationships from meaningless relationships. Often, therefore, AID would select relationships that were the result of random fluctuations in the data set. As a result, these decision trees frequently did not reflect the actual data patterns that affected the question under examination.

In the mid-1970s, G. V. Kass published a method of addressing the shortcomings of AID. His approach applied the lessons of statistical hypothesis testing to the decision trees produced by AID. Kass reasoned that the branches identified by AID could be tested by using a standard statistical test to determine whether they were the result of a chance effect of fluctuations in the data. He found a way to apply modern statistics to determine the statistical strength of each of the decision tree branches. When the branch was too weak statistically, it would not be displayed. In the early 1980s, a *validation approach* emerged to further remedy the problems with the AID technique. This approach complements Kass's statistical approach because although statistical approaches are based on statistical theory, validation approaches are based on an examination of the actual properties of the data. Validation looks closely at the data used to build the decision tree. If too many fluctuations are observed, then as in the statistical approach employed by Kass, the branch is rated poorly and is not presented in the final decision tree display. This validation approach is also used in a modern decision tree product called KnowledgeSEEKER, marketed by Angoss Software International. This product is covered in Chapter 5.

Current Data Mining Methods

A starting point for data mining methods and software available from vendors is a brief introduction to how data mining works. Typically, a decision maker feeds a business goal and corporate data into data mining tools, which then use a variety of methodologies to model the data. The outcome is a set of factors in the data that are related to, or predictive of, the business goal in the form of data visualization. Using data visualization software that presents a picture for users to see, an enormous amount of information is presented in a concise format. A very wide range of information presented to the user, including knowledge, allows peaks or valleys to stand out.

Many methods currently used in data mining are natural extensions and generalizations of analytical methods that have been used for decades. Neural networks, a special case of projection pursuit regression, were developed in the 1940s. CART (classification and regression trees) methods were used by social scientists in the 1960s. K-nearest neighbor, a form of density estimation, has been used for a half-century. Other methods include rule induction, discriminant analysis, and logistic regression. Basically, these methods, just like regression techniques, model relationships between a set of profile variables and an outcome. However, what is new is that these methods are now being applied to more general business problems, caused by the increased availability of data, inexpensive processing power, and user-friendly software for implementing these methods. The recent interest in data mining is in part due to the improved user interfaces. Varieties of regression techniques, discriminant analysis, and even simple graphs can help reveal hidden patterns. Because no single method solves all or even a majority of problems, successful data mining requires a portfolio of tools, both old and new. To assist the reader in placing current data mining methods in their proper perspective, reference can be made to Figure 3-3. Software that makes use of these methods and others are set forth in Chapter 5.

Figure 3-3
Typical Data Mining Methods, Including Advantages and Limitations

Data Mining Method	Advantages	Limitations
Neural networks—programs that mimic the brain's ability to learn from its mistakes.	Usable even when relationships among variables are unknown, and models nonlinearity and interaction well.	Solutions can be uninterpretable, and there still can be no convergence to a solution.
CART (Classification and regression trees)—branching that shows relationships in the form of a hierarchy.	Handles all types of predictor variables, and the resulting model is easy to understand.	Does not always find the optimum solution and develops discontinuous rules, even with continuous data.
K-nearest neighbor—a classification technique that classifies each record based on the records most similar to it in a historical data set.	Does not require equations and is easy to understand.	Requires large amounts of data for each new prediction, and needs large amounts of storage and computing power.
Rule induction—the extraction from data of useful rules based on statistical significance.	Useful in the development of "If-Then" rules, which can be easily understood.	Creates non-hierarchical sets of conditions, which may overlap.
Discriminant analysis—the ability to differentiate between good and indifferent factors in the analysis.	Solutions are easy to understand and it is very sensitive at finding patterns,	Tends not to work well if predictor variables are not normally distributed.
Logistic regression—statistical modeling method to discern trends over time.	Generally, can be used on any data and the rules are easy to understand.	Can be difficult to model for large numbers of variables.

SECURE DATA USING RAID TECHNOLOGY

To help secure data, many data storage managers are resorting to RAID (Redundant Array of Independent/Inexpensive Disks) technology. RAID is basically a fault tolerant solution that improves hard disk performance and reliability. It represents disk arrays in which two or more drives work together to provide increased performance and various levels of error recovery and fault tolerance. Most RAID units are based on racks of 3 ½-inch drives that provide 2GB or 4GB of capacity each. RAID technology is "smart" because it generates extra bits of data from existing data, allowing the system to create a "reconstruction map" so that if a hard drive fails, it can rebuild lost data.

RAID is known for its ability to access data fast. Since data access is measured in milliseconds instead of tens of seconds, RAID systems data transfer rates are typically faster than optical and offer significantly higher I/O rates than tape. Speed is not all that RAID has to offer high-volume environments consisting of large networks and fast workstations. These systems need high-performance data storage capacity. Currently, disk drive capacity can reach at least 9GBs on one disk. Inherent in the design of RAID is a significant amount of built-in data protection; hence, the term ''redundant.'' Most levels of RAID copy the data written on one disk to another. Some RAID levels even reserve a specific disk for parity which lets one regenerate unretrievable data.

RAID can be implemented at different levels. RAID subsystems duplicate the data on drives. This process, called mirroring, provides an exact copy that protects users fully in the event of data loss. However, mirroring means higher costs. If full copies are to be kept current, users need to double the amount of storage capacity that is kept on-line. Other RAID levels are less expensive because they only partly duplicate the data. This permits data storage managers to minimize the amount of extra disk space (or overhead) they must purchase in order to protect data. Although RAID does not fully guarantee that users will always have access to data, a properly configured subsystem is the best way to limit costly downtime.

SUMMARY

Data storage in the form of data marts and data warehouses was the main focus of the chapter along with their underlying framework and current directions in how the data is stored. Building upon this discussion was a tie-in with data mining (i.e., the ability to sort through large volumes of data and discover patterns, trends, associations, and relationships, including those not previously suspected). As such, data mining was shown in the chapter to be the process of turning raw data into useful knowledge that can give a company a strategic advantage. This background on data storage and data mining will be helpful in gaining an understanding of how to build knowledge-based systems in Chapter 5 as well as knowledge-management applications in Chapters 6 through 10. In the next chapter (Chapter 4), the focus will be on the practice of data communications and networking in knowledge management systems.

NOTES

1. Tom Coffing, ''Teradata Territory, The Database of Choice,'' *DM Review*, May 1998, p. 56.

2. Neil Raden, ''Data, Data Everywhere,'' *InformationWeek*, October 30, 1995, pp. 60–65.

3. Katherine Bull, ''Data Warehousing: The Ideal File Cabinet,'' *InformationWeek*, January 16, 1995, pp. 43–48.

4. Alan Radding, ''Warehouse Wake-Up Call,'' *InfoWorld*, November 20, 1995, pp. 1 and 57–62.

5. David Baum, ''Warehouse Mania,'' *LAN Times*, November 20, 1995, p. 70.

6. Herb Edelstein, ''Mining Data Warehouses,'' *InformationWeek*, January 8, 1996, p. 49.

4

Networking Within a KMS Environment

Issues Raised:

- What are the key technologies driving widely dispersed knowledge management systems?
- How important is collaborative computing (i.e., groupware) in acquiring and sharing knowledge?
- What are the current approaches to networking within a KMS environment?
- Of what use are the Internet and a company's intranets and extranets within a knowledge management system environment?
- How do network computers and personal computers fit into the future of a KMS operating mode?

Outline:

INTRODUCTION TO CREATING A NETWORKING ENVIRONMENT CONDUCIVE TO ACQUIRING AND SHARING KNOWLEDGE

Well-known authors such as Peter Drucker and Alvin Tofler have been writing and talking for years about the principal role of the global economy which is now fully upon us. Companies need the knowledge of all their workers, not just the insight of those in top management. They need to establish bidirectional paths to the knowledge of suppliers and strategic allies. Most of all, companies need firsthand knowledge about what customers and prospects want and must be able to turn these perceived needs into successful products and services. As noted throughout the text, the best way to develop the appropriate knowledge is to create a networking environment conducive to knowledge sharing. By bringing all sources of information together and providing universal access to decision makers, it is possible to build an *integrated knowledge management system environment*. To be effective, this environment must reinforce the networking infrastructure already in place, tying them together and delivering a product that is greater than the sum of all its parts.

Additionally, within an integrated KMS environment, there should be provision for supportive collaborative computing that supports workflow communication. Decision makers should be able to obtain information and knowledge from anywhere, in an ''any-to-any'' approach, without regard for their sources and types. Within such an environment, there should be the capability for decision makers to ''pull'' information and knowledge from data warehouses or have both ''pushed'' to them, using terminology they understand. An integrated KMS environment should be able to interpret important elements, text elements, and multimedia. To ensure 100 percent accuracy, it should be reliable, available, and scalable (RAS), thereby meeting the requirements of decision makers.

Needless to say, an integrated KMS environment has raised the importance of managing data communications and networking. The complexity of tools, people, and processes needed to build, operate, and monitor these networks has become apparent to more and more users, especially decision makers, throughout the organization. The way an organization approaches the design, implementation, and operation of data communications and networking can make or break the quality of its network services. More than ever, networks of all types—whether they are LANs (local area networks), MANs (metropolitan area networks), WANs (wide area networks), virtual networks, intranets, extranets, the Internet, or some combination of these—are at the very heart of a company's operations.

In this chapter, there is also a discussion of network computers versus personal computers within a KMS operating mode. All networking operations must be managed with greater levels of reliability and security today as well as in the future. From this broad-based approach, it is easier to develop and monitor a networking environment that really is conducive to acquiring and sharing information and knowledge.

Key Technologies Driving Widely Dispersed Knowledge Management Systems

Since knowledge management is the process, the culture, the technology, the infrastructure, and the content that surround managing all of a company's intellectual capital, it includes warehousing a company's internal intellectual capital as well as supplying the capability for people to collaborate and provide ways for company personnel to find their own internal experts. It also involves acquiring external content and deploying that to company personnel. For John Peetz, who is chief knowledge officer of Ernst & Young, a KMS environment that is widely dispersed has certain key technologies that drive it. *First*, there are collaborative technologies that enable a company's professionals to work together and work virtually. Those technologies enable the company to organize itself without respect to geography. For example, since Ernst & Young is a heavy Lotus Notes user, Notes is the space within which its professionals collaborate and work together virtually. Notes is also a knowledge management container technology because the firm has found collaborative technologies to be the best place to put portable knowledge. Since its professionals are constantly on the go, they need to carry a good part of what they need with them.

Second, there is the need for web technology that allows the firm to build more robust knowledge management systems and processes that can handle large volumes of information and knowledge and can be accessed on-line. It provides a platform that links together disparate sources of knowledge and content, and it provides a platform for searching. It also enables the firm to interconnect globally on an efficient basis. A *third* key technology driving widely dispersed knowledge management systems is search technology. Currently, the firm is using Verity's (Sunnyvale, California) Intelliserve search engine. One of the ways its professionals search is by browsing. It is like reading the *Wall Street Journal* every day. The firm employs something called *power packs*, which are collections of the firm's best intellectual capital in each of 120 different subjects. They are portable, and the company's professionals carry them around.

Underlying much of these key technologies is *document management*. At a fundamental level, the individual unit of measurement of intellectual capital is the document. The firm refers to it as its corporate intranet, the EY/Knowledge Web which consists of documents that are grouped and cataloged in a variety of ways. At this fundamental level, there is a very simple document management system that stores, collects, catalogs, and deploys those documents. At a higher level, for certain knowledge bases or other applications that contain knowledge, more sophisticated document management systems are used. The basic knowledge management system does not care from where the document came or how it was authored. It centers more on what is in it, who needs it, and how to get it there. In contrast, imaging is somewhat unimportant to the firm. It is used in certain parts of the firm's operations, but most of the content is created digitally and acquired.

Currently, *workflow* is used to help the firm acquire, store, and catalog content. Globally, the firm has 75,000 employees who are organized into a very complex collection of organizational units with many subject-matter specialties. Although there are a lot of different ways of getting things done, they are combined through workflow techniques in order to be able to acquire content. Thus, there is an architecture that has a centralized infrastructure but decentralized content management, and the firm combines those two to put the management of each of those in the right place. Workflow helps the firm connect them.[1]

EMPLOYMENT OF COLLABORATIVE COMPUTING TO ACQUIRE AND SHARE KNOWLEDGE

As indicated above, collaborative computing is an effective approach for acquiring and sharing knowledge. Essentially, collaborative computing is using computer networking technology in a group environment to share information and knowledge in order to make intelligent decisions. Collaborating over computer networks has become increasingly common as organizations of all sizes use groupware to connect people with information and knowledge. Just as LANs created workgroups by connecting individuals, the World Wide Web is now transforming workgroups into working groups—the distinction being the modifier "ing." While workgroups are static, working groups are dynamic. Working groups connect to one another at random, make their connections from disparate and changeable locations, collaborate in real time via data, voice, or video, and make decisions based on up-to-the-minute information and knowledge.

Today's collaboration by computer or groupware aids in the three C's—*c*ommunication, *c*ollaboration, and *c*oordination. Groupware allows users to interact with both people and databases. It facilitates collaboration, let users better manage workflow, and allows them to interact with stores of information, such as a calendar on an executive's desktop PC. However, in a few short years, collaborative computing will become a most significant category of multimedia application delivered over the corporate Internet. These applications will find their way into widespread use, evolving from simple information sharing to screen sharing that can be linked to knowledge. As companies move from text-based to multimedia to real-time collaborative systems, there are three categories of applications that are evolving: (1) files transfers such as browsing, E-mail, and simple workflow; (2) two-way screen sharing of important information and knowledge; and (3) more advanced real-time applications that use knowledge.

Integration of Collaborative Computing with the Internet

Currently, there are a number of groupware packages available. Among them are: IBM's Lotus Notes, Microsoft Exchange, and Novell GroupWise. Lotus Notes is a most comprehensive groupware environment since it focuses on user customization and application development. Lotus relies on a legion of integrators and third-party developers to help users with an investment that usually is more training-intensive than a basic messaging system. Notes is centered on group access to sychronized Notes databases. In significant upgrades, Notes has features that include the look and functionality of a traditional web browser and an upgrade to Domino that includes an expanded development environment, improved scalability, and increased Internet support. Microsoft Exchange is a message-based system tied tightly to Microsoft's Windows NT Server, which is the server platform on which it will run. All communication is accomplished by E-mail messages, including replication. There is no integrated development environment, but users can create simple form-based applications or go outside to Visual Basic to write programs. Novell GroupWise software includes document management, forms, and workflow modules, but it is tightly tied to the NetWare network operating system, much as Exchange is tied to NT. GroupWise is also message-based, and XTD (i.e., GroupWise XTD) allows users to do most tasks from the E-mail interface.

In addition, groupware vendors currently incorporate support for Internet standards. In most cases, that takes the form of support for the Hypertext Transport Protocol (HTTP), the backbone of Internet technology. HTTP is the mode by which Hypertext files move across the Internet. For example, IBM's Lotus Notes uses a groupware platform that boasts advanced integration with Internet technologies including HTTP. Notes features Domino, an HTTP interface to the Notes object store that enables access to Notes data from a browser.

So the question can be asked: Is the web a direct threat to Notes? The answer is no. At the very least, the two are complementary and will be increasingly used together. Notes, for example, got its start by supporting fairly simple collaboration using discussion databases and E-mail, which are capabilities provided by the Internet today. However, Notes has evolved into a far more sophisticated product that goes beyond the simple document sharing and publishing capabilities offered by the web. The web has been successful because it does not attempt to do everything for everyone. It provides a nice graphical environment for publishing and sharing information and knowledge, and it supports all platforms. The bulk of what happens on the web today is browsing and downloading. To become a real competitor to Lotus Notes, the web must be capable of supporting complex business applications in a secure and reliable fashion.

An effective way to introduce collaborative computing is to start at the top of the organization, where the rate of change acceptance is much higher. If top executives are enthusiastic about electronic meeting software that is used to facilitate the annual board meeting, there is generally improved productivity. This positive experience will filter on down to the lower levels of a company's operations. On the other hand, if a company starts with the members of a team that is redesigning access to the mail room, real collaborative computing will not reach key decision makers. In addition to considering the starting level, the main criteria useful in introducing collaborative computing center on the company's business requirements and its current computing infrastructure. It is necessary to understand the company's business needs and think about what the infrastructure is today. Making a decision that dovetails with the current infrastructure is important. Otherwise, it is important to understand the ramifications and cost of replacing that infrastructure.

CURRENT APPROACH TO NETWORKING WITHIN A KMS ENVIRONMENT

Computer technology has moved and continues to move in the direction of networks to support mission-critical and newer applications, such as on-line analytical processing and knowledge processing. From this view, the complexity of tools and processes along with people that are needed to build, operate, and monitor the networks has become visible to more and more computer managers and users throughout the organization. The way an organization approaches the design, implementation, and operating of networking can make or break the quality of its network services. More than ever, networks of all types, whether they are LANs, MANs, WANs, intranets, extranets, linkage to the Internet, or a combination of these, are at the very heart of a company's operations. They must be managed with greater levels of security, reliability, and service quality today as well as in the future. The information and the resulting knowledge derived from a company's networking infrastructure are at the very essence of running a company effectively as well as making its people productive.

Integration of Client/Server Architecture with the World Wide Web

Going beyond the basics of networking useful within a KMS environment, it is helpful to take a look at a client/server architecture that is tied in with the World Wide Web. In traditional enterprise computing, a client machine is typically a PC that runs a highly complex operating system and uses much of its substantial supply of memory and local storage to house an assortment of resource-intensive applications, including E-mail and other network access software. These are ''fat clients'' and they tend to be high in costs. By comparison, the kind of ''thin client'' that Java computing makes possible costs substantially less. Part of that substantial price difference can be attributed to the original price tag: thin Java clients need less local storage, since all code, data, and configuration information are stored and managed centrally.

Most of today's client/server tools, such as decision support and knowledge management, perform most processing functions on the client which leads to heavy network traffic and poor response time. Performance of client-centric tools degrades further when they are used to access large corporate databases, execute complex queries/reports or serve a large number of users. The solution is a three-tiered architecture that partitions data access and reporting functions to take advantage of the respective strengths of clients and servers. Many of today's fat client tools, which place most processing on the client computers, work well with small databases but fail in medium- to large-scale deployments. Enterprise-wide knowledge management systems and data warehousing, for example, require a different approach.

A three-tiered architecture addresses these issues by optimally partitioning the processing among the clients and servers. The first tier (the client) is used primarily for creating and defining queries and reports. One server tier processes queries and formats results while a second server tier hosts the database. The two server tiers can reside on a single server or be divided among two or more servers. The three-tiered approach leverages powerful servers to perform query and report processing while taking advantage of client capabilities for creating, defining, and viewing queries and reports. Restating the three-tiered architecture within the context of the World Wide Web, web browsers become a new front-end option, another way to present the application. Existing database and transaction processing resources remain in place, and the web server becomes the middle tier between the two, distributing queries and requests from web users to the database and transaction processing resources of the organization. Hence, it is necessary to rethink the entire application infrastructure just to accommodate the web.

It is expected that web browsers accessing multiple web servers will form the architecture for the next wave of client/server computing. Carrying this approach a little further centers on the resurrection of big applications running on big servers that are accessed by thin or skinny clients running web browsers—the modern equivalent of massive time-sharing machines connected to thousands of terminals. In the latter part of this chapter, reference will be made to the three tiers of Oracle's Network Computing Architecture (NCA)—a thin client for the presentation layer, an application server for business rules, and a database server for data storage and manipulation. Overall, the emergence of complex web applications has revalidated multitier client/server architectures.

LOCAL AREA NETWORKS (LANs)

Local area networks (LANs) meet the increasingly vital need to interconnect computers, terminals, word processors, fax machines, and other office machines within a building, campus, or a very small geographic area. A local area network may be designed to support only one vendor's terminal equipment, or it may be designed for multivendor support. Network logic may be embedded in the terminal equipment, in bus/network interface units or in central controllers. Overall, LANs are flexible and cost-effective tools in comparison to computer mainframes that greatly expand the variety of services that can be performed by microcomputers and workstations. A model based on the International Standards Organization's open systems interconnection (OSI) helps explain the software and hardware charateristics of LANs. Fundamentally, the OSI model describes the seven layers of activity for typical LAN communications.

Underlying any local area network is the physical wire connecting computing devices. Some LANs use either coaxial cable or twisted-pair wire. Each has advantages and disadvantages, depending on the particular application. However, fiber optic cable is a somewhat newer alternative to both coaxial and twisted pair. It offers higher bandwidth than both. Not only is the fiber optic cable used for LANs, but it is also often used to connect separate LANs that are located at some distance from each other. Fiber optic networks are typically used as backbone links connecting islands of office networks, minicomputers, or shared peripherals. Fiber links are also employed as point-to-point data highways connecting computer mainframes to distributed systems or other LANs. In such applications, high bandwidth and distance—fiber links can stretch as far as four kilometers unrepeated—are the prime considerations. Even in office applications, fiber is preferable to copper wires because it suffers no bandwidth degradation due to signal reflection and is easier to maintain.

Wireless LANs

Today, wireless LANs are emerging as important additions to present-day offerings of wired LANs because of cost, compatability, and ease-of-use issues. Although wireless networks are unlikely to replace wire-based systems (as set forth above), they offer an attractive alternative for those who want to add new users to corporate LANs and support mobile workers who telecommute from far-flung locations. There are two kinds of wireless network operating mode. Wide area wireless networks, like cellular and public packet switching wireless networks, cover relatively long distances (metropolitan areas) with modest data communications performance. On the other hand, local area wireless networks cover a shorter distance (a floor of a building or a corporate campus), but offer a much higher bandwidth.

Virtual LANs

Another important direction in LANs today is the virtual LAN. LANs are virtual in the sense that no physical wire or backplane necessarily defines them. Because of the switching technology, a virtual LAN has many times the bandwidth of a regular LAN. Essentially, virtual LANs (VLANs) are logical groupings of network addresses organized independently from the physical networks on which they reside. They therefore have the ability to make the network configuration transparent so that users can communicate freely without knowledge of the network. They are simply a broadcast domain that ties together any group of end users on a switched network at wire speed. The objectives of VLAN technology are threefold: (1) to provide and manage scarce bandwidth for the high-performance applications like graphics, CAD/CAM, and multimedia that are seen on current networks; (2) to separate the logical network management from the physical network infrastructure; and (3) to facilitate network node moves, adds, and changes. At their best, VLANs transcend both physical networks and geography, thereby allowing network administrators to change logical configurations and manage bandwidth as needs dictate.

METROPOLITAN AREA NETWORKS (MANs)

Going beyond the confines of a LAN existing within a building or several buildings in close proximity to one another, there are metropolitan area networks (MANs). A MAN has limited geographic range, generally defined as within a 50-mile radius. In the past, a number of small companies have begun businesses by installing fiber optic cable in metropolitan business areas. Their primary customers are companies of all sizes that need to communicate within the metropolitan area. The customer is usually responsible for providing equipment. The primary market is the customer that needs a lot of high-speed digital service. The MAN providers typically offer lower prices than the telephone companies, diverse routing, and backup in emergency conditions. Because of the pressing need to link a typical organization with other organizations locally, nationally, or internationally, the discussion below takes this important direction into account.

WIDE AREA NETWORKS (WANs)

Today, wide area networks (WANs) are generally considered to be those that cover a large geographic area, require the crossing of public right-of-ways, and use circuits provided by a common carrier. WANs may be made up of a combination of switched and leased, terrestrial and satellite, and private microwave circuits. The WAN for a large multinational company may be global, whereas the WAN for a small company may cover only several cities or counties. General Electric, for example, has a private global network to transmit voice, data, and video signals to GE offices in 25 countries.

To overcome difficulties experienced by users in wide area networks, there is the need for a new approach. The problem is that the farther the computer is from the data, information, and knowledge, the harder it is for the user to get to it. This is especially true if it is found in another city or across the nation. Trading the security and relative speed of a LAN for the sluggishness and uncertainty of a wide area network creates unforeseen data bottlenecks. A new universal network transport mechanism, called *asynchronous transfer mode* (ATM), gives the user easier access between a Token Ring or Ethernet local area network and wide area mechanisms, such as T1 and X.25. By providing a common infrastructure that is suitable for everything from desktop and LAN applications to campus, metropolitan, and global networks, ATM offers a new direction in network technology.

Until recently, LAN and WAN technologies have approached data transmission differently. The driving force behind ATM is a new class of applications involving voice, video, multmedia, imaging, and client/server functions. These broadband applications demand much higher network capacity than the traditional personal productivity, on-line transaction processing, and database programs. The disparity between LAN and WAN transport protocols makes it difficult to create broadband enterprise networks. Regarded as a universal protocol for high-speed networking, ATM has been chosen by the CCITT (the international data communications standards organization) as the transport layer protocol for emerging broadband integrated services digital networks (BISDNs). Basic ISDN will be discussed later in the chapter.

Wireless WANs

Wireless WANs are being put to use in a variety of applications, although current technology limitations make wireless WANs unsuitable for many applications now common on LANs and internetworks. Wireless services are well suited mainly for applications that involve short, bursty messages. Wireless data networks already have become a critical advantage in many industries. An example is the courier industry. In the late 1970s, Federal Express Corporation revolutionized the overnight delivery business by building a private wireless network to track its packages. The Federal Express network was not low in cost. It cost the courier hundreds of millions of dollars. But it helped propel the company to the front of a very competitive industry.

Although wireless WAN services are found in organizations of varying sizes, the next few years will be critical in deciding how important they become in corporate networks. One of the most important issues that must be resolved is the matter of standards. Today's wireless WANs are based on proprietary technology, even though several carriers have thrown open their systems to third-party developers. Until standards are in place, many organizations are reluctant to make major commitments to wireless WANs. As is the usual case with all standards, progress toward the development of standards for wireless WAN systems and equipment is slow.

INTEGRATED SERVICES DIGITAL NETWORKS (ISDNs)

One way of bringing together the preceding discussion on data communications and networking is to think in terms of total communications for a typical organization. Although this can take many directions, only one is discussed below due to space limitations. The focus is on integrated services digital networks (ISDNs), which can provide users with a total network in which compatible voice, data, and video configurations will be transported on a single pair of wires, eliminating leased line and digital circuits for data, voice lines for telecommunications, and cable services for video. ISDNs can offer users a multifaceted communications network to transmit and receive information worldwide. The concept behind ISDN is a standard protocol that is used to link private and public networks to receive and transmit digital information. Compatibility stems from predetermined standards, allowing all types of equipment to interface, provided they are manufactured to accepted standards.

The ultimate goal of ISDN is to combine all of the telecommunications services that are currently being provided by different networks into one large-scale network. Services to be offered through ISDN include telephone services (call forwarding, transferring, conference calling, automatic wake-up calling), data services (closed user groups, called and calling line identification, multi-address calling), teletext services (delayed messages, multiple addressing, Telex access, and a graphic mode), facsimile services (delayed delivery and multiple designations), and video-text services (transactions, such as reservations and shopping, and special character sets). In preparing for ISDN, companies need to consider whether their current data communications decisions are compatible with an evolution to ISDN-based communications. In addition, companies should examine their internal structure for planning voice, data, and office facilities to ensure that internal conflicts between separate voice and data departments are minimized.

In summary, ISDN is an ideal technology for remote LAN access/work-at-home settings, satellite offices, Internet access for individuals, and computer-based video conferencing. It is an international network architecture that offers a standard universal interface for voice, data, and video, thereby allowing highly efficient, interactive use of the public telephone network. In contrast, open network architecture (ONA) is a regulatory development that will allow specialty information services, such as messaging, electronic mail, security, and answering services, to take place over a local telephone network. Although the implementation time of ISDN and ONA technologies is uncertain, it would depend in large part on public demand. One probable effect of this implementation will be an increase in *telecommunicating* on a broad basis that was not possible before now. Thus, the home computer will be an essential storage and communications device, much like the telephone.

RELATED NETWORKING TECHNOLOGIES

Complementary to the preceding discussion are electronic mail systems, voice messaging and speech recognition systems, and video conferencing. If fast and accurate communications are needed and overnight couriers and telexes are too expensive in volume, there is a need to consider *electronic mail systems* (E-mail). Because E-mail distributes messages from one computer to another, transactions are both very fast and cost-effective, and run 24 hours a day. This is especially helpful across time zones. Some E-mail systems even offer the ability to transfer entire desktop publishing programs, recalculable spreadsheets, revisable word processing documents, and updatable databases—something a fax machine will never do. To use E-mail, the user enters the system and types a message. Tagged with an electronic address, the message is then transmitted to a "mailbox"—a point in the main computer's memory where it is stored until called up. The message can be funneled into the PC of a specified system user or sent to a middle person who can print and deliver the message. Because typical E-mail works through PCs, a user can work up a document on a PC and send it instantaneously without the hassles of couriers or post office schedules.

Currently, there are over six million E-mail subscribers in the United States. Communication is increasingly available for companies with as few as six locations through public E-mail systems, such as Western Union's EasyLink, Dialcom, and MCI Mail. All of these firms are integrating E-mail with other telecommunications methods, enabling the computer to transmit via fax, telex, or cablegram—almost unlimited information and communication delivery capabilities. E-mail subscribers can often get access to a variety of public databases, financial reporting services, news clipping services, and news wires. Western Union, for instance, offers FYI News, a service that provides up-to-the-minute reports on business, finance, politics, entertainment, and more.

For company employees wishing to receive, use, and distribute calls and messages, *voice messaging* can be helpful and can dramatically speed up the communication process while making it more accurate. Essentially, voice messaging technology eliminates intervention between a caller and the intended message recipient. Messages incorrectly taken, lost, or forgotten are becoming a thing of the past. With a high-quality voice messaging system, company employees have to make only one telephone call to retrieve all their messages. In essence, voice messaging can become the hub of all potential communication centers: business, home, car, pager, electronic mail, telephone answering service, facsimile machine, and push-button telephone. Voice messaging connects all of these spokes into one central message system, thereby saving the executive time, money, and energy.

Speech recognition systems are related to voice messaging systems. Speech recognition software packages have two basic purposes: to accept voice commands to streamline the operation of the computer or to take verbal dictation that can be saved as a text document. The former class basically accepts verbal input to activate macros, many matching spoken words to a list of menu commands. For example, Voice Blaster from Covox, Inc. automatically creates a list of an application's menu items; the user trains the software to respond to his or her voice as commands are spoken. The program requires a sound card, yet supplies a microphone-and-earphone headset. All in all, it is expected that speech products in the coming years will be mature enough to warrant serious consideration for everyday business use.

Video conferencing, which is available for business units that are widely dispersed geographically, is designed to be used as a business tool to assist in overseeing widespread operations. There are two distinct types of video conferencing. The first, "person-to-person," links one PC to another, thereby allowing two people to share moving pictures and some type of shared workspace. Usually these systems transmit postage-size images over ISDN, regular phone lines, or Switch-56 via a little video camera mounted on the monitor. The second type is "group-to-group" video conferencing that tries to merge two or more conference rooms. Large monitors, multiple microphones, and dedicated transmission lines are usually required for this type of sharing, resulting in better picture and sound quality than person-to-person. Of course, the cost is much higher.

In group-to-group video conferencing, there can be an exchange of ideas that involves company personnel from distant operations. The accent may be on a free exchange of potential answers to specific questions that arise in the normal course of conversation. From this perspective, the interaction among participants who are geographically separated from one another may signal the need to develop specific computer programs for answering the questions posed. At the next video conference, a presentation can be made that focuses on potential answers to the important business questions posed earlier.

Currently, several vendors are offering public rooms or sharing their private rooms with others. In a similar manner, many large corporations are currently bringing private satellite broadcasts directly into their own facilities or into hotel meeting facilities to deliver corporate communications or training to employees. As they have gained experience with corporate video, companies have installed their own private networks with satellite receiver dishes located at their corporate facilities that enable employees to watch regularly scheduled company programs.

There are many benefits from utilizing video conferencing. First, there is a reduction in travel costs. By eliminating many trips, a company cuts out the unproductive time people spend on traveling, thereby resulting in increased productivity. The ability to hold a meeting almost instantly in a relaxed atmosphere with less time away from office and home has removed a lot of stress often involved with meetings. In addition, video conferences enable the company to involve more people in meetings. These individuals might include experts or scientists, who would rather be at work in their labs than traveling to a meeting.

MERGER OF TRADITIONAL ELECTRONIC COMMERCE WITH THE INTERNET AND INTRANETS

A logical starting point for a discussion of the Internet and a company's intranets and extranets within a KMS environment is the area of *electronic commerce*. Traditionally, electronic commerce has utilized such means as electronic document or data interchange (refer to Chapter 1), fax communication, symbol technology, bar code and inter-enterprise messaging. While the deployment of this information and communications technology has grown steadily over the years, traditional electronic commerce has never reached the level of acceptance that has been accorded to electronic commerce on the Internet. This is because traditional electronic commerce relies for the most part on the value-added networks (VANs) and private messaging networks that generally involve high costs and offer limited connectivity. Connectivity on VANs reaches only other paying enterprises and relies mostly on store-and-forward methods. While quite adequate for electronic commerce functions such as passing purchase orders and invoices (which can be processed in a batch mode from a store-and-forward mailbox), VAN connectivity is too limited for advertising and interactive functions such as browsing product and service text and graphics. Its chief advantages are relatively good security, reliability, and confirmation of receipt.

The Internet, on the other hand, has worldwide connectivity that is growing at a rapid rate in every segment of society, can be interactive, and is relatively inexpensive to use. The major disadvantage is that there is no central authority for managing the Internet. Also, there is a problem of reliability which, while improving at this time, is still sometimes questionable. Security must be considered nonexistent unless the user provides it. But relatively new Internet services, such as the World Wide Web and the technology advances behind it, make it possibly the most exciting development for business today and tomorrow.

The Internet's potential for offering nearly unlimited electronic communications with a world of trading partners—not just those who subscribe to one private network—has stirred the imagination of EDI users and software vendors. Software such as Premenos Technology Corporation's Templar now offers companies the alternative of Internet-based EDI. The traditional EDI VANs are looking at the Internet as a logical extension of the core commerce services that they provide anyway. The attraction of the Internet and other Internet protocol–related technologies for business EDI is the same as in other areas of use: lower cost, greater speed, and the potential for vastly wider interoperability.

Where VANs charge by every thousand characters of data transmitted, an Internet connection entitles users to transmit countless documents for flat monthly fees. For a medium-volume EDI program, this can mean a total cost of hundreds of dollars a year over the Internet versus thousands with a VAN. In addition, Internet transmissions usually range from 9.6Kbps to 1.5Mbps (on a T-1 line), which is up to 300 times as fast as the typical 4.8Kbps of VANs using the X.25 standard for data transmission. To protect their territory, a number of VANs have responded with Internet-based products and services. These come in two principal types: traditional store-and-forward document transmission using the Internet as a transport mechanism, which usually includes encryption for security; and a web-based EDI service that allows small trading partners to exchange documents with their larger partners using only a basic Internet connection and document forms found with a World Wide Web browser.

The merger of electronic commerce with the Internet can be extended to include a company's intranets. However, the accomplishment can be somewhat difficult if a company's commerce and web-related projects are spread across departments, which is usually the case. Often, the computer department owns the intranet, marketing runs the corporate World Wide Web, and traditional EDI is specific to each business unit. Nonetheless, the potential payback of unifying various endeavors under a web-fired vision of electronic commerce is enormous and well suited for strategic-minded intranet managers.

To get a feel for the tie-in of electronic commerce with a company's intranet, consider Chrysler's Supply Partner Information Network (SPIN), a browser-accessible resource for information and transactions that is part of the company's Extended Enterprise extranet. (Extranets will be explained below.) SPIN includes resources such as equipment purchasing policies and guidelines for doing business with Chrysler. It also supports real-time procurement applications, so parts suppliers can check the status of orders and submit invoices. SPIN is used by 3,500 of the 12,000 suppliers working with Chrysler (Auburn Hills, Michigan). However, additional users and access to additional databases are being added weekly.[2]

Linkage of Electronic Commerce to Extranets

Related to the foregoing discussion is the relationship of electronic commerce to extranets. Basically, electronic commerce has the capability to create instant electronic partnerships among suppliers and customers nearly anywhere in the world. An extranet provides desktop access to product catalogs, purchase orders, shipping records, secure E-mail, invoice status, and videos. In short, an extranet provides information that enables business to take place. It can take a community of trading partners and bind them together electronically far more efficiently than is possible with traditional methods. The idea behind the extranet is quite simple: Live data stored in operational databases and HTML-based information can be shared by connecting two or more companies' intranets via a secure link over the Internet. Encryption, password protection, and firewalls protect the exchanges. The Gartner Group predicts that more than 40 percent of business-to-business electronic commerce applications, including traditional EDI and forms-based EDI, will be replaced by extranets by 2002. Within five years, the firm estimates, 80 percent of companies will use extranets, compared to about 30 percent at present. Overall, although the World Wide Web may have ushered in a new era of communications, the most direct route to success is via an extranet for many organizations.[3]

AN INTRANET IN A TYPICAL COMPANY

With the phenomenal popularity of the Internet as a means of accessing information and knowledge (as discussed above as well as in the next section of the chapter), it is viewed today as a messaging model. The result is an "intranet," a private-network version of the Internet, or simply an internal Internet modeled after the global Internet and its World Wide Web. Intranets employ the hypertext and multimedia technologies used in web pages, but they do so for applications internal to an organization. They provide a standard browser-based window in which all information is displayed the same way, and all processes interface the same and work the same. As such, intranets enable companies to make massive amounts of information and knowledge available to their employees locally and remotely and to improve their messaging strategies.

Typically, intranets are erected to support one or more publishing applications that, while not mission critical, offer a real payback. For example, staff directories, product data sheets, employee handbooks, and other human resource materials fit into this category. Essentially, these are read-only data sets where user response is not required. These applications can be easily achieved at low cost. On the other hand, more ambitious applications use web pages linked to back-end applications that retrieve or store data in databases. For example, many companies are building web-based human resources applications that allow staff to check on vacation entitlements and other benefits. Overall, intranets change the way a company thinks about information access and distribution as well as transform network infrastructures.

Essentially, a typical intranet's key to creating a boundaryless enterprise lies in its ability to share not only information and knowledge but also processes across the entire value chain of activities, from production to consumption, through a single universal interface, thereby collapsing transfer times and creating a new level of intimacy with customers, suppliers, and teams. Within this context, there are four basic classifications for intranets:

1. document-based—concerned with the archiving and/or distribution of documents
2. process-based—focused on automating processes within a company
3. commerce-based—used to facilitate business-to-business information and knowledge exchange or useful as a replacement for EDI
4. knowledge-based—concerned with the management and sharing of a company's centralized and decentralized knowledge bases

When a company designs and implements an intranet, there is a need to decide whether the intranet will use an internal wide area network and local area network as the communication path between the employees and the intranet. If so, there is need to be aware of the possible traffic load that may be generated and determine if the WAN/LAN connection can handle the increased traffic. If a company decides to use an external network, such as the Internet, as the communication vehicle, there are concerns about the security and privacy aspects of the intranet. With company information flowing around between the employees at their PCs and the web server connected across the public Internet—perhaps information such as a company's policies and procedures—it is possible that outsiders could tap into the information and use it for their own purposes.

Essential Elements of an Intranet

The main building blocks of an intranet are shown in Figure 4-1 and related to the Internet. More specifically, a typical intranet consists of servers, databases, browsers, firewalls, and dynamic HTML pages. At the heart of most intranet systems are *web servers*. These simple but effective information distribution mechanisms are becoming increasingly sophisticated as vendors extend and en-

Figure 4-1
The Building Blocks of an Intranet and Its Relationship to the Internet

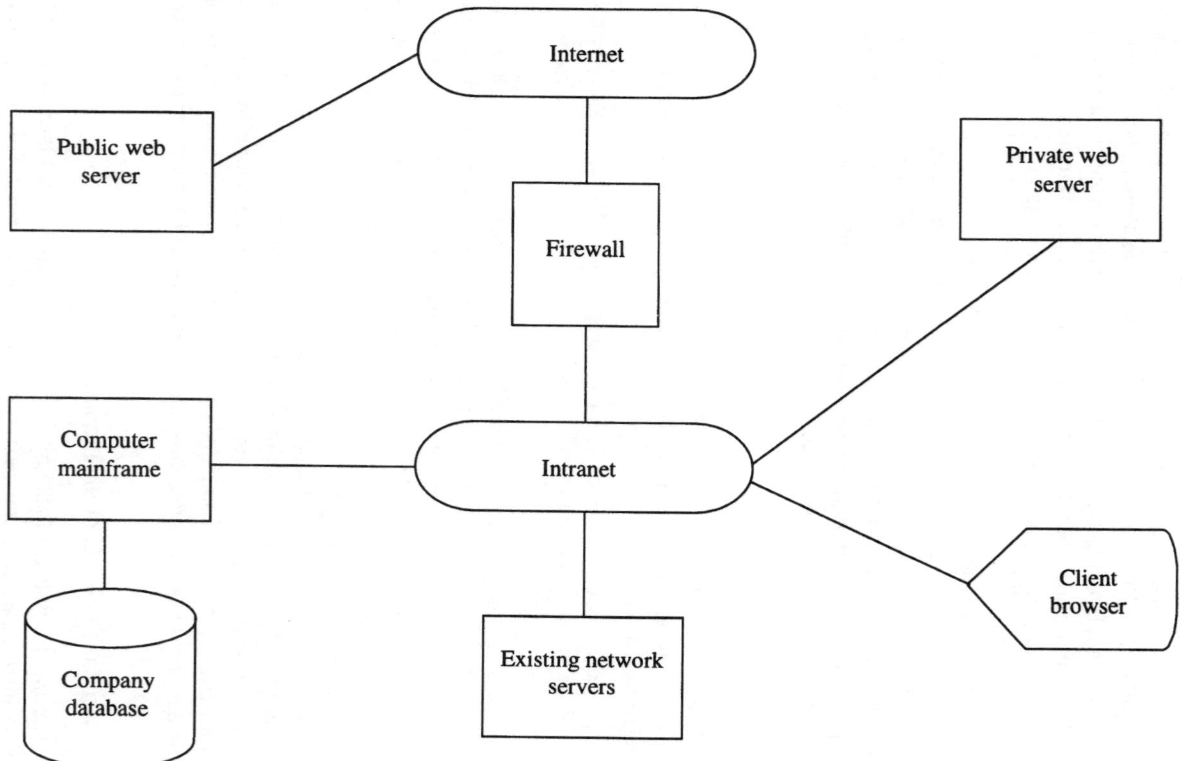

hance their basic functionality. Intranets can also involve the use of TCP/IP (transmission control protocol/Internet protocol) as a transport and a number of TCP/IP applications that range from file transfer to audio and video distribution. As shown in the illustration, web servers are integrated with *databases*, linked to mainframes and other legacy systems, and provide workflow services. Combined with the high bandwidth capacity of corporate data networks, a company can capitalize on advanced features, such as real-time audio and video as well as collaborative applications and 3-D data representation.

A client *browser* is the means by which the user interfaces with the intranet. The most sophisticated browsers include Netscape's Navigator, Microsoft's Internet Explorer, Attachmate's Emissary, and Sun Microsystems' HotJava. These products will allow the user to support advanced presentation techniques and a whole range of add-on products. In contrast, a *firewall*, essentially a computer connected to both the corporate network and the Internet, is the main line of defense. Once companies create direct links between their private networks and the global Internet, their internal network is open to attack from anyone. Because of this, the need for a firewall is paramount for security reasons. Additionally, there is generally a need to convert the scanned documents into a text format suitable for web access (i.e., a format known as HyperText Markup Language or *HTML*).

Beyond these basic building blocks, there are a number of specialized tools to help a company build an intranet. There are video conferencing systems, such as the low-cost VideoPhone from Connectix Corporation (San Mateo, California), web-based bulletin boards, such as the WebBoard product from O'Reilly & Associates, Inc. (Sebastapol, California), and conferencing systems, such as OpenMind from Attachmate Corporation (Bellevue, Washington). VideoPhone could be used for meetings, even over slow WAN links, while WebBoard could be used to maintain discussion areas for work groups or the entire company. Although finding products is easy, deciding what is best for a company's intranet can be difficult. The key is to employ those products that address clearly identifiable needs, offer a quick payback, and are simple to implement.

The most important benefits of an intranet involve new methods of information distribution and collection, new opportunities to involve staff in the process, and the cost benefits of recentralizing some of those functions that are difficult to manage in a distributed environment. Companies that build intranets will find that information publishing becomes a way of corporate life, and the result is improved internal communications and a more effective community culture. Overall, intranets are here to stay and, as shown in Figure 4-1, they can be linked directly to the Internet.

Using an Intranet Within a KMS Environment

Knowledge-based intranets serve as a means to access various databases, generated reports, and other information and knowledge. These knowledge-based intranets tie together knowledge otherwise locked up in disparate applications. To illustrate, HBO (Home Box Office), a division of Time-Warner Entertainment, provides programming via both the HBO and Showtime cable networks to nearly 30 million viewers throughout the United States. HBO uses an intranet to provide enterprise-wide access to information and related knowledge needed to make informed television programming decisions and to assist its sales force in selling its premium television services. In the past, the sales force would learn of new marketing campaigns once a month, when HBO's marketing department sent the large boxes of marketing materials, video tapes, and other collateral to its 200 to 300 sales representatives nationwide. Now this information is rolled out via the intranet, eliminating costs for printing and video duplication. Furthermore, the intranet provides the sales force nearly instantaneous access to time-sensitive market intelligence that used to take weeks for sales representatives to receive under the previous system.

From the company's intranet, HBO employees are able to access crucial information on virtually every movie ever made (including those in the process of being made) within the company's corporate database. The database tracks various information related to each movie, including its cast, director, distributor, gross earnings, and details on HBO's rights to sell it. It is also linked to a Nielsen database that tracks ratings of each show. Previously, this information could be accessed only as paper reports. With HBO's intranet, users can execute SQL queries to the database from within HTML forms. The server then dynamically generates a graphical representation of the requested information. HBO's ultimate goal is a single point of access to all the line-of-business information and resulting knowledge spread throughout the organization, thereby providing one common interface to all corporate information and knowledge, including such items as network programming, HR policy manuals, the employee database, and organization charts.[4]

THE INTERNET AND THE WORLD WIDE WEB

Over time, the Internet has been called by different names, among them are the information superhighway, the digital expressway, or just plain cyberspace. It utilizes the World Wide Web, which is a vast, interlinked network of computer files from all over the world that a user can access by clicking on a mouse. The web is the place on the Internet where organizations post a home page. The web can be thought of as the Internet's multimedia subuniverse. CompuServe, Prodigy, and America Online all feature the web, as do many smaller services. A web "browser" is essentially the software that gets the user from file to file. Although there are several currently being offered, the most popular one is Netscape Navigator, which the user can download free of charge. The Internet started out as an ad hoc computer network that was started in the late 1960s by the Defense Department. Fundamentally, two events converged to create the Internet: (1) technology and (2) necessity. The *technology* was the packet-switched switching. The *necessity* was the perceived threat of thermonuclear war. That is, the U.S. Air Force was interested in building a computer network that stood a chance of surviving a major attack. Therefore, they built a network without a central control point so that it could lose one, or several, computers and the computers remaining could still communicate with each other. This led to the creation of the ARPANET, the progenitor of today's Internet.

HTML and VRML Used in the World Wide Web

To better understand the Internet's use of the World Wide Web, consider the fax. When one sends a fax, the page sent is actually broken down into light and dark images. This graphical method of transmission is inefficient and slow, and does not work with colored images. The World Wide Web, on the other hand, uses HyperText Markup Language (HTML) to break up a document into simple text elements that are reconstructed by the ''browser.'' The browser is what makes the web possible. The first browser, NCSA Mosaic, has spawned dozens of competitors, all of which are vying for market share and acceptance. Standards are lagging way behind the release of new language enhancements and browser developments. The result is that every one of the 30 or more available browsers will display a document differently. HTML 4.0 is the latest published standard. It builds on Version 3.2 by adding new elements, deprecating some elements, and making a few others obsolete. It should be noted that some HTML standards are not supported by all browsers.

In an effort to spruce up web pages, there is the Virtual Reality Modeling Language (VRML), a standard-file format for describing virtual worlds. It is designed to bring real-time interactive, three-dimensional graphics to the Internet via the World Wide Web. VRML allows prospective world builders to sit down at their keyboards and build full-fledged 3-D environments, then make their creations available over the Internet. Users running web browsers can click on a link that takes them into a virtual world, and a VRML browser running on their local machine will take over the task of rendering that world and letting the user navigate through it. VRML can be used for everything from visualization of a building layout to representation of complex data. For example, the dynamics of the stock market or a complex industrial process as a moving, 3-D image can be represented. Instead of trying to determine cause and effect using static numbers, employees will be able more easily to grasp the forces driving the information and its resultant knowledge.

A marketing manager, for example, might find VRML useful when creating a pricing model. With VRML, the manager could plot a 3-D graph that charts the number of units shipped against the profit margin and against the return on investment. Then, the individual could watch the graph change as the variants are altered. If the manager wants to project the impact of a drop in units shipped, for instance, the individual can simply push down the shipment curve and watch what happens to the profit margins and return on investment. There is no need to spend time crunching numbers and interpreting the results. Longer term, VRML supports 3-D-rendered data and processes that let the user walk or fly through virtual worlds. The ability to mainpulate one's viewpoint and interact with virtual objects brings a new understanding of details, structure, and relationships.

Overall, the capability to navigate around a conceptual space is an important asset to applications such as workflow for accounts payable or the sales department. The spatial characteristics allow identifying locations and 3-D characteristics. Instead of entering a flat page, a person can enter a city, a business, or a drawing. In fact, industry experts believe that the beginnings of tomorrow's important applications are starting to be developed today. These include 3-D simulation and training, visualization of financial data, virtual retail stores, visualization interfaces to data warehouses and executive information systems, network management, and corporate presentations.

Essential Elements of the Internet

The essential elements of the Internet differ from those set forth previously for intranets. The transition to web-based on-line transaction processing calls for different application architectures. To provide proper support for the Internet, an application needs to be built in a three-tiered manner (as set forth previously in the text). By way of review, they include: (1) the user interface on the browser, (2) application logic on a middle-tier server, and (3) data on a back-end data server. The key issue is to insulate the middle-tier business logic from the front-end clients and back-end data servers. By doing so, changes can be made at any tier without affecting the others. As shown in Figure 4-2, a three-tiered architecture is used for the Internet and its tie-in with the World Wide Web.

Besides running the business logic, the middle tier hosts some transaction middleware. This type of software gives the web a memory (technically called "state") so that a transaction can consist of several separate actions taken by a user. It also provides integrity for the transaction so that customers are not charged for a purchase that is never recorded. Transaction software typically includes security features, supports other security products, or does both. Lastly, transaction middleware can run on several servers so that the user can add servers as the traffic load increases to balance the load among them.

Doing Business on the Internet

Although establishing a direct connection to the Internet was somewhat difficult in the past, it is easy today. More commercial Internet service providers have sprung up to meet business demand and as increasingly powerful computers and software make it possible to hide the Internet's Unix command system behind graphical, point-and-shoot interfaces like Mosaic or even Microsoft

Figure 4-2
The Utilization of a Three-Tiered Architecture for the Internet

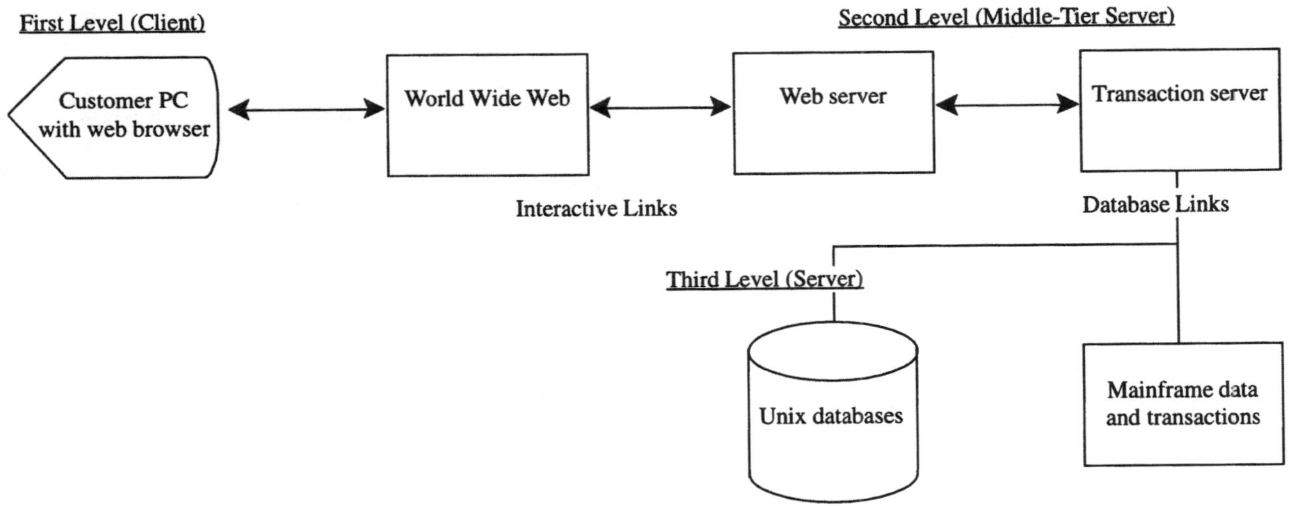

Windows. In the immediate past, most of the Internet's traffic consisted of E-mailing, browsing the web, reading and posting network news, or just languishing in artificial role-playing and interaction environments. Today, the orientation has broadened to include such items as high-volume trading of stocks and bonds by the likes of Bank of America, Merrill Lynch, and Fidelity Investments to consumer purchases of everything imaginable. Products and services are being bought and sold every day on the Internet. While consumer sales on the Internet will continue to rise, the real growth will be in business-to-business commerce. That is, for large companies, an emerging crop of products that support EDI over TCP/IP makes the Internet a more attractive, cost-effective medium than traditional VANs. Meanwhile, small companies are moving to capitalize on the Internet and are challenging even the biggest conglomerates in the Internet marketspace. Products that secure large-scale transactions on the Internet are being developed, which will further increase the Internet's attractiveness.

Although the Internet's role as the new "global business village" is still evolving at this time, there is one thing that is clear: the Internet is linked to the need for communicating business information about a company's products and services. The Internet has the capability to communicate with customers, potential customers, partners, distributors, and employees. Over the Internet, consumers can place an order, brokerage customers can make a stock trade, and suppliers can even update a manufacturing database that, in turn, could alter a production schedule. These capabilities apply equally to users accessing a web site via the Internet or an intranet. The Internet's allure is that it provides a relatively cheap, rapidly updatable, easy-to-distribute medium with a rich environment of text, graphics, sound, and video. Today, any size company must be involved in the Internet using the World Wide Web in some shape or form as way of doing business if it wants to survive in the long run.

Emergence of Internet II

Currently, the Internet is so saturated with commercial and other informed users that it can no longer provide the speed, access, and reliability needed for interactive and high-density transmissions. In fact, the Internet has become so popular with household computer users that the Internet's originators—universities, industries, and the federal government—are being crowded out. So the developers have created Internet II, which they plan to keep all to themselves. Internet II is designed to be a private network owned by its charter members. The charter members are 100 universities that do a lot of research. However, these schools are not excluding everybody from their Internet II club. They are cutting in the federal government and big industries because that is where universities get most of their research money.

At the university level, the current Internet restricts classroom demonstrations to simple computer drawings akin to stick figures. Connections are not good enough to produce complex teaching aids without unpredictable delays. On the other hand, Internet II seeks to fix that by improving computer connections among and within campuses and by developing ways to sort and priortize information to allow real-time video presentations to cruise past less urgent E-mail on the information superhighway. The ultimate goal of Internet II's enhanced voice, video, and data capabilities is to create a network that researchers can rely on to obtain the high-volume computer files they need when they need them. The bottom line is that professors can effectively reserve network capacity.

Utilization of World Wide Web to Tap into Corporate Knowledge

As stressed in this text, no company regardless of size can compete effectively without taking advantage of its documented knowledge. A typical company finds itself amassing an ever-growing pile of paper and electronic documents in file formats as various and incompatible as word processing texts, scanned drawings, spreadsheets, and other types. Intranet technology can add to this difficulty by introducing HTML and its associated objects—Graphical Interchange Format (GIF), for instance—as standards. Thus, the ability to manage, navigate, and access documents across diverse standards has become a strategic requirement for World Wide Web developers. To meet this challenge, solution providers are lining up behind two distinct, complementary approaches to web-based documents; conversion to HTML and accommodation of non-HTML formats.

Most companies will benefit from a hybrid of these approaches because each has distinct benefits and drawbacks. Conversion takes a web-centric view, based on the tenet that HTML is a common language suitable for distributing every document. The challenge in this approach is to convert legacy documents automatically to HTML from the widest array of native formats and with the best practical fidelity. A number of software conversion packages are available from a wide variety of vendors.

THE ORIGINS OF NETWORK COMPUTERS

There are a number of networking technologies—as set forth in this chapter—that are useful to assist users in sharing company knowledge no matter where they are located. As a starting point, it would be helpful to look at the origins of networking terminals. In the late 1950s, *dumb terminals*, which can be defined as display machines that lack processing ability but are connected to computer mainframes, started to appear. In some cases, the dumb terminal was used to enter and print data, while the host computer did nearly everything else. In the late 1970s, dumb terminals cropped up by the millions in banks, insurance companies, factories, schools, and libraries. While most terminal users would only type in data, a few could print out what appeared on screen. By the end of 1981, there were approximately one million IBM 3270-type terminals installed in the United States, making up the largest single segment of the data entry market.

The important benefit of dumb terminals was that they were virtually tamperproof and gave the computer department control over data and programs. However, at this time, the development of the microprocessor, which gave users control over their own data and applications, was in process. IBM entered the PC market in 1981 and created a standard for the industry. In the same year, dBase II and other tools arrived that allowed computer mainframe data to be downloaded to and mainpulated on a PC. As a result of this computer revolution, worldwide sales of dumb terminals grew until 1984 when the PC's impact began to be felt. Although the IBM 3270-type dumb terminal essentially was pronounced dead by *Computerworld* in 1990, actually dumb terminals still sell today.

Even though there were a number of attempts to prolong the life of dumb terminals in different forms, it was about 1985 that another player appeared—the diskless PC (a computer without a disk but with a CPU chip). With this system, users could store their applications on a central server. In creating the diskless PC, vendors were responding to a need for machines that cost less than PCs but still provided some functionality, such as word processing. In essence, the diskless PC was a good in-between step from a 3270 to a fully operational PC. The diskless PC failed to gain popularity because users wanted to run the software applications of their choice. Corporate networks, which were not as predominant then as today, presented another obstacle. Nevertheless, the diskless PC, though a minor player in the immediate past, is becoming the network computer (NC). Notables in the computing field, such as William Gates and Larry Ellison, agree that the diskless PC is essentially a network computer.

Currently, network computers employ *thin clients* that give users much functionality. Thin clients maintain a centralized management scheme, give users more power, and offer networking administrators more options. Most thin clients are smaller than a toaster, holding little more than a processor with limited memory. Because centralized management drives the client to uniformity, any complexity in the system must be moved from desktops to a back-end server. For users who need only a few, simple applications to get their jobs done, thin clients fit the bill very well.

Basics of Network Computers

Because the Internet has had a major impact on the way goods and services are bought and sold, there is a need for Internet access that is simple and inexpensive. This access is found in a network computer that utilizes the Java language (or similar language) to write straightforward programs quickly within a network computing architecture (NCA). Combined, these technologies—Java, NCs, and networking computing architecture—provide a robust framework for Internet commerce. Since NCA is the architecture that can make the Internet a ubiquitous resource, the NC is the device to explore the Internet market. Generally, the PC is cumbersome and complicated for average users, including most home users. But the NC simplifies access and lowers cost, which will drive business to the home market, and the home market will in turn drive more businesses to the Internet. NCA provides the backbone architecture that can manage the different elements and scale to the higher transaction numbers the larger audiences bring.

In terms of its *hardware* (as noted in the previous discussion), the NC is a much less expensive device than the traditional PC. Typically, the NC has a processor and memory and gets all of its information from the application server and data systems. Under the network computing paradigm, instead of housing and maintaining all the word processing, E-mail, spreadsheet, and other client tools on the PC, the most up-to-date applications are obtained from an application server. The NC terminal is a fast-processing graphical terminal instead of a dumb, character-based terminal. NCs have powerful processors without the cost of disk space and the time and money required to maintain and house applications and software locally.

Additionally, NCs use a smart card that is much like a credit card or bank card. The card has optional memory capabilities of up to 8 kilobytes for data and program storage. The NC card is the user's network passport. When inserted into the machine, the card provides network connection information, user information, and additional security information. After the user enters a personal identification number, the NC connects to the appropriate network, databases, and services, such as E-mail, Internet applications, and electronic commerce applications. NCs are capable of quickly delivering data with only a 28.8-kilobit-per-second modem connection, and they support cable modems, which are capable of delivering data hundreds of times faster than a 28.8-kbps modem.

A most important feature of NC *software* is the utilization of new languages, such as Java, to write small, straightforward applications—called *applets*. Like components, applets can be combined with each other or with other software to create applications. There is the ability with Java to run in a Java ''virtual machine'' (an emulation) on any computer and operating system so that software only has to be developed once to run anywhere. The network computer operating system (NCOS) and software stored on the ROM (read-only memory) chip in many of the NCs available is provided by Network Computer, Inc. (NCI), a wholly owned subsidiary of the Oracle Corporation. The features of NCOS include:

- a small operating system
- storage of applications as operating system modules in ROM (such as a browser)
- availability of standard compilers (such as C/C++) to produce native code
- a standard UNIX-based TCP/IP network implementation

- extendability through dynamic addition of modules
- support for graphics and multimedia

Other software provided by NCI includes the NC Desktop, an interface for managing and using NC applications, and NC Connect for Windows, which enables users to run Windows applications and access Windows documents via an NC device.

An underlying framework for network computers is the notion of a thin client (which was mentioned previously in the chapter), whereby the desktop device is linked via network to one or more servers. Everything that constitutes a state—the operating system, applications, data, integrity, etc.—has been relocated from client to server. Although this thin client network computer is ''skinny'' in terms of desktop management costs, it is actually remarkably rich in functionality due to the Internet and the nature of the Java language.

Just recently, Oracle's Network Computer, Inc. subsidiary announced Network in a Box, a *hardware/software combination* for seamless installation of network computers. By selling Network in a Box as a prepackaged client, NCI is focusing on schools, small companies, or other agencies that may lack an internal computer department. Network in a Box is available with two smart cards, now referred to as NC Cards, from Schlumberger Electronic Transactions. The cards act as pass cards that enable multiple users to access network-based information and services from any NC. A typical value added reseller (VAR) that sells the package is Propeller Portable Computer Products Inc. The package includes two Intel-based NCs, server software, network connectivity hardware, NC management software, E-mail, and productivity applications as well as NCI's NC Desktop NC software. Although the package includes server software, the server must be purchased separately.

Major Issues Centering on Network Computers

There are a number of major issues centering on network computers that need to be addressed before spending considerable sums on the technology. *First*, and foremost, is NC technology really necessary to meet and possibly beat competition? The answer is typically no since NC offerings, such as those by Oracle, Sun, and IBM, are basically remastered versions of the dumb terminal outfitted with the Java capability. In most cases, this technology is not replacing PCs per se, but rather serving as upgrades to the millions of dumb terminals still in existence. *Second*, will the NCs reduce the cost of ownership for desktops? The answer is generally yes and no—that is, studies seem to indicate that the cost of ownership of NCs can or cannot be about the same as that for fully optimized and well managed PCs. *Third*, what are the hidden costs to installing a NC network? There are several, including costs for servers, routers, switches, and related networking equipment associated with the NC network. Also, there is the cost of developing in-house applications for the NCs. *Fourth*, before buying PCs, it is necessary to be able to answer this question: Are the capabilities of bandwidth suppliers adequate? Some suppliers have overcommitted their bandwidth to subscribers, agreeing to contracts that go beyond their ability to perform. Typically, an increase in bandwidth required by network computers is dramatic. WAN charges alone could negate any savings realized by buying network computers over PCs. Users will need network upgrades—from hubs and routers to LAN switches—to assure proper performance for network computer users. The increase in traffic will depend on which applications network computer users access.

Fifth, are current services adequate to meet the needs of a NC environment? Generally, the answer is no since users with local servers will need Ethernet switches to provide dedicated bandwidth to each network computer and a fatter pipe to the server. In addition, most users locate servers centrally in data centers on backbone networks. *Sixth* and last, are a company's NC human resources adequate to meet the demands placed on it? Networking personnel are going to require new skills. There will be a need for expertise in the platform-independent programming languages Java, JavaScript, and Active X along with knowledge of small-scale operating systems to run the NC. Those who have skills in administering LANs will have to broaden their skill sets on larger server computers. Those servers will contain all of the applications, content, and information being provided to the network. In addition, network administrators will have to learn more about computer-telephone integration. The increase in bandwidth, through communications technologies, such as ISDN or ATM, will create greater demands on the network. Overall, a hard look at these issues will dictate the real economics of network computers. It is expected that NCs will never eliminate PCs from the desktop since there will always be a segment of the market that will require PCs, such as CAD/CAM, virtual reality, and other advanced applications.[5]

Economics of Network Computers versus Personal Computers

The economics of network computers versus well-managed computers has been the subject of considerable debate recently. Typically, NCs can increase the efficiency of managing large numbers of desktops and significantly decrease the per user cost of ownership. Assuming that the cost of PC ownership and maintenance is $8,000 to $12,000 per user on an annual basis, the total cost of NC ownership can be (but not always will be) several thousand less per year. From this view, a typical NC offers a richer and easier-to-use computing environment, without the hardware or support costs of a well-managed and fully-configured PC. It should be recognized that companies are increasingly realizing that not everyone needs or uses all the functionality that is provided by a traditional PC. In fact, most users employ only about 20 percent of the function, such as spreadsheets, office suites, and word processors, provided by fully loaded products. New or basic users can get lost in these broad products, which offer everything for everyone. For the most part, smaller, more focused devices are actually more productive. Many users employ their PCs only to access E-mail or vertical applications that are specific to their company or their job. In that case, the PC is really being used as an expensive terminal.

Fundamentally, the economics of network computers versus fully configured PCs centers on the reducing the cost of ownership for desktop systems. Network computers are designed to give users access to applications as well as information and knowledge stored on a centrally managed server or computer mainframe. They have the potential to reduce support and administration costs for large numbers of desktop users. Currently, companies are intrigued by network computers because considerable sums of money are being spent on PC upgrades and maintenance. Network computers run Sun's Java Internet programming language, which takes central management from the computer mainframe world and local processing power from the PC world and puts them together. It is expected network computers will succeed mainly as terminal replacements in the commercial market and for lightweight PC users.

In the business world, where practically everyone is networked, the need to make every computing node complete and independent is decreasing. There is no need to put storage and software on every PC desktop when a network computer can provide fast, cheap, and transparent access to software and storage. Additionally, millions of users are browsing the Internet where immediate access to millions of documents provides them with information, knowledge, education, and entertainment. This ready-made and constantly growing content provides a reason for a network computer that does not have to store its own content. Instead, users can reach out for instant information and knowledge on a million varied topics, each of which are continually refreshed by the content providers.

Typical Network Computer Applications

The world's largest florist, 1-800-FLOWERS INC., is utilizing network computers that replace its terminals. For years, the company has given its employees in its eight national telecenters character-based terminals hooked to NCR 3550 midrange Unix computers. While the system was adequate to handle telephone orders, it offered little to help its representatives forge the kind of personal customer relationships that are needed for higher sales. In the past, while in an order-entry mode, the only way to access information that contributed to customer conversation was by bringing up mulitple windows over the order-entry screen. With the development of a custom Java application, representatives have a scrolling window on the side of the order-entry screen that gives them database information about that particular customer. This helps them build the kind of rapport that encourages more volume per sale and repeat business.[6]

Another network computer application is found at Pro Staff Inc., a temporary services company (in Minneapolis, Minnesota). It is an early adopter of thin-client network computers. The NCs let Pro Staff employees access the company's customer management application and other Windows-based applications, all running on servers housed at the company's data centers. In retrospect, the company concluded that this could never have been done if PCs were utilized.[7] Overall, companies are building applications where the benefits are expected to outweigh the problems that go with being early adopters of NC technology.

The Future of Network Computers and Personal Computers to Share Knowledge

Network computers, as discussed above, represent the third wave in client desktops. That is, they follow the dumb terminals of the 1960s and 1970s and the fully loaded desktop PCs of the 1980s and 1990s. Basically, these stripped-down NCs, versus fully loaded desktop PCs, use Internet technologies for core functions. In order to be called a network computer—as defined by Oracle, Sun, IBM, and others—a device must be able to run a World Wide Web browser and support Sun's Java application environment. As noted previously, because the NC has little or no local storage, the bulk of data and applications reside on a network server. This means a network computer communicates over a network via standard Internet protocols, and it exchanges electronic mail through several established Internet mail protocols. It must also be able to read several file formats, such as HyperText Markup Language. In the future, all network computers will be performing these same basic functions.

A critical difference between network computers and desktop PCs today and tomorrow is that the network computer ''reference profile'' standard does not specify the underlying operating system, hardware, or CPU. This leaves it wide open for adoption or retrofitting by any existing platform, ranging from Unix workstations and Macintoshes to Intel Corporation's based PCs. Networking problems will be handled in the future much the same as they have been in the past. For example, if there is a problem in one of a company's plants, there is no need to have someone dedicated to fixing computer systems on site. This means that a significant amount of time is not spent on the telephone with PC-related problems. Needless to say, network administrators especially like the idea of being able to support applications from a central location. It allows them to update and troubleshoot client machines.

As network computers begin trickling onto enterprise desktops, another future direction will be portable NCs. About a dozen hardware and software companies use a set of specifications for building portable NCs in sizes ranging from pagers to notebook PCs. The mobile NC Reference Profile builds on the desktop NCRP. Neither relies on any particular processor or operating system, and both use current Internet standards such as HTML and HTTP to build interoperable devices. The specification covers three types of portable NCs: what the reference profile refers to as a ''professional assistant,'' which is most similar to a notebook PC; information access devices such as smart phones; and basic messaging devices such as pagers. All in all, switching to network computers by business firms is a move that they are not likely to make immediately. International Data Corporation (Framingham, Massachusetts) estimates that there will be 80 million PCs and about six million network computers by the year 2000.[8]

Major stumbling blocks for network computers are likely to be user loyalty to the local storage capabilities of PCs and corporate hesitation about introducing yet another machine into the current infrastructure. In the final analysis, the true role of NCs lies not in displacing the personal computer, but rather in expanding the market. Because a network computer is really a virtual device (i.e., the generic Java-enabled browser), it is not important whether the physical access device is a PC or an NC for sharing information and knowledge throughout an organization.

NETWORK SECURITY

Companies around the world are working on tightening electronic links with their customers and suppliers in an effort to create dynamic supply chains that can thwart competitors at a moment's notice. Often, this approach means the need to incorporate the virtual corporation concept. No matter which approach is taken, the typical company is subject to a variety of electronic break-ins that include planting of viruses and E-mail bombs as well as theft of money, information, cellular phone numbers, and checking account numbers. Every month the security advisories broadcast on the Internet are full of new vulnerabilities in marketed systems and devices and new ways hackers are attacking them. In fact, hackers themselves are posting information on the Internet about how to break into systems and enlisting hoards of other hackers to exploit these vulnerabilities. All of this can happen within an hour. Needless to say, there is a great need for network security of all types. A number of standard and newer security procedures along with computer virus procedures and firewall protection are discussed below.

Standard Data Security Procedures

Recognizing the vulnerability of the data stored on and accessible by PCs via on-line networks, a number of control procedures have been developed to deal with security problems. A primary approach is to protect personal computers, software, and data physically by making unauthorized access more difficult. A starting point in controlling who can use computers and data involves restricting physical access to the equipment. This includes locking rooms that contain PCs or terminals when they are not in use and using locks to prevent unauthorized people from accessing keyboards. Going beyond this general approach, other control procedures include sign-on logs (users must sign a log sheet showing when and for what purposes they are acessing the computer), a data and program library (users must formally request the data and software applications they wish to use from the library), password systems (users who want to access data on the central computer mainframe must key in their passwords before the connection can take place), user authentication (verification that users are who they claim to be), call-back routine (after determining the authenticity of the user's request, the host computer then calls back the user's PC at a predetermined, approved phone number), token devices (a physical key, much like a key to a house or automobile, that permits access to specific computer systems), and biometric devices (which rely on a physical attribute of the user and includes fingerprint systems, retinal scan systems, signature recognition systems, facial recognition systems, and voice verification systems).

In today's networking environment, *data encryption* is particularly helpful since it protects data in several ways. It protects against unauthorized access and eavesdropping, prevents alteration, and authenticates users. Although encryption will not protect against viruses that enter the system through authorized channels such as disk media, it can prevent unauthorized callers from gaining access and using the system. The most commonly used encryption technique is DES (Data Encryption Standard), which scrambles data by using a complex nonlinear ciphering algorithm. The key used to perform this operation is a 56-bit binary word, usually a random number. If the user on the receiving end has an encryptor with the same key, that user can decrypt the ciphertext to produce the original data. If the sender's key does not match the receiver's key, the data cannot be decrypted, but it will not be destroyed. To make it even more difficult, the cipher can also be fed back to the encryptor in one of serveral approved modes of operation to make the ciphertext dependent upon the characters preceding it. This makes repeated messages and blank fill (in which even the spaces between messages and message elements are encrypted) produce a different stream of ciphertext each time they are sent, thereby frustrating attempts at data substitution or attempted analysis by an eavesdropper. As a result, commercial networks have a high degree of protection. It should be noted that a 56-bit key has 72 quadrillion possible combinations.

Newer Data Security Procedures

Going beyond the above standard data security procedures, the next generation of security technology will include the use of artificial intelligence (i.e., expert systems), fiber optics, satellite communication, and advancements in biometrics. For example, *expert system–based security systems* consist of software and hardware that monitor essential data within an information system 24 hours a day. Monitoring handles stored or active information and provides an audit trail of the data. *Fiber optics* technology uses light pulses traveling over optical fibers that do not emit electromagnetic radiation and therefore are less vulnerable to remote monitoring devices. It is almost impossible to detect signals on a fiber optic cable without cutting and splicing the cable. While not foolproof, *satellite technology* may prove to be more secure than traditional networks. On satellite networks, signal channels are assigned to each user, and that makes it difficult to locate the code.

In the near future, *biometrics* are expected to be packaged into ''smart cards''—cards containing an integrated circuit chip. Smart cards are used as debit cards, access tokens, and cellular communications devices. By adding biometric technology, they can be made less prone to fraud. In one use of the technology, users will place a finger on a point-of-sale device, and the system will compare the finger scan with biometric data stored on the smart card, activating a transaction. The transaction data can be stored on the card as well. Eventually, smart cards will have their own embedded scanners, eliminating the need for a separate POS (point-of-sales) device.

Computer Virus Procedures

Basically, a computer virus is a program that ''infects'' other programs by modifying them to include a copy of itself. With an ''infection,'' a virus can spread from one program to others, one user to other users, one computer to other computers, and one network to other networks, thereby corrupting programs and data. Some viruses lie dormant for months, even years, thus corrupting backups made over a long period. Because a virus can spread far and wide, a single programmer with a PC can cause worldwide computer problems. Many known viruses have spread to thousands of computer systems, crossing both national and geographical boundaries. From a risk assessment viewpoint, this changes the very nature of the threat. Even a highly improbable attack can have globally catastrophic effects.

In view of these comments on viruses, it is recommended that users abide by the following guidelines: *First*, software disks should be scanned for viruses before installing the software; this includes shrink-wrapped commercial software packages. *Second*, users' disks should be scanned before they are used in public computer facilities. Some sites have dedicated virus-scanning solutions for this. *Third*, locked (write-protected) backup copies of master software disks should be used and the master disks should be kept in a safe place. *Fourth*, important data should be backed up frequently. A rule of thumb is that if one would not want to redo all the work done since the last backup, the next backup is overdue. *Fifth* and last, if a virus warning appears, the user should know whom to contact for assistance or what to do to remove the virus independently. If these guidelines are followed, it is very likely that virus infections can be prevented or, at least, reduced drastically.

It should be noted that the threat of viruses is compounded by the use of groupware products, such as Lotus Notes and Microsoft Exchange, and has anti-virus vendors scrambling to prevent attacks. Anti-virus products often do not catch every virus because protection is limited either to the desktop or the server. To improve the odds of catching a virus before it infiltrates the network, companies need to implement anti-virus measures across the board—at the server, the desktop, and Internet gateways. That brings up another issue that plagues security experts: managing all these different components.

To be effective, anti-virus software must be updated often. With multiple machines and anti-virus utilities to manage, administrators can have a difficult time keeping up. Regional offices probably have the most problems with virus protection. For example, a company could have strong protection at all entry points in the corporate headquarters, but the branch offices might not have the required computer talent to maintain the system. Anti-virus vendors are attempting to simplify the management of their software. Many vendors post virus updates on their web sites, letting managers pull down the patches or implement a ''push'' software distribution method whereby the updates are automatically delivered. Also, many anti-virus packages now have the capability of checking the status of all the installed software components through a single console.

Firewall Protection

Firewalls are a necessity today since companies expose their networks to Internet traffic. Though no firewall is quite as stalwart as the name implies, it is an important security bastion, protecting a company's network or intranets from most unauthorized intruders. It should be noted that it is unwise to rely entirely on the firewall. The best approach is to pair firewalls with the other types of security protection noted above. A firewall is usually placed between internal LANs and WANs and external networks such as the Internet. Its main purpose is access control. Essentially, a firewall creates a kind of Checkpoint Charlie, where users must stop to have their credentials examined. The firewall, in effect, identifies names, applications, Internet Protocol (IP) addresses, and other characteristics of the incoming call. It then checks this information against the access rules the administrator has programmed into the system.

The growing and volatile firewall industry has provided nearly as many ways to meet this need as it has vendors. These products originated in a new and fast-growing market and offer varied approaches to their tasks. At the same time, they reflect the evolution of a maturing market. While a typical firewall product used to be based on a single technology, today's sophisticated offerings use hybrid technologies to extend an administrator's range of security options. For example, it is now possible to grant one group of users full access to the network while restricting another group to use of Lotus Notes—and only during business hours. With this wider range of options comes greater complexity. Fortunately, graphical interfaces in many of the products help firewall managers make and implement many decisions.

A TYPICAL REAL-WORLD EXAMPLE OF SHARING KNOWLEDGE THROUGH NETWORK COMMUNICATIONS

AMP Inc. offers a typical real-world example of sharing knowledge through network communications. AMP is a world leader in the development and manufacture of electronic/electrical interconnection devices. For a number of years, AMP has spent about 12 percent of its sales dollars on research, development, and engineering. Its commitment and ability to develop and share valuable knowledge—both with customers and its employees around the world—is a key enabler of AMP's success. Tools used to transfer knowledge range from highly sophisticated electronic delivery to face-to-face meetings.

A key objective of the AMP Business Excellence process (which is based generally on the Baldrige award criteria) has been to integrate excellence, quality, and business goals across the global enterprise. AMP has created a variety of unique ways to share knowledge with customers, including such things as engineering consulting services, digital engineering data on-line and on disk, and the AMP FAX system, which gives customers immediate access to more than 70,000 AMP drawings, specifications, instruction sheets, and related documents, all of which can be automatically transmitted to customer fax machines within minutes.

The company's recent customer-driven innovation is AMP Connect, a multilingual Internet catalog of AMP products that allows customers to quickly, easily, and electronically tap into a wealth of data 24 hours a day. From virtually anywhere in the world at any hour of the day or night, customers can search alphabetically, by product picture, or by part number for detailed information on more than 67,000 parts. The electronic catalog is available in eight languages: English, French, German, Italian, Japanese, Korean, Mandarin Chinese, and Spanish. A recent refinement in the catalog introduces 3-D models of over 6,000 AMP connectors that design engineers can download and drop into their own design projects, thereby shortening their time to market.

SUMMARY

In this chapter, the fundamentals of networking that are essential in developing a KMS environment were discussed. Underlying such a networking infrastructure is collaborative computing that enables company personnel to work together as well as work virtually. Today, this includes the utilization of not only groupware but also web technology that links together disparate sources of information and knowledge globally and provides a platform in the search for appropriate knowledge. This background will be helpful in gaining an understanding of how to build and implement knowledge management applications as set forth in future chapters.

NOTES

1. John Peetz, Jr., "CKO's Define What Needs to Be Shared," *Imaging World*, October 6, 1997, pp. 20–21.
2. Peggy Watt, "IntraNet, Take Charge," *Intranet*, November 1997, pp. 7–10.

3. Samuel Greengard, ''Extranets, The E-Business Link,'' *Beyond Computing*, June 1998, pp. 38–41.

4. Thomas M. Koulopoulos and Nathaniel Palmer, ''Intranets: A New World Order,'' *Virtual Workgroups*, September–October 1996, pp. 9–12.

5. Gene Koprowski, ''The Truth About NCs,'' *Client/Server Computing*, March 1997, pp. 23–28.

6. Jane Morrissey, ''NCs in Blossom,'' *PC Week*, June 25, 1997, p. 10.

7. Edward Cone, ''NCs Impress,'' *Imaging World*, March 31, 1997, pp. 84–85.

8. April Jacobs, ''The Network Computer,'' *Computerworld*, December 23, 1996/January 7, 1997, p. 41.

5

Implementation of Successful Knowledge Management Systems

Issues Explored:

- What is the essential focus of knowledge management systems?
- How does one justify the implementation of knowledge management systems?
- What software can be used to implement an effective knowledge management system?
- What are the key steps to implement a successful knowledge management system?
- What are some typical examples of companies that have implemented knowledge management systems successfully?

Outline:

GETTING STARTED ON IMPLEMENTING SUCCESSFUL KNOWLEDGE MANAGEMENT SYSTEMS

Today, knowledge (as stressed in prior chapters) can represent the know-what, the know-how, and know-why of a company's overall picture as well as its functional areas. Knowledge is acquired by managers and analysts, including their staffs, by examining and investigating areas under study. This is different from the acquisition of specialized skills that are learned by performance over time. Typically, *knowledge work* is performed by company personnel who possess a high level of expertise in their respective functional areas, such as strategic planning, marketing, manufacturing, accounting and finance, and human resources. In addition, there are other company positions that involve some type of knowledge work, directly or indirectly. These include administrative office assistants and factory supervisors who have acquired important knowledge based on their years on the job. Knowledge work can therefore be defined as "the acquisition, creation, packaging, or application of knowledge."[1]

At the outset, it should be stated that there is no single hardware or software product or combination of the two that can provide a comprehensive approach to knowledge work. If a comprehensive KMS environment is the ultimate goal, hardware and software products cannot be used in isolation. Building a corporate-wide knowledge management infrastructure requires the integration of many different technologies. For a company to unlock successfully its collective knowledge for companywide use, it is necessary not only to implement integrated hardware and software technology but also to integrate a company's personnel and their related business processes with this knowledge management technology. If company personnel are not working in a collaborative environment or if no procedures and processes are in place to share the knowledge, no amount of KMS technology can change that. For a KMS environment to work effectively, it must be viewed by company personnel at all levels as a strategic means for the company to become more competitive and ensure success in the long run.

To better understand what needs to be done to develop knowledge management systems successfully, it is best to start with past and current approaches to knowledge acquisition in the form of expert systems and then go on to different levels of knowledge acquisition and use—ranging from operational knowledge to tactical knowledge to strategic knowledge. This chapter also covers the possible need for redesign to accommodate changing knowledge work processes and cost justifications for KMS. An integral part of developing knowledge management systems is selecting appropriate software, and therefore software selection is also discussed in the chapter. This discussion is related to the key steps for implementing successful KMSs as well as for continuing support of such systems. Finally, typical successful knowledge management systems by leading organizations are set forth.

Essential Focus of Knowledge Management Systems

Currently, to achieve good results, a typical organization needs newer methods and procedures to improve its knowledge work. This ties in with the essential focus of KMSs, which is to provide the means for professional and technical workers to capture knowledge and allow it to be accessed easily so that it can be applied effectively to achieve improved results. Knowledge work processes can center on *finding existing knowledge* (i.e., searching for it, among multiple sources) or center on *creating new knowledge* from resources unused in the past. *Knowledge can also be created externally*—for example, the development of new knowledge about financial reporting by an outside auditor or during the course of the regular annual audit. Similarly, the knowledge work process can focus on the *reuse of knowledge*, such as when adopting object-oriented technology in the computer field.

The task of implementing a successful knowledge management system may seem insurmontable. But in reality, most computer consultants offer a different view. Some have stated that up to 90 percent of the infrastructure required for knowledge management is already in place. This refers in most organizations to the existing structure of their computer networks and servers. Hence, only a small shift in the total computer technology budget is required to make the change to a knowledge management system.[2]

REDESIGN MAY BE NECESSARY FOR CHANGING KNOWLEDGE WORK PROCESSES

To acquire and disseminate narrow- to wide-based knowledge for an organization's personnel, the present knowledge work processes may have to be improved. From an overview standpoint, this may involve reengineering in which knowledge work processes have to be revamped so that knowledge flows freely to every functional unit and subpart that needs it. In order to achieve this ambitious knowledge work redesign, several approaches can be undertaken by knowledge management system developers. For one, an organization can *change the content of knowledge* by expanding or contracting what it encompasses in order to better meet desired objectives, such as a one-to-one tie-in with the company's critical success factors. For another, an organization can *reorder the composition of work* so that company personnel may change the focus of their jobs from information to knowledge. This change may require the use of more work teams so that knowledge learned from previous projects, job assignments, and the like can be shared on current work assignments. From another perspective, the change can focus on the *employment of new networking technology that lends itself to groupware*. Employing this technology allows employees to access individual knowledge bases and global knowledge bases in order to bolster the effectiveness of their work. Overall, the above changes are quite consistent with reengineering-oriented approaches to work and, at the same time, bolster the efforts of workers using knowledge to perform their jobs more effectively.

Choose the Appropriate Knowledge Orientation

In order to determine which approach is the proper direction for reengineering knowledge work processes, it is necessary for the knowledge system developers to specify which knowledge orientation is required by the organizational unit and its personnel. Is there a major or minor emphasis on knowledge among organization personnel for the work process under study in the functional unit? Additionally, there are other factors that can affect which direction to take. These include the competitive environment, corporate culture, organizational strategies, problem-finding approach, and the information technology infrastructure—each of which could be study unto itself. By establishing an effective relationship among knowledge work processes, organizational personnel, and the items set forth above, knowledge system developers can sort out the important factors and set forth ones that are useful in the final design.

Although knowledge system developers can sort out which needs should be emphasized or be deemphasized, it is necessary to create a corporate-wide or global knowledge base that brings together the diverse elements of knowledge found throughout the organization. Many of the important elements to consider in developing a corporate-wide knowledge base were included previously in the text, especially in Chapter 3, and therefore will not be repeated here. In addition, knowledge system developers need to develop lists of company experts, information maps, and corporate yellow pages that are sources of knowledge. Other possible items for determining an appropriate knowledge orientation include the age of the work force, educational level, and time on the job. Based on a thorough analysis of these items, an appropriate knowledge orientation can be developed for management, their staffs, and technical workers to help them become more effective in their jobs.

COST JUSTIFICATION FOR KNOWLEDGE MANAGEMENT SYSTEMS

An often asked question by corporate sponsors of knowledge management systems is, ''How does one justify the cost in terms of a traditional cost-benefit analysis?'' The answer given by those within or outside the computer department who have tried is that one does not. For the most part, the payoff from knowledge management systems are different from other types of information systems in that they are often less tangible, less quantifiable. For example, in the implementation of a new accounting system for accounts receivable, an information systems manager is able to estimate specific savings from tracking accounts receivable more closely. However, these new knowledge management systems focus on providing managers, their staffs, and technical workers with improved knowledge via some type of information analysis over time. The real payoff is in giving them quick access to analytical knowledge that shows patterns, trends, and projections that may lead to new ways of thinking and better decisions.

On the other hand, there can be instances where savings or gains can be tied directly to knowledge management systems. For the most part, however, no one has been able to come up with a model or system for justifying the cost of these systems. Typically, cost-benefit analysis is not used. In its place, the focus is on the value of these systems to managers, support staffs, and technical workers. Also, it is not easy to predict the total cost of such systems in an accurate manner. The largest expense generally comes from ongoing knowledge acquisition and dissemination to organization personnel as they become more familiar with the system and seek more knowledge about patterns and trends that can be related to future projections to assist them in doing a better job of problem finding.

The difficulty in justifying the cost of these systems keeps many computer departments from proposing them in the first place. If those at the top of the organization are pushing for these systems and have enough clout, however, the cost-justification issue usually fades into the background. Often the cost of a knowledge management system gets justified by one or more managers high up in the organization saying, ''Give me this new knowledge management system or else,'' which implies that they may look elsewhere for employment. Overall, justifying the cost of knowledge management systems tends to be an evasive compared to the situation for traditional mission-critical information systems.

SUCCESSFUL KNOWLEDGE MANAGEMENT SYSTEMS INCLUDE SELECTING APPROPRIATE SOFTWARE

Knowledge management systems represent a new business intelligence technology that has become popular because it allows decision makers to access and analyze large quantities of information that can be used to distill knowledge concerning current and future patterns and trends. In addition, these systems are attractive because they provide decision makers with faster access to desired knowledge which can be presented in new ways that do not require extensive custom programming. Their most appealing feature is that they assist decision makers in making better informed decisions rather than making decisions for them. The rationale is that decision makers have a wide base of resources at their command to use on problems facing them. Since no one software product can serve the full range of user knowledge needs, there are a host of products available today, which is the subject matter of the next section of the chapter.

Successful knowledge management systems require the cooperation of the vendors, the computer department, and the company's decision makers and their staffs. Most outside vendor products have limitations that will be reached the first time a user (i.e., decision maker) says, ''I need . . .''. What the person then finds is that the package has provided what is thought to be needed. The vendor can do little to adapt it. So instead of simply acquiring this package, it is necessary to look for one or more software packages that provide capabilities for adapting it to the needs of company decision makers.

This naturally leads to the next group that must be involved, the computer department. Working with the computer department rather than treating it as an outsider will result in a knowledge management system much better suited to the users' needs. These computer professionals, after all, have been providing much of the information that managers and their staffs use. Hence, they understand what some of the decision makers' needs are already. They will also be the individuals who will develop and implement the system and adapt it to decision makers' requirements.

Finally, decision makers are the most critical element in a successful knowl-

Figure 5-1
Summary of the Critical Factors for Determining the Appropriate Software Useful in Providing Knowledge for Decision Makers and Managing the Software

- Is the software easy to use for the development and use of knowledge?
- Does the software provide for in-depth analysis of patterns and trends?
- Does the software actually do what decision makers want here and now?
- Does the software allow decision makers to access and analyze large amounts of information in order to get at pertinent knowledge?
- Is the software generally a combination of packages designed for the organization's size or will it be outgrown in a few years?
- How are changes and updates in the software handled?
- Is the software reasonably priced?
- Does the software provide flexibility in the development of pertinent knowledge to meet decision makers' needs?
- Will the vendor support the installation adequately?
- On what hardware does the software run?
- Is all of the documentation clear?
- Can the user visit at least one other user of the software package(s)?

edge management system. It is important that they know what they really need to guide them to make better decisions. Since it is important that decision makers get involved and support the effort to get the system up and running, they need to take the time to sit down with the computer department and discuss their real needs. Which knowledge-based systems are currently available (i.e., what nuggets of knowledge exist in a company that have been codified and are available now for use by decision makers)? In addition, does the current knowledge systems approach need to be improved to make the decision makers' jobs easier? In particular, should a broad-based, global knowledge base be installed that encompasses all knowledge elements found throughout the organization? What are the new knowledge requirements of decision makers? Is there something they need that they have not asked for? Overall, decision makers can explore with computer professionals some of the knowledge-based systems currently in place and see how they can be improved using a knowledge management system approach to provide for more effective decision making.

Critical Factors for Evaluating Knowledge Management Software

In order to determine the appropriate software to provide abundant and rich knowledge for decision makers, it is necessary to evaluate a package's critical factors. A representative listing of these factors is given in Figure 5-1. As a starting point, the package should be easy to use. It should be designed to assist decision makers in the development and use of knowledge. In other words, the software should be designed to help decision makers make better decisions, not dictate their actions. The software should also provide for analysis of patterns and trends not only in the past but also for the present and future, thereby allowing decision makers to focus on projections. The software should respond readily to decision makers' requests (i.e., their wants here and now).

The software package should allow the decision maker fast access to knowledge that can be presented in very sophisticated ways without custom programming. Similarly, it should allow access to a very large amount of knowledge in a format that allows decision makers to find their own answers as problems and opportunities arise. Because some of the knowledge-based software precalculates and aggregates values, decision makers should be able to slice and dice quickly using a variety of keys to get at important knowledge. Additionally, the software approach, generally a combination of software packages, must be able to handle the organization's size or it will be outgrown in a few years. The software should allow for changes and updates as deemed necessary.

The software should be reasonably priced and flexible to meet the decision makers' needs. It should be flexible to allow for different types of analysis in order to manipulate the knowledge in whatever form is considered to be most useful. As specific knowledge analysis is required, they must be able to be added without losing other functions or requiring changes in the basic software. Other factors come into play that can be asked as questions: ''Will the vendor support the installation adequately?'' ''Will the software run on the organization's hardware?''

''Is the documentation clear?'' Needless to say, these questions must be answered to evaluate critically the decision about whether to proceed with a specific software package. It should be noted that it is helpful to visit one other user of the software to get a firsthand look. If multiple software packages are to be acquired, it would be helpful to pay a brief visit to users of each package.

It is highly recommended that the above factors be investigated fully before signing a contract for purchase or lease of the software operating in a networked or mainframe environment. The computer department, working with decision makers, should resist the temptation to sign the vendor's standard agreement. If possible, the matter should be referred to the company's legal department, rather than trying to handle the matter alone. In the final analysis, the key to the longevity of various types of software designed to develop narrow- to broad-based organization knowledge is flexibility to meet the changing needs of users.

SOFTWARE USEFUL IN KNOWLEDGE MANAGEMENT SYSTEMS

Today, knowledge management systems often integrate a variety of off-the-shelf software products, such as groupware, document management systems, E-mail, relational databases, and workflow, with knowledge extraction tools, knowledge management software, knowledge management intranet search engines, knowledge management alternatives (Lexis-Nexis), and knowledge-discovery or data mining software. In addition, knowledge management systems can employ OLAP software, statistical analysis software, and GUI/4GL software packages to assist decision makers in getting at the knowledge at hand. Depending on the nature and purpose of a knowledge management system, there can be still other software products and hardware needed to form a complete KMS package to gather, organize, collaborate, refine, and distribute knowledge. Essential to capturing and making individuals' knowledge available to the entire organization is the ability to deal with heterogeneous information. Although data warehouses are useful for collecting and storing structured information in an organization, a large amount of information resides in unstructured text—E-mail messages, documents, presentations, etc. Knowledge extraction tools to get at appropriate organizational information will be covered next. Then the popular software approaches mentioned above will be set forth in some detail to complement the discussion of knowledge management software.

Knowledge Extraction Tools

A starting point within a KMS environment is extracting information initially in the entire knowledge acquisition process. Other than the laborious task of manual mining of information, the preferred way is to make this information structured and readily accessible—that is, turn it into organizational knowledge by identifying and extracting important content from the text automatically. Knowledge extraction from text involves several underlying phases of document and linguistic analysis: breaking the document into units (titles, paragraphs, sentences, and words), determining the linguistic role of each word in each sentence (i.e., noun, verb, adjective, etc.), normalize different surface representations of the same word (i.e., bought, buys, etc.), and identifying and classifying patterns within the analyzed, normalized text that constitute content-rich structures—noun phrases (''stock market decline''), people (''President Clinton''), and organizations (''Treasury Department). In turn, these extracted objects can be indexed by search engines, for example, in order to support better retrieval, categorization of topic area, and message routing and filtering.

The challenge for providers of knowledge extraction tools is to provide a product that is very fast, accurate, and extendable. Because organizations deal with hundreds of gigabytes of textual information, system throughput is critical, as are precision (correctness) and recall (completeness). For many companies, knowledge extraction tools must deal with text in several languages. Above all, the tools must be able to be tailored to the customer's domain and to the KMS environment. Due to the complexity of knowledge extraction tools, they have not been developed overnight, but rather over a long period of time. For example, Inxight's LinguistX product line is the result of 20 years of research and development at Xerox PARC. This product line provides multilingual natural language processing components to extract knowledge at very high speeds. It supports a range of functions, from automatic language and character-set identification to phrase extraction to automatic summarization in 11 European languages and Japanese, with others to follow. Today, LinguistX is incorporated into major applications from companies, such as Infoseek, Excite, Oracle, Textwise, and Verity. These products along with many others are covered in the material to follow on knowledge discovery software.

Knowledge Management Software

Knowledge management software shares its borders with search and knowledge discovery or data mining tools where the differences are somewhat subtle. That is, search tools ferret out information known to be present, but they do not necessarily reveal anything inherent in the data. Data mining focuses on legacy data that is more transactional and financial in nature for extracting patterns, trends, and rules. In contrast, knowledge management software provides the capability for users to collect and organize information and knowledge, search for what is needed, and share the findings with others. As will be seen in the exposition to follow, knowledge management software varies from one vendor to another. Thus, it is helpful to look at these software tools from this perspective. It should be noted that identifying the intended purpose of knowledge management tools will go a long way toward choosing the appropriate one(s).

GrapeVine for Lotus Domino and Lotus Notes is a groupware management system that helps companies classify and index corporate knowledge using charts and profiles. It is highly scalable and follows earlier release of its client/server version. If a company has deployed Notes, employees are already using it to exchange information about their projects, sales leads, and the like. GrapeVine attempts to discover and route existing information stored in Notes databases or on local area networks that it thinks company employees have an interest in. With this approach, users might even find the new project they are embarking on overlaps with one already in progress in another part of the company.

Typically, GrapeVine is the best solution for companies that rely heavily on Lotus Notes for messaging, collaboration, and document storage. The application sits on top of the Lotus Domino server and pulls information from Notes databases and other external files. It then distributes the information to users through the Notes messaging system. Integrating GrapeVine with Notes should be straightforward for a Notes administrator, but GrapeVine does provide a consultant for three days (at no charge) to help with the details. Users familiar with Notes will take to GrapeVine quickly. It is available from GrapeVine Technologies, Inc., Troy, Michigan (248-680-6685) <http://www.grapevine.com>.

Wincite is a Windows-based knowledge management system that has fast data retrieval, flexible report distribution, and graphing and support using an Oracle client/server architecture. The Wincite solution tackles the knowledge management system from a conventional approach. It is aimed at analysts who track market conditions, competitors, and other information. This tool organizes intelligence and distributes it to employees within a business. If analysts are knowledgeable, Wincite will amplify their aptitude; if their insight is less keen, it will distribute those findings as well.

This solution approach to knowledge management requires in-depth customization by the vendor to define the content users want to track, design the data entry screens, and set up the briefing books. Wincite consultants work on site for about six days and then complete the job back at the Wincite office. The entire process takes about one month. Because the Wincite approach to knowledge management is straightforward, it does not profess to find any hidden relationships within the data. However, it organizes what analysts feed into the knowledge base and distributes it throughout the organization. The knowledge base is easily built by linking Wincite to external files or inserting data directly into the system. Findings are consolidated into tailored reports that can be posted to a web site or sent by E-mail. It can be obtained from Wincite Systems LLC., Chicago, Illinois (312-630-4848) <http://www.wincite.com>.

Another knowledge management software package is KnowledgeX. By feeding it pieces of information, KnowledgeX can discern relationships that the user might otherwise overlook. For example, by feeding it with public documents about management and investment policies, the solution might reveal hidden relationships that might be indicative of how future management decisions will be made. Similarly, KnowledgeX is a useful tool for tracking the career paths of the competition's chief executives and displaying the results graphically. KnowledgeX displays its output either in a hierarchy or in a "spider web" form. Generally, since KnowledgeX is easy to implement for users familiar with SQL databases, it requires little maintenance and lets users create some custom reports. Additional information examples about KnowledgeX will be given in the next chapter. It is available from KnowledgeX Inc., Atlanta, Georgia (404-816-4807) <http://www.knowledgex.com>.

Other knowledge management tools include the following: Sovereign Hill provides a search and index tool, a web access layer, and a sophisticated database that understands people, places, and things. The software parses free-form data and distills it into the core relationships. For example, after supplying it with industry news, users can query Sovereign Hill about competitors. Its answer will not just incorporate hits on a competitor, but also identifies the relationships the competitor has with employees, customers, or competitors. It is available from Sovereign Hill Software Inc., Dedham, Massachusetts (781-407-7700) <http://www.sovereignhill.com>. KnowledgeShare (from Cambridge Technology Partners, Inc.) is a client/server-based system for developing and managing an enterprise-wide repository on intranets. Lastly, Decision Suite 3.0 (from Information Advantage) is an integrated suite that lets a user navigate, filter, visualize, and share live analysis and information. Overall, these knowledge management tools are designed to help typical companies manage corporate knowledge effectively and disseminate it throughout the organization as needed to assist appropriate company employees.[3]

Knowledge Management Intranet Search Engines

Knowledge management software that utilizes intranet search engines is the most basic and widely used tool for finding and accessing information housed on companies' Internet-based computer networks. Many of these products came from earlier ones designed to locate and retrieve data from databases, file systems, and other legacy systems before intranets took hold across companies. Typically, search engines often make up just one part of a broader-based knowledge management product package. Typical intranet search engines are set forth below.

The Knowledge Access Suite from Information Discovery (Hermosa Beach, California) was the first and only set of products to provide business users with a gateway to knowledge that has been predistilled from data and is stored in a Pattern Warehouse. Business users need not perform data analysis but simply query explainable knowledge on the intranet that has been automatically premined. At the heart of the Knowledge Access Suite lies PQL (Pattern Query Language) which is a pattern-oriented query language specially designed to provide business users access to refined information, just as they use SQL to access data.

Originally a supplier of software and services to the CD-ROM market, Dataware Technologies, Inc. (Cambridge, Massachusetts) developed NetAnswer, knowledge management technology that utilizes its own database. Once information is found, it is placed in the database, thereby eliminating the chance of its disappearing from a non-Dataware data source. The current Dataware NetAnswer release is a query-and-retrieval system featuring relevance ranking and natural language processing. It is compatible with major web browsers and consists of a server and database.

Excalibur Technologies Corporation (Vienna, Virginia) developed Visual RetrievalWare software specifically for finding data in a multimedia age. The software is designed to index and retrieve text, photos, video, audio, and animation via Boolean language as well as statistical, semantic, and pattern recognition. Excalibur also has a product specifically for text searches.

Another intranet search engine is one that is available from Fulcrum Technologies, Inc. (Ottawa, Canada), which pioneered "brokering technology." Brokering technology allows users to index information residing on networked computers and execute simultaneous inquiries across network resources. The key to the company's Knowledge Network product is a feature called Knowledge Map, a folder hierarchy that shows users the information sources available to them through the corporate intranet. Knowledge Network consists of software that sits on a web server and can be accessed via standard web browsers.

Information Dimensions, Inc. (IDI) (Hermosa Beach, California), a spin-off from the Battelle Memorial Institute, first developed a product called Battelle's Automated Search Information System (BASIS). IDI has since developed a BASIS intranet package for UNIX and NT networks that includes a document manager, a web server gateway, and client software. Another important company in this category of knowledge management intranet serarch engines is Verity, Inc. (Sunnyvale, California). Verity's flagship product is SEARCH '97, an application platform containing a group of tools designed for accessing information from many data sources across an enterprise. It features agent technology designed to proactively search, filter, categorize, and deliver information to users; database gateways that allow for cross-database searching; and an intranet spider for indexing data. It includes a user interface for the desktop, an information server, and an agent server.[4]

Knowledge Management Alternative—Lexis-Nexis

Setting up a program with Lexis-Nexis is an alternative to the knowledge management software mentioned above. This company provides businesses with information collected from a wealth of news sources and public records that users can search and retrieve over the Internet. Currently, it houses more than one billion documents in a massive central repository (located in Dayton, Ohio) and adds almost 14 million documents to the pool each day. Actually, Lexis-Nexis consists of two separate services. The Lexis is a full-text legal information service that was started in 1973 to help legal professionals more efficiently research the law. Lexis has evolved into 40 specialized libraries covering all major fields of practice, including tax, securities, banking, environmental, energy, and international law. On the other hand, Nexis news and information service, which began in 1979, is a leading news and business information service. It contains more than 13,500 sources, including regional, national, and international newspapers, news wires, magazines, trade journals, business publications, and public records.

The Lexis-Nexis system is somewhat similar to the Wincite software mentioned previously. It searches for information based on specific criteria and delivers it to the users in a company who need answers. In the early stages of implementation, a Lexis-Nexis representative meets with the knowledge manager to determine the type of information that needs to be collected and the relevant topics that need to be covered. The representative gets a firsthand view of the type of user that the system will serve and the person(s) who will be in control of the information pool. Next, the Lexis-Nexis representative determines which product best serves the needs of the company. Lexis-Nexis offers a number of services, among them Tracker, Info Tailor, and Requester. Tracker is a software program that lets the knowledge manager search for information and publish the results on the corporate intranet or in other common areas, such as a Lotus Notes database. Info Tailor is a personal information agent that brings customized news to the user's desktop every morning. Requester is a search tool designed for users who need to track their own information from their desktops. Users can request information on a variety of topics including news, company financial and personnel statistics, industry forecasts, and product data. Among the companies using the Lexis-Nexis system are utility companies, which use it to track their competitors and new regulations that affect the utilities industry. These utilities can also prospect companies that are relocating to other local areas to win new accounts. Lexis-Nexis can be reached at http://www.lexis-nexis.com.

Knowledge Discovery or Data Mining Software

Knowledge discovery or data mining software provides an important means for decision makers in a KMS environment to uncover patterns and trends as well as rules for today and tomorrow. Among the major players are: Angoss Software International, Business Objects, Cognos, DataMind, IBM, Information Discovery Inc., Magnify, NeoVista Solutions, Pilot Software, SAS Institute, and Thinking Machines. A listing of popular knowledge discovery or data mining vendors and their software products is found in Figure 5-2. In future chapters, specific reference will be made to KnowledgeX (Chapter 6), Pilot Discovery Server (Chapter 7), KnowledgeSEEKER (Chapter 8), KnowledgeMiner (Chapter 9), and DataMind (Chapter 10). Additionally, more detailed information will be given later in this chapter about KnowledgeSEEKER, along with a sample application. Other applications of KnowledgeSEEKER will be given in Chapters 6 through 10.

The Data Mining Suite is an integrated set of products that provide a powerful, complete, and comprehensive solution for large-scale enterprise-wide decision support and data mining. The system works directly on very large SQL repositories with no need for sample or extract files and delivers results on the web. Over 90 percent of computations are performed on the server, in parallel if desired. The system directly accesses large volumes of OLAP and relational data, incrementally discovers powerful patterns that are very general and go far beyond decision trees and simple rules. The system delivers automatically generated English text and graphs as explainable documents on the intranet.

Another typical software product is the Intelligent Miner from IBM that runs on AIX using a 5-node RS/6000 SP. Analyses are performed from Intelligent Miner clients on Windows NT. This software package serves as the core technology for Loyalty Consulting's data mining services for clients in finance, retail, telecommunications, and other industries. Intelligent Miner's full range of data mining capabilities help users to acquire more intimate knowledge of their customers, predict customer behavior, and find the most cost-effective way to influence that behavior. Most importantly, Intelligent Miner meets users' key criterion for data mining: the ability to deliver measurable results, such as increased revenues and lower selling costs. It provides a wide range of algorithms for clustering (both demographic and neural), classification (tree induction and

Figure 5-2
A Listing of Popular Knowledge Discovery or Data Mining Vendors and Their Products

Company and Product

American Heuristics
Profiler
Triadelphia, WV (304-547-4201)
http://www.heuristics.com

Advanced Software Applications
ModelMax
Pittsburgh, PA (412-429-1003)
http://www.advancedsoftware.com

Angoss Software International Limited
KnowledgeSEEKER
Toronto, Canada (416-593-1122)
http://www.angoss.com

Attar Software
XpertRule Profiler
Harvard, MA (800-456-3966)
http://www.attar.com

Business Objects
Business Minder
Cupertino, CA (408-953-6000)
http://www.businessobjects.com

Data Mind
DataMind Professional
Redwood City, CA (415-364-5580)
http://www.datamind.com

HNC Software
DataMarksman
San Diego, CA (619-546-8877)
http://www.hncs.com

HyperParallel
Discovery
San Francisco, CA (415-284-7000)
http://www.hyperparallel.com

Information Discovery Inc. (IDI)
Data Mining Suite
Hermosa Beach, CA (310-937-3600)
http://www.datamining.com

Integral Solutions
Clementine
King of Prussia, PA (610-768-7725)
http://www.isl.co.uk/clemdist.html

Company and Product

IBM Corporation
Intelligent Miner
Armonk, NY (contact local sales rep)
http://www.ibm.com

Lucent Technologies
Interactive Data Visualization
Murray, Hill, NJ (908-582-8500)
http://www.lucent.com

NCR
Knowledge Discover Workbench
Dayton, OH (800-447-1124)
http://www.ncr.com

NeoVista Solutions
Decision Suite Series
Cupertino, CA (800-800-6427)
http://www.neovista.com

Pilot Software
Pilot Discovery Server
Cambridge, MA (800-944-0094)
http://www.pilotsw.com

SAS Institute
SAS/Insight, SAS/Spectraview
Cary, NC (919-677-8200)
http://www.sas.com

Seagate Software System (Holistic Systems)
Holos 5.0
Edison, NJ (908-321-6500)
http://www.holossys.com

Silicon Graphics
MineSet
Mountain View, CA (800-800-7441)
http://www.silicon.com

SPSS
SPSS
Chicago, IL (800-543-9262)
http://www.spss.com

Thinking Machines
Darwin
Bedford, MA (617-276-0400)
http://www.think.com

neural induction), value prediction, association discovery, sequential pattern discovery, and predictive modeling. Essentially, Intelligent Miner allows users to build better data mining models than are available with many other tools since it offers a broad range of data mining algorithms that can be combined to provide greater value to users.

Server data mining software licenses typically cost $150,000 to $200,000, while desktop or ''micromining'' software licenses typically cost $500 to $50,000. For example, IBM's Intelligent Miner can deal with data warehouses containing hundreds of gigabytes or terabytes of information. Its licenses range in price from $25,000 to $150,000 for systems from Risc/6000 UNIX machines to System/390 mainframes. Although these costs may appear to be somewhat high, some vendors and users note that data mining offers a good return on investment and an important competitive advantage.

Database and Computer Vendors Incorporate Knowledge Discovery or Data Mining Capabilities

Today, database vendors have integrated their products with the data mining capabilities of other vendors. This decision support strategy pairs the processing horsepower of relational databases with the discovery-driven analysis capability of data mining. This combination improves the scalability and performance of data mining applications, and simplifies their management. For example, Brick Systems (Los Gatos, California) has integrated its RDBMS technology with data mining technology from Data Mind (Redwood City, California). DataMind Professional Edition provides scalable data mining software that builds a model from historical data via an automatic discovery process, thereby allowing business professionals to explore relationships in historical company data.

In addition, data mining vendors are cooperating with computer vendors. For example, several vendors, like Information Discovery Inc., NeoVista Solutions, Pilot Software, and SAS Institute (as found in Figure 5-2), are linked with Hewlett Packard. They are part of HP's OpenWarehouse Alliance Program which focuses on selecting best-in-class warehouse component providers to ensure compatibility and to maximize functionality on HP computing platforms. Information Discovery System is a collection of client/server data mining tools that work with Oracle, Sybase, and Red Brick relational databases and also perform data mining on the Internet. This software takes advantage of the parallel processing technology of an HP 9000 Enterprise Parallel Server by decomposing its analysis and sending it to the separate processors automatically. In a similar manner, NeoVista Solutions' Decision Suite Series provides comprehensive, enterprise level, data mining solutions, and associated professional services to Global 2000 companies. Products are based on a comprehensive suite of automated knowledge discovery software—the Decision Suite Series—designed to be highly scalable and to integrate easily with legacy and open systems decision-support environments, such as HP's Enterprise Parallel Server.

The Pilot Discovery Server (a key component in the Pilot Software Decision Support Suite) is a sales and marketing product that uses data mining to help users increase sales and acquire and retain customers. Seamlessly integrated within a large relational data warehouse, Pilot Discovery Server analyzes all available information in customer activity and demographics. The product runs on HP 9000 Enterprise. Similarly, the SAS Institute's software—SAS/Insight and SAS/Spectaview—offers various tools for the exploration of data to uncover anomalies in the data tools for modeling as well as analytical tools, such as multi-dimensional analysis. SAS software runs on HP computing platforms.

Essentials of KnowledgeSEEKER

To encourage a better understanding of a typical knowledge discovery (data mining) tool, the essentials of KnowledgeSEEKER are set forth below. As noted in the preceding discussion, one of the key features of a knowledge discovery tool is its ability to uncover relationships in the data that reveal those patterns that characterize the operation of the phenomenon being investigated. An effective knowledge discovery tool must be able to detect either subtle and complex or obvious and simple relationships as will be evident in the discussion to follow.

The first step in knowledge discovery is to define a business goal (i.e., what question must be answered). For example, if the question concerns profitability, then a measure of profitability must be identified in the database. Similarly, if a manufacturer's goal is to find which variables influence assembly-line parts defects, a question concerning quality, then a measure of quality must be identified in the database. Once the question is determined, the next step is to consider the various factors that could influence the outcome. When looking at profitability, for example, the determining factors would include selling price, quantity sold, manufacturing cost, and discount rate. The database, therefore, must be examined to identify those data fields which provide measurements of potential dependencies. A subset of the database containing only those data fields is then created.

If a data set contains a huge number of records, KnowledgeSEEKER can be instructed to take a *sample* from the main data set in order to get a more manageable, yet still representative, subset of records with which to operate. With a data set of 5 million records, for example, a 1 percent sample would produce 50,000 records. KnowledgeSEEKER would then carry out its analysis in the same way it would with the complete data set and would provide the calculations with which the results would be tested for accuracy. KnowledgeSEEKER imports the data set to be analyzed and stores it in its own file format, ready for analysis. In addition, KnowledgeSTUDIO, a data mining workbench from Angoss Software International Limited, allows decision trees to be grown on data sets with hundreds of millions of rows by using a highly scalable three-tiered architecture.

To perform a KnowledgeSEEKER analysis on that data set and grow a decision tree, the user is asked to select one of the data fields as the starting point of the analysis—that field is known as the *dependent variable*. The data field selected as the dependent variable can contain either categorical or continuous data. If, for example, the purpose of the analysis is to find ways to increase profitability, gross margin (a continuous variable) would be an appropriate dependent variable. KnowledgeSEEKER then automactially scans all the fields in the data set, summarizes the statistically significant patterns and relationships among the fields, and displays the result as a *graphical decision tree* or as a *knowledge base of rules*.

Statistical rules guide the selection of fields—and values within combined fields—that form the optimal decision tree. All possible field and field-value combinations are examined and the most promising split in the tree is displayed. The decision tree in Figure 5-3(a) shows a typical split at the start of the analysis. This example was taken from a hypertension study that was analyzed by KnowledgeSEEKER. Blood pressure (a categorical variable) was selected as the dependent variable, and the strongest predictor that KnowledgeSEEKER found within the study's data was "age," which it automatically split into three separate categories. As displayed in Figure 5.3(b), the user then asked KnowledgeSEEKER to grow the tree, by selecting one of the "age" nodes and once again asking KnowledgeSEEKER to find the most significant relationships and perform a split. At any time, the user can select any node and ask KnowledgeSEEKER to perform a split based on any of the other significant relationships which KnowledgeSEEKER has identified.

The decision tree can be grown until no further significant relationships are found. A very large tree can be easier to interpret by reducing its "bushiness" (i.e., how many branches are displayed). The bushiness of the tree depends on the statistical significance of each split. At any time, the user can alter the tree size simply by resetting the split criteria and significance level. The higher the significance level, the more confident the user can be that the differences between the groups are real and the less bushy the tree will be. When there are no further significant splits, KnowledgeSEEKER will stop growing the tree. Significance is determined by a rigorous test that employs standard statistical hypothesis testing procedures. In practice, three to four levels in the decision tree are usually all that are required to determine the important features of any area under investigation.

The predictive information discovered by KnowledgeSEEKER that is shown on the decision tree can be used to formulate policy, make operating decisions, and direct an appropriate effort. KnowledgeSEEKER will also convert the decision tree into a set of rules or SQL (Structured Query Language) select statements. That output can be used to build rule-based expert systems, (i.e., knowledge-based systems). The rules can be generated for individual nodes or for the whole tree. These options convert the tree into a series of generic If . . . Then statements or Prolog programming language statements that reflect the

Figure 5-3
(a) Decision Tree That Uses Blood Pressure as a Dependent Variable for the Knowledge Discovery Tool, KnowledgeSEEKER, and (b) Tree Grown by Selecting One of the "Age" Nodes in KnowledgeSEEKER

(a)

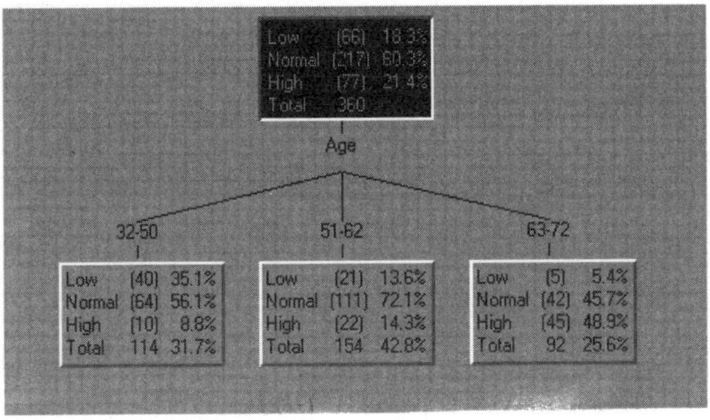

(b)

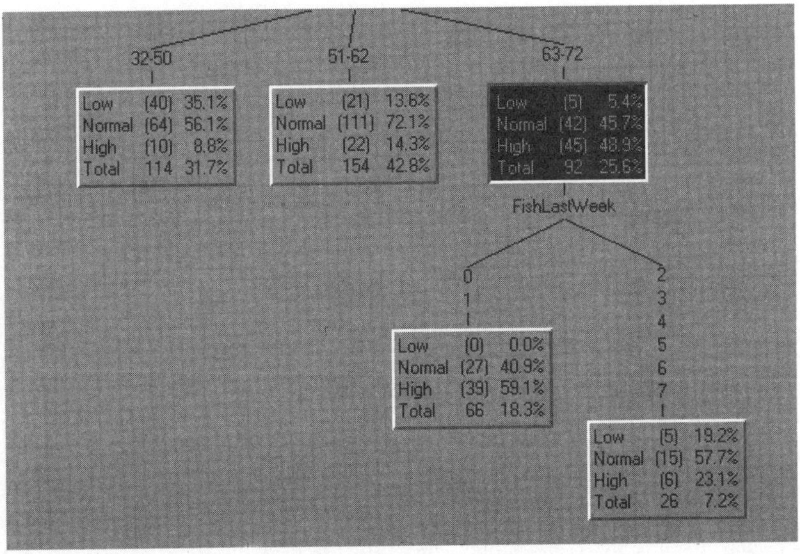

Source: Angoss Software International Limited.

splits expressed in the tree. KnowledgeSEEKER can produce a SQL select statement that will, when submitted as a query to a database, extract all records in the database that conform to the SQL rule. SAS procedure code and SPSS command syntax can also be generated.

To ensure that a rigorous, scientific approach is used to identify the data relationships that are displayed on the decision tree, KnowledgeSEEKER provides a validation facility that ensures both the accuracy and the validity of any results. This software uses a statistical hypothesis testing approach as its primary method of identifying any strong relationships in the data. This approach relies both on statistical theory and on empirical, reproducible statistical results to calculate the probability of error associated with each identified relationship. This means that if a result is reported as being 99 percent statistically significant, then 99 times out of 100 the results are true. Overall, KnowledgeSEEKER not only discovers any underlying data patterns but also ensures that they are the ''right'' or ''best'' patterns. Moreover, it presents the results in a decision tree format that is easy to understand and is capable of communicating the results to others for implementation.

OLAP Software

OLAP software centers on *multidimensional analysis*, which is an architecture for performing computer analysis in new and different ways. OLAP software packages can be used to uncover new patterns and knowledge about a company's operations. Typically, this analysis divides data into the important dimensions used to manage the business. For example, dimensions for marketing applications might include products, market areas, distribution channels, and time periods. In turn, these dimensions can be used to describe each data point in the database, such as selling price, units sold, total revenue, and market share. Dimensions can be further described by attributes, such as location, size, or year. Attributes can also describe hierarchies within a dimension, even overlapping and inconsistent hierarchies.

From an end user's perspective, multidimensional analysis provides for selection, analysis, summarization, and reporting by dimensions and attributes within dimensions. Multidimensional analysis can support virtually any time-series application. These include forecasting and budgeting. Most current spreadsheet, database, and reporting tool vendors offer simplistic multidimensional tools. However, some of these vendors and others are offering more sophisticated tools. That is, all multidimensional engines are not created equal. There is a need to look for engines than can work with any data warehouse, use meta data, and use any PC development tools for the user interface. Not only should the engine be robust to support an unlimited number of dimensions, custom groupings, and automatic and custom calculations but the engine also needs to reside on a server large enough to support hundreds of users, large volumes of data, and intensive processing.

The major OLAP software products include Essbase from Arbor Software, Inc. (Sunnyvale, California); Commander from Comshare, Inc. (Ann Arbor, Michigan); Express from Oracle Corporation (Redwood Shores, California); KnowledgePoint from Knosys Inc. (Boise, Idaho); and LightShip Suite, from Pilot Software, Inc. (Cambridge, Massachusetts). They exhibit some interesting and helpful features to users. For example, some software products handle up to six dimensions with ease. In addition to this software, some users are turning to alternative products because they are considered easier and faster to implement. For example, Business Objects from Business Objects, Inc. (San Jose, California) gives managers the ability to perform complex multidimensional analysis, thereby allowing them to follow lines of questioning on their own. As another example, SAS/EIS from SAS Institute (Cary, North Carolina) uses fourth generation language-based packages that are designed to provide multidimensional views and analyses.

Statistical Analysis Software

Although many of the current software packages have statistical analysis capabilities, there are those that are designed primarily as statistical analysis systems for uncovering important relationships and trends. For a typical business situation, a series of data is used to see what the results look like when plotted under a certain set of conditions. Interactively, the set of conditions can be changed and new output plotted. Needless to say, there are a whole series of business problems that benefit from graphic solutions: project planning, break-even analysis, learning curves, and so forth. Since a picture is often worth a thousand words, a thousand lines of printout, or ten minutes of discussion, decision makers are able to absorb a tremendous amount of information when it is shown graphically. Because knowledge management systems make great use of computer graphics, they allow organizational personnel to build models and speculate with their computers using graphic output concerning how hypothetical decisions might translate into reality.

A number of statistical analysis packages currently available include SAS (Statistical Analysis System) from the SAS Institute, Inc., SAM (Strategic Analysis Model) from Decision Sciences Corporation, SPSS from SPSS, Inc., STATSII from CompuServe, and DISSPLA and Tell-A-Graf from Integrated Software Systems Corporation. SAS is used for most statistical applications that are widely found in business today. SAM has been used for expediting strategic planning by generating alternative future scenarios. SPSS is useful in market-research studies; STATSII centers on business statistics, forecasting, and econometric modeling. DISSPLA is a graphics software system with a high-level subrouting plotting language for producing graphs, surfaces, and maps. Tell-A-Graf enables users to call up graphs, charts, and plots using simple English-like statements.

GUI/4GL Software

Currently, there are a large number of GUI (graphical user interface)/4GL (fourth-generation language) packages that epitomize the term ''client/server development tools.'' At the outset, it should be noted that although today's more advanced GUI languages have replaced the fourth generation in many situations,

4GL remains the tool of choice for many straightforward and basic adminisrative jobs, large reporting tasks, and screen setups that require page breaks, margins, and specific page formatting. These GUI/4GL packages offer a broad range of features and functionality. Ease of use and RAD (rapid application development) via iterative prototyping are important hallmarks of this group. While CASE (computer-aided software engineering) and ''pure'' 4GLs provide integrated support for many of the functions required for building complex systems (data modeling, version control, software distribution, interapplication middleware), GUI/4GL tools typically, but not exclusively, provide this same functionality by way of vendor alliances.

Generally, products in this group can be differentiated according to their functionality. Some products are strongly object oriented (OO), fully supporting multilevel and multiple inheritance, while others are more object based, limiting OO support to encapsulation and single-level inheritance. Also, GUI/4GLs can be distinguished by whether they generate compatible code or interpreted code. Since many of the 4GLs lack the highly optimized ''pure'' 4GLs, this issue becomes important as systems are scaled up to serve more users. All tools in this class use a high-level 4GL to specify applications.

A class of tools that is very similar to the GUI/4GLs is the visual 3GLs. Originally, these products were not considered client/server tools per se, but this has changed recently. The explosive growth of Microsoft's Visual Basic (VB), coupled with VB 4's greatly improved database access capabilities and Borland's phoenix-like rise on the strength of its Delphis tool, now positions these products as front-rank client/server tools.

Typical GUI/4GL tools include Powersoft Corporation's PowerBuilder, Forte Software's Forte, Uniface Corporation's Uniface, and Oracle Corporation's Developer 2000. Rapid application development is an integral part of PowerBuilder. Within the boundaries of its client-side OOP (object-oriented programming) paradigm, the applications are quite usable and maintainable. The developer can build screens, input some data, and thereby allow users to give feedback. In total, PowerBuilder is an object-oriented client/server development system that is quite useful for mission-critical Windows applications.

A specialized form of fourth generation languages include financial planning languages. When users find that their models are too large for electronic spreadsheets and need advanced features such as risk analysis, linear optimization, and goal seeking, financial planning languages that operate in conjunction with microcomputers and computer mainframes are used. They are high-level financial generators designed to excel in a certain class of applications that includes financial planning and analysis, strategic planning, budgeting, modeling, and business simulations. Actually, they are quite useful in handling any problem whose answer is likely to end up on a row-and-column format or whose complex nature reflects logic and data manipulation rather than support for managers. Their statements must resemble a typical person's vocabulary and must track unstructured and continually changing thought processes. Furthermore, these generators must react in sufficient time to allow a person's attention to remain focused on the problem. Decision-making support is further promoted by permitting the language statements to appear in any order.

Financial planning languages, such as Comshare's Commander and Information Builders's Focus, enable managers and their staffs to become competent in building and solving models in an interactive, exploratory manner. Typically, users of financial models are found in manufacturing as well as banking and finance where corporate planning and finance are the largest user groups. Modeling applications most frequently used center on cash-flow analysis, short-term investments and debt structure, accounts payable, and inventories. Other typical uses include pro forma financial reports and financial forecasts, investment analysis, profit planning, sales forecasts, budgeting, merger-and-acquisition planning, and project models.

METHODOLOGIES FOR DEVELOPING SUCCESSFUL KNOWLEDGE MANAGEMENT SYSTEMS

Just as there are a number of software packages and languages that are useful within a KMS environment, there are also methods for developing knowledge management systems successfully. Popular ones include joint and rapid application development (JAD and RAD), windows-based application development, visual programming development, and object-oriented (OO) technology development. These packages are discussed below, as is their tie-in with the World Wide Web.

It is essential that knowledge system developers get a firsthand look at what is currently going on in the organization's operations (i.e., learn how people actually work). The result will be usable knowledge about the organization's internal operations that can be applied to functional units and their subunits. Similarly, knowledge system developers should learn something about their competitors. Perhaps, a tie-in with their auditors or an outside consulting firm who maintain knowledge bases about specific industries can be of assistance here. The essential message is that knowledge system developers should understand rudimentary methods and procedures involved in how people work. In some cases, it may be useful to move into different areas of the company for several weeks so that real, usable knowledge and not theoretical knowledge is gathered.

Experienced knowledge system developers emphasize the need to start with knowledge work processes. Knowledge work processes drive a successful knowledge management system, not the technological issues. The rationale is that these newer systems are helping decision makers make better decisions in terms of their work activities. The technology is incidental to this critical issue. Examples given in this text have focused on knowledge work processes and how they can be developed further to assist decision makers. Additional examples will be given later in the chapter.

For example, Cigna's Property and Casualty Division has created a new desktop knowledge system for underwriters. There was a two-day "innovation workshop" to encourage creative suggestions from users. Half-day feedback sessions at dozens of field offices also were held. Now, with a few mouse clicks, underwriters can call up dozens of worksheets, forms, motor vehicle and financial reports, and lists of company experts to improve their knowledge work processes. Substantial user input and speedy development using Microsoft Corporation's Visual Basic was crucial in improving these work processes.[5]

Joint and Rapid Application Development (JAD and RAD)

Joint application development (JAD), which is basically a systems design technique, has as its goal to improve the quality of project specifications by engaging users in the requirements definition process. JAD is performed in structured workshops driven by a JAD leader and documented by a scribe. Over time, a quality systems specification evolves and becomes a blueprint for project development. Typically, computer projects are prone to delays, errors, and failure for a number of reasons. Poor communications, a protracted systems development process, a "we-they" environment, and massive, incomprehensible, and inconsistent documentation are some of the symptoms.

To be responsive to organizational needs, computer projects must be completed before the problem parameters change. By having computer professionals and a group of users work together in a nonthreatening series of analysis and design sessions, the total time to understand and document the requirements for a new system can be greatly reduced. The goals of JAD are to accelerate the development process, increase productivity, improve quality, and build better developer-client relationships.

Overall, joint application development facilitates the interaction between systems analysts and users. Much of the value in this approach is that it requires consensus. Conflict can be used to energize the group so that they accept differences, focus conflict on substantive (rather than personal or political) issues, promote deeper communication and understanding and, in the end, achieve a superior quality product. It has been said that the value of JAD is not so much in the end product but in the discovery process.

Rapid application development (RAD), on the other hand, represents the body of development approaches that use JAD, CASE tools, and 4GLs to build systems faster. RAD is a systems development approach that has gained acceptance in the computer development community. It combines elements of JAD and automated prototyping techniques with a stringent time limit to create an environment that fosters rapid systems development and maintenance. RAD employs small teams with specialized skills. Unlike other development approaches, it has no interim deliverables. Each RAD team simply builds a piece of larger prototype and refines it until it becomes a working system. Some computer development experts have noted that using JAD and RAD together represent a good way to achieve internal customer needs for quality and speed.

Currently, many software vendors are offering their own RAD products and services. Rapid application development tools include Microsoft Corporation's Visual Basic and Powersoft Corporation's PowerBuilder. While vendors offer widely differing products, their approaches to RAD are characterized by some key common elements: an interactive development approach; great emphasis on enterprise and data modeling; use of automated tools for rapid prototyping and code generation; active end user involvement throughout systems development; and reliance on reusable code, forms, and modules. Since most businesses revolve around a few critical success factors, the reason for centering on data modeling is to identify just what those success factors are and how the pieces fit together. In turn, this foundation can be utilized for building and prototyping system applications.

A most important distinguishing factor of RAD is its time limit. Projects typically run from 60 to 120 days. While this short time limit can be a motivator, it can also become the single greatest reason for employee dissatisfaction and turnover. Careful planning and execution are needed to make RAD projects work. Rapid application development calls for leaders who are forward thinking and confident enough in their staffs to empower them to get the job done. Overall, most system developers agree about the benefits of RAD tools: development is faster and easier and code can be reused and ported across platforms. Because end users are involved in prototyping, chances are that they will be satisfied with the final product.

Going one step further, RAD technology is making use of modeling that allows all information about a complex application to be stored in a repository. This allows the application to change as business rules change, with new application code being reflected in the model. Many modeling tools are being combined with CASE tools, which allow users to create complex data models for applications used in enterprise environments. Tight integration between these tool sets is important to ensure that changes in an application are reflected in the CASE data model and vice versa.

Current RAD tool vendors have decided to offer CASE-like modeling. For example, Powersoft acquired S-Designor, a database modeling tool that has been integrated with PowerBuilder, and it has added process modeling as well. Similarly, Forte, Oracle, and others have integrated analysis-and-design tools into their own development environments. Analysis-and-design tool vendors have also formed alliances with RAD tool vendors. For example, Visible Systems has coupled with Unify Vision and provides bidirectional integration with PowerBuilder, Uniface, and SQLWindows. Bidirectional integration automatically reflects changes during the coding that affect the design back to the model, ensuring that the design as captured by the model and the application code remain synchronized. Without such synchronization, the organization loses the benefits of having a model when the need for maintenance arises. Generally, experienced RAD programmers do not like the discipline imposed by model-based analysis and design. However, given the complexity and risk of enterprise-scale client/server computing, this is a good alternative to system development.

Windows-Based Application Development

There is currently a new set of development tools available to systems analysts and programmers: windows-based application development. The most popular representatives of this new breed of high-level development languages and/or frameworks include Borland Turbo C++ for Windows, Microsoft Visual Basic with Professional Toolkit, Asymetrix Toolbook, the Whitewater Group's Actor, and Microsoft Visual C/C++. These products and many more have sprung up to assist system developers in making the change to developing for, and sometimes within, a graphical environment. Many Windows programs are graphically based versions of existing text-based applications. But as Windows 3.X has gained unprecedented market penetration along with the next generation of Windows (NT), there has been and continues to be more interest in developing new types of applications geared to the operating environment.

Because Windows is event driven, Windows programmers are freed from thinking in the traditional logical and sequential manner of DOS (disk operating system) programming. Windows programmers construct applications in an environment that allows them to think in a much less linear fashion. Since events can be invoked from all parts of the screen (menu, toolbar, dialog, box, etc.), a Windows programmer needs to anticipate all the actions a user might like to perform and take into account any order that the user decides. To this must be added the fact that other programs may be running and interacting with the program under development. One of Windows' greatest strengths is its multitasking capability. Typically, windows-based application development gives programmers an easy way to get up to speed.

The development of Internet applications, including intranets, has become a high priority for many development teams. For example, Sun has created much excitement with Java, which has the ability to embed Java applets within HTML-based documents and support dynamic content and access to other applications. Java-specific tools are now available in the Windows NT market, but most lack integration with applications on computer mainframes or other servers. Microsoft has added to the momentum by developing the ActiveX control strategy, which allows authors to integrate BackOffice data, Java applets, and older OLE-based applications. Microsoft has moved to leverage its visual development tools by releasing a Java development environment called J++. Several other vendors have moved to provide Internet/intranet controls for the Windows NT development environment.

Visual Programming Development

A more current approach is visual programming development that is tied in with the World Wide Web. Visual programming tools simplify the overall development process and create a synergy between end users and developers. They let developers create applications using point-and-click and drag-and-drop techniques instead of text-oriented methods. Code is generated on behalf of developers, and visual techniques let them more easily organize development tasks. Simplifying the application development process is considered to be a big advantage of visual programming tools. In the text-based world, the difference between textual and visual would be similar to that between character-based and graphical. Programming with visual tools is faster and requires fewer skills and less training.

Currently, data visualization software—initially found in scientific research laboratories—helps improve comprehension of complex business data. That could mean displaying the information on a map, a chart, or even an animated, virtual-reality scene that shows changes over time. For example, Silicon Graphics uses its internally developed Data Navigator to monitor sales activity in geographic regions. Using a mouse, analysts can ''fly'' through sales territories and manipulate the level of detail shown. Sales targets are portrayed as hovering disks that are broken when the target is exceeded. From this view, data visualization is a pictorial representation of data. It can be sliced, diced, or plotted to create a ''landscape'' of the data and information. For improved clarity, color and time-elapsed motion can be used. The bottom line is that data visualization software can turn large, complex data sets into patterns that are easily recognized.

In the World Wide Web universe, visual programming tools are quite useful. As Web applications become a necessary component in enterprise development, users will expect more from developers in terms of support. The Web has brought developers and end users closer. Netscape Communications Corporation, for example, is driving its development effort off the Internet. The company puts beta software on its web site, lets users work with it to discover bugs and suggest changes, and then modifies it for general release. As developers of web applications focus on the client, they will demand some of the traditional back-end services, such as data integrity, protection, recovery, and joining, to be delivered to them.

Object-Oriented (OO) Technology Development

A widely used methodology for any type of system development, including a KMS operating mode, is object-oriented (OO) technology. It is useful to increase the productivity of systems analysts and programmers by giving them a single construct with which to address analysis, design, and related activities. The fundamental construct is the object, which combines both data structure and behavior in a single entity. Object models are particularly valuable for communication and documentation. And they serve well as the framework for program code and database schemas. With object-oriented methodology, the result is a much better understanding of requirements, cleaner designs, and more maintainable and reliable systems.

Object technology is sometimes considered to be a subset of CASE because the two share the characteristic of reusable programming modules. However, there are important differences. While CASE is a semiautomated form of structured programming in which each function is broken down into sets of instructions, object-oriented programming is based on modeling the physical aspects of the business rather than the procedures themselves. Objects contain programming and data so that the object knows what it is and how it behaves. While a CASE module could be reused in a similar application with a little extra coding, a well-designed object could be used in any application, regardless of its type. Object modularity also means that a designer need only make changes to a single object in order to modify a program, rather than having to modify hundreds or even thousands of lines of code, because one change causes a chain reaction. Such modularity is a primary reason why many organizations are moving to this important direction in systems development and maintenance.

Currently, the World Wide Web has kick-started objects into broad acceptance. Next-generation web applications, such as electronic commerce, will depend on distributed-object technology, particularly CORBA-compliant ORBs, to become a reality. Object Request Brokers (ORBs) are a type of middleware that enables objects to pass messages among themselves. Objects will be able to interact with each other over the Internet, providing services such as transaction processing, replication, fallback and recovery, and multilevel security, that are difficult if not impossible to build into applications created using other programming technologies of HTML.

The transition to object technology is currently being undertaken by companies in a evolutionary fashion. Because there is a steep learning curve, thinking in terms of objects may take some time. Typically, it takes close to a year to make the shift. It should be recognized that class construction or the building of objects is a complex business. Every object can have hundreds of relationships with other objects, and its creation requires strong analysis and design skills. If applications are being downsized or moved to a client/server environment, systems analysts and programmers are likely to be more open to object technology. If deemed appropriate, external training and consulting organizations should be used for the transition to object technology.

KEY STEPS IN IMPLEMENTING SUCCESSFUL KNOWLEDGE MANAGEMENT SYSTEMS

Knowledge management systems were described earlier as a group of related technologies that assist in the collection, organization, and transfer of knowledge among company employees. Sometimes, a company's customers can be involved in the whole knowledge process. A knowledge management system should function as a knowledge warehouse where users have easy access to the knowledge contained in disparate information systems as well as have the ability to contribute valuable knowledge. Because there is no comprehensive KMS software approach available today (or anticipated in the near future), a number of steps for implementing a successful knowledge management system are suggested. Underlying all of these steps is the empowerment of employees (and customers) to have more control over their operations. Finally, it should be noted that the ultimate goal of a knowledge management system is not to capture all possible knowledge in people's minds, but rather to do a better job of using the individual's knowledge to run the company more effectively in the short to long run.

Typically, these steps are taken in the following order:

1. Get support by starting at the top of the organization.
2. Appoint a chief knowledge officer (CKO) to manage knowledge.
3. Select an experienced team to implement the system.
4. Select an appropriate methodology to develop the system.
5. Select appropriate knowledge software that meets users' needs.
6. Determine a proper organization to acquire, renew, and disseminate knowledge.
7. Develop initial knowledge applications.

Each of these steps is covered below.

1. *Get Support by Starting at the Top of the Organization.* The first step in implementing a knowledge management system is to obtain executive sponsorship (i.e., to identify a *corporate sponsor*). No KMS system will succeed without a strong advocate at the very highest level. Ideally, it should be the number one or two executive in the organization. If top management support is not there, the system is not going to go very far. This is like trying to undertake a knowledge management system from a grass-roots effort. Overall, getting started centers on obtaining the support of the president of a company or, at least, the support of the company's executive vice president.

2. *Appoint a Chief Knowledge Officer (CKO) to Manage Knowledge.* Additionally, sponsorship must go beyond a corporate executive sponsor and include a day-to-day operating sponsor. Today, this person is the *chief knowledge officer* (CKO), who makes the initial request for the system and oversees its continuing development over time. Sponsorship means more than sitting back and saying, "I'm for this project and will be its champion throughout the development process," and then delegating all of the work to others. A successful KMS implementation requires a total commitment from the company's chief knowledge officer. This person must be capable of managing old and present knowledge as well as putting in motion what it takes to acquire new knowledge. The individual must equip the organization to respond to as-yet-unknown forces for change. That is, the CKO must question assumptions, learn new technologies, and thrive in the face of uncertainty. The CKO must therefore be capable of operating comfortably in either the business or technological areas of an organ-

ization. Additional information will be set forth in Chapter 10 on human resources regarding the job requirements for a chief knowledge officer.

3. *Select an Experienced Team to Implement the System.* After the appropriate chief knowledge officer has been recruited and has his or her job under control, there is a need to establish a project team that is capable of carrying out the implementation of the knowledge management system on a corporate-wide basis. The head of the KMS project team should be knowledgeable and receptive to the new knowledge technology set forth earlier in the chapter. Ideally, this person should be able to work on the project full time, have an excellent understanding of both the organization's and management's knowledge needs, and have priority access to the chief knowledge officer. Overall, the KMS manager should have the proper credentials to head the project team.

Because knowledge is a level higher than information and uses information as its raw material, the recruitment of a KMS project team must take this important fact into consideration. A balanced mix of technology specialists and business analysts is needed. Technical specialists from the information systems department who are knowledgeable about data mining, data warehousing, network computing, capacity planning, and security issues need to be recruited. Similarly, business analysts who are knowledgeable in identifying, locating, and utilizing knowledge required by the company's management at all levels need to be recruited in order to complement the information systems professionals. Ideally, these business analysts, representing the various business/financial areas, should be providing information and current knowledge to the company's managers that focus on the accomplishment of a company's objectives, goals, and strategies.

4. *Select an Appropriate Methodology to Develop the System.* Underlying the appropriate methodology to develop a successful knowledge management system is the consideration of whether to go with a "push" or "pull" philosophy for delivering knowledge. If the *push approach* is utilized, the knowledge necessary for company employees, managers, and others to do an effective job is relayed to their desktops. The knowledge produced by the knowledge management system is pushed forward to users on a routine basis to assist them in their day-to-day tasks. In contrast, if the *pull approach* is employed, users are provided the tools needed to find the knowledge they need. Earlier in this chapter, a wide range of knowledge management tools and related information software were discussed as possible candidates to assist in this pull approach. Needless to say, two different system methodologies have a decided impact on the design architecture.

The design methodology set forth below focuses on the push design approach since the pull design approach is very open ended and varies from one installation to another. An important part of this first approach is the development of a corporate-wide knowledge base. Typically, such a knowledge base consists of various kinds of knowledge, such as established facts, rules, heuristics, strategies, procedures, and standards, along with an explanation of this knowledge.

The capability of modeling knowledge and using fuzzy knowledge can also be included under the heading of the corporate-wide knowledge base. A well-designed, corporate-wide knowledge base assists a company in such processes as knowledge acquisition, knowledge inference, and explanation, including validation of the software quality assurance process.

Concurrent with the development of the corporate-wide knowledge base by the KMS project team is the design of a user-friendly interface for knowledge base construction and validation as well as implementation. A user-friendly interface is also helpful for knowledge retrieval and updating. For example, this can take the direction of a graphical user interface (GUI). Related to these design activities is the selection of a suitable underlying methodology for knowledge representation. An object-oriented method, or one of the other methods set forth earlier in the chapter, should mesh with the objective of establishing a knowledge management system and meeting users' needs.

In total, the appropriate KMS design methodology for a push or a pull approach is not a product or a total solution that the project team can buy off the shelf. Rather, it focuses on the capability to link important structured and unstructured factors over time with the changing rules by which people apply knowledge. The methodology must provide the basis for learning and the compounding of learning—that is, the ability to create longer-term intelligence. Essentially, an effective KMS design methodology is a process that is, in actuality, implemented over years and focuses on the effective interfacing of human minds with the best of business practices.

5. *Select Appropriate Knowledge Software That Meets Users' Needs.* An integral part of the above KMS design methodology by the project team is the selection of the appropriate knowledge tools that meet users' needs. The result of using these tools is an efficient and effective mechanism for knowledge acquisition, knowledge inference, and knowledge explanation. Some of the knowledge tools (i.e., knowledge extraction tools, knowledge management software, knowledge management intranet search engines, knowledge management alternatives [Lexis-Nexis], and knowledge discovery or data mining software) set forth earlier in the chapter are excellent candidates for adoption. As will be seen in the remaining chapters of the text, KnowledgeSEEKER will be employed as a typical knowledge tool to demonstrate its usefulness for a typical company's functional areas. For the most part, it is prudent to build flexibility into the knowledge management system as users' needs multiply over time.

Appropriate knowledge tools today include using the company's intranets, extranets, and the Internet along with some type of groupware, such as Lotus Notes. By adopting an easy-to-use platform plus standardizing on a single-technology platform, there is easy access to knowledge as well as the ability to connect everyone in the company. They are useful for indicating trends and identifying opportunities for improvement. From this view, the "best practices" for a company in a specific industry can be shared throughout an organization.

Additionally, appropriate knowledge tools include those that create rich meta-data structures for capturing information about the knowledge assets. For example, was a proposal successful or not? What did the individual learn? This enables the capture of tacit knowledge that can be more useful than merely reading an archived document. It allows the capturing of knowledge in a more structured form, which allows users to perform fielded searches on classes of knowledge assets and enables uniform presentation of the resulting information. However, organizational knowledge goes beyond mere documents, web pages, and other explicit forms. Finding out who knows what in an organization has always been a time-intensive process. An effective knowledge management system should provide the capability to find people based on their skills and areas of expertise so that company members can quickly find the experts for whom they are looking.

The selection of appropriate knowledge tools by the KMS project team centers around their capability to meet users' needs—that is, their contribution to assist managers and analysts, including their staffs. Obviously, a knowledge management system will not provide all possible knowledge, nor should it attempt to be a total solution, because people are the problem solvers. The system is simply a tool to support company personnel. Ultimately, they will have to ask "why," and they will have to come up with the solution. Overall, not only do knowledge tools need to be selected carefully so that they provide *flexibility* for users, but also the output from these tools should provide the capability to improve their *effectiveness* in everyday operations.

6. *Determine a Proper Organization to Acquire, Renew, and Disseminate Knowledge*. Once the appropriate knowledge tools have been selected, it cannot be assumed that data and information exist that can be converted into knowledge. If they do, it cannot be assumed that the data and information are compatible with a KMS environment. Because a knowledge management system represents a key tool for leveraging the contents of an organization's current databases plus data and information stored in its data warehouse, the system must be properly organized to acquire, renew or refresh, and disseminate a company's knowledge. In working through these issues, the KMS project team must give users the capability to acquire (knowledge capture), renew (knowledge inventory), and disseminate (knowledge transfer) knowledge in new and different ways. These important organizational issues are discussed below.

In terms of *acquiring knowledge*, the capture and collection of tacit knowledge is related to an organization's corporate-wide knowledge base (as noted previously). No matter what the size of the organization, knowledge is not a static source. True knowledge is found, to a large degree, in the sophistication of the methods and processes by which that knowledge can be consistently renewed. From this perspective, knowledge cannot be preserved for very long without losing its inherent value, which is *timeliness*. While the accounting knowledge base changes little in a five-year period, the knowledge base for engineering and designing integrated circuits changes every few months. Effective knowledge capture is based on its relevance to today and tomorrow. Having instant access to yesterday's best practices does nothing for a consulting firm if the knowledge is outdated. Hence, replacing knowledge is much more difficult than simple knowledge capture.

Once procedures have been established by the KMS project team to capture relevant knowledge for the times, there must be procedures put in place to *catalog this knowledge*. In the past, cataloging information meant searching and finding a set of documents. However, with knowledge links, any single document can lead to an indeterminate number of other links, making navigations almost impossible. To resolve this difficulty, there is a need for intelligent inventory systems that catalog knowledge as it is needed rather than in advance. This approach recognizes that knowledge is changing constantly. Today's knowledge extraction tools, such as Inxight's LinguistX product line, support a wide range of functions from automatic language and character set identification to phrase extraction to automatic summarization.

The *dissemination of knowledge* or knowledge transfer means transferring the implicit nature of both the "what" and the "how" of what should be done. While prior information systems, such as OLAP systems, placed the burden of asking the right questions on the users, knowledge management systems shifted the burden to a large degree, to the system. At the same time, a knowledge management system provides users with the ability to expand their understanding of the company's operations over time as they discover new areas that they did not think to ask about in the first place. From this view, the KMS project team can pinpoint new directions for transferring knowledge to system users that were not obtainable with past information systems.

7. *Develop Initial Knowledge Applications*. The KMS project team should start with one or more important knowledge applications that have wide appeal across the organization. Typical applications could focus on a company's critical success factors (CSFs). CSFs center on performing those factors that are critical to the survival of a company (and will be expanded upon in the next chapter). If, for example, customer satisfaction or quality are two important CSFs, what information as well as knowledge should be retrievable by managers to evaluate and improve these areas. In terms of an OLAP system, for example, new sales to existing customers might be the measure of customer satisfaction, or quality might be measured by the volume of product defects. In contrast, knowledge of customer satisfaction would go a step further by starting with the customer as the focus for improvement. This would entail utilizing in-depth customer surveys, examining point-of-purchase information, forming customer focus groups, and employing knowledge discovery techniques. In reference to knowledge discovery or data mining techniques, a store could collect useful information about their customers by asking them for their ZIP codes and correlating this with bar-coded data collected at the cash register.

This approach could also be applied to the quality of goods and services. The focus would initially be on how customers perceive the quality of the company's offerings—good, bad, or indifferent. In turn, this could lead to internal improvements that impact the goods or services offered to customers. The linkage between a company's customers and the employment of knowledge within a KMS environment is essential if the project team wants to show important results for initial knowledge applications. Overall, companies that utilize knowledge management systems are capable of adding to their top and bottom lines through the greater use of superior solutions across the organization.

CONTINUING SUPPORT OF KNOWLEDGE MANAGEMENT SYSTEMS

If a corporate-wide knowledge management system is developed and implemented correctly, some type of formal training is needed for managers and their staffs. Typically, managers and their staffs need to know how to use the knowledge that can be displayed on their screens. This knowledge may tend to change over time depending on the industry in which the company operates. If hand-holding of the company's personnel is undertaken, the KMS stands a much better chance of being accepted. Managers and analysts tend not to bother with a user's manual or even a user's pamphlet.

In some cases, a company may supplement the KMS project team with outside consultants. The use of consultants during development, implementation, and support phases does not relieve the company from acquiring expertise in knowledge management. Usually, the consultants have a broader perspective that may help avoid pitfalls and may speed up the learning curve. Outside consultants can give the KMS effort an extra boost and ensure its final success.

For effective continuing support within a KMS environment, essentially the project team becomes the support team. However, it usually takes fewer people to support the knowledge management system than to develop it initially. The KMS support team members should have a continuing interest in the system's success. Needless to say, the implementation of a knowledge management system can cause major changes throughout the organization in terms of altering the flow of information and knowledge to and from the top of the company. Within this context, managers and their staffs can spend more time analyzing and improving the company's strategic business direction. Whereas most of a manager's time was previously spent gathering data and information, the time has been greatly reduced by requiring less than 20 percent of the manager's effort. Thus, time savings allow more time for intensive analysis to improve a company's operations. As the world renowned management consultant Peter Drucker has said, "That which is measured ultimately improves." Updating this concept to the present time, a KMS environment must provide a basis for learning and the compounding of learning in order to create relevant knowledge for improving a company's performance over time. In turn, this relevant knowledge becomes an important company asset that needs to be managed effectively.

REAL-WORLD CASE STUDIES OF SUCCESSFUL KNOWLEDGE MANAGEMENT SYSTEMS

An important reason behind the implementation of knowledge management systems is the ability for organizational personnel to share knowledge via some type of on-line forum. As one person put it, "Why reinvent the wheel if organization personnel can share company experience and knowledge to solve an internal or external problem?" Building systems to manage organizational knowledge or know-how goes beyond the needs of CPAs and consulting firms. Today, information systems professionals in various industries around the globe are engaged in a wide variety of knowledge management system installations. Although approaches tend to vary, knowledge management systems organize and make available important know-how wherever and whenever it is needed. This centers on "best practices" or guiding principles, projected forecasts, reference sources, proven processes and procedures, patent information, established formulas, corrective fixes, and similar items. Data warehouses, computer networks, company intranets, extranets, groupware, bulletin boards, and video conferencing are the technological tools for storing and distributing appropriate knowledge—as stressed previously in the text. Typical examples of knowledge management systems case studies are given in Part III (Chapters 6 through 10) of this text, in addition to the sample real-world case studies provided below.

Because there is no single approach to knowledge management systems, the aerospace giant, Hughes Space & Communications Company (El Segundo, California), decided that the best approach was to create its own Hughes Knowledge Highway. Described best as a human network that uses technology, the highway employs video conferencing, Notes, employee home pages, and other technologies. Among other things, the highway is used to spread new management practices, track patents and licenses, and gather competitive intelligence.

Another firm—the Bechtel Corporation—decided the best foundation for its emerging knowledge management effort was an enterprise document management system from Documentum, Inc. (Pleasanton, California). Since authoring, managing, and controlling requisitions, reports, and purchases orders drive its business, the company, aided by EDS Strategic Desktop Services, has installed Digital Equipment Corporation's VAXstation and Alpha servers in five U.S. offices to serve its 4,000 to 5,000 users worldwide. For example, a civil engineer using the system will be able to access vast amounts of resources on past projects, including plant designs and equipment specifications. Internet links let users download earthquake and weather data directly from the World Wide Web.

Along the same lines, Buckman Labs has created a knowledge web for its 1,200 employees in 80 countries. They have round-the-clock access to K'Netix, which is a rich global web of electronic forums, bulletin boards, virtual conference rooms, on-line libraries, knowledge bases, and electronic mail that can be accessed via IBM's ThinkPad 755s. Recently, the company has added Notes and Internet support. It has overhauled its worldwide network to TCP/IP and is employing information and related knowledge from its databases onto internal web servers.

From a different perspective, the primary focus of Monsanto's efforts in knowledge management is connecting people with people and encapsulating that knowledge so it can be shared. The company has gone from pioneering knowledge management in Monsanto's Ceregen unit to rolling out the chemical giant's first enterprise-wide data warehouse for development of pertinent knowledge. Its client/server system uses MicroStrategy's DSS Agent front end and an Oracle back end on a Digital Alpha workstation. The company's warehouse contains "a genetic map" that includes charters, organizations, and geographics.[6]

SUMMARY

Today, knowledge management systems are useful to managers and analysts, including their staffs. These systems provide on-line access to knowledge needed in these competitive times. A typical KMS environment brings together the application of technology, people, and work processes. It gives companies the capability to uncover important patterns and trends that are timely for beating or, at least, meeting competition. This chapter has looked at the factors necessary for installing a successful knowledge management system. Among the important factors treated were getting started on implementing a knowledge management system, the possible need for redesign to change knowledge work processes, critical factors to evaluate knowledge software, data mining and other software found in knowledge management systems, current methodologies for successful KMS development, and key steps for implementing a successful knowledge management system. In addition, cost justification for a typical knowledge management system was examined initially in the chapter. Although cost justification is somewhat elusive, a KMS operating mode basically makes a company *more effective*. By mobilizing the intellectual resources of a company's people, a knowledge management system creates longer term intelligence that results in effective operation of a company over the short to long term. Lastly, several KMS case studies were presented to demonstrate the wide range of these newer type systems.

NOTES

1. Thomas H. Davenport, Sirkha L. Jarvenpoa, and Michael C. Beers, "Improving Knowledge Work Processes," *Sloan Management Review*, Summer 1996, p. 54.

2. Harry H. Lasker and David P. Norton, "The New CIO/CEO Partnership," *Computerworld* (Leadership Series), January 22, 1996, p. 2.

3. Bill Ginchereau et al., "Knowledge-Management Solutions; Knowledge Equals Power," *InfoWorld*, November 17, 1997, pp. 116–128.

4. Chris Nerney, ''Search Engines, Searching for True Knowledge,'' *Network World*, June 16, 1997, p. 42.
5. Joseph Maglitta, ''Know-How, Inc.'' *Computerworld*, January 15, 1996, pp. 74–75.
6. Ibid., pp. 73–75.

PART III

Typical Knowledge Management Systems Found for Functional Areas in Business

6

Application of Strategic Planning Knowledge

Issues Explored:

- What is the tie-in between executive visioning and long-range strategic planning within a KMS environment?
- What important principles underlie strategic planning knowledge?
- How useful is problem finding in discovering strategic planning knowledge?
- How can a typical company benefit from a KMS operating mode in the area of short-term to long-term strategic planning?
- How can a knowledge management system help in establishing global best practices?

Outline

USING KNOWLEDGE MANAGEMENT SYSTEMS TO MAKE STRATEGIC PLANNING MORE EFFECTIVE

A number of leading futurists have predicted that today, as well as into the 21st century, there will be times of great change. Many of the anticipated changes are not minor perturbations, but rather major adjustments in business and social environments. Several of the driving forces behind these changes are global competition, the restructuring of business organizations, the aging of the U.S. population, continued variations in the inflation (deflation) rate, the volatility of the stock market, periodic energy shortages, and accelerating technological changes of all types. Top-level managers are going to be hard-pressed to deal with this new environment without changing the process of solving problems. Future decisions will involve more complex ones than in the past. To be effective in the future, decisions must merge quantitative and qualitative analyses. Solving the problems of the near future and beyond requires the use of advanced computer systems, like knowledge management systems, to provide top-level managers and their staffs with a more effective approach to strategic planning.

At the outset, it would be helpful to distinguish between strategic thinking and strategic planning. *Strategic thinking* involves intuition and creativity as well as being concerned with a synthesis of what is to come. It is an integral part of executive visioning in a changing world. The outcome of strategic thinking is a forward-looking perspective and an articulated vision of the direction that a company should take at the appropriate time and place. Knowledge is useful in articulating an executive vision within a strategic thinking framework. This will be evident in a future section of this chapter. In contrast, *strategic planning* is more about analysis—that is, breaking down a company's mission and its objectives into measurable goals. In turn, the expected consequences of these goals are articulated in the form of short- to long-range plans and reports that appear in the form of budgets. Hence, strategic planning from this viewpoint centers on financial measurement and improvement using knowledge that is obtained over time. This point of reference will be evident throughout the chapter.

To assist the typical manager in obtaining a good understanding of this important area relative to knowledge management systems, the first part of the chapter examines the need for top-level managers and their staffs to have a real feel for the underlying principles and important factors associated with strategic planning. For the most part, strategic planning needs for top-level managers and their staffs need to be tied in with executive visioning and problem finding. All of these newer directions set the stage for strategic planning areas that lend themselves to a KMS operating mode—in particular, short-range to long-range strategic planning. In addition, the utilization of knowledge management systems for global best practices provides a means for extending the capabilities of these systems.

SHORT- TO LONG-RANGE STRATEGIC PLANNING IN A CHANGING WORLD

As will be emphasized in this chapter, every organization should recognize that *change can be the engine of growth.* The challenge lies not in embracing this business tenet, but in anticipating, adapting to, and generating fresh ideas that exploit change. Because strategic planning is a logical means for adapting to change, it centers on setting or changing organization objectives and goals as deemed appropriate, obtaining the resources to meet these objectives and goals, and determining the strategies and programs to govern the use and disposition of these resources. Because it occurs at the highest level and is related directly to top-level executives and their corporate planning staff, strategic planning merges the appropriate external and internal factors that are critical to setting the proper present and future direction for the organization. In turn, it provides input for lower- and middle-level managers.

Strategy considerations relative to future market opportunities and products to fill them are basic to *long-range strategic planning*. A distinctive characteristic of this highest planning level is the use of marketing facts to discover opportunities and then develop effective strategies and programs to capitalize on these opportunities. Similarly, the focus is on bringing future problems back to the present for solution. The long-range strategic plans that embrace all aspects of the organization and its environment provide a basis for more detailed medium-range strategic planning.

Medium-range strategic planning, sometimes called *tactical planning*, is concerned primarily with financial planning to place the organization in the best financial position for the next several years. This fiscal planning involves developing the operating programs and associated budgets for the next several years. On the other hand, *short-range strategic planning*, or detailed operating planning, is related to the financial plans of the current year only. For an organization that has practiced formal planning on a regular basis, it is normal for every major functional area to prepare annual plans for the coming year. Essentially, these financial plans are brought together from a detailed examination of the key measures of the business for the coming year, such as product-line profitability, variable and fixed costs, inventory turnover, manufacturing capacity, and financial ratios.

Utilization of Knowledge in Executive Visioning

An important element underlying strategic planning from the short range to the long range is *executive visioning*. Many times, executive visioning is tied in with problem finding. An executive view entails farsightedness along with an eagerness to look ahead. But at the same time it must be practical. Effective executive visionaries are not necessarily those who can predict the 21st century and beyond accurately. Rather, they are the decision makers who can draw a conceptual road map from where the company is now to some imagined future, who can say, "This is how we get there." Visioning implies a change from the status quo, which helps explain why visionaries are overrepresented in the ranks of entrepreneurs. It also explains why they come in handy to an organization in deep trouble. Think of Mr. Lee Iacocca saving Chrysler. Vision is not for the complacent. While the executive visionary sees things a bit differently, this individual is no mystic. The person's sources of information are down to earth—customers and suppliers, for example—and extend beyond his or her gut-level feelings. The most visionary executive can take in large amounts of information and knowledge, not just what is inside himself or herself.

Typically, a broad grounding in a particular industry is almost always a prerequisite to successful direction setting. It is helpful to look at the early career of an executive who comes to be regarded as visionary. Usually, the individual finds an assignment or a series of assignments that enable him or her to see the company from many different perspectives—for example, the individual has served as vice president of marketing, then production, then, finance, or has had a tour as executive assistant to the president. Jan Carlzon, for instance, held all sorts of positions in the travel business before becoming head of SAS, and Louis Gerstner studied the financial services industry as a McKinsey consultant before taking over American Express's credit card and traveler's check businesses.

There can, however, be situations in which the executive does not need to be steeped in an industry to conceive a vision of its future. Upstarts like Steve Jobs dwell on the dangers of falling prey to the "standard world view," thereby missing opportunities that arise when that standard world begins to show a few cracks. The skeptics concede, though, that someone who has grown up in the business stands a better chance of realizing his or her vision.

Executives with vision typically share a couple of other characteristics. They have a high degree of self confidence. It takes a lot of inner strength to imagine a future at variance with the common expectation and to sustain that vision in the face of responses ranging from incredulity to derision. The visionary may also be a bit of a loner. Ego strength can mean that the individual has less need of other people. But executive vision has a way of exciting others somehow. An executive visionary appeals to the emotions and aspirations of people in a way that goes beyond the usual carrot-and-stick approach.

Most corporate visions come out looking like tarted-up strategies. William Hewlett and David Packard established a company that is dedicated to producing the best instruments for the world's scientists. That surely counts. Ray Kroc built McDonald's and Kemmons Wilson founded the Holiday Inns chain—both visionary achievements of 20th-century American capitalism. Vision by itself, however, is not enough. The executive visionary must be able to communicate what he or she has dreamed, and the company must have the required skills to execute the dream. The leaders of the organization must act consistently with the vision in everything they do. Too often in the past, top-management teams have worked up a statement of corporate vision, promulgated it, and then have thought their work is done. What they overlooked, and what dooms this kind of superficial effort, is the need to plan and manage this vision over time. A knowledge management system, backed up by appropriate information systems, is an excellent vehicle for assisting in the fulfillment of the executive vision.

Strategic Planning Principles Based on Knowledge of Total Business Operations

Numerous strategic planning principles that are discussed in this chapter and in the next four chapters will highlight those that provide an underlying framework for a typical company (manufacturing or service oriented). One of these principles serves as a starting point. It is the recognition that *change is a constant.* Generally, fundamental changes to an organization can take from five to ten years to complete, while superficial improvement can be achieved in a much shorter time frame. The first step in successfully managing any change is analyzing the gap between the present situation and the intended goal. It is vital for management and employees to work together toward the final goal. Secondly, there must be a plan in place to reach the final destination. The focus is on short-range to long-range corporate plans. It is necessary to break down these plans into manageable pieces so that relatively simple steps, accompanied by progress reviews at each stage, make the change less difficult. Finally, it is necessary for managers at all levels to manage the transition to the intended goal. Even the most detailed planning will not fully anticipate myriad unexpected events. It is best to manage the process of change by responding with needed training and support.

Because change is considered to be a constant in today's business world, there is a need to consider this factor in determining (1) a company's mission, (2) identifiable objectives, and (3) measurable goals and strategies. A company's mission gives overall direction to its entire organizational efforts. For example, say that a company's mission is to be the dominant supplier of widgets to the most profitable domestic market segments and to provide a high-quality employee work environment. Identifiable objectives, regardless of how general they may be in their conception, become a measure of success in very real terms. They should be looked upon not as a reactive approach to setting direction for a company, but rather as a proactive force to realize organizational goals successfully. These objectives, such as to compete in profitable market segments and be the low-cost producer in the company's market segments, provide the basis for determining measurable goals, such as increasing market share by 12 percent in high-profit market segments while reducing manufacturing costs by 8 percent per unit and achieving a 22 percent return on investment. In turn, these goals provide a basis for developing appropriate strategies that realize the company's mission. For example, strategies could include expanding market research activities to identify high-profit market segments and developing one or more product lines that fit the requirements and needs of these high-profit market segments. The successful linkage of a company's mission to its objectives, goals, and strategies requires knowledge of a company's total business operations. The principle of effective use of resources applies here and underlies the entire strategic planning function.

Another important strategic planning principle is one that relates to a company's long-term strategy. Competitive strategy is about being somewhat or completely different in the eyes of customers. Essentially, a company can outperform its rivals only if it can establish a difference that is perceived by its customers. This difference must also be preservable over the long haul. This approach contrasts with concentrating on operational effectiveness, where techniques can be duplicated over time by competitors. Creating a successful long-term strategy involves choosing activities that are desired by customers and that are somewhat difficult for the competition to match. The essence of an effective long-term company strategy, then, is choosing to market goods and services differently from rivals. Otherwise, such a strategy is nothing more than a marketing ploy that will not withstand competition over time.

Related to the previous principle is one that allows a company to transform new technologies of products and services into an important advantage, not only for itself but also for its customers. Too often, companies experience a technological breakthrough but are not capable of capitalizing on it. It cannot succeed without capable management to define or redefine the company's goals and its core competence. Without the proper managerial guidance, these pioneering efforts can result in disastrous forays into unknown territories. On the other hand, development of carefully prepared corporate short- to long-range plans that are supported by an appropriate organizational structure and effective marketing can thrust a company into a position of market leadership. Over time, it is necessary that technological pioneering efforts be maintained by continually bringing out important customer-oriented features ahead of competition.

For companies that are not engaged in technological pioneering but are operating in established industries, there is a need for top management to step back and take a hard look at its operations. This ties back to the principle of strategic thinking—that is, thinking in terms of strategies that are linked to today and tomorrow. Thinking involves identifying and mapping the driving forces that the company needs to evaluate. The mapping power provides top management and the corporate planning staff with visual representations of possible solutions and results, thereby helping them to achieve consensus in determining the driving forces. Once top management and its staff has formulated a new strategy, it must align the strategy with the company's resources to make sure that implementation is possible. In turn, this strategy can be translated into action by using aggregate project planning, as discussed below.

An important guiding knowledge principle of strategic planning is one that recognizes the need to develop project plans that focus on the development of new products and services. To map out and manage a group of strategic development projects effectively, there must be a total project plan in place. Getting to the point of an aggregate project plan is not easy, but working through the detailed process is a critical part of developing a sustainable development strategy. While the specific plan is extremely important, the planning process itself is even more so since the plan will change as events unfold and managers make adjustments. But choosing the right mix and determining the number of projects the resources can support, as well as picking the right projects, raise essential questions about how product and process development ought to be linked to the company's competitive opportunities. Overall, creating an aggregate project plan not only gives direction and clarity to the overall development effort but also provides a framework for outstanding performance.

In the development of a company's strategic plans, the principle of examining the best- and worst-case scenarios comes into play. The best-case scenario is based on an economy that is experiencing a 5 to 6 percent growth rate where profits are very high. In contrast, the worst-case scenario considers the financial results of natural disasters like fires or floods. These are usually short lived and can be solved quickly, though at high cost. The types of disasters referred to here are conditions that prevent a company from fulfilling its long-term mission, objectives, and specific goals. Also, a worse-case scenario can refer to a reduction in business volume. Knowledge of these unfavorable conditions is necessary if an effective job of short- to long-range corporate planning is to be undertaken. While most corporate planners think in terms of good times, realistic projections should also include provision for bad times, especially when global operations are used in developing realistic short- to long-range plans.

For effective corporate planning under any scenario, a most important principle recognizes the importance of short- to long-range strategic planning. Essentially, these strategic plans, which will be explored in more detail later in the chapter, recognize that the company knows what its customers want and need before they do. (This concept will be explored in more detail in Chapter 7.)

This proactive stance will help a company gain a competitive edge in the marketplace. At this point, it is safe to say that financial plans need to incorporate this important fact of competitive advantage. A company's short- to long-range corporate plans should also be related to its strategies (as discussed in a previous principle) so that the right hand knows what the left hand is doing. They should not only be realistic in financial terms but also should challenge management and employees to meet financial targets that go beyond what a company has done in the past. Knowledge of past operations coupled with the challenge of the future should provide the company with opportunities to develop new ideas and concepts in order to meet these future projections. Essentially, long-range strategic plans provide a basis for action which, in turn, drives medium-range and then short-range strategic plans.

A principle that ties in with the need for short- to long-range strategic planning is one that cultivates a new style of corporate behavior that encourages changing established views of the company's products and services. There is also a need to encourage creativity in strategy and business processes. From this view, innovation is a style of corporate behavior that is comfortable with, even aggressive about, new ideas, change, and even failure. It must permeate an organization. Although it is not necessary to abandon a healthy business just for the sake of trying to be innovative, it is important to make sure there are many good ideas in various stages of fermentation. When the time comes, the company needs to be willing to take risks. If a company waits to move until everything is certain, competition will have been there first. Thus, innovation can be the lifeblood of a company that uses vast amounts of internal and external knowledge to keep ahead of competition.

To assist management and its staff in getting a handle on important factors affecting a company's total operations, including innovative directions, the principle of spending time with customers goes a long way toward understanding their point of view. This recognition about the customer's importance suggests that the customer is more than the next step in the distribution chain. Senior managers and their staffs need to spend several days in the lives of their key customers. There is no substitute for senior executives' instincts, imagination, and personal knowledge of the marketplace. Creativity on their part can bring insights and expertise to their customers' problems. Hence, the strategic planning process for all of a company's functional areas can be improved by making the customer the focus of investigation. In turn, knowledge that is learned about a company's customers can help provide an underlying framework for a KMS operating mode.

An integral part of the preceding principles is the element of risk (covered briefly in one principle above). Essentially, a company's risk-management strategy needs to be integrated into its overall corporate strategy. A small company, for example, can ill afford to have "all of its eggs in one basket," since a disaster in the one area could bankrupt the company. In contrast, a large company can take on risks in one or more areas of its business. If this area(s) fails, it can be written off against other profitable areas of operations. However, a large company has to be cautious, since many times the level of risk is affected by its competitors' strategies. Overall, an effective strategic planning principle states that the level of risk needs to be balanced with the company's ability to withstand significant losses and survive in the long run.

Underlying all of the above strategic planning principles (based on knowledge of total business operations) is the fact that management and its staff have the authority and responsibility over a company's operations. Not only does management assisted by its staff have the *authority* over developing and implementing short- to long-range strategic plans, but it also has the *responsibility* to carry out these strategic plans. Knowledge gained from within and outside the company provides management with the the means to discharge its duties in an effective manner. The fact that authority and responsibility are linked to *accountability* is often overlooked. Accountability means that management is held accountable for operating results, financial or otherwise. Thus, a most important strategic planning principle ties in authority and responsibility over operations with accountability for results. Needless to say, a knowledge management system can assist management in tying together these three items successfully as well as maintaining them over the long term. Strategic planning principles based on knowledge of total business operations are displayed in Figure 6-1.

IMPORTANT FACTORS THAT ARE USEFUL IN DISCOVERING STRATEGIC PLANNING KNOWLEDGE

Today, the changing world, as discussed previously in the chapter, should be regarded as a *constant*. Change creates important opportunities but, if ignored or unanticipated, it can be devastating. The business community showcases change and its consequences like no other. The $30 billion-a-year package delivery business, for example, would be significantly smaller had Federal Express and UPS not anticipated a surge in worldwide demand for time-guaranteed delivery. To assist corporate management in adapting to all types of changes, including changing computer technology, important factors that are useful in discovering strategic planning knowledge within a KMS environment are set forth below. These center on the following: (1) problem finding in discovering strategic planning knowledge, (2) enlarged view of core competence to develop new opportunities, (3) importance of a company's critical success factors (CSFs) and their measurement, (4) benchmarking the company to detect the best business practices, and (5) software useful in discovering strategic planning knowledge.

Related to the foregoing factors is the need for a company's managers to translate the executive vision that revolves around a company's strategies and express it in terms that guide action at the local level. Needless to say, it is helpful that this executive vision be based on knowledge of a company's operations. To help get a grip on the knowledge base, companies today are em-

Figure 6-1
Strategic Planning Principles Based on Knowledge of Total Business Operations

- Recognizing that change is a constant, fundamental changes to an organization can take from five to ten years to complete, while superficial improvements can be achieved in a much shorter time frame.
- Change is a most important factor affecting a company's mission, identifiable objectives, measurable goals, and corporate strategies. As such, there is a need for the effective utilization of a company's resources for changing times.
- A company can outperform its rivals only if it can establish a difference that is perceivable by its customers. A long-term company strategy is to market goods and services differently from its rivals.
- Technological breakthroughs should provide an important advantage not only for a company but also for its customers. This approach can propel a company into a position of market leadership.
- The need for strategic thinking is paramount in order for a company to identify and map its driving forces. The mapping process provides management with visual representations of possible solutions and end results.
- To map and manage a group of strategic development projects effectively, there must a total project plan in place. An aggregate project plan not only gives direction and clarity to the overall development effort but also provides a framework for outstanding performance.
- While most corporate planners think in terms of good times, realistic projections should also include provision for bad times. The development of a company's strategic plans, then, should include examining the best- and worst-case scenarios.
- A company's short- to long-range strategic plans should challenge its management and employees to meet financial targets that go beyond what has been done in the past.
- Short- to long-range strategic planning should include cultivating a new style of corporate behavior that encourages changing established views of a company's products and services so that innovation is the order of the day.
- There is no substitute for senior management and its staff spending several days in the lives of their key customers. This approach can bring insights and expertise to their customer problems.
- The level of a company's risk is related to its size and needs to be balanced with the company's ability to withstand significant losses and survive in the long run.
- Although authority and responsibility are widely discussed in describing a manager's limits, an often overlooked fact is their linkage to accountability for operating results under the manager's jurisdiction.

ploying a chief knowledge officier (CKO) to harvest and distribute professional expertise via information technology. As indicated previously in the text, the chief knowledge officer, also called the chief learning officer or VP of information strategies, identifies what corporate knowledge needs to be developed and retained as well as what knowledge is useful in strategic planning. The focus is on seeing patterns and trends that enable decision makers to make the transition to insight and prediction. This focus is particularly useful in short- to long-range strategic planning.

Problem Finding in Discovering Strategic Planning Knowledge

For effective problem finding, strategic planning must be undertaken from a proactive standpoint where external and internal environmental factors that affect the organization, from the short range to the long range, are taken into consideration. Many times, such information is found in the company's data warehouses. The most important *external environmental factors* focus on customers, suppliers, the government, investors, the public, financial institutions, and competition. The most important *internal environmental factors* center on organizational strengths and weaknesses, objectives and goals, functional areas, and personnel. Obtaining and using this information and knowledge is an integral part of the strategic planning process. Overall, the raw material of strategic planning is needed by top management and its corporate planning staff to initiate problem finding. Likewise, it is the means by which strategic decisions are made to further organization's objectives and goals.

To have an effective planning process, top-level managers and corporate planners need to identify potential problems in the future and bring them back to the present for resolution. Problem finding tends to center on finding solutions to problems that many deem impossible to solve. Going one step further, there is the need to *identify opportunities* that are related to future problems. As in the past, top-level managers and corporate planners must also be involved in problem solving. Thus, they need to go beyond problem solving and be actively involved in problem finding to allocate and use the organization's resources effectively.

To assist this highest-level group in problem finding, knowledge discovery tools along with mathematical and statistical models can be employed to develop appropriate analyses. Because the highest-level problems tend to be semistructured and unstructured, a series of "what if" questions can be asked and answered to get a feeling for future problems that are poorly defined. Hence, the needs of top-level decision makers, when they are oriented toward the near future, usually center on using multidimensional analysis but, more importantly, on knowledge discovery as a means to answer pressing questions. However, as the time frame is extended further into the future, the problems become even more unstructured and may require heuristics (i.e., rules of thumb) based on past strategic planning principles (such as noted previously). Due to the vast number of uncertainties over time, the reliability of answers to these ''what if'' questions are, needless to say, less accurate. Nevertheless, top-level executive needs are being met as well as possible based on a magnitude of unknowns. For more information on problem finding, reference can be made to Chapter 2 and a number of publications by the author.[1]

An important benefit from problem finding is that a manager can prevent a molehill from becoming a mountain if the manager is warned early enough to take corrective action. What is it worth to a manager to be warned of a business problem sometime sooner? What it is worth to the manager and to the company is the avoidance of a crisis. Often, it is too late to react to problems that are already out of control. This strategic advantage from using problem finding within a KMS environment, while difficult to quantify, is very significant and real for the typical company today.

Enlarged View of Core Competence to Develop New Opportunities

In order to create new markets for products and services, early and consistent investment in what is called ''core competencies'' is one important factor. In turn, corporate imagination and expeditionary marketing are the keys that unlock these new markets. A company that underinvests in its core competencies, or inadvertently surrenders them through alliances and outsourcing, generally robs its own future. But to realize the potential that core competencies create, a company must also have the imagination to envision markets that do not yet exist and the ability to stake them out ahead of the competition. In a few words, a company must anticipate what the customers want before they are aware of what they want. [2]

A company will strive to create new competitive space only if it possesses an opportunity perspective that goes far beyond the boundaries of its present businesses. This perspective identifies, in broad terms, the marketing territory top management hopes to stake out over the coming years, a terrain that is unlikely to be captured in anything as precise as a five-year marketing plan. The initial enthusiasm that several Japanese companies brought to developing high-definition television (HDTV) grew out of just such a vision. Creative considerations of the many new opportunities that might emerge if HDTV could be made a reality led them beyond the traditional boundaries of color television business to identify potential markets in cinema production, video photography, video magazines, electronic museums, product demonstrations, and training simulations, among others.

As this example demonstrates, a company's opportunity perspective represents its collective imagination of the ways in which an important new benefit might be harnessed to create new competitive space or reshape existing space. Commitment to an opportunity perspective does not rest on ROI (return on investment) calculations but on an almost visceral sense of the benefits that customers will finally derive should pioneering work prove successful. The more fundamental the envisioned benefits and the more widely shared the enthusiasm for the opportunity, the greater the company's perseverance will be.[3]

Although there is a need for core competencies to create new markets, there is also the need for an enlarged view of these competencies. Conceiving a company as a group of core competencies rather than as a group of products and services is one way to extend the opportunity perspective considerably. Because Motorola sees itself as a leader in wireless communications, it is not just a producer of paging devices and mobile telephones. Instead, the company's charter permits it to explore markets as diverse as wireless local area computer networks and global positioning satellite receivers. Ajinomoto, a giant grocery products company, is not only in the food business but also applies the skills it has mastered in fermentation technology to produce an elastic paper for Sony's top-end headphones. The point to be made from these examples is that if company managers are not able to think outside current business boundaries, they will miss important new opportunities that depend on the combination of skills from several sources. Core competence with the proper application of knowledge should prosper and flourish over the years to the betterment of all parties concerned. Dominance in core products and services, then, allows companies to shape this evolution to keep one step ahead of competition.[4]

Importance of a Company's Critical Success Factors (CSFs) and Their Measurement

For any business, critical success factors (CSFs) are the limited number of areas in which results, if they are satisfactory, will ensure successful competitive performance. They are the key areas where things must go right if the organization is to flourish. If results in these key areas are not adequate, the organization's efforts for the period will be less than desired. As a result, the critical success factors are areas of activity that should receive constant and careful attention from management. The current status of performance in each area should be continually measured, and that information should be made available to the higher levels of management.

Typically, critical success factors support the attainment of measurable organizational goals. These goals represent the end points that an organization hopes to reach. Critical success factors are the few areas in which good performance is necessary to ensure attainment of those goals. For example, the automobile industry has four industry-based CSFs: having the right styling for the times, having a good-quality dealer system, having effective cost control over selling and manufacturing operations, and having the capability to meet current energy standards in terms of average mileage per gallon for all cars produced. Though the automobile manufacturers must pay attention to many other factors, these four areas represent the underpinnings of successful operations.

From a broad viewpoint, the principal sources of critical success factors have been identified by John F. Rockhart at MIT's Sloan School of Management. They are as follows:[5]

- *Structure of a particular industry.* Each industry by its very nature has a set of CSFs that are determined by the characteristics of the industry itself.
- *Competitive strategy, industry position, and geographic location.* For smaller organizations in an industry that is dominated by one or two large companies, the actions of the major companies will often produce new problems for the small companies. The competitive strategy for the latter may mean establishing a new market niche, getting out of a product line completely, or redistribution of resources among various product lines.
- *Environmental factors.* As the economy changes as potential factors change, as energy problems become more acute, and the like, critical success factors can change for an organization.
- *Temporal factors.* Internal organization considerations often lead to temporal critical success factors. Inventory, for example, which is rarely a CSF for top management, might become a high-level CSF if there is far too much or too little stock.

Although these four sources for identifying CSFs are determinable, critical success factors are different for an individual industry and even for companies within that industry.

Going one step further, the concept of *key performance indicators* (KPIs) is a way of formalizing and describing critical success factors. Fundamentally, a comprehensive CSF system has four basic components which are shown in Figure 6-2. *First*, executive visioning that centers on broad-based knowledge of a company sets the company's overall direction and is linked to its corporate objectives and goals. *Second*, general company objectives are related to overall corporate goals, which are then broken down into appropriate measurable goals for divisions and business units. These goals provide the means for developing appropriate corporate strategies and programs. *Third*, each business unit identifies a number of critical success factors that must be performed well to achieve its goals and strategies as well as carry out its programs. These activities are then assigned to the people responsible for their completion. *Fourth*, each business unit establishes a measurement system to quantify success. These measures are the key performance indicators, which normally include a number of financial ratios. Reference to KPIs and financial ratios is also found in Chapter 9.

For example, a company has decided that one of its corporate goals is to improve customer satisfaction by 10 percent this year. At the corporate level, a periodic survey of customers would be a key performance indicator, since corporate managers are responsible for the overall corporation effort. Measurable activities that contribute to improvements might be improved product quality, improved customer service and support, improved delivery times, and more customer-suggested product improvements. Each of these activities suggests its

Figure 6-2
From Executive Visioning to Corporate Objectives and Measurable Goals to Critical Success Factors to Key Performance Indicators (KPIs) and Financial Ratios Within a KMS Environment

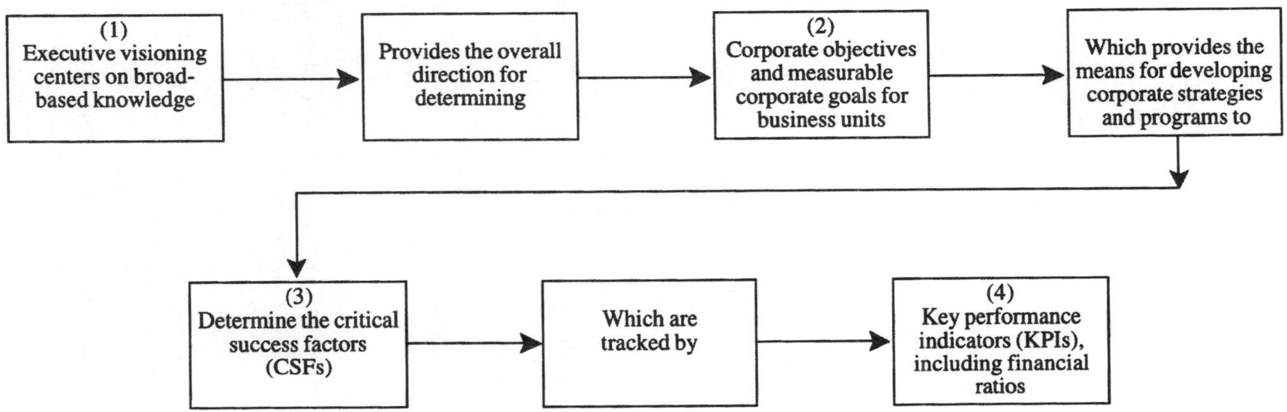

own set of key performance indicators. The most important part of this process is that the KPIs are measures that the people responsible for them can actually control and for which they can be held accountable. And because of this combination of responsibility, control, and accountability, these KPIs, including financial ratios, are certain to be relevant and important to the managers assigned to them.

Benchmarking the Company to Detect the Best Business Practices

An important way to judge the performance of a company is to compare it not only with other units within the company but also with outsiders that represent the best industry practices. Commonly, this technique is called *benchmarking*. When the Xerox Corporation started using benchmarking not too long ago, management's aim was to analyze unit production costs in manufacturing operations. Uncomfortably aware of the extremely low prices of Japanese plain-paper copiers, the manufacturing staff at Xerox wanted to determine whether their Japanese counterparts' relative costs were as low as their relative prices. The staff compared the operating capabilities and features of the Japanese machines, including those made by Fuji-Xerox and tore down their mechanical components for examination.

As somewhat expected, the investigation revealed that production costs in the United States were much higher. Discarding their standard budgeting processes, U.S. manufacturing operations thereby adopted the lower Japanese costs as targets for driving their own business plans. Top management, gratified with the results, directed that all units and cost centers in the corporation use benchmarking.

In contrast, distribution, administration, service, and other support functions of Xerox found it difficult to arrive at a convenient analogue to a product. These nonmanufacturing units began to make internal comparisons, including worker productivity at different regional distribution centers and per pound transportation costs between regions. Next, they looked at competitors' processes. In logistics that meant comparing the transportation, warehousing, and inventory management of Xerox's distribution function with those of the competition.

The initial step in the process is to identify what will be benchmarked (i.e., measured): expense-to-revenue ratios, inventory turns, service calls, customer satisfaction—whatever the "product" of the particular function is. Then it is necessary to pinpoint the areas that need improvement. In Xerox's experience, managers tend to concentrate first on comparative costs. But as they become more knowledgeable about benchmarking, managers discover that understanding practices, processes, and methods is more important because these define the changes necessary to reach the benchmark costs. Moreover, as managers become more confident about benchmarking, they can readily extend it beyond cost reduction to profit-producing factors, like service levels and customer satisfaction.[6]

Annual reports and other easily available publications are important sources for the purpose of comparison. They can uncover gross indicators of efficient operation. Universally recognized measures like return on assets, revenue per employee, inventory turns, and general and administrative expenses will help identify well-managed companies. To identify superior performance in specific functions, a company can utilize trade journals, consultants, annual reports, other company publications in which ''statements of pride'' appear, and presentations at professional and other forums. The same well-run organizations keep turning up.

Software Useful in Discovering Strategic Planning Knowledge

To assist small businesses in enhancing their planning efforts, software packages provide an effective starting point and can lead the planner through the process of generating an effective business plan. The software planning packages are not only easy to install in standard hardware but also easy to use. They also provide some capabilities to carry out ''what if'' analysis. In addition, they offer the capability to utilize historical and current knowledge in the preparation of a business plan.

While there are variations in business planning software, typically a formal business plan consists of several common elements: executive summary, company overview, products/services, market analysis, marketing plan, and financial plan.[7] A snapshot of the whole plan is represented by the *executive summary*, which highlights the company's mission, measurable objectives and goals, product and marketing strategies, and the financial plan. When preparing the executive summary, keep it short and simple. From one to several pages is ideal. Following the executive summary is the rest of the business plan. The *company overview* sets the stage for the venture and provides details of its history and ownership, operating structure, management team, and business purpose. *Products/services* describes what the company sells and how it develops, produces, and distributes products and services. This section also offers an analysis of competition and future plans. This is followed by the *market analysis*, which describes current and potential customers and the demographics of the marketplace. In addition, the *marketing plan* reveals the company's strategy for reaching its markets through advertising, alliances, distribution channels, promotions, and a sales force. Finally, the *financial plan* sets the words to numbers and shows the recent operating history. It projects the next three to five years' worth of cash flow, profits, and asset and liability balances. It also typically contains a break-even analysis, financial ratios, capital requirements, and the timing and amount of the return on investment.

Typical business planning software packages include the following: Avantos ManagePro helps managers plan and track goals and progress while fostering success through focused management activities. It includes goal planning and tracking tools, such as the Top Level Goal Planner, for planning and delegating key business objectives, strategies, and tactics. The Goal and People Status Boards enable managers to monitor the status of primary business goals and obtain at-a-glance reinforcement of where to focus attention. Jian BizPlan Builder is a complete business plan template on disk with more than 90 typed pages of example text that are formulated into word processing files. Templates use standard spreadsheet applications like Excel or Lotus 1-2-3 to calculate financials and generate graphs. The step-by-step format guides the user through, explains issues, and gives clear and sensible advice.

Once a company's business plans have been developed (from the short-range to the long-range), software can be employed that is useful in determining the company's overall financial performance. Such software goes beyond the monthly actual reports and budget reports that are routinely produced by today's information systems. Currently, companies are employing corporate scorecard software, which is a sophisticated business model that helps a company understand what is really driving its success. In effect, it acts like the control panel on an airplane—that is, the business equivalent of a flight speedometer, odometer, and temperature gauge all rolled into one. A corporate scorecard keeps track of a company's financial progress as well as its softer measurements. Ranging from customer satisfaction to return on investment, these areas need to be managed to reach a company's final destination (i.e., profitable growth). A scorecard, for example, might graph customer service to determine if it is improving or deteriorating and, at the same time, tally product defects to determine if they are rising or falling—and where. Going a step further, scorecard software, which is usually distributed throughout a company's computer network, lets company employees across the entire organization be certain they are talking about like items when they get together. If customer satisfaction is declining, sales, manufacturing, and research and development will all be reading the same score and thus will be able to tackle the problem from a common perspective.

Today, there are two views on the utilization of scorecard software. One is that a company's yardsticks should be purely financial. Managers should employ indicators like revenue growth and return on investment to guide a business. The other is that a corporate scorecard should be balanced. A company, for instance, should not only keep close watch on performance numbers like gross profit margins on new products but should also use softer measurements. Other softer measures include the number of new products, product development cycle times, and the rate of on-time deliveries. The bottom line from this view is that a company is forced to evaluate critically those drivers that really determine its performance over the short run to the long run.[8]

Although business planning software and scorecard software is useful in a typical information system mode, no technique or software can replace experience and knowledge about a business or its markets, which is necessary for effective strategic planning. In contrast, knowledge discovery and data mining can make business knowledge and experience more valuable than ever. They provide a means for conducting complex data analysis to discover patterns, relationships, and associations within a set of data and information. Such patterns and the rules inferred from them can be used to guide decision making and even predict the outcome of those decisions by corporate planners.

An example of knowledge discovery software that can be of assistance to management and its corporate planning staff is KnowledgeX. Essentially, this software can discern hidden relationships among people, organizations, and positions. It is able to take information, organize it, and extract from that material the connections and webs of relationships. Using Intelligent Knowledge Exchange, KnowledgeX can perform a text processing task called "SmartParse" to select and extract textual information. If it encounters terms it already knows, it will automatically assign the correct set of connections to that term. If it does not know the term, the user can define it once and all future uses of that term will be connected according to rules. KnowledgeX is object oriented. It allows multimedia information to be accessible from within the program.

Once the relationships are established, KnowledgeX has the ability to display these connections in a graphical way or as a text outline. The graphical display is easy to grasp and often reveals relationships that have been buried within the text and not obvious to the researcher. By creating maps showing relationships among customers, companies, individuals, and organizations, KnowledgeX makes it easy to grasp how these people and organizations are interconnected. The more information the knowledge base contains, the better KnowledgeX is at finding unknown and unnoticed relationships.

In addition, KnowledgeX can combine information entered by many people on the network and find the connections within that information. Fragments coming from other people can therefore be converted into something like a centralized knowledge source. That is, KnowledgeX takes information and knowledge coming from many sources and reveals relationships that had never been known before because the pieces were too fragmented and dispersed among too many people. From this perspective, this knowledge discovery software is quite useful in bringing together diverse elements needed for resolving critical strategic planning issues.

✓ KNOWLEDGE MANAGEMENT SYSTEMS IN STRATEGIC PLANNING

In order to understand knowledge management systems better in corporate strategic planning, marketing, manufacturing, finance, and human resources in this chapter and the following ones, reference can be made to either a manufacturing-oriented company or a service-oriented company. In either company, the corporate strategic planning system is linked directly with other systems. That is, planning activities are related to external environmental factors through a company's mission to its organization's objectives and goals. In turn, these important relationships are related to a company's internal environmental factors (i.e., marketing, manufacturing, finance, and human resources). All of these external and internal environmental factors form the basis for short- to long-range strategic planning within a KMS operating mode. The capability of the knowledge management system to extract on-line knowledge, facts, information, and the like now makes this system a forward-looking one for answering questions about the future. From this viewpoint, an effective strategic planning system makes great use not only of multidimensional analysis but also of whatever software is useful for answering tomorrow's questions in view of today's projections.

Areas That Lend Themselves to Discovering Strategic Planning Knowledge

In view of this current approach using a KMS operating mode, an effective strategic planning operating mode needs to translate visioning down to a practical level. That is, *executive visioning* can be used to help managers build a consensus around its strategies and programs so that it guides action at the lower or local levels. This necessitates letting managers *communicate* these strategies and programs up and down the organization and, at the same time, linking them to each business unit and individual objectives and goals. This planning model enables the company to integrate its *business and financial plans* at the lower levels. This model also allows for *feedback*, since it gives the company the capability of studying alternatives for strategic improvement. Strategic improvement consists of continuous feedback—that is, testing the environment on which the strategies are built and making the necessary adjustments where deemed necessary.

Since short- to long-range strategic planning in a typical company makes use of this broad-based approach, this will be the essential focus of the areas that lend themselves to discovering strategic planning knowledge. Typically, a company's corporate planning staff, which undertakes strategic planning activities, is responsible directly to the president or chief executive officer (CEO), has relatively few members, exists at the corporate level, and operates on a full-time basis. This corporate planning staff operates in an environment characterized by product and technological change. Also, the character of a company's departmentalization seems to influence the organization structure for strategic planning. An important part of the corporate planning staff's time is spent determining and analyzing a company's critical success factors as well as related key performance indicators, including financial ratios. For example, say that a staff has determined CSFs to be: (1) prices (responsiveness to competitive pricing), (2) cost control (reducing the cost of plant and office operations), (3) inventory turnover (improving the times the inventory turns over yearly), and (4) product mix (having the right products for the times). These CSFs are in line with those set forth earlier for other industries and can be related to key performance indicators and financial ratios. Knowledge about a company CSFs, which is obtained from its current operations via its KPIs and financial ratios, may indicate that there are subtle changes occurring currently. The end result is that there may well be a shift in what constitutes an effective way to evaluate a company's performance.

LONG-RANGE STRATEGIC PLANNING

Within a KMS environment, corporate planners view decision making as a *continuous decision process*. It centers on setting appropriate corporate objectives and measurable goals, employing strategies and programs to achieve these desired objectives and goals, allocating a company's resources in an optimum manner, specifying the critical success factors, and determining the key performance indicators and financial ratios to measure the CSFs. As shown previously in Figure 6–2, all of these planning and related activities are influenced by visioning that is based on a comprehensive knowledge of a company's operations. The implemented plans are then monitored to keep them on course and to correct any deviations from the original or revised plans. Revisions are usually necessary since change is integral to the nature of strategic planning and its decision process.

Since there is a need to evaluate planning alternatives continuously for achieving stated objectives and measurable goals, the capability for studying various aspects of the long-range plans in its various stages becomes critical. In practical terms, this means producing many runs or variations of the same plan, using different sets of assumptions and perhaps different logic. In *evaluating resources*, for example, varying combinations of resources can be applied, and numerous questions concerning their nature and size can be posed. "Do we have the necessary resources to achieve our objectives, or must they be acquired? If resources are to be acquired, at what cost will they be acquired and in what time span? Will they be operational in time to achieve the corporation's objectives within a given schedule? What are the optimum mixes of resources to satisfy different objectives under different sets of conditions? What are the likely effects of miscalculating availability and cost of equipment, personnel, or funds to acquire the needed resources? What can happen for every one percent of error in the forecast and, therefore, how critical is it that we hold strictly to the plan?" Similarly, in *evaluating strategies*, for example, various questions can be asked concerning improved revenues, lower costs, higher reliability, meeting customer requirements, relationship to other products, enhanced image in customer eyes, better information, and relationship to organizational plans and derivative programs.

The anticipation of consequences of given assumptions and the evaluation of alternatives is a major activity of a company's managers at the highest level and of the corporate planning staff. The utilization of appropriate information and its resulting knowledge is helpful because it provides the means whereby the final strategic plan mirrors the real world as closely as possible. Knowledge discovery can help corporate planners evaluate alternatives and (usually) choose the best one. Such evaluation has come to be known as the ''what'' is likely to happen ''if'' the company takes or does not take a certain course of action. As will be seen in the materials to follow, a KMS operating mode can prove to be extremely useful for a company's corporate planners.

Integrate Changing Times with Long-Range Strategies and Resources

An integral part of the entire strategic planning process is the integration of changing times with long-range strategies and resources. A Labor Department study, for example, forecasts a slowdown in future economic growth. It estimates that the country's gross domestic product, adjusted for price change, will grow at annual rates of just over 3 percent. That would be about 25 percent below the average growth rate of about 4 percent that has prevailed during much of the time since World War II. In addition to the external long-range factors, a typical company's executives and their corporate planning staff should consider the internal factors that affect the long run. Essentially, they include the factors mentioned above (marketing, manufacturing, financial, and human resources). The interplay of these internal environmental factors and the external environmental factors can have a dramatic impact on a company's strategic plans. In fact, incorrect information concerning the internal and external environmental factors may lead a typical company down the wrong planning path.

To get a better idea of how to adapt to changing times as reflected in a company's long-range strategies, reference can be made to Figure 6-3 for three typical situations. First, a company can invest available resources in order for the business to *grow* and thereby strengthen its profitable position. Second, it can *protect* business strengths in order to maintain a strong position in a moderately attractive and mature market. Third, it can *divest* the business in order to exit from a weak position in a relatively unattractive market. Based on these three typical situations, allocation of a company's resources differs as noted in Figure 6-3. Similarly, measurement and analysis using KPIs and financial ratios also differ based upon the situation. In all three situations, the discovery of new knowledge can be useful to management in getting a complete understanding of a grow, protect, or divest long-range strategy.

Once a company defines its current state and its long-range strategy, it can and should match its people to that strategy. These three typical strategies require distinct sets of managerial characteristics and management styles. Broadly speaking, an entrepreneur is needed for the *grow* situation, a competent manager for the *protect* situation, and a critical manager for the *divest* situation. Not only do these three types of organizations differ in the optimum management style of their executives, but also in the way they are organized and the climate that exists within each organization as well as the current economic climate. For

Figure 6-3
Relationship of Company Long-Range Strategies to Allocation of Company Resources, Including Their Measurement and Analysis Using Key Performance Indicators and Financial Ratios

Company Long-Range Strategies	Allocation of Company Resources	Measurement and Analysis Using Key Performance Indicators and Financial Ratios
Grow	Improve market share	Market share
	Develop new products	Sales volume growth
	Increase manufacturing capacity	Capitalized ROI
	Expand sales force	Relative quality
Protect	Maintain market share	Marketing expenses/sales
	Optimize margins	R&D expenses/sales
	Differentiate products	Investment/sales
	Increase efficiency	Capacity utilization
Divest	Forego market share for profits	ROI
	Hold prices and margins	Net cash flow/investment
	Prune product lines	Pretax profit/sales
	Shrink sales force	Sales/assets

example, in the *grow* situation, corporate planning for problem solving and problem finding is longer term in its outlook and there is a great deal of delegation of authority. There is considerably less freedom to act independently in the protect organization and planning is more medium-term in nature. The successful manager in either situation is one who thrives in the company's culture and feels most comfortable within its organizational structure.

Using Knowledge to Improve Long-Range Strategies

Related to a company's long-range strategies are a number of underlying concepts. A popular concept that embodies many of the strategic planning principles set forth previously is this: The essence of strategic unity between business and technology is manifested in changing roles and structures, high expectations, and a collaborative spirit. From this view, long-range strategies are broad visions of the future that are adaptable to a changing environment. They encourage corporate planners to think about the future in creative and productive ways. Such planners see their job as getting others to question conventional wisdom. To perform their jobs, corporate planners have to resort to provocation or shock tactics like raising difficult questions and challenging conventional assumptions. A number of the strategic planning principles set forth previously may be of help in changing the status quo. The knowledge contained in these principles may well provide the impetus for improving a company's long-range strategies. Overall, development of long-range strategies is the process of discovering and understanding broad visions of the future as opposed to the strategic planning process, which is about turning these visions into action.

A very important long-range strategy that is widely used today to improve customer service and lower operating costs is the Internet and its corporate equivalent intranets. All elements of a company's supply chain, for example, can be linked by electronic networks. If a person buys a pair of Nike running shoes, that information can be transmitted back to the plant in Taiwan where the shoes are made and the shoes can be express mailed directly to the person's home. Similarly, items purchased electronically from several suppliers in the same region could be shipped in a batch using electronic interfaces. A whole host of intermediaries in the chain who used to make their living coordinating and moving information can be eliminated. Intranet-to-intranet communication is blurring the lines between companies. The notion of where a corporation starts and stops is very different today. As another example, a company's expertise might be harvesting timber or processing lumber, but the company also needs to move its products to the construction industry. Traditionally, all those steps were brought together in a soup-to-nuts operation. Now, given interconnectivity, someone else can run a company's truck fleet, but it will still operate like one's own fleet.

For some companies, the growth of network computing offers new business opportunities. QuickResponse Services Inc. (based in Richmond, California) provides electronic links between manufacturers and retailers, thereby becoming an information switch for several large apparel manufacturers, including Liz Claiborne and Perry Ellis. By collecting information from the retailers about which products are selling, the company then works with manufacturers to restock their inventories. The Microsoft Corporation has handed off troubleshooting responsibilities for its in-house computers to an outside vendor that uses the software maker's intranet to get at faulty computers. Another example of network computing is the Chicago-based Navistar Inc., which no longer maintains a tire and rim inventory at its Springfield, Ohio, truck-assembly plant. That responsibility is now handled electronically by Goodyear Tire & Rubber Company, one of Navistar's tire suppliers. Basically, a Goodyear office in New York receives Navistar's manufacturing schedule and tire-and-rim requirements by electronic data interchange (a proprietary electronic network). The information is then sent to a Goodyear plant in Ohio where tires are mounted on rims. The completed assemblies are shipped to the Springfield plant, arriving just eight hours ahead of when they are needed. The tire-and-rim assemblies come in the same order as the trucks that are coming down the assembly line.[9]

To assist its clients in using knowledge to improve their operations and assist in developing appropriate long-range strategies, Andersen Consulting has developed Knowledge Xchange. Essentially, Knowledge Xchange creates *virtual communities of* practice: Lotus Notes groupware and Microsoft OfficeSuite run on a Novell NetWare-based LAN. The LAN is connected to a proprietary client/

server-based WAN. Because the value of this consulting firm is in its knowledge capital, Knowledge Xchange makes all of the firm's accumulated knowledge and skills immediately available to each of its consultants, and, therefore, to every client. It is a virtual place where all of the firm's 27,000 consultants can share their knowledge and expertise in global communities of practice. Knowledge Xchange is available to each consultant on desktop and laptop computers and affects the work done on a daily basis. In fact, it lets a consultant find out who has skills out there that he or she does not have so that the consultant can quickly put together an on-line team to help solve a client's problem. This way, the proper skills can be brought to bear on developing a company's strategies and meeting its strategic planning needs. The knowledge obtained from Knowledge Xchange can make an important difference between success or failure.

Long-Range (Five-Year) Strategic Planning

Typically, a company's strategies that need to be translated into action take the form of long-range (i.e., five-year) strategic plans. To assist in the development of these long-range plans, corporate planners need to begin with a knowledge and understanding of existing products, divisions, margins, profits, return on investment, cash flow, availability of capital, research and development capabilities, skills and capacities of personnel, etc. For a manufacturing-oriented company, this understanding needs to be extended to an in-depth analysis of manufacturing operations that is tied in with centralized operations at the corporate level. There is a need to examine performance over the past few years as well as the current year as part of an initial overall review process. Evaluating significant aspects of past and current operations is the basis for determining how well the organization objectives and goals are being met. In like manner, plans for the coming five years, based on short- to medium-range plans for improving operations, become an essential part of getting started on long-range strategic planning.

A typical five-year plan for a manufacturing-oriented company includes the *external environmental factors* shown in Figure 6-4. These are generally not controllable, such as customers, government, public, competitors, suppliers, investors, and financial institutions. On the other hand, four *internal environmental factors* that are controllable by the company center on the following:

- *Marketing planning* focuses on expanding current product lines and entering new product markets. This involves increasing use of selling outlets and/or distribution to sell the company's products, changes in pricing policy and pricing practices to effect higher sales, and consideration of new advertising media for more effective penetration of the company's markets.
- *Manufacturing planning* centers on major facilities contemplated and improvements in processing efficiency, including the percent of capacity that is now and will be em-

Figure 6-4
Relationship of External to Internal Environmental Factors for Short-Range to Long-Range Strategic Planning for a Typical Company (Operating at the Corporate Level Within a KMS Environment)

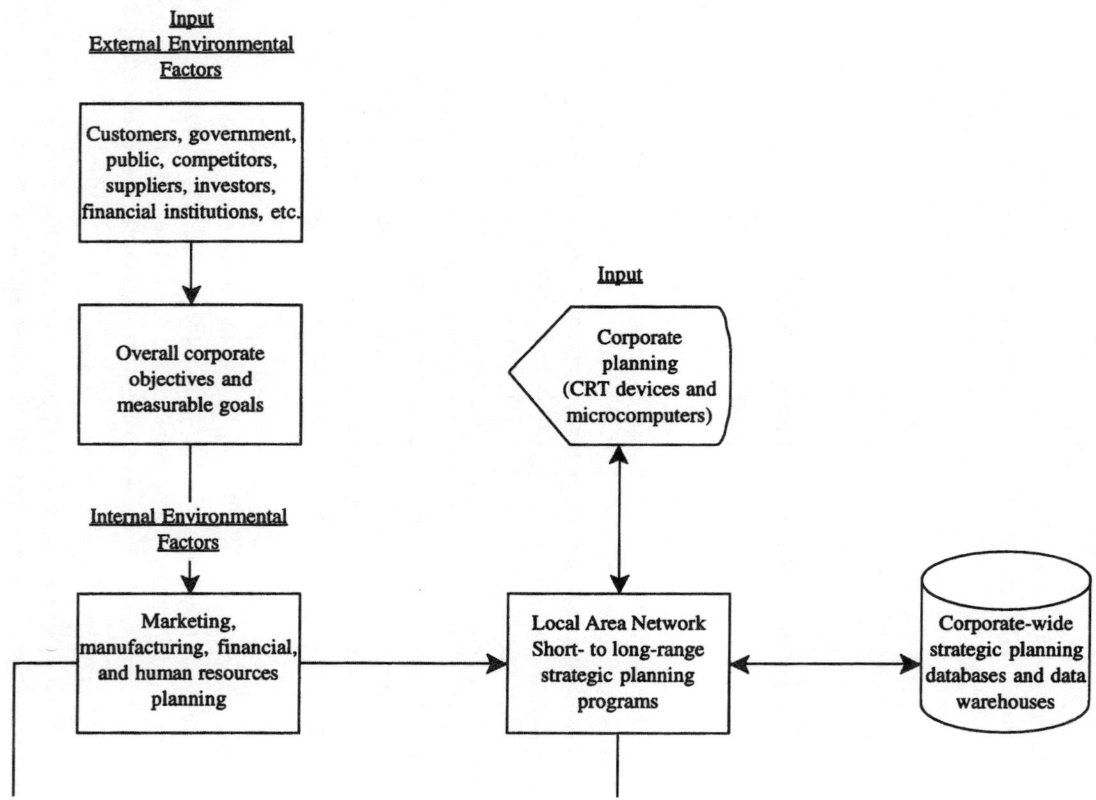

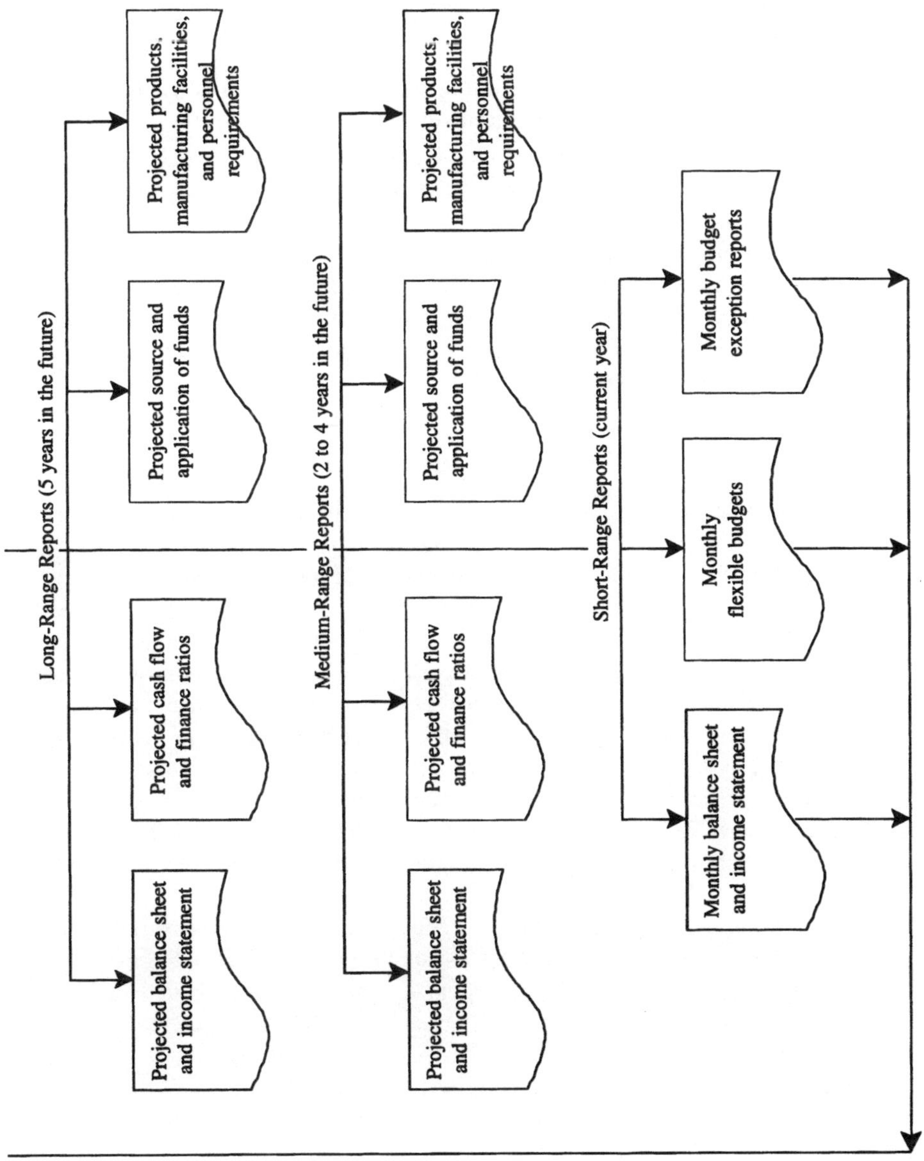

Long-Range Reports (5 years in the future)
Projected balance sheet and income statement
Projected cash flow and finance ratios
Projected source and application of funds
Projected products, manufacturing facilities, and personnel requirements
Medium-Range Reports (2 to 4 years in the future)
Projected balance sheet and income statement
Projected cash flow and finance ratios
Projected source and application of funds
Projected products, manufacturing facilities, and personnel requirements
Short-Range Reports (current year)
Monthly balance sheet and income statement
Monthly flexible budgets
Monthly budget exception reports

ployed with current facilities and machinery as well as the steps that are being taken to use any excess capacity.

- *Financial planning* relates to projected sales by product lines, contribution (sales less direct manufacturing costs) by product lines, indirect manufacturing costs plus sales and general and administrative expenses, net profits before federal income taxes by product lines, fixed and working capital needs, return on investment by product lines, and comparable financial ratios and analyses.
- *Human resources planning* centers on projected requirements for key management personnel and production labor when considering turnover and future growth.

To develop projected strategic plans, the corporate planning staff employs the company's corporate databases and data warehouses to analyze meaningful long-range information as well as to discover new knowledge about a company's operations over time. In turn, this output is used to finalize the company's five-year strategies and programs.

Problem-Centered Approach to Long-Range Strategic Planning

The knowledge obtained to improve a company's long-range strategies can be integrated with problem finding. Because company executives and their corporate planning staffs must combine knowledge of today's marketplace, including economic and political analysis, with a vision of the future, strategic planning does not involves forecasting of the future in the conventional sense, but rather a projection of a variety of possible scenarios under good, average, and poor economic conditions. Against these scenarios, corporate planners analyze the strengths and weaknesses of the company and evaluate its resources under these conditions. This includes a rigorous study of the finances. Market forecasts and financial modeling can provide the foundation for a company's strategic plans. To illustrate the problem-finding process (as set forth in Chapter 2), the problem-centered approach is applied to strategic marketing plans in the discussion to follow.

In this illustration, the corporation is engaged in selling products to the home market. Its president recognizes that its future markets may well change drastically over time. In fact, the individual is convinced that about half of the present products will not be sold five years hence. In view of this potential major upheaval in the marketplace, he has enlisted the services of a national consulting firm. The consultants who were assigned to this marketing project formed a group of high-level management personnel, consisting of the executive vice president, the marketing vice president, four regional sales managers, and themselves.

As a starting point, the group met for two days at corporate headquarters and initially centered on *problem generation* (first step) regarding present and future products using decision conferencing. Under the direction of a senior consultant, the group examined marketing problems by using a brainstorming approach.

The major discussion focused not on the products being marketed under good, average, and poor economic conditions, but rather on the changing nature of customer buying habits. Due to the continuing trend toward smaller living quarters and smaller families caused by inflationary times and other factors, the corporation is faced with developing new products to reflect the changes that affect the home market. The group also brainstormed the trend toward more people living alone.

Based on the information displayed on a public screen, *evaluation* (second step) consisted of reviewing the marketing areas of the future and their related problems. As it turned out, all of the areas displayed on the public screen were determined to be valid for managerial concern in the *validation* stage (third step). The trend toward smaller living quarters represents a major problem for the corporation. In contrast, its current products are oriented toward medium- to large-sized homes where there is ample space to accommodate them. In light of this major problem and its related problems in the future, the group spent some time *establishing boundaries* (fourth step). Although the home market in foreign countries was considered to be a viable one, it was decided to put first things first by channeling the corporation's resources into the development of new products for the domestic market.

Although a number of problems needed to be solved, the major one was the first one solved—that is, developing over the next five years a wide range of new products that would be more compact and, at the same time, capable of performing a wide range of services to meet homeowner needs. The *solution* took the form of having the group employ knowledge discovery software within a KMS environment. In turn, this collected knowledge was useful in passing judgment on the profitability of the proposed products and comparing one to another for implementation. The profitability of the products (i.e., net profit on sales and return on investment) were determined in terms of modeling the anticipated revenues and costs over their life. Overall, the employment of the problem-centered approach resulted in identifying future product problems. In turn, these problems were brought back to the present time for solution. As a result, management by perception was put into practice by this high-level executive task force for determining future strategic marketing plans.

SHORT-RANGE AND MEDIUM-RANGE STRATEGIC PLANNING

Short-range strategic planning, sometimes called operational planning, is a derivative of medium-range strategic planning which, in turn, comes from long-range strategic planning. For a typical company, short-range strategic planning is concerned with the efficient use of available capacities. It is a detailed financial plan that specifies both how the company's objectives and goals for the coming year will be attained and the operational procedures for managing daily operations. As such, the short-range plans outline the specific steps for accomplishing the medium-range plans. Also, they play a major role in implementing business strategies by translating long-range plans into action.

Additionally, short-range plans center on detailed objectives and specific measurable goals and strategies of the company and the means for achieving them—usually in the form of flexible budgets or profit plans by product groups. Management needs cost and revenue margin information so that it can identify areas of strength and weakness. Knowledge about a company's product margin (contribution information) and its competitors over time is also needed to measure the profit impact of alternative courses of action. Hence, approved short-range strategic plans become budgets so that actual results can be measured and compared with them monthly for more effective control.

Using Knowledge to Prepare Short-Range and Medium-Range Profit Plans

For a typical company's products, an annual profit plan is an integral part of corporation-wide strategic planning. In a similar manner, overall profit plans are determined for two, three, and four years hence. Reference can be made to Figure 6-4 for typical output. As information about changing times becomes available, profit plans for the coming year must be revised to reflect the changes and expected changes in the business environment. Effective profit planning, therefore, must be a continuous effort rather than a periodic one, within a KMS operating mode. Although budgets for profit planning are generally prepared by the accounting department, the responsibility rests with the corporate planning staff, who must not only select the appropriate financial information for specific planning decisions but must also combine this information from corporate databases and data warehouses in useful and meaningful ways. Many times, there is a need to employ knowledge discovery techniques to extract financial trends and patterns. Staff members must also review and coordinate the estimates provided by the functional managers involved in a particular decision. They must measure the profit impact of alternative courses of action and offer advice on the meaning and significance of financial analysis. In summary, long-range strategic plans within a KMS environment are translated into medium-range plans for the next several years and finally into short-range strategic plans, or annual profit plans (including budgets) for the coming year (refer to Figure 6-4).

Flexible budgets or detailed profit plans for the coming year are developed to take into account planning for marketing, manufacturing, human resources, and finance that have an impact on the current year. Similarly, overall profit plans for medium-range strategic plans can be developed. To assist the corporate planning staff, appropriate software, such as an OLAP software package, can be used to answer a series of "what if" questions about planning and to perform sensitivity analysis to determine the impact the change of one or more variables might have on the final profit plans. As shown in Figure 6-5, managers and their staffs interact with the company's information to answer "what if" ques-

Figure 6-5
Typical Short-Range Planning Analysis (Forthcoming Six Months) to Answer "What-If" Questions During the Budgetary Process About the Profitability of New Products

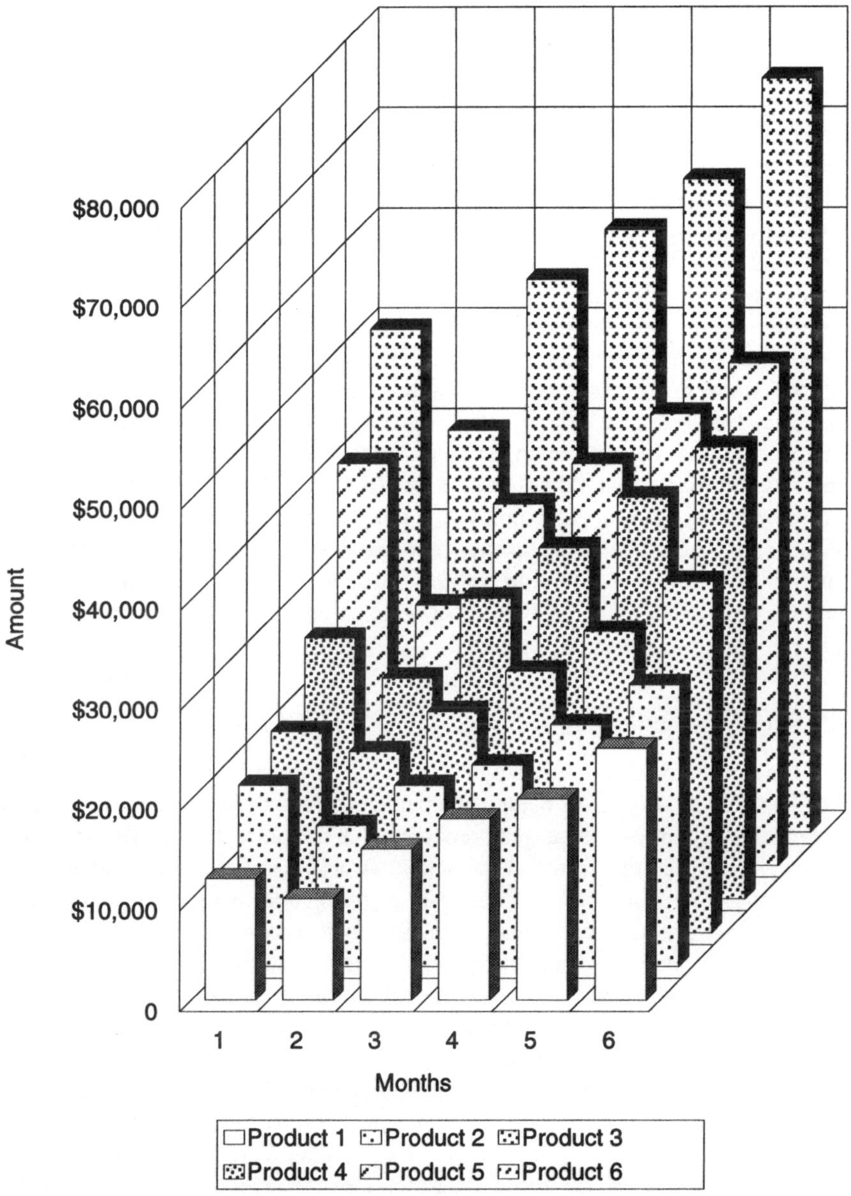

tions and to undertake sensitivity analysis. In this case, there is a six-month analysis of six new products in terms of profitability. As shown, profits increase over the months due to a number of factors, including a reduction in production times, larger sales volumes due to the acceptance of the product, and a reduction in scrappage as the learning curve improves. A variety of answers, then, can be obtained to assist in the development of profit plans—the corporate strategic plans for current and future operations. The development of a company's profit plans can benefit from the use of knowledge management techniques, particularly knowledge discovery (data mining) software.

Going beyond the preparation of short- and medium-range profit plans, it is helpful to measure actual performance against these profit plans. In terms of the short range of the current time period, the scorecard software mentioned previously in the chapter can help management at this point. Besides getting an overview of how a company is doing, specific areas of a company can be measured and evaluated for performance. For example, the scorecard software can check on defect rates plant by plant and see how each plant's quality is improving. It can link measurements like on-time deliveries to certain financial indicators. The software can measure the percentage of sales due to new product introductions, gross margins on new products, and corporate-wide indicators like revenues and return on investment. It should be noted that different companies at different times have different needs and aims. For example, a service company that has just merged would not build a strictly financial model that focuses, say, on productivity. Output per employee is not a driver for that business. The real value of scorecard software is that it forces a company to reexamine its assumptions about what really drives performance. It forces a company to focus and become much more explicit about what matters to its customers and, ultimately, what matters to its stockholders.

Using Information and Knowledge to Finance an Expansion

To assist in short-range strategic planning, information and knowledge can be helpful in the review of quarterly financial forecasts to finance an expansion. For example, top-level managers can apply for a loan to finance an expansion although they lack the historical financial data necessary for a statistical analysis of earnings. The solution is to construct a four-quarter earnings forecast combining present market conditions with their best knowledge about the future. The gathering process is started by polling the managers for number estimates and market assumptions. For this type of modeling process, there is almost complete consensus among all managers on all assumptions other than unit sales and selling price. The importance of unit sales and selling price growth, coupled with the range of estimates received, makes the use of multiple projections prudent. Consequently, the model provides the best-case and worst-case scenario forecasts for review by top-level managers and their staffs.

Basically, the model incorporates assumptions for several variables, including growth factors for unit sales and selling prices for the next four quarters. Also, current sales along with the actual cost of goods sold, sales commissions, administrative expenses, and federal income taxes are needed for the current quarters. Using the estimates based on assumptions, projected quarterly income over four periods can be displayed for high-growth and low-growth projections in unit sales and selling prices along with income, representing the best-case and worst-case forecasts. Additionally, sensitivity analysis allows the company's managers to examine the impact of a change in one variable. A more rigorous multidimensional analysis can be performed by varying a number of variables to see what impact each change has on net profit on sales. In this way, managers can evaluate how sensitive the model is to changes in given variables.

Another forecasting approach is to utilize one of the popular software packages available today. For example, Forecast Pro for Windows allows users to let the package—via its expert system—determine the best forecasting model based on the software's observation of the data. The software package recommends a forecasting model and will even explain why a particular model was selected. This feature provides an accurate model as well as teaches the user what to look for when analyzing a data series.

Comparison of Company Against Competitors and Noncompetitors

Going beyond assistance in the preparation of final flexible budgets and review of quarterly financial forecasts, a KMS approach is also helpful in measuring a company's operations against competitors as well as noncompetitors. To enable corporation executives to accomplish such analysis, there may be a need for information and knowledge from external databases. That is, specific information and knowledge for such analysis must be stored on-line for later use by executives. When executives develop plans that center on improving productivity for manufacturing operations, adequate information and knowledge are available to set the wheels in motion for developing short- to long-range strategic plans for beating or, at least, meeting competition. Similarly, external financial information and knowledge about competition can be stored on-line so that executives can measure their own corporation's performance against the competition. In this manner, executives can see where the corporation is experiencing good, average, or poor performance in its major areas of operation against the best of its competitors.

It should be noted that benchmarking against the competition poses problems. For one thing, comparisons with competitors may uncover practices that are unworthy of emulation. For another, while competitive benchmarking may help a corporation meet its competitors' performance, it is unlikely to reveal practices for beating them. Moreover, getting information about competitors is obviously difficult. Finally, it has been observed that people are more receptive to new ideas that come from outside their own industry. A noncompetitive investigation can give executives information about the best functional practices in any industry. These may include technological advances unrecognized in their own industry (like bar coding, which originated in the grocery industry but has since been widely applied). Adoption of these practices can help a corporation achieve a competitive advantage.

To place the preceding discussion in its proper perspective, one of the Xerox Corporation's most valuable and memorable benchmarking experiences was with L. L. Bean, Inc., the outdoor sporting goods retailer and mail order house. It was carried out by Xerox Logistics and Distribution (L&D), which is responsible for inventory management, warehousing, and transport of machines, parts, and supplies. Historically, productivity increases of Xerox's L&D had been 3 to 5 percent per year. Recently, it became clear that improvement was necessary to maintain profit margins in the face of industry price cuts.

The inventory control area had recently installed a new planning system, and the transportation function was capitalizing on opportunities presented by deregulation. Warehousing was next in line for improvement, and the distribution center managers wanted a change. They identified the picking area as the worst bottleneck in the receiving-through-shipping sequence. A new technology, automated storage and retrieval systems (ASRSs) for materials handling, had appeared on the scene and was the subject of hot debate in Xerox's distribution function. The corporation had just erected a high-rise ASRS warehouse for raw materials and assembly parts in Webster, New York, in the same complex as a large finished goods distribution center. Internal benchmarking evaluations by L&D showed that heavy investment in capital equipment for ASRS could not be cost justified for finished goods. They needed a different way to boost warehousing and materials handling productivity. But what?

The L&D unit assigned a staff member half-time to come up with a suitable noncompetitor to benchmark in the warehousing and materials handling areas. The staff member combed trade journals and conferred with professional associations and consultants to find the companies with the best reputations in the distribution business. He then targeted those companies with generic product characteristics and service levels similar to Xerox reprographic parts and supplies. The staff member had singled out L. L. Bean as the best candidate for benchmarking in terms of their warehouse operations.

The staff member was particularly struck with the L. L. Bean warehouse system design. Although extremely manual in nature, the design minimized the labor content, among other benefits. The operation also did not lend itself to automation of handling and picking. The design therefore relied on very basic handling techniques, but it was carefully thought out and implemented. In addition, the design was selected with the full participation of the hourly work force. It was the first warehouse operations designed by quality circles.

To the layperson, L. L. Bean products may bear no resemblance to Xerox parts and supplies. To the distribution professional, however, the analysis was striking; both companies had to develop warehousing and distribution systems to handle products diverse in size, shape, and weight. This diversity precluded the use of ASRS. Later, a Xerox team visited Bean's operations in Freeport, Maine. Besides the person in charge of benchmarking in L&D, the team consisted of a headquarters operations executive and a field distribution center manager. These two people represented the line employees who would ultimately make any changes. The findings resulted in L&D incorporating some of L. L. Bean's practices in a program to modernize Xerox's warehouses. These practices included materials location arranged by velocity, to speed the flow of materials and minimize picker travel distance as well as enhanced computer involvement in the picking operation. Xerox plans to put together a totally computer-managed warehouse.[10]

Knowledge Discovery Is Useful in Environmental Awareness Analysis

From a slightly different perspective, planning can take the form of environment awareness analysis, where the past is indicative of the future. Using a knowledge discovery package (i.e., KnowledgeSEEKER), national survey respondents were asked whether they could distinguish among ''reduce,'' ''reuse,'' and ''recycle.'' Presumably, those who perceive a difference are more sensitive to environmental issues and interventions. Thus, they would be more likely to distinguish among the three R's. As shown in Figure 6-6(a), 64.2% of the population distinguish among the three R's—that is, approximately two-thirds of the survey respondents were environmentally aware. In Figure 6-6(b), the effect of educational background on environmental awareness is shown: 80% of people who have graduated from a university are environmentally aware (as judged by the distinction they make among the three R's). Also, the incremental effect of ethnic background on environmental awareness (among those who had graduated from a university) is shown. A French Canadian, Bristish, French, or Eastern European ethnic background increases the respondent's likelihood of distinguishing among the three R's to 88.4%. The incremental effect of age is depicted in Figure 6-6(c). In those age categories between 18 and 64 (i.e., less than 65), environmental awareness increases to 90.9%. Finally, community size has an additional effect on environment awareness. As noted in Figure 6-6(d), 92% of the survey respondents from communities that are over 50,000 in population were environmentally aware. Overall, the tree diagram in Figure 6-6 indicates that environmental awareness is the combined effect of education, ethnic background, age, and community size.[11]

ESTABLISHING A KNOWLEDGE MANAGEMENT SYSTEM FOR GLOBAL BEST PRACTICES

Today, an effective KMS operating mode extends the flow of knowledge beyond national boundaries. Sales executives, for example, need to share vital

Figure 6-6
Tree Diagram Showing the Results of Environmental Awareness Analysis: Output from KnowledgeSEEKER

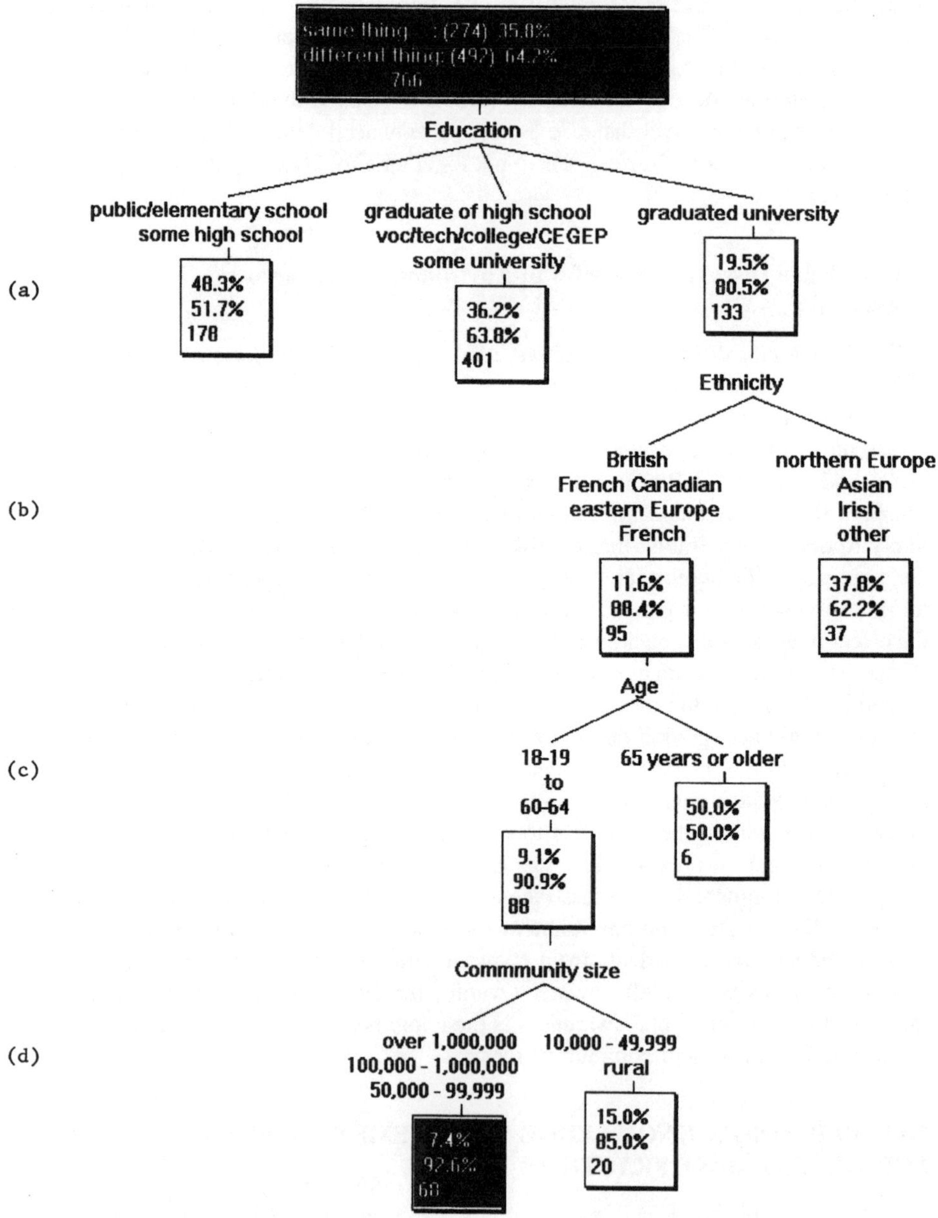

Source: Angoss Software International Limited.

statistics about customers, products, services, competitors, and selling techniques around the world. In order to do this, it is necessary to develop a KMS that encompasses the entire business world. Such an approach was taken by Arthur Andersen. Going beyond Knowledge Xchange—an in-house version of the kind of consulting help it sells its clients—Arthur Andersen in the early 1990s began creating the Global Best Practices (GBP) knowledge base.

Basically, the GBP is a central repository of knowledge about world-class business practices. The goal was to capture qualitative and quantitative information and knowledge about how companies achieve best-in-the world standards of performance in activities that are common to most companies regardless of their industry. This would then be used by Arthur Andersen's professionals to provide clients with an ever-growing body of knowledge that could serve as a reference point for performance improvement. The contents of the knowledge base include the following: best practices information, best company policies, top ten studies and articles, world-class performance measures, diagnostic tools, customizable presentations, process definitions and directory of internal experts, best control practices, tax implications, and relevant Arthur Andersen engagement experience.

Arthur Andersen gathers knowledge in different ways from a number of sources. The Global Best Practices hot line receives more than 250 calls each month. Calls are tracked on a Lotus Notes database and sorted into business process categories. This knowledge, combined with ongoing research into emerging areas, is used to determine which process areas will be developed or enhanced for an upcoming release. Research analysts team with content experts who serve clients to develop best practices content and diagnostic tools, about 250 pages per process. Quantitative and qualitative information and tools are released on a CD that can be accessed by all Arthur Andersen professionals worldwide and used in the field with clients. Best practices information is also generated through suggestions received by the hot line or captured through formal and informal surveys.

The impetus for building GBP came from the outside. Arthur Andersen needed to leapfrog competitors in the then-emerging area of best practices, so it set a three-month timetable to start advertising a resource tool to give clients access to best-practice insights. Although the tool did not exist at that time, the firm began to create, develop, and release the GBP knowledge base. The four-year initiative has taught the project's development team some unexpected lessons about implementing changes that fundamentally shift a company's culture and the way it does business. Many of these lessons contradict generally accepted ideas about what constitutes good planning and execution. A thorough reading of the important strategic planning principles set forth earlier in the chapter are indicative of these lessons.[12]

SUMMARY

The central theme of this chapter concerned strategic planning within a KMS environment to assist corporate managers and their corporate planning staffs in the proper acquisition, use, and disposition of an organization's resources. Because corporate strategic planning is an important focal point of information-based and knowledge-based systems, its purpose is to decide *what to do* in terms of strategic plans based on a company's mission, objectives, and goals, *how to* implement specific strategies and programs on time, and *when to* perform them to meet short-, medium-, and long-range strategic plans. Important relationships and feedback that exist among these basic elements were explored throughout the chapter. As a means of giving direction to a typical company in a changing world, the chapter examined initially the utilization of knowledge in executive visioning and strategic planning principles underlying knowledge of a company's total operations. Next, the important factors useful in discovering strategic planning knowledge were explored. A KMS approach was presented in the long run and the short run for a typical company to demonstrate the usefulness of knowledge to support managerial decisions. Finally, the establishment of knowledge management systems for determining global best practices was set forth.

NOTES

1. Robert J. Thierauf, *A Problem-Finding Approach to Effective Corporate Planning* (Westport, CT: Quorum Books, 1987); *User-Oriented Decision Support Systems—A Problem-Finding Approach* (Englewood Cliffs, NJ: Prentice-Hall, 1988); *Group Decision Support Systems for Effective Decision Making* (Westport, CT: Quorum Books, 1989); *Creative Computer Software for Strategic Thinking and Decision Making: A Guide for Senior Management and MIS Professionals* (Westport, CT: Quorum Books, 1993); and *On-Line Analytical Processing Systems for Business* (Westport, CT: Quorum Books, 1997).

2. Gary Hamel and C. K. Prahalad, "The Core Competence of the Corporation," *Harvard Business Review*, May–June 1990, p. 79.

3. Gary Hamel and C. K. Prahalad, "Corporate Imagination and Expeditionary Marketing," *Harvard Business Review*, July–August 1991, pp. 81–82.

4. Ibid., p. 83.

5. John F. Rockhart, "Chief Executives Define Their Own Data Needs," *Harvard Business Review*, March–April 1979, pp. 86–87.

6. Frances Gaither Tucker, Seymour M. Zivan, and Robert C. Camp, "How to Measure Yourself Against the Best," *Harvard Business Review*, January–February 1987, pp. 8–9.

7. Gerald Herter, "Practice Development, Business Planning Boosts Your Chances," *Accounting Technology*, April–May 1995, pp. 21–30.

8. Joel Kurtzman, "Is Your Company Off Course? Now You Can Find Out Why," *Fortune*, February 17, 1997, pp. 128–130.

9. Bill Richards, ''Working Together, The Business Plan,'' *The Wall Street Journal*, November 18, 1996, pp. R10 and R16.

10. Tucker, Zivan, and Camp, ''How to Measure Yourself Against the Best,'' p. 9.

11. Angoss Software, ''Study 9: Environment Awareness Analysis,'' *Knowledge-SEEKER in Action* (Toronto: Angoss Software International Limited, 1996).

12. Wendi Bukowitz, ''In the Know,'' *CIO*, April 15, 1996, pp. 24–32.

7

Application of Marketing Knowledge

Issued Explored:

- Why is it important to rethink the marketing mix for knowledge management systems?
- What marketing principles have been developed over time that are based on a thorough knowledge of customers?
- How can problem finding be used by marketing decision makers as a starting point in discovering marketing knowledge?
- What marketing areas typically lend themselves to discovering knowledge?
- How can knowledge discovery be used to develop an overall marketing strategy?

Outline:

USING KNOWLEDGE MANAGEMENT SYSTEMS IN MARKETING TO GAIN A COMPETITIVE ADVANTAGE

To better understand knowledge management systems in marketing, it is first necessary to focus on a company's customers and how they should be served. Information that is currently collected about customers and about products and services that can be provided to meet their current needs is related directly or indirectly to those marketing endeavors that focus on meeting customers' needs over time. From this perspective, effective knowledge management systems in marketing pay off in improved products and services, quicker problem solving for new products and services, reduced market research and development costs, and enhanced customer relations, to name a few. A leading-edge company therefore has the ability to gather, analyze, and distribute knowledge that keeps it ahead of competition.

Based on this knowledge orientation for marketing, the whole marketing function needs to be rethought from a long-range viewpoint. This discussion is found initially in the chapter along with the marketing principles that are based on a knowledge of customers. This background serves as a means for exploring the important factors that are useful in discovering marketing knowledge. Next, typical marketing areas that lend themselves to discovering knowledge are explored. Areas examined in more detail relate to marketing strategy and product pricing. Also, a typical marketing application using KnowledgeSEEKER is set forth. Finally, the relationship between competing on knowledge and competitive wisdom is highlighted.

RETHINKING THE ENTIRE MARKETING MIX

At the outset, it would be advisable to take a look at the entire marketing mix today and tomorrow. The focus is on rethinking how the typical marketing manager views the marketing mix—product, price, place, and promotion—in light of knowledge about these four items. For a company to be successful in the future, it must offer the *right products* at the *right price* in the *right place* along with the *right promotion.* Needless to say, a successful company must change with the times. There are fundamental changes in demographics and consumer preferences in the 21st century that will force companies to rethink their marketing mix.

In the retailing field, for example, marketing executives must be responsive to altering *product offerings* at the appropriate time. Traditionally, retailers selected their merchandise assortments for breadth and depth. To meet ever-changing consumer preferences, however, retailers need to change their thinking. For example, retailers such as the Limited Stores and The Gap have stuck with their original formulas of offering a small focused assortment in great depth. A stroll through any of the regional malls reveals many similar specialty merchants—stores that sell exclusively sunglasses, nuts, brushes, bathing suits, and so forth. These specialty stores represent the traditional departments in a department store. However, these changes for the times may be inappropriate in the near future.

Regarding *pricing strategy* and *promotion*, retailers, for example, have a method for carving out a niche for themselves. The meteoric rise of discounters in the past reached its peak primarily because of heavy competition in that market. Currently, growth appears greatest among those firms that dominate their categories. The reason is that they have become market leaders within a chosen segment. The ability of these super discounters to offer both broader and deeper assortments within a limited category ensures them steady traffic without extensive promotional price cutting. Currently, many pricing trends focus on everyday low prices and high/low promotional pricing. Although promotions encourage comparison shopping to obtain the best price, many people with demands on their time cannot do that and instead will trade potential savings for time. This partially explains the success of Wal-Mart. From a management perspective, everyday low pricing means labor savings because of reduced marking and remarking of price tags, and fewer stock shortages on the promotional items.

The changing demographics are best illustrated in the emergence of *new channels of distribution* and the resurgence of some old channels of distribution. The demand for convenience, not just price, has allowed nonstore retailers to flourish. Since the technology is changing so rapidly, it is impossible to know exactly what the future will bring. Currently, some of the important trends are: hypermarkets, electronic shopping, mail-order catalog/direct mail, and manufacturer's outlets.

Knowledge Is Customer Focus

Attemps to get a handle on the marketing mix today tend to focus on some type of information analysis that is multidimensional in nature. More specifically, this centers around on-line analytical processing that helps marketing managers explore the effectiveness of their marketing operations. Although this approach has proven to be helpful, there is a need to go a step further and center on knowledge that has the customer as the focus. In essence, any company that hopes to win over its customers in the long term must have in place a process to identify and meet customer expectations on at least three levels. These include basic expectations of the product or service before purchasing, stated performance requirements of the product or service after purchasing, and arising needs for newer additions to the product or service over time.

Typically, where the customer is the focus of marketing efforts, there is an emphasis on these key points: who are the customers; what do they need or want; how does the company deliver satisfaction today, how can the company improve the delivery; and what measurements does the company need to build in to make sure those requirements are being meet. As a result of this far reaching approach to knowledge about its customers, a company maintains a broad-based orientation that allows it to understand them holistically.

Going one step further, by being knowledgeable about its customers, a company can gain important knowledge about its industry. It can pull together and aggregate knowledge to provide it with benchmarks to compare against industry averages. Focusing on industries rather than on its products or services allows the company to leverage knowledge to add value beyond the basic product or service. The bottom line is that customer knowledge gives the company a real competitive advantage in the short to long run.

Marketing Principles Based on Knowledge of Customers

Over the years, a number of marketing principles based on a direct or indirect knowledge of customers have been developed. One important principle revolves around the development and maintenance of core competencies of a company's products and services. Core competencies are the backbone of business development since they constitute the focus for strategy at the corporate level. They represent the core of a company's operations in terms of its products and services. Generally, if a company is conceived of as a hierarchy of core competencies, core products, and market-focused business units only, then it will be able to survive in the long run. Cultivating core competence does not mean outspending rivals on research and development or becoming more vertically integrated. Rather, the focus is on doing what is necessary to ensure the continuing success of the company's basic businesses today and tomorrow. Essentially, core competence should grow and not deteriorate over time.

To assist marketing management in getting a handle on the changing times and the changes affecting their core products and services, there is a need for market research information gathered internally as well as information gained from market research forms. It should be noted that market researchers can also obtain appropriate information from magazines and newsletters, conferences, financial reports, trade and government organizations, and the Internet. No matter what the sources of market research used, it should be employed carefully. That is, it should be more than a mere guide for marketing managers to develop and support market-based decisions. Market research information should assist marketing management in anticipating what customers want before they are aware of their needs for products and services. As such, market research information over time can be assessed in terms of what has and is happening and what probably will happen to customers' needs for goods and services tomorrow. This broad-based approach to market research will give corporate management some insight into knowledge about the company's core products and services and where the company should be heading.

Typically, successful products today are the result of small and incremental innovations in design and manufacturing as well as marketing over the years. Management must maintain a commitment to the product or service over a long period of incremental improvements. For example, Procter & Gamble persisted with research for 10 years to make Pampers affordable for the mass market. Because marketing management requires vision and persistence over many years against great odds, companies need to commit finances for the long run. Specifically, they need to address access to financial resources and willingness to use those resources. Enduring market leaders are companies that commit the required resources at the proper time.

When consideration is given to the development of new products and services, corporate management needs to know how many projects its organizations can handle and how quickly those projects can deliver new products and services to market. From this view, product development can be thought of as a production process in which projects move through a knowledge work process equivalent to that of a job shop operation. Typically, companies that have applied process management to product development have found that projects get finished faster if the company takes on fewer at a time. Investments to relieve bottlenecks also yield improved time-to-market benefits. Overall, a company may be able to beat its competitors to market for new goods and services.

To assist large companies in meeting marketing challenges from smaller companies, newer information technology such as knowledge management systems is helping them to sort massive amounts of information to target small groups of responsive customers almost automatically. For example, a large supermarket chain can use point-of-scale scanning and frequent shopper programs to build a sophisticated customer database. Extensive consumer information enables this supermarket chain to stock each store according to the preferences of local customers at the same time that it centralizes its buying process. Also, such customer purchasing programs can be used to target individual consumers and, eventually, individual households. Overall, massive amounts of information can be culled to discern trends and patterns that are useful in targeting small groups of highly responsive customers.

Although newer information technologies allow companies to get a better understanding of their customers, there still seems to be a feeling among marketing managers that there is a straightforward linear relationship between customer satisfaction and loyalty. In reality, in markets where customers have a choice, the difference between the loyalty of completely satisfied customers and somewhat satisfied customers is quite different. In essence, competition can change somewhat quickly. Marketing managers who do not put forth their best efforts to satisfy their customers totally are at risk. In contrast, providing customers with outstanding products and services works in a positive way to achieve sustained customer satisfaction. For the most part, marketing managers who push excellence in satisfying customers are good at listening to their customers and in interpreting what customers with different levels of satisfaction are telling them.

Current thinking in marketing processes goes outside the typical operations of the marketing department. The focus is on tying together a company with its suppliers and customers by integrating processes and information flows with theirs. The real advantage is not in cost savings, but in interlinking businesses so they can help one another better. A progressive company today no longer battles its suppliers, but rather joins forces with them to bring products to market faster or to achieve other mutual advantages. For example, Wal-Mart, which started out with electronic data interchange in the early days, has moved far beyond that technology to a system developed in-house through which the company openly shares information with its suppliers. In fact, that system, called RetailLink, goes so far as to put each supplier roughly on an equal footing, in terms of information, with Wal-Mart's own internal buyers and financial analysts. In effect, Wal-Mart has moved its integration up and down the supply and demand chain to better meet customer needs.

In addition to the above, a number of other marketing principles that are based on knowledge of customers have been developed over time. A most notable source is Profit Impact of Marketing Strategies (PIMS), a computerized approach for planning market strategy run by the Strategic Planning Institute. It is a data pool of information on the marketing experiences of its members.[1] Several hundred corporations submit data annually on a total of about 3,000 of their business units, each of which is a distinct product-market unit. Each member provides PIMS with the most intimate details on matters such as its market share, investment intensity, product quality, and total marketing and R&D expenditures. Through computer simulation the company can then test its own market strategies against the real experiences of hundreds of comparable companies, including competitors. What it receives are answers to questions such as these: What is the normal profit rate for a business or a product line given its combination of circumstances, and why? If the business continues on its current track, what will its future operating results be? What will happen to short- and long-term performance if certain strategic moves are made? What changes will create the best profits or cash returns?

One of the findings that has emerged from the PIMS computer models of the real-life experiences of its corporate members is that there is a set of operating rules that governs all businesses. Some 37 factors—including market share, capital intensity, and vertical integration—jointly explain 80 percent of the success or failure of any business; only 20 percent of a business's return-on-investment can be attributed to factors that are unique or special, such as the quality of working relations. Other PIMS findings indicate that a larger market share is strongly linked to higher profits and that product quality is also very positively related to return on investment. When product quality is low, it does not pay most companies to have high marketing expenditures. High research and development spending hurts profitability when market position is weak but increases it when market share is high. In this situation, copying competitors' products rather than inventing new ones is probably the best bet. In addition, higher investment intensity (i.e., ratio of total investment to sales) is associated with lower ROI, and high investment intensity combined with low market share is an ROI disaster.

Typically, what a member wants from PIMS is to find out what it will cost to make a particular strategic move and how much better off the business will be afterward. For example, consider return on investment, which PIMS considers one of the best measures of how a business is doing. The PIMS models can forecast how much ROI for a business line will change because of a strategic move involving more marketing, research and development, capital equipment buildup, or whatever—both what the return on investment will be immediately following the move and what it will be several years in the future. Principles that have emerged from the PIMS computer models of the real-life experiences of its corporate members plus others are summarized in Figure 7-1.

IMPORTANT FACTORS THAT ARE USEFUL IN DISCOVERING MARKETING KNOWLEDGE

To have global success today and tomorrow, companies need to focus on corporate visioning (refer to the prior chapter) rather than a "me-too" product attitude. *Visioning* of the marketing function is envisioning markets for products and services that do not exist today. For example, "smart" or knowledge-based products are coming that gather and interpret information over time to enable customers to act more effectively in their daily routines. A typical company should generate new products and services so that the company is out there ahead all on its own, as Raytheon should have been with the microwave oven and variations of it many years ago. In the 21st centry and beyond, marketing battles will be won by companies that can build and dominate fundamentally new markets.

Creative new smart products, such as speech-activated appliances, household microrobots, and self-parking cars, not only make the inconceivable conceivable but also allow a company to influence the direction of a current well-established market. As more and more companies close the gap with their rivals on costs,

Figure 7-1
Marketing Principles Based on Knowledge of Customers

- The focus of core competencies is to do what is necessary to ensure the continuing success of the company's basic businesses today and tomorrow.
- The main thrust of market research information is to assist marketing management in anticipating what customers want before they are aware of these needs for goods and services.
- Successful products are the result of small and incremental innovations in design, marketing, and manufacturing over the years.
- Development of products and services can be thought of as a productive process in which projects move through a knowledge work process like that of a job shop.
- The capability of today's information technology to sort through massive amounts of information to target small groups of highly responsive customers allows large companies to own market niches the way small companies do.
- Listening to customers and interpreting what customers with different levels of satisfaction are saying on the part of marketing management is the difference between the loyalty of completely satisfied customers and somewhat satisfied customers.
- Successful marketing efforts integrate a company's operations, from its suppliers through to its customers, and feedback is an important part of the entire integration process.
- Some 37 factors, such as market share, capital intensity, and vertical integration, explain 80 percent of the success or failure of any business, while only 20 percent of a business's return on investment can be attributed to unique or special factors.
- High marketing expenditures for low-quality products can have a devastating effect on profits.
- Larger market share is strongly linked to higher profits.
- High product quality can offset a weak market position.
- Anything more than a minimal research and development program does not make sense for a company with a weak market position.
- Weak companies should not become vertically integrated, whereas strong ones should.

quality, and delivery, they need to have the capability to stake out new territories with products and services. Hence, there is need for a new direction that is tied in with the ability to analyze via a knowledge management system where the company has been over time as well as where it should be headed.

Some of the important factors that are useful in discovering marketing knowledge are given below. They are: (1) problem finding in discovering marketing knowledge, (2) expanded view of market research and analysis, (3) database marketing to discover knowledge about customers, (4) using the Internet to take advantage of marketing opportunities, and (5) software useful in discovering marketing knowledge.

Problem Finding in Discovering Marketing Knowledge

Typically, marketing planning and control for a company are related directly to knowledge management systems since the obtainment of market planning information often involves the employment of computerized mathematical and statistical models that enable marketing managers to retain control over problem solving. In addition, these models are useful in problem finding in that marketing managers can solve complex marketing problems. Since marketing managers are leaders who communicate with work groups, motivate employees, and supervise ongoing organizational activities, the computer is an extremely important tool that can assist them in decision making. From this view, marketing managers are able to increase their effectiveness by employing knowledge management systems to get a grip on future opportunities that are afforded by newer directions in marketing, such as the smart products mentioned above. Marketing managers need a knowledge of surrounding environmental factors and a vision of their responsibilities. They must also take the initiative to cope with change. A knowledge management system, then, can assist them in the analyses of problem solving and problem finding as well as resolving problems and identifying future opportunities for developing new products and services.

For example, the use of the problem-finding process for a typical manufacturing company centers on marketing managers seeking satisfactory solutions to their problems. In a similar manner, production and financial managers seek good answers to their problems. Unfortunately, each has a different, and possibly narrow, perspective. To manage the marketing area (as well as other areas) effectively, the company needs to utilize problem finding for future problems so that the marketing-manufacturing interface clearly produces the best results for the company. Seasonal sales can be forecast and slack periods can receive the benefit of promotional efforts in order to smooth sales and reduce variations in production and inventory levels. In addition, production savings can be compared with promotional costs, and a coordinated budget can be developed to reduce overall costs. Problems of conflicting objectives, underutilization of resources, overreaction to changing economic indicators, and rigid budgetary constraints that prohibit the company from optimizing its overall objectives can be overcome. The solution, then, is to implement planning of the marketing function with the company's other functional areas through a problem-finding approach. In effect, the company needs to look out into the future and to bring its problems back to the present for solution, relating its marketing area to other functional areas. From this enlarged perspective, a knowledge management system in marketing is an important link in a company's total corporate strategy for meeting the needs of its customers today and tomorrow.

Expanded View of Market Research and Analysis

An important part of market research is to lead a company's customers where they want to go before they know it themselves with help from marketing knowledge. For example, NEC pursues a telephone that will interpret between callers speaking in different languages, while Motorola envisions a world in which telephone numbers are attached to people rather than places, and where a personal communicator allows millions of out-of-touch business travelers to be reached anywhere. In a similar manner, smart or knowledge-based products, such as diapers that change color when wet or a tire that alerts the driver of its low air pressure, diagnose and interpret the immediate environment to enable customers to act more effectively.[2] From this expanded view of market research, market research analysts are examining new opportunities that require in-depth insight into customers' needs, lifestyles, and aspirations. Needless to say, companies that are competent in utilizing marketing knowledge rather than just information will be more successful than those that do not.

Companies that succeed in educating customers about what is possible develop both marketers with technological imagination and technologists with marketing imagination. For example, in one Japanese company, senior technical officers spend as many as 30 days a year outside Japan talking to customers. The aim is not to solve technical problems or to close a sale, but rather to listen and observe customers and absorb their thinking over time. In another example, a Japanese chief engineer of a major new business development program lived for a time with an American family thought to be representative of the customers his company hoped to win. Again, the goal is not to improve the flow of information between marketers and engineers or to manage the balance of power between the two groups, but rather to blur organizational and career boundaries by ensuring that both communities have a large base of shared experiences. The net result is a good mixture of market and technical imagination which, in turn, underlies marketing knowledge over time.[3]

An expanded view of market research and analysis centers on virtual reality systems (for more about this, see a recent book by the author).[4] Recent advances in three-dimensional modeling along with computer graphics have made it possible for market researchers to recreate an actual retail store on a computer screen. Virtual shopping simulations are easy to undertake and low in cost. Being extremely flexible, market researchers can change the assortment of brands on display within seconds to minutes. The virtual store gives market researchers the freedom to exercise their marketing knowledge early in the product development process without risk. As such, virtual reality can be used as a strategic tool that can change the way companies approach issues ranging from entering new markets to responding to new competition. The capability to compare one marketing approach against another gives market researchers new knowledge within a short time frame that was not possible with prior approaches.

Database Marketing to Discover Knowledge About Customers

As markets grow more competitive and companies focus on competitive advantage, it becomes increasingly clear that marketing management needs to keep existing customers happy while trying to find new ones. For the most part, database marketing is a *customer-centric approach* that helps a company discover what individual customers are buying, know how often they have been contacted, and see which marketing strategies have been most effective for individual customers. Giving customers what they want is more essential than ever, and database marketing is a key to reaching this goal. Recent studies have shown that approximately 80 percent of recurring revenues come from 20 percent of a client base. As such, database marketing provides the tools to discover who makes up that 20 percent of this base so that marketing management can target campaigns to those customers or look for replacements.

Database marketing can be looked upon as an extension of the data warehouse concept (as set forth in Chapter 3). In a broad sense, database marketing is a set of activities ranging from promotional selling to strategic market analysis that centers on the collection, analysis, and use of individual customer attributes and behavior patterns. In the past, marketing databases were built on mainframes or mid-range systems. The trend is to distribute query and analysis functions through client/server architectures. Client/server configurations provide flexibility, high speeds, and user-friendly interfaces. Additionally, they can easily be linked to PC-based applications for additional analysis and presentation, all at a fraction of mainframe computer costs.

Some companies develop marketing databases strictly as analytical tools to maintain, consolidate, and analyze information captured by other transactional processing systems, while other companies use them to automate both transaction and analysis functions. Typically, companies gather large amounts of data on customers and their buying habits. In turn, marketing database software helps companies merge data from separate files, thereby yielding new information about customer attitudes and preferences, while computers and analytical tools help marketers discover knowledge to gain a deeper understanding of marketing trends in consumer behavior. In this process, raw data is transformed into useful information and, through the use of sophisticated tools, converted into useful marketing knowledge. Overall, database marketing is enabling companies to learn more about their customers so that they can better anticipate what products and services customers are likely to buy.

Using the Internet to Take Advantage of Marketing Opportunities

The Internet (as discussed in Chapter 4) has opened up new opportunities for a typical company to market goods and services. In turn, new knowledge can be gathered about a company's customers. However, determining how to take advantage of the opportunities this new channel is creating is another matter for a typical company. Essentially, the Internet poses a challenge for established businesses. The opportunities presented include providing for direct links to anyone anywhere, thereby allowing the Internet to be used to build interactive relationships with customers and suppliers as well as deliver new products and services at very low cost. It should be noted that established businesses that have carefully built brands and physical distribution relationships risk damaging all they have created when they pursue commerce in cyberspace. In addition, because Internet commerce is such a new phenomenon, it is difficult for top managers at most companies (new or old) to decide the best way to utilize the channel.

Nonetheless, top managers cannot afford to avoid thinking about the impact of the Internet on their businesses. At the very least, they need to understand the important opportunities available to them and recognize how their companies may be vulnerable if competitors seize those opportunities first. To determine what opportunities and threats the Internet poses, top managers should systematically focus on what the Internet can allow their particular organization to do. Essentially, the Internet presents several opportunities. The first of these is the establishment of a direct link to customers or to others with whom they have important relationships (such as critical suppliers or distributors) to complete transactions or trade information more easily and at lower cost. Next, the technology lets companies bypass others in the supply chain. A publisher, for example, could bypass retailers or distributors and sell directly to readers. Companies can also use the Internet to develop and deliver new products and services for new customers. Lastly, a company could conceivably use the Internet to become the dominant player in the electronic channel of a specific industry or segment, controlling access to customers and setting new business rules.

To place the foregoing into perspective, consider how the Internet could affect companies like Dell and Compaq as suppliers of computer equipment to General Electric. Several major divisions of General Electric are completing plans to put parts and equipment up for bid on the Internet. These divisions intend to deal directly with suppliers over the Internet and to receive multiple bids for every part. Based on early tests, General Electric estimates that many millions can be shaved off its purchasing costs and its purchasing cycle times can be cut by as much as 50 percent. The company expects that it will purchase the majority of everything it buys through this web-based bidding system. Because Dell sells computer equipment directly to its customers, sometimes over the Internet, while Compaq sells through distributors, Compaq could be placed at a major disadvantage for GE's business. Its distribution costs are higher, its pricing and information systems are designed for conducting business through distributors, and any move Compaq makes toward accepting orders over the Internet could threaten those distributors. Overall, the utilization of the Internet has become a requirement for most companies. For a multinational company whose global customers demand an even higher level of service, making better information and resulting knowledge available to more of the people who need it is a competitive imperative.

Software Useful in Discovering Marketing Knowledge

In Chapter 5, the employment of data mining software in knowledge management systems along with other software was emphasized. Some of the software vendors that centered their products around on-line analytical processing have upgraded their product line to include data mining. In the past, OLAP tools have provided companies with multidimensional analysis to better understand, for example, point-of-sale and competitive data. These tools give them the insight they need to meet their competition. Today, data mining tools provide the capability to go a step further by being able to analyze a customer database and identify groups of customers who have similar characteristics and make predictions for those groups. As noted throughout the text, data mining is the act of drilling through huge volumes of information in order to discover relationships or to answer specific questions that are too broad in nature for traditional query and OLAP tools.

In the recent past, data mining has been mainly used for specialized applications, such as analyzing credit card data or supermarket retail information. However, now a much wider range of companies are seeking ways to mine large data warehouses. For example, profiling and segmenting customer data helps a company to know its customers better. Marketing managers can be assisted in looking at products to which customers are most likely to be attracted and looking at the best ways to sell these products.

To help marketing managers gain a better understanding of marketing knowledge software, vendors are teaming up to assist typical companies in their data mining efforts. For example, Lightbridge, Inc. (a leading provider of integrated customer acquisition and retention solutions for the wireless industry) has partnered with Pilot Software to develop a set of applications that provide wireless carriers with detailed intelligence about their customers, sales channels, trends, and patterns. Using predictive data mining, carriers can predict the future and determine which customers are most likely to switch carriers. Analyzing the history of customers, Pilot Discovery Server from Pilot Software, Inc. predicts future customer behavior by creating a predictive model from the information in the data warehouse. The predictive model analyzes the customers who have disconnected and those who have renewed, determining the probability that a current customer with a particular profile will disconnect. The results of the model help the carrier understand the factors that influence churn—that is, which customers are most likely to defect to another company and why.

Lightbridge had two major requirements that the Discovery Server addressed, allowing the company to be successful in solving the churn problem. Lightbridge needed a product that could be developed quickly against substantial data warehouses, and the results had to be both understandable and directly accessible by business users. By utilizing SQL (structured query language) to obtain the data, Pilot's Discovery Server works directly in the warehouse. Unlike other products, Discovery Server does not require any special extracts or duplication, thereby making the process easier and also minimizing data redundancy. The resulting predictive model provides customer profiles that make it very easy to understand each segment and the differences among them.

Because an important goal of data mining is to discover hidden facts contained in databases, data mining is among the most strategic applications in companies when it is applied correctly because of the enormous payoffs it brings. Other applications for data mining include fraud detection, identifying good credit risks, product warranty management, evaluating the effectiveness of retail promotions, and reducing customer turnover for service companies. Data mining centers on finding answers to questions that marketing managers do not know enough to ask. It allows marketing managers to discover new marketing knowledge. Thus, a company can harness its intellectual assets by getting the right information quickly into the hands of the right marketing personnel via its knowledge management system.

KNOWLEDGE MANAGEMENT SYSTEMS IN MARKETING

The ultimate accomplishment of knowledge management systems is their ability to respond instantaneously and effectively to marketing opportunities, improve customer satisfaction, and help beat competition. Within this framework, knowledge management systems in marketing need to have a company's collective ''sixth sense.'' That is, they need to embody the marketing principles set forth previously plus those that are relevant to future markets. Similarly, knowledge management systems in marketing need to incorporate the important factors that have been found to be helpful in discovering marketing knowledge. The net result of this knowledge is that a company has the the capability of being one step ahead of competition. A company's competitors can copy all they want, but they cannot copy the real collective marketing wisdom of its marketing management. As a result, competitors find themselves repeating what is already in the marketplace and are always a year or two behind.

This collective sixth sense approach by marketing management and their staffs accents the need for a *proactive* approach to meeting the needs of customers instead of being *reactive*. For example, say a customer phones to reserve a room at a hotel for an eagerly awaited out-of-town vacation. After the dates and rates are agreed upon, the reservations operator begins to ask the usual questions. The customer responds that he is a member of the hotel's frequent guest program. After the customer gives his account number, the operator informs him that this frequent hotel account has been terminated because of inactivity. Although the customer has an urgent impulse to tell the operator what he really thinks about the guest program, good judgment prevails. In retrospect, the chain's lack of marketing savvy to collect information on customer preferences that it could have used to lure this customer back relatively easily with targeted marketing is simply a poor marketing strategy. In essence, the lack of a creative sixth sense caused this hotel chain to focus its sales attention on serving and expanding their relationships with active customers, thereby bypassing a huge potential market of inactive customers with some type of special offers.

Too often, companies purge their databases of inactive customers so that they do not waste data storage. But reducing costs this way is not a creative method for expanding a customer base. In effect, these companies are throwing away customer names while their advertising and marketing departments are spending many thousands, even millions, of dollars to identify and entice prospective customers. The cost of storing the data describing an inactive customer is generally much less than a penny, while the cost of identifying a new prospect can range from tens to hundreds of dollars. Moreover, every company knows more about the preferences and buying habits of the inactive customer than of the prospective customers. Why not, then, design a marketing program to induce inactive customers to do business again? A company that undertakes a creative, proactive approach to inactive customers can utilize a knowledge management system to help get a better handle on its customer base. A company cannot reap the rewards of marketing knowledge simply by buying some hardware and software. Instead, it must take a longer range view and acknowledge that ongoing marketing knowledge and intelligence is critical to new product development.

Areas That Lend Themselves to Discovering Marketing Knowledge

Marketing areas that lend themselves to discovering knowledge are varied, as will be seen in this second half of the chapter. The capability of sales and marketing decision makers to spot trends in the marketplace will be apparent in the following discussion. The capability to analyze key aspects of the changing marketing landscape and the capability of marketing managers to make key decisions about the present and future directions of markets will make a very important difference between being somewhat successful and being extremely successful. Related to these factors of marketing strategy is the issue of pricing a company's products and services to meet changing times. Other areas that typically lend themselves to discovering marketing knowledge include advertising, market research, and physical distribution. Due to space limitations, only the areas of marketing strategy and product pricing are treated below.

MARKETING STRATEGY

In a business environment characterized by global markets, faster product cycles, and shrinking profit margins, companies are spending millions of dollars annually on their marketing efforts. Success means that companies must constantly focus on identifying market changes. Their mission is to search the vast amounts of corporate data and information for answers that enable their companies to develop intelligent overall marketing strategies. Marketing managers therefore need a knowledge management system that delivers a wide range of marketing information and knowledge to their desks every day—information that allows them to spot market trends, rank products, analyze channel performance, or create quickly ad hoc views of sales by account or region. To be useful to the manager, the system must be timely, flexible, and intuitive. Such an approach is possible in marketing and its related functions with a knowledge management system.

Knowledge Discovery to Develop an Overall Marketing Strategy

In the development of an overall marketing strategy, discovery of marketing knowledge can be helpful initially in gaining an understanding of who the customer really is. As a starting point, it would helpful for marketing managers to internalize the marketing principles based on knowledge of customers set forth previously in Figure 7-1. As stated previously in the chapter, the customer is the most important entity in the distribution channel. That is why marketing managers need to consider the present needs and future wants of their customers in every step of the distribution channel. It is helpful for managers to spend a typical day in the lives of their small-, medium-, and large-size customers from the standpoint of meeting their needs today and their wants tomorrow. For example, even though a company shiping might think it is doing well by 95 percent of its orders on time on the average, the customer may view things differently, since its order must be 100 percent complete before it can introduce the item into production. This is where on-line analytical processing can come into play. Multidimensional analysis can be used to help understand the customer's viewpoint. In the example given, multidimensional analysis of three variables (percent of shipments received on time, percent of shipments received late, and days late for remaining items) may give marketing managers a better perception of its operations through the eyes of a typical customer. Although the results may not be very positive, OLAP is capable of presenting a realistic picture to marketing managers—good, bad, or indifferent.

Knowledge of customers' needs is critical, as is an understanding of how a company can assist its marketing managers to develop an overall marketing strategy by concentrating on customer satisfaction. Typically, retaining existing customers is usually much more profitable than focusing on acquiring new customers. Even though many companies state that customers are important, often company employees do not rate customer satisfaction as a top priority of their company. Many times, there is a large gap between what a company says it does and what its customers perceived it as doing. Hence, knowledge of customer needs and how the company has or has not met those needs can be used to determine the degree of customer satisfaction or lack thereof.

An effective way to employ knowledge in order to develop an overall marketing strategy can be found in the marketing efforts of well-known companies. For example, the Procter & Gamble Company has undertaken a global initiative to make its marketing efforts more efficient. In its Market Breakthrough 2000 plan, the effects of P&G's effort to find more efficient ways of marketing its wide array of products can already be seen in the Cincinnati-based company's United States operations. In the United States, P&G is building closer ties to a reduced number of outside companies that do everything from artwork to package design to printing materials for promotional campaigns. Procter & Gamble is looking at its whole system of developing and executing its marketing programs with its suppliers to find ways to improve flexibility, save time, and get the results it seeks at a lower cost. Additionally, P&G is leveraging its size as the nation's largest advertiser in terms of spending by using one agency to make all of its media purchases.

Knowledge of Customers to Select a Specific Marketing Strategy

Using knowledge of customers over time, marketing managers in a typical company can create a marketing strategy for next year. As a beginning point in this example, there are comparable data to work with: surveys, market tests, and market audits performed by the market research department. But none of them answer the important questions. What would happen to contribution to fixed costs and profit if the number of users increased next year for the company's products—that is, the "proportion usage" increased over the current year? Similarly, what would happen to contribution to fixed costs and profit if the "rate of usage per year" for the current number of users increased next year over this year?

To answer these two questions, it is necessary to analyze the past and future possible demand for the company's products in order to develop specific knowledge. In turn, a particular marketing strategy based on this analysis can be developed by marketing managers to change certain events and thus increase sales. For example, a most important element is the market segment of newly formed families who are concerned about using the product. As noted above, there are two possible strategies for increased demand: (1) increase the proportion of buyers in this market segment or (2) increase the usage rate of those who current buy the product. In addition, these strategies can be developed over optimistic, average, and pessimistic conditions.

Although in this example multidimensional analysis can be used to analyze the components of the problem in order to answer the preceding questions, generally, historical data on the number of persons, proportion buying, and rate of buying per year are given along with the unit price and variable costs percentage, and the number of buyers expected must come from a knowledge of the company's customers over time. To increase the proportion-using category, say from 60 percent to 65 percent under *pessimistic* conditions (first case), 70 percent under *average* conditions (second case), and 75 percent under *optimistic* conditions (third case), appropriate multidimensional analysis can be undertaken in terms of contribution to fixed costs and profit by products and cases. An alternative is to accept the 60 percent proportion, for example, and find a way to increase the usage rate next year for products, say from 1.95 to 2.15 people under *pessimistic* conditions (fourth case), 2.25 people under *average* conditions (fifth case), and 2.35 people under *optimistic* conditions (sixth case). In each of these six cases, a strategy can be translated into an estimated contribution to fixed costs and profit by products and time periods. Based upon the circumstances, the best marketing strategy is selected—such as an increase in buyer usage—to give the greatest return for the company's products under study for future time periods. However, it should be noted that there might be shifts in the company's markets over time. Hence, knowledge of the company's customers may indicate the need to redo the study to ensure that the company is pursuing the best marketing strategy.

Advertising Strategy for a Direct Mail Campaign

An example of using KnowledgeSEEKER (from Angoss Software) is one that revolves around the use of direct and database marketing.[5] Telemarketing and direct mail can be cost-effective ways of getting a company's sales message across. Like all sales efforts, these are most effective if sales prospects are qualified first. Current statistical recordkeeping technology offers a number of advantages to direct mail and telemarketing managers who are looking for ways of stretching their marketing dollars. Many data sets contain vital demographic and purchase pattern data about potential buyers, including their postal codes. Zip codes can be translated into a targeted mailing or, when cross referenced to telephone numbers located in the target area, can be translated into a qualified list of potential purchasers.

Initially, it is necessary to generate the desired purchase profile according to postal area, followed by a product to sell. In this case, the product is a retirement savings plan investment package. The company wants potential contributors to subscribe to its financial services and plans to sell to them on the basis of the performance of its investment fund over the past and on the basis of endorsements of the service that have been received from previous customers. The company identifies a relevant data set that contains information on the retirement savings plan contributions that have been made by individuals in the target area, taken from their previous year's tax records. The data has been aggregated so that each record contains summary information for a number of reporting units (to preserve the confidentiality of individual tax filers). In addition, the company has on file information about average retirement savings contribution, postal area, neighborhood age profile, and income and tax paid. The results are presented in a tree format per Figure 7-2.

Figure 7-2
Tree Diagram About Customers for a Telemarketing and Direct Mail Campaign Using KnowledgeSEEKER

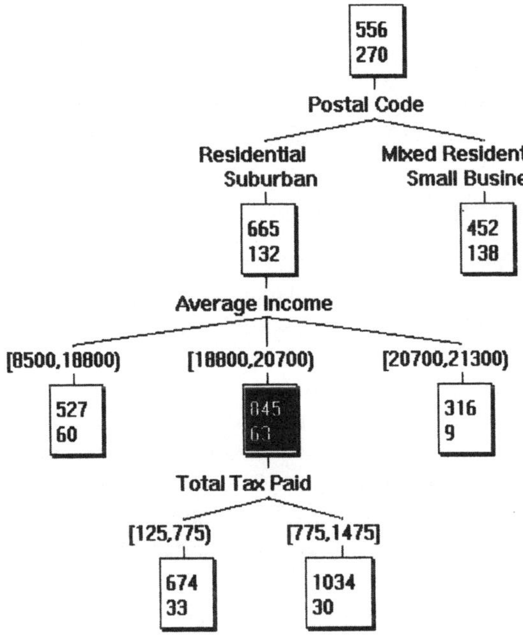

Source: Angoss Software International Limited.

As shown in this figure, the focus of the company's marketing campaign could be improved considerably if it just narrowed in on the residential and suburban postal code areas because the average retirement savings plan was $665 (132 summary record reporting). This is considerably more than the other areas. Within these postal areas, the next best bet is to target people whose average income is between $18,800 and $20,700. These people make greater average retirement savings plan contributions than even higher income earners (an average contribution of $845). Within this group, the best bet is to focus on people who paid a higher than average tax, (i.e., those whose taxes were higher tended to have a large contribution). At this point, the company has developed an appropriate advertising strategy and a specific range of addresses. The advertising strategy is simple and time-tested. Retirement savings plan contributions are an investment in one's future and a way of reducing the amount of money that one would have to spend for taxes anyway. The company could quote specific figures, based on actual tax records, that could be used to compare prospective buyers to other contributors.

Additionally, addresses could be identified by the number and block face codes that are attached to the postal code. These could be automatically generated from the company's file. These codes could have been used to focus on telephone numbers, but the company elected to pursue a direct mail and advertising strategy since the message—the tax savings of retirement savings plan contributions—is ideally suited to this kind of approach. Overall, a direct mail and advertising campaign for residential suburban people of average income proved to be the best strategy, based upon an in-depth knowledge of potential customers from the company's data files.

PRODUCT PRICING

Pricing of a company's products (as noted previously in the chapter) is one of the four elements comprising the marketing mix. Because of the complexity of the marketing environment, there is a great need for setting correct prices. Pricing is a problem when a new product is being introduced, when a price change is contemplated in the face of uncertain customer and competitor reactions, or when a company must react to a competitor that has just changed its price. Pricing is also a problem when sealed bids must be submitted. And it is a problem when the company's product line is characterized by substantial demand and cost interdependencies. In view of these problems, new product pricing can best be determined by applying appropriate statistical or mathematical models as well as data mining tools to proposed selling prices and estimated demand. Such an approach can be an integral part of venture analysis of a new product or service (as discussed below). In addition, there is a need to evaluate pricing as it relates to competition as well as the relationship between product quality and price charged. It should be recognized that low-quality products mean that premium prices cannot be charged. Similarly, a weak market position has a detrimental affect on prices charged to customers. Many of these product pricing areas are addressed below.

Using Knowledge to Price Products over Their Life Cycle

One of the most extensive and sophisticated marketing mathematical models is *venture analysis*. It is an investment planning system for analyzing new opportunities and encompasses such techniques as probability, decision theory, and the time value of money as well as mathematical modeling. Because it is a massive system of gathering, relating, appraising, and projecting all data pertinent to a complete business venture over its life cycle, this mathematical technique stores many kinds of information. All costs involved in the product project are developed. Manufacturing costs include raw materials, direct labor, depreciation, and overhead. These data are modeled for each step of the production process. For the pricing and promotional effort, product prices are estimated at various desired levels to determine the optimum price. All promotional costs involved in marketing the product are broken down by media selected and projected. Research and development costs plus general and administrative costs are scheduled to make the data complete.

An important part of the venture analysis model is knowledge on the part of marketing modelers about the proper determination of prices at various stages over the life cycle of the product. Utilizing a pricing approach within venture analysis, the model relates an array of price, advertising, personal selling, and sales promotion combinations for the product under study and pertinent facts about competing products. Essentially, the venture analysis model hypothesizes about the degree to which competitors will react to a price change and in what form this reaction will occur. Using an appropriate statistical and/or mathematical model, it analyzes what blend of marketing decisions will go best with a given price. In turn, it determines what effect the given price will have on the sales of other products in the product line. The pricing aspects of a new product, then, are included in the venture analysis model along with the prices charged by competition. However, it is up to the marketing managers to review these prices and make appropriate adjustments based on their knowledge about what is reasonable as well as their experience and judgment. Otherwise, unrealistic prices will be used to evaluate a product over its life cycle. In turn, the product will be priced unrealistically in terms of its competition.

Of paramount importance for venture analysis is knowledge about specific variables, assumptions, constraints, and like items to be considered for inclusion in the model by marketing modelers. For example, an itemization of all candidate variables based on the subjective judgments of marketing executives is necessary. Knowledge of the marketing and pricing environment and the relative importance of various factors is necessary. It is imperative to build a data warehouse of historical marketing data, including pricing data, covering not only this company's new products but also all new products introduced in the industry over the past few years for which adequate source data are available. It is from these data that the statistical and/or mathematical relationships subsequently expressed in the model are derived. Thus, it is apparent that considerable pertinent data are needed before a new product can be effectively evaluated.

Utilizing the venture analysis model for a new product or service, a marketing modeler can meet with a company's marketing managers who will supply various estimates as they are called for by the model, including the estimated size of the target group, recent product trial data, repeat purchases, the promotional budget, size of investment, target rate of return, product price, and gross profit margin for each product under study. The model will analyze this information under computer control and display a forecast for price along with the total number of customers, company's market share, windfall profits (if applicable), period profits, and discounted cumulative profits. The marketing managers can alter various input estimates and readily ascertain the effect of the altered data on sales and profits. Additionally, prices can be varied over the life cycle of the product. That is, the first year(s) allows a company to charge higher prices due to the newness of the product. As competition moves in, prices are generally lowered and profits tend to fall per unit. When the product is removed from the market or changed to meet emerging customer needs, there can be a change in the pricing structure of the product or service to meet changed conditions in the venture analysis model.

Although the foregoing analysis has centered on one product or service, in actuality there are generally a number of products or services that undergo the venture analysis model. After all analyses have been performed by the marketing modeler that are deemed appropriate for the new products or services under study, there is a comparison of alternative product or service ventures by marketing managers to determine which is the most viable one. For example, as shown in Figure 7-3 for five different products, Proposed Product 2 gives the highest return on investment over the next five years for upgrading the company's product line within an OLAP operating mode. However, if new knowledge is discovered and brought to bear in this example (which can eminate from any possible source), it may well be that Proposed Product 2 is not the best choice. For example, knowledge from outside the company—such as the possible side effects of air pollution or impeding legislation in the judicial system that adversely affects Product 2—may signal that all information and knowledge have not been brought to bear on a definitive solution.

Currently, variations of venture analysis are offered by a few software vendors. For example, Cincom Systems Inc. (Cincinnati, Ohio) is marketing a suite of software products, called Control:Acquire, to automate and support the tasks required to bid on new business. This software package manages an entire sales cycle from prospecting for business to estimating costs and developing proposals. One feature of the software is called Workbench Configuration. It can process product requests from customers so that a sales staff has a complete picture of the components needed to meet a customer's needs. The Workbench feature can lead the company through the selection of product parts and tasks. The software can then compare those choices to a knowledge bank of product information to make sure that the company has selected a buildable product. A second feature is called Estimating, designed to give timely and accurate cost estimates when developing proposals. A third feature is Proposal Management, which automates the job of maintaining information on sales proposals and can also send sales orders. A fourth feature, Work Breakdown Structure Planner, automates the task of scheduling and monitoring the implementation of a customer's order. Essentially, this product is designed to reduce sales overhead costs, order-to-shipment cycle times, and expensive order revisions.

Using Knowledge to Relate Product Quality to Pricing

The Profit Impact of Market Strategy (PIMS), as discussed previously in the chapter, yields knowledge about what works, what does not, and why. Although PIMS principles are set forth by Robert Buzzell and Bradley Gale in their book, the most important single factor affecting a business unit's performance in the

Figure 7-3
Proposed Product 2 Out of Five Products Gives the Highest Return on Investment Over the Next Five Years

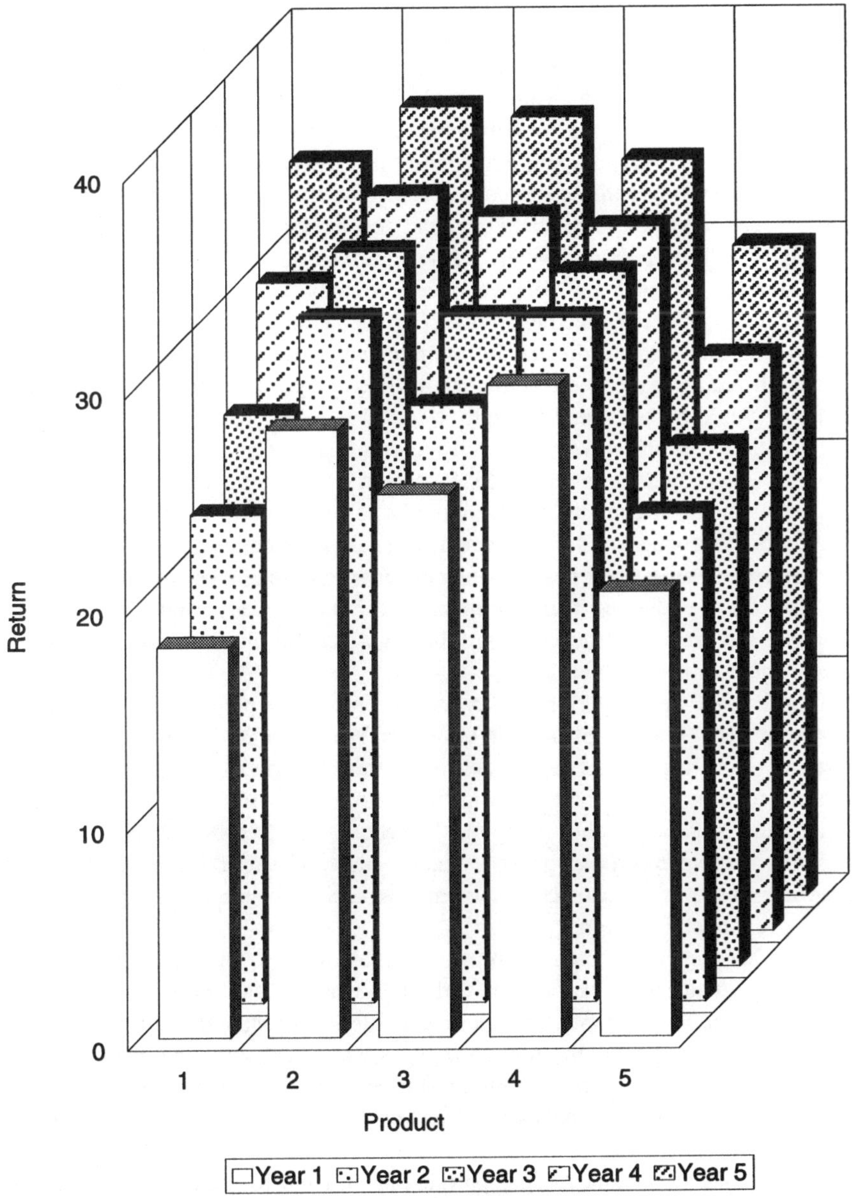

long run is *the quality of its products and services*, relative to those of competitors. Buzzell and Gale illustrate the linkage between relative quality and business performance in their Purdue chicken example.[6] Chickens have as strong a claim to commodity status as pork bellies or crude oil. In the Buzzell and Gale example, the performance of each competitor was the same for each product and service attribute. (This was actually ranked by the PIMS study.) This placed Purdue and his representative competitor at the 50th percentile on relative quality, neither ahead nor behind. With no difference in performance on product and service attributes, the customer basically bought on price.

After Frank Purdue took over the chicken business from his father, he pulled ahead on almost every nonprice attribute that counts in the purchase decision. His research showed that customers in his served market prefer their chickens plump and yellow. Careful breeding and the judicious use of food additives enabled Frank to produce meatier, yellower chickens than his competitors. Over time, Purdue initiated capital investments to improve the real and perceived quality of his chickens. Needless to say, Purdue's company executed an effective advertising campaign dedicated to communicating the quality of its chickens. Although such analyses were not called on-line analytical processing at the time, today it would be construed as such.

Essentially, Purdue invested heavily to create a real quality difference in its product. According to extensive PIMS research and as noted above, the most important factor affecting a business unit's performance in the long run is the quality of its products and services relative to those of competitors. Purdue built its advertising around a big idea—namely that Purdue chickens were superior. In turn, Purdue charged a premium price for its chickens. Major advertising research indicates the price of a product or a service must be consistent with the image it is trying to build.

In the short run, superior quality yields profits via premium prices. PIMS businesses (3,000 business units in total) that ranked in the top third on relative quality sold their products or services, on average, at prices 5 to 6 percent higher relative to competition than those in the bottom third. In the long run, on the other hand, superior quality is the most effective way to grow. Quality leads to both market expansion and gains in market share. The resulting growth in volume means that a superior-quality competitor gains economies of scale advantages over its competition.

From another view, many companies today need to maintain the product quality for which they are known and, at the same time, reduce the price of their products. For example, Procter & Gamble is currently slowing the growth of its marketing budgets in order to try to lower prices on some of its brands. It has cut its spending on coupons in half over the last several years because the low redemption rate makes them an inefficient marketing tool. In its core suppliers program, P&G is working closely with several key suppliers to study processes and save money. That partnership has led to improved results and reduced expenditures. In essence, Procter & Gamble is trying "to do more with less.'' It is cutting selling prices and finding ways to cut costs even more than the corresponding drop in prices.

COMPETING ON KNOWLEDGE IS RELATED TO COMPETITIVE WISDOM

Building upon the concept of competing on knowledge is the related concept of competitive wisdom. As discussed in Chapter 1, *wisdom* is the ability to judge soundly. It requires the intuitive ability, born of experience, to look beyond the apparent situation and recognize the big picture. It involves identifying exceptional factors and anticipating unusual outcomes. In marketing, this means that some marketing people see things in competitive situations that others do not see. This requires getting marketing personnel out of their job-specific myopias and getting them involved in the big picture. Salespeople talking to customers about other suppliers, marketing personnel attending scientific conferences, and marketing staff perusing comments and complaints posted to Internet-based newsgroups can all help marketing groups recognize good competitive information that can be turned to the company's advantage. All of these marketing people are potentially analysts. They must be given an ongoing view of what is happening in the company at large as well as beyond its borders.

From this view, competitive wisdom of marketing personnel needs to be actively sought, recognized, nutured, and refined over time. There is nothing unusual about the observation that business information is not limited to standard reports such as market-share statistics and profit-and-loss statements. On the other hand, the information gathering process is eclectic, and while managers will always need repetitive reports of regularly occurring information, they need direct observation inside and outside the company, meetings, informal notes on the Internet, and impromptu conversations, even in restrooms. Outside the company, an ever-growing treasury of information sits in databases, government agencies, trade journals, and scientific papers, just waiting to be exploited. Every company, in reality, has access to essentially the same information and knowledge. So the challenge is not simply to locate critical information and derive appropriate knowledge for competing in the marketplace but also to apply it better and faster than the competition. That requirement leads to the conclusion that a successful company has the capability to absorb a wide array of external data, information, and knowledge and, in turn, combine it with up-to-the-minute internal reports to produce sound business decisions. In effect, competitive wisdom views every employee as an enlightened knowledge gatherer, capable of recognizing important information and knowledge and passing it quickly to the right person in the right format for making the right decisions.

SUMMARY

The initial focus of this chapter was on the need to rethink the entire marketing mix in order to make the most effective use of knowledge management systems in marketing. In addition to presenting important marketing principles, significant factors that are useful in discovering marketing knowledge were set forth. They included a problem-finding approach, an expanded view of market research and analysis, database marketing, using the Internet to sell goods and services, and data mining software. Essentially, this exposition centered on market leaders who know what customers want when developing a company's products and services. Or to state it another way, the company knows what its customers want before they know themselves and influences the direction that the market will take today and tomorrow. Such an approach is found in smart or knowledge-based products and services. In the second half of the chapter, applications that showed the relationship between rethinking the marketing function and discovering knowledge for the areas of marketing strategy and product pricing were presented. Additionally, the integration of marketing knowledge with competitive wisdom was highlighted.

NOTES

1. Paula Smith, "Unique Tool for Marketers: PIMS," *Management Review*, January 1977, pp. 32–34.
2. Stan Davis and Jim Botkin, "The Coming of Knowledge-Based Business," *Harvard Business Review*, September–October 1994, pp. 165–170.
3. Gary Hamel and C. K. Prahalad, "Corporate Imagination and Expeditionary Marketing," *Harvard Business Review*, July–August 1991, pp. 85–86.
4. Robert J. Thierauf, *Virtual Reality Systems for Business* (Westport, CT: Quorum Books, 1995), chapter 7.
5. Angoss Software, "Study 6: Direct and Database Marketing," *KnowledgeSEEKER in Action* (Toronto: Angoss Software International Limited, 1996).
6. Robert D. Buzzell and Bradley T. Gale, *The PIMS Principles: Linking Strategy to Performance* (New York: The Free Press, 1988).

8

Application of Manufacturing Knowledge

Issues Explored:

- How important is a broad-based view of manufacturing in a KMS environment?
- What are the important principles and factors that underlie effective knowledge for manufacturing?
- What areas typically lend themselves to discovering manufacturing knowledge?
- How can knowledge discovery assist management in the areas of purchasing plus production planning and execution for a typical manufacturer?
- What approach is helpful to manufacturing management in discovering and tracking quality problems?

Outline:

USING KNOWLEDGE MANAGEMENT SYSTEMS TO TURN MANUFACTURING INTO A COMPETITIVE WEAPON

The marketplace, as highlighted in the prior chapter, is rapidly changing in ways that are different from the past. Since worldwide competition demands a renewed emphasis on product and service quality, a product needs to be examined in great detail in the design stage before it is produced. In turn, the manufacturing process is engineered to be stable and reliable. If the design is good and so is the process, quality is inherent. It is necessary not only to build a product faster and cheaper but also to make that product better. This approach to quality emphasizes the need for cost-effectiveness of productivity in all areas of a company—from design to the assembly line.

Also noted in the prior chapter, an important focus of marketing knowledge is to help marketing managers think like their customers, including how their customers view and measure satisfaction. Taking this concept one step further, a typical company needs to relate its customers and their resulting satisfaction (or lack thereof) to its manufacturing operations. Within a combined marketing-manufacturing framework, manufacturing managers need to measure their companies not by measures of labor efficiency, cost reduction, overtime, variance, and absorption. Rather, they need to compare the company to its competition on such items as product, quality, delivery, price, and service. Such an approach is possible using knowledge management systems in manufacturing. In fact, it is possible for a typical company to turn its manufacturing operations into a competitive weapon.

It is from this perspective that there is a need to rethink the manufacturing function from a broader perspective—the subject matter of the first part of this chapter. This rethinking centers on many items, including computer integrated manufacturing and total quality management. In addition, manufacturing principles based on knowledge of the total supply chain of a company's customers are set forth. This background ties in with the important factors that are useful in discovering manufacturing knowledge. Next, appropriate knowledge applications in purchasing and production planning and execution are presented along with the underlying concept of total quality management. The use of the Internet to tie in manufacturers with suppliers is presented to demonstrate an alternative means of obtaining and using knowledge. Also, the utilization of on-line analytical processing and virtual reality is set forth and illustrated where appropriate. Overall, a knowledge management system approach to manufacturing allows for improving customer satisfaction up and down the supply chain. In addition, it gives managers and their staffs access to knowledge and analyses that are not generally found in prior information systems.

A BROAD-BASED VIEW OF MANUFACTURING OPERATIONS

At the outset, it should be noted that labor costs in manufacturing operations amount to only 10 percent to 15 percent of total cost, with material costs representing another 30 percent to 40 percent and overhead representing 45 percent to 60 percent. Since overhead is allocated by direct labor hours, companies often try to reduce indirect labor and increase direct labor, which amounts to an accounting game, since true overhead still stays the same. In contrast, a company's manufacturing management should be attacking queue and wait times, which have no labor associated with them but which affect lead time, inventory and its associated carrying cost, material handling equipment and storage, insurance, and like items. Hence, a broader perspective of manufacturing operations is needed today and tomorrow much more than in the past. Knowledge and application of appropriate changes can turn a company's manufacturing operations into a competitive weapon for attacking its current problems and for achieving profitable growth.

As will be seen in this chapter, knowledge is useful for the creation and control over both current and future manufacturing operations. This relates to problem solving for current manufacturing operations along with internal knowledge integration across functions and projects as well as innovation and experimentation to build for the future. It also involves problem finding, in which there is need to integrate external flow with a company's internal flow in the manufacturing process. Within this framework, the company's management is open to change and can learn from its past—good, bad, or indifferent. The bottom line is that the total organization, including its manufacturing operations, center around the discovery and use of knowledge on a daily basis.

Knowledge About a Company's Products Is Not Fixed

An important lesson learned by a typical company's knowledge-driven manufacturing operations is that such knowledge is not fixed and immutable. Yesterday's brilliant insight can quickly become today's competitive noose. For example, consider the automobile industry where quality is still defined as the absence of manufacturing defects. In years gone by when there was a large gap between the product quality of American and Japanese vehicles, that was certainly a valid measurement because it had a direct impact on customer satisfaction. Today, the difference in defect rates among the major automakers is somewhat indiscernible to customers. So the question can be asked, what drives satisfaction and loyalty today for a car manufacturer's products? Typically, research indicates that customers feel that a good measure of vehicle quality is a balance between minimizing the *things gone wrong* and maximizing those attributes that customers consider *things gone right*. Essentially, it is not just one or the other but a complex blend of both. Most car owners today say they are satisfied with their cars. It is only when the impact of the customer's total experience with the product and the dealership is measured that one can begin to understand the perception of quality and how it affects customer satisfaction and loyalty.

Additionally, knowledge about a car company's customers today center on other factors that they say are important, including comfort, thoughtfulness of design, handling, power, style, convenience, helpful innovation, and even their interactions with the dealer. Success in the marketplace implies that people want cars they can get excited about, not just more of the same. If customers were concerned only about defects, for example, car manufacturers would never have put sliding doors on minivans, since there are many more things that can go wrong with sliding doors than regular doors. Overall, although car manufacturers care about eliminating defects, their driving force is defect-free vehicles that people love to own/rent and drive.

Expanded View of Computer Integrated Manufacturing

As a starting point, it is helpful to look at the total framework that underlies all manufacturing activities in a typical company. Such a framework today and in the future centers on a broad-based view that can be called computer integrated manufacturing (CIM). For the most part, CIM means blending manufacturing with marketing, finance, accounting, and human resources as well as other functional areas where deemed necessary. CIM is currently crucial to the survival of manufacturers because it provides the levels of planning and control for manufacturing along with the flexibility to change with the times. The basic objective of CIM is to change management's thinking by establishing a framework within which manufacturing operations are defined, funded, managed, and coordinated. This framework requires specific mechanisms for production planning, cost control, projection selection and justification, project management, and project performance monitoring. The role of the enterprise view of CIM is to ensure that the appropriate levels and types of integration are appropriate.

Related to the CIM concept is the whole idea of *flexibility*. Flexibility at the plant level refers to the ability to adapt or change. However, there are many ways to characterize such an ability. One plant manager might be talking about the cost of changing from one product to the next. Another plant manager might be talking about the ability to increase or decrease production volumes to fit the market demand. Yet another might be talking about the ability to increase the range of available products. All these abilities refer to flexibility but they require different courses of action to develop. Essentially, the type of flexibility a given company should employ is determined by its competitive environment. Whether one is referring to products, production volumes, or manufacturing processes, flexibility is about increasing or decreasing output, or achieving a uniform output. As such, the CIM concept not only depends on the technical factors to make the appropriate changes but also on the people factor to achieve desired results.

A current trend that centers on *agile manufacturing* is updating the flexibility concept. Agile manufacturing is currently defined as the ability to respond quickly to rapidly changing markets driven by customer-based valuing of products and services. It says agile companies have the ability to reconfigure operations, processes, and business relationships swiftly. Thus, the agile concept emphasizes ultraflexible production facilities; constantly shifting alliances among suppliers, producers, and customers; and direct feedback of sales data into the factories.

Using state-of-the-art design and manufacturing technologies, many companies have gotten better at meeting customers' needs, responding to changing markets, and producing higher quality products. They have reduced paper flow, prototyped products quickly, shortened cycle times, linked supply lines electronically, created virtual inventory and companies, and given customers more choices. Some results have been widely reported, such as Motorola's customized pagers and Levi Strauss's customer-tailored jeans. Others not as widely reported include the Big Three automakers, the aerospace industry, semiconductor makers, the computer industry, and pharmaceutical companies. All have been able to speed up design, manufacturing, and customization using the agile concept to meet changing customer needs.

A further broadening of the CIM concept includes *supply chain management* (SCM). The focus is on the whole supply chain, which includes where and how the products are sourced, delivered, and merchanised to the customer. Its primary goal is to supply high-quality, low-cost products with a fast turnaround time. Although this is applicable to many environments, it focuses more on distribution environments. This integration requires a seamless link that shares information among marketing, sales, purchasing, finance, manufacturing, distribution, and transportation. Advances in information technology provide this through methods such as electronic data interchange (EDI), faster transportation systems, and distribution requirements planning. By achieving this kind of integration, a company can maximize its supply chain value with a lower landed cost of product from a vendor on one side of the supply chain and pass this value to the customer on the other side of the supply chain. Overall, for manufacturers, efficiency comes from integrating distributed data sources to better link segments of the supply chain.

Finally, the CIM concept needs to be expanded to include *virtual worlds.* More to the point, expanded CIM virtual worlds have the potential to assist management in reengineering their operations—manufacturing or otherwise—to improve the productivity of the company. As discussed later in the chapter, reengineering focuses on doing more with less so that the productiveness of personnel and equipment is improved. For example, an experimental assembly modeling system that radically changes the way aircraft are produced has been tested at the Northrop Corporation. The prototype system makes use of 3-D stereo display and input devices to simulate the assembly process. The system could save money in development costs by eliminating the need for full-scale mockups. Thus, Northrop's assembly modeler is a good example of the benefits of stereo viewing and desktop VR in manufacturing.[1]

Total Quality Management Focus

After being viewed as a manufacturing problem in the past, quality has become a service issue—not just for service-sector businesses like communications, health care, and finance but for the service side of manufacturing companies as well. The focus is on *total quality management* (TQM)—that is, quality in the offering itself and in all the services that come with it. If product quality is essentially the same across the industry, service becomes the distinguishing factor. Overall, TQM has become a prerequisite for survival today and tomorrow.

With TQM, the postwar quality movement has moved into its third stage. When the growing popularity of Japanese automobiles, televisions, and radios forced U.S. manufacturers to take another look at themselves in the late seventies, most companies were still in what quality experts call the first or inspection phase, relying on sampling techniques to get rid of defective items. Too often, however, they did not. In 1980—the year an NBC White Paper introduced audiences to W. Edwards Deming, the American statistican who had shown the Japanese how to use process controls to catch defects at the source—manufacturers who took the issue seriously started moving into the second or quality-control phase. Now, with TQM, quality is no longer solely in the quality-control department. It is sponsored by top management and diffused throughout the company.[2]

Essentially, employees see a gap between what the company says is important in regard to quality and the company's follow-through. Needless to say, this is less than a rousing vote of confidence in the quality performance of American businesses. Employees want to see better results. Substantial proportions of survey respondents say that the quality programs in their companies have had either no effect or a negative effect in specific areas (ranging from 22 percent negative on communications to 42 percent negative on their pay and benefits). Workers state that the two most important ways a company can make it easier for them to do high-quality work are, first, to provide more training in job skills and, second, to offer job security. Going beyond these two items in order of importance to workers are the following: have a more supportive attitude from top management, train workers in interpersonal working skills, respond faster to employee ideas, offer more up-to-date tools and technology, have a more supportive attitude from middle management, and offer better access to available information.

Take Federal Express which handles 1.5 million packages per day as an example. The reason that customers can rely on such a complex organization is that Federal Express has made a 100 percent service level and a 100 percent customer satisfaction level as its key goals. Every employee has the right, the authority, or backing to do whatever is necessary to satisfy the customer. Essentially, Federal Express has put a lot into mechanisms to feed information back to the people who are doing the job so that if they have a quality problem or an error, they know it and can fix it. The company has spent a lot of time training its people in quality methods. Company employees are educated about how important good quality is to the company's future viability. In each of the preceding six points, monetary issues play a role, but they are consistently ranked by the survey respondents below other concerns. The points are a road map to quality by the people who work with the company's customers.[3]

Manufacturing Principles Based on Knowledge of Operations

Essentially, the manufacturing principles set forth below are based on knowledge of the total supply chain. This chain encompasses customers, suppliers, manufacturers, wholesalers, and retailers and the interaction among them. To turn the supply chain into a competitive weapon, product designers must initially be teamed with customers as well as personnel from their own marketing and manufacturing operations. Typically, a company finds it necessary to tear apart and rebuild its approach to product design. This means that designers spend time using such electronic means as groupware to get at all the facts involving a proposed new product. A business team would normally consist of a representative from marketing, finance, and manufacturing and quality control.

The flow of information begins with customer requirements. The team works on a conceptual design and then goes back and forth with the customer to formulate a detailed design. In turn, the business team designs, manufacturers, markets, and sells the product. For instance, say a team wants to design a new vacuum cleaner. After consulting with representative customers and its retailers, marketing knows just how it wants the product to look, (i.e., what shape it should take and how large it should be). The engineer is concerned about the product's size and shape, not for appearances's sake but rather because the casing needs to house the inside circuitry that makes the product run. After the design process is complete, the computerized system also generates a bill of materials that will eventually feed automatically into the company's manufacturing resource planning system. Based on this newer design process, an important starting manufacturing principle requires that all appropriate personnel within and outside the company participate and are involved in product development.

For a company to maintain manufacturing dominance in its core products, it must employ the appropriate resources to reshape its product line to meet changing times. Control over core products allows a company to shape its evolution of applications and end markets. As a company multiplies the number of application arenas for its core products, it must consistently reduce the cost, time, and risk in new product development. The bottom line is that well-targeted core products can lead to economies of scale. Unlike physical assets, competencies do not deteriorate as they are applied but can grow over time to the company's competitive advantage.

Related to the foregoing is another important manufacturing principle. Since product life cycles have shortened dramatically in the recent past, companies have been forced to develop and commercialize new technologies faster than ever. As a result, competitive advantage now often goes to the company that is most adept at choosing among the large number of technologies and not necessarily to the company that creates them. This change in thinking by U.S. companies helps explain the resurgence of the U.S. electronics industry. It should be noted that a company's approach to this technology integration should suit the way it operates (i.e., its culture) and its resources.

In the past, many manufacturers have viewed their markets in terms of mass production. They have produced a great variety of goods and services. A better approach is to focus on customization. While mass marketing and mass production require that customers sort through a variety of options, customization offers them exactly what they want at a time, place, and price they want. By making the job easier for their customers, manufacturers gain allegiance for the long term. In essence, an effective marketing and manufacturing team finds and produces products and services for customers and not customers for its products and services.

Another manufacturing principle that has undergone change is the following: Manufacture products in long runs and move large quantities in as few shipments as possible. Today, there is agreement that companies must move products faster, fill orders more accurately, and do it at less cost. Reducing manufacturing cycle times enables better planning by more closely aligning production with demand. In some industries, such as apparel and high technology, market demands change every quarter, which means the need for reduced inventories.

Today, the hallmark of an efficient manufacturer centers on cheaper and faster inventory turns. Turning over inventory faster is related to *just-in-time inventories*, which are designed to deliver raw materials and finished parts to where they are needed as close as possible to when they are needed. For example, car manufacturers operate on inventory that is delivered on a just-in-time basis, no more than two to four hours before it is needed. Thus, the manufacturer's investment in inventory is cut dramatically today compared with just a few years ago. This has been made possible by giving suppliers access to sales data in total supply chain management.

To quote another manufacturing principle, the key to reducing total inventory costs further is to recognize that for every dollar cut from inventory, companies save an additional dollar in warehousing, transportation, and other carrying costs each year. Needless to say, these cost savings can be substantial for any manufacturer. In addition, it may be possible to cut costs related to safety stock or buffered inventories. In terms of the total supply chain, all parties can benefit from a reduction in inventory costs.

Related to the above lean inventory techniques is the concept of continuous improvement, which is an important element of total quality management (TQM). Continuous improvement is what it names implies—making small, incremental improvements to products over time to meet customers' changing needs. Similarly, customer service improvements provide a competitive edge in industries where fast response times are critical. For example, hospitals require shipments of replacement parts because they cannot afford to have their MRI machines down for long.

A comprehensive manufacturing management approach to continuous improvement also includes bringing order to operations. This centers on a consistent set of procedures and techniques to address price, delivery, service, quality, and time to market. Its elements include determining the causes of material backups, which are often due to combining batches to optimize setups or to combining like-size materials to optimize yield. A helpful approach is to diagram and analyze the movement of parts needed to make an assembly and fulfill shipments to ensure parts will end up in the right place at the right time.

To improve work-in-process in a company's manufacturing operations, only material in process for actual orders is worked on while other material is moved to the side. Orders are processed on a first-in, first-out basis by customer due date. To improve the work-in-process flow, machine setup and workflow operations can be videotaped. Tapes can then be analyzed by breaking them down into time elements to spot areas for improvement. It may be necessary to reorganize work areas to improve manufacturing cycle time. From this view, manufacturing operations may show significant improvements in lead-time reductions, inventory reductions, partial elimination of overtime, reductions in scrap and rework, and the need for training of workers.

An often overlooked manufacturing principle relates to a company's benchmarking of its own performance in logistics and other areas. For example, a company can track on-time delivery rates—that is, how fast it delivers its products. It can assess its accuracy rate. Delivery of the wrong product on time pleases no one. It can measure cycle time by recording the number of inventory turns achieved in a year with the view of cutting inventories in all of the right places. Logistics costs as a percentage of sales can also be tracked by the company. In all of these benchmarking examples, a company can compare itself to its competitors and companies in other fields in order to get a handle on how the company is performing—good, bad, or indifferent.

Last, but not least, using a company's current knowledge base in a productive manner is a most important challenge facing knowledge managers. Because closing gaps is primarily achieved by connecting knowledgeable people from both inside and outside the company, knowledge managers need to draw upon their established networking skills and use their traditional cross-functional roles to give them unique perspectives on effective knowledge-base solutions. From this enlighted view, a company can utilize marketing and manufacturing knowledge as well as knowledge from a company's other functional areas to meet its challenges. For example, an engineering firm found itself under pressure as clients began demanding fixed-price contracts instead of traditional cost-plus arrangements. The firm needed to ensure more predictability and efficiency in its design and construction projects. It was clear that project teams working independently were not benefiting from one another's experience. A group of executives, including the information systems manager, was forced to implement a knowledge management process that would allow project teams access to the relevant cumulative intelligence from inside and outside the organization. The net result was that the company's knowledge management process was highly effective because it focused on key decision points, thereby making the desired knowledge easily accessible through the enterprise computing and communications infrastructure at the time it was needed.

A summary of the above manufacturing principles is found in Figure 8-1. Essentially, many of these principles are linked with other functional areas, in particular, marketing.

IMPORTANT FACTORS THAT ARE USEFUL IN DISCOVERING MANUFACTURING KNOWLEDGE

Important factors involved in discovering manufacturing knowledge are generally complex because there is a need to relate manufacturing activities to many other functional areas of the organization. To produce meaningful and operational information for planning and executing manufacturing operations, changes must be made to the decision processes. In addition, newer manufacturing and related software that allow manufacturing managers to control their activities on a *now* basis need to be introduced to assist them and their support personnel in performing their daily tasks. In the material to follow, a number of important

Figure 8-1
Manufacturing Principles Based on Knowledge of the Total Supply Chain

- Redesign of the whole development process centers on including customers, suppliers, manufacturers, wholesalers, and retailers in the total supply chain.
- For a company to maintain manufacturing dominance in its core products, it must employ the appropriate resources to reshape the evolution of its products over time.
- In a fast-changing world of shortened product life cycles, competitive advantage goes to those companies that are most adept at choosing the appropriate technologies from among the large number available for use rather than to those creating these technologies.
- The customization of products in the manufacturing process gets around the problem of trying to unload the output of mass production on a manufacturer's customers.
- Due to changing times, manufacturing products in long runs and moving large quantities in as few shipments as possible is no longer a viable option for most manufacturers. The reverse is true.
- The concept of just-in-time is related to faster inventory turnover so that raw materials and parts are delivered to where they are needed as close as possible to when they are needed.
- For every dollar cut from inventory, an additional dollar is saved in warehousing, transportation, and other carrying costs every year, not to mention lower costs for safety stock or buffered inventories.
- The concept of continuous improvement (an important part of the TQM approach) centers on making small, incremental improvements to a company's products and services over time to meet the changing needs of customers.
- To bring order to a company's manufacturing operations, managers need a consistent set of procedures and techniques to address price, delivery, service, quality, and time-to-market factors.
- To improve work-in-process flow for manufacturing operations, machine setup and workflow operations can be videotaped and then analyzed by breaking them down into time elements to spot areas for improvement.
- To better understand a company's manufacturing operations and related areas, it is helpful to benchmark operations against competitors or companies with similar operations in other fields.
- Project teams must be capable of accessing relevant cumulative knowledge from within and outside the company so that needed expertise is employed to its fullest.

factors that are useful in assisting manufacturing managers and their staffs include the following: (1) problem finding in discovering manufacturing knowledge, (2) reengineering to improve productivity, (3) utilization of manufacturing mathematical and statistical models, and (4) software useful in discovering manufacturing knowledge.

Problem Finding in Discovering Manufacturing Knowledge

Within a knowledge management system operating mode, a problem-finding approach provides manufacturing decision makers with a broad view of production planning and a wide span of control over manufacturing activities. In an environment of rapid change, this is accomplished by a forward integration of information and knowledge. External environmental factors must be integrated with forecasting information. This, in turn, feeds the material requirements plan, the output of which goes into the purchasing and production planning and execution systems. New information is captured at all points and provides information for inventory and accounts payable. Although much of the need for manufacturing information and its resulting knowledge over time comes from increased integration, there is also a need for effective management of the production processes. More effective material acquisition policies and better production planning demand more accurate and timely information and knowledge to support their operations. Overall, the integration of manufacturing with other related systems centers on the need for improved information and knowledge for effective day-to-day operations.

For a manufacturing-oriented organization, the integration process starts with a five-year strategic plan. More specifically, in terms of the manufacturing area, it relates to product-line planning, facilities planning, and personnel planning as developed by the corporate planning staff for top management. Next, these manufacturing-oriented, long-range plans are translated into medium-range plans and finally into short-range plans such as current-year plans. In effect, the long-term strategic plan that locates future marketing problems and solves them in terms of future opportunities is eventually refined into integrated plans for this year's manufacturing operations. From this view, it is easy to understand why timely planning and control of manufacturing resources through problem finding and the resulting information integration can be a vital factor in the long-term success of an organization.

To assist in the information integration process for effective problem finding and problem solving, the manufacturing and execution system utilizes appropriate mathematical and statistical models along with knowledge developed to date to assist in planning and control of its resources. Some of the knowledge to date centers around the manufacturing principles, such as those set forth earlier in the chapter. It is a logical approach for overcoming common management problems encountered in manufacturing operations, such as the misuse of available productive capacity. *Productivity* sometimes is far less than it should be or could be. Techniques to plan and control manufacturing resources are readily available, but only a few manufacturers have learned to use this combination of mathematical models, computerized systems, company personnel and appropriate knowledge effectively. Those manufacturers that have will be able to utilize their productive capacity in a world of persistent uncertainty and growing complexity.

Reengineering to Improve Productivity

Reengineering has been and continues to be an important direction for business because the most successful and promising companies develop new techniques that allow them to survive in an increasingly competitive climate. To reengineer (i.e., reinvent their companies), managers need to abandon past organizational and operational principles and procedures and create entirely new ones. No matter what industry a company is in, how technologically sophisticated its products or services are, or what its national origin is, basically it traces its work styles and organizational roots back to the prototypical pin factory that economist Adam Smith described in *The Wealth of Nations* (published in 1776). Smith's principle of the division of labor embodied his observation that some number of *specialists*, each performing a single step in the manufacture of a pin, could make far more pins in a day than the same number of *generalists*, each engaged in making whole pins. Today's airlines, car manufacturers, accounting firms, and computer manufacturers, to name a few, have all been built around Smith's central idea. Typically, the larger the organization, the more specialized is the work and the more separate steps into which work is divided—and this is true of both manufacturing and nonmanufacturing firms.

Business reengineering means starting from scratch. It centers on forgetting how work was done in the past and deciding how it can best be done now. Old job titles and old organizational arrangements—divisions, departments, groups, and so forth—cease to matter. Instead, what matters is how work is organized given the demands of today's markets and the power of today's technologies. At the center of business reengineering is the concept of discontinous thinking (i.e., identifying and abandoning the outdated rules and fundamental assumptions that underlie current business operations). Every company is replete with implicit rules of the past: for example, that local warehouses are necessary for good customer service or that local marketing decisions are made at headquarters. These rules are based on assumptions about technology, people, and organizational goals that no longer hold.

To reengineer a company's business procedures, it is necessary to rethink these procedures and redesign the *business processes* to achieve improvements so that a company's employees go from being specialists to generalists to improve productivity. A business process is a collection of activities that take one or more kinds of input and create an output that is of value to the customer. For example, in filling an order, the delivery of finished products is the value that the process creates. However, Adam Smith's notion of breaking work into its simplest tasks and assigning each of these to a specialist tends to lose sight of the larger objective, which is to get the goods into the hands of the customer who ordered them.

As an example of reengineering where employees go from specialists to generalists, consider the accounts payable department of the Ford Motor Company. Previously, 500 accounts payable clerks (specialists) spent the majority of their time straightening out the problems when purchase orders, invoices, and receiving documents did not match. However, with the new system, the clerk at the receiving dock takes in the goods and depresses a button on the terminal keyboard that tells the company's database that the goods have arrived. Receipt of the goods is now recorded in the database, and the computer automatically issues and sends a check to the supplier at the appropriate time. On the other hand, if the goods do not correspond to an outstanding purchase order in the database, the clerk on the dock will refuse the shipment and send it back to the supplier. Thus, payment authorization, which used to be performed by the accounts payable specialist, is now accomplished by the receiving dock generalist. The old process fostered enough complexity to keep 500 clerks busy. The new process comes close to elimnating the need for an accounts payable department altogether. Ford now has just 125 people involved in supplier payment. In some parts of Ford, the head count in accounts payable is a small fraction of its former size.[4]

Within a current KMS operating mode, it is conceivable that a newer redesigned approach to the accounts payable department may signal the need for fewer people. That is, a comprehensive evaluation using a cost-benefit analysis of basic accounts payable functions may indicate that certain peripheral functions are not worth the cost of maintaining them. As noted previously in the text, knowledge tends to change over time along with changing technology. Hence, further improvement in this accounts payable department is quite possible to meet the demands of changing times.

Utilization of Manufacturing Mathematical and Statistical Models

Manufacturing mathematical and statistical models that are used in conjunction with a company's data marts, data warehouses, or databases provide an excellent way of developing knowledge about a company's manufacturing operations. For example, from future forecasts of a company's sales using a statistical model, management can determine efficient manufacturing schedules. Drawing from the company's current database, monthly capacities can be accessed along with the variable costs of manufacturing for the company's products. By utilizing a mathematical model (i.e., the simplex method of linear programming), manufacturing loads can be calculated based on the forecasted period's sales. In turn, information about the company's operations in terms of loading its manufacturing plants can be evaluated over time, thereby providing knowledge to manufacturing management. The knowledge gained may reveal important insights about how the company can reduce its cycle times, cut inventories in all of the right places, and even develop a vendor alliance that is based on ordering material according to consumption rates and replenishment cycle times and not on customer sales forecasts. A thorough evaluation of manufacturing knowledge can focus on changing measures to take into account the customers' criteria and build in team measures so that workers, management, and the support organization are held accountable for the common goal of customer satisfaction.

Other models that are applicable to manufacturing operations include queuing, PERT/Cost, PERT/LOB (Line of Balance), and simulation. These can be used for loading machines, scheduling operations, and revamping manufacturing operations. Still other mathematical and statistical models are useful to evaluate the performance of manufacturing management and its staff over time. Such an approach is found in purchase performance models that center on evaluating *price, quality*, and *delivery* along with a *purchase performance index*. The weights selected for price, quality, and delivery represent the judgment of the purchasing department as well as that of manufacturing executives. No matter what weights are agreed upon, they form the basis for evaluating vendor and buyer performance. Due to the importance of purchase performance later in the chapter, they are discussed below.

Price. To measure the price variable, past costs provide the best available standard for the present. Current costs that are considerably above those of the previous period are a signal that purchasing might be performing poorly. Of course, it is possible that an increase in price is due to a general rise in prices throughout the economy. But such an all-encompassing movement would tend to affect all prices; in such situations, management should be able to filter out the impact of this general increase. More typically, variation of prices is due to a variety of causes. It is this type of variation that management wants isolated and remedied if possible.

Quality. Price is not the sole determinant of a "good buy." The firm must also consider the quality of goods it needs before it is possible to evaluate whether it really did get a good buy. The receiving department must examine the goods to determine whether or not incoming shipments contain defective items. Although the typical corporation does not employ extensive statistical sampling of incoming parts and materials, many other firms have an extensive and organized inspection procedure. No matter what procedure is employed, a measure of the proportion of deliveries that actually are accepted is useful for measuring the effectiveness of purchasing.

Delivery. Late deliveries, like poor-quality materials and purchased parts, can negate a seemingly good buy. At their worst, late deliveries may result in closing down a production line or even in the loss of future sales. From this viewpoint, it is easy to visualize why a measure of how well vendors meet their specified delivery dates is essential for evaluation purposes. Also, such a measure is useful in evaluating the delivery dependability of particular vendors and in evaluating the buyers who choose to purchase regularly from such vendors.

Purchase-Performance Index. The aggregate of the price, quality, and delivery indices is a purchase-performance index, sometimes called PPI. The purchase performance index (a single value) summarizes the actual performance against expected performance, stated on a quarterly basis or some other time period. It is a composite index, requiring some kind of averaging or weighting process in order to combine these three indices into one. The weights depend on purchasing management's judgment concerning the relative importance of each index factor. Common weighting factors are to assign a weight of 50 to the price index, and 25 each to the quality and delivery indices. Such an assignment of weights indicates that the organization places twice the emphasis on price when compared to the remaining two factors.

In the following example, the purchase-performance index, based on the foregoing weighting factors, is 105; its price, quality, and delivery indices are 94, 107, and 125, respectively.

Index	*Index Value*	*Weight*	*Index Value × Weight*
Price	94	50	4,700
Quality	107	25	2,675
Delivery	125	25	3,125
		100	10,500

PPI = 10,500/100 = 105

The PPI, which is over 100, represents an improvement over the prior period. A value of less than 100 indicates just the reverse.

Software Useful in Discovering Manufacturing Knowledge

Software that is useful in getting a grasp on manufacturing knowledge started out from an information-orientation focus. Oliver Wight, a leading proponent of manufacturing process automation many years ago, used the term "MRP-II" (manufacturing resource planning) to distinguish this manufacturing development from the narrower approach found in the discipline of MRP (material requirements planning). In effect, Wight was peering into the manufacturing side of the enterprise from a business view—from accounting, purchasing, marketing, customer service, sales, operations, and information systems. Today, however, a major problem is the lack of integration with nonmanufacturing systems. Most of today's MRP and MRP-II packages fail to allow an employee to look into the computer and get a snapshot of the status of any customer order, whether it's a production, marketing, or a finance view. Yet this is exactly what a company needs to do today. The reason for this problem is that most MRP and MRP-II packages on the market work off large computer mainframes and cumbersome languages. Writing links to corporate accounting or marketing databases is possible but fraught with expense and frustration. The primary goal of manufacturing software today should be customer service—getting the right product to the right place at the right time at the right price.

Because traditional MRP and MRP-II systems, even in client/server environments, are too rigid for some users, some developers are already reslanting their products to newer manufacturing models: Enterprise resource planning (ERP) and customer-oriented manufacturing management software (COMMS). Typically, MRP-II is host-based, proprietary, and hard to modify, while ERP systems are open systems, based on RDBMS software in 4GL client/server environments.

Fundamentally, enterprise resource planning is real-time manufacturing software that incorporates the entire supply chain from sales and ordering to production, inventory, and distribution. It comes under the umbrella of the CIM concept set forth previously. Since companies are implementing client/server systems that manage the entire supply chain (from the time a product order comes in until the moment it is delivered), ERP systems represent an integrated set of applications modules that ties together a host of functions. As such, they are highly integrated application suites that support many processes, including sales forecasting, order management, purchasing, production scheduling, inventory management, distribution, scheduling, engineering, maintenance, and accounting. These systems become the nerve center of a manufacturer. Overall, enterprise resource planning systems have the capability of providing competitive advantage through lower costs and faster response time.

While many vendors sell systems that manage different parts of a manufacturer's business, only a few actually offer client/server software that spans most of a manufacturer's needs. It should be noted that the skills necessary to create ERP systems for client/server are expensive. Hence, some organizations that previously generated their own core applications are now outsourcing software development to package vendors.

In contrast, some developers are proponents of COMMS, which unites a manufacturer's departments and suppliers around its customers. COMMS allows a company to be more responsive to customers in terms of quality and ability in order to meet their needs on a timely basis. Because the entire manufacturing order is organized with the customer at the hub, managers can tell at a glance which plant has excess capacity and provide accurate price and delivery costs if a product is not in stock.

Although the newer manufacturing models, such as ERP and COMMS, offer a broad-based approach to computer integrated manufacturing, their primary focus is on information. Information is also the primary focus of manufacturing execution systems (MESs) software. As will be seen later in the chapter, MES applications guide manufacturing processes through each step and collect information about what was done to what by whom on which machine. Detailed instructions and shop-floor data capture allow other applications to analyze what has already happened and what needs to happen next. There is a need, however, to take the output of these manufacturing models and go a step further in terms of discovering new knowledge that can assist manufacturing decision makers at all levels of a typical company. One approach is to employ data mining tools in order to extract patterns, trends, and rules. Not only is data mining applicable to marketing (as noted in the prior chapter) but it is also useful for discovering manufacturing knowledge. For example, the data mining software from Angoss Software (namely, KnowledgeSEEKER) is used extensively by Hewlett Packard in their U.S. manufacturing plants as a process control tool for analyzing factors impacting product quality as well as for generating rules for production control systems. KnowledgeSEEKER was used to trouble-shoot quality assurance problems in the production process for the HP IIc color scanner. It identified the critical factors, several of which had been completely unsuspected. This information allowed the engineers to correct the problem quickly. In another case, KnowledgeSEEKER derived the rules necessary to identify situations where a manufacturing process was about to go out of control. This allowed intervening actions to be taken that prevented the problems from ever arising.[5]

Another approach that is useful in discovering manufacturing knowledge is the utilization of neural networks (refer to Chapter 3). Take the example of a farm tractor manufacturer that uses neural networking software to run the machine that produces special sand for making cast-iron molds. The idea is that the software will ensure that the sand comes out just right. Neural software can be thought of as a sophisticated note-taker. As sensory devices constantly measure variables such as temperature and moisture, the software stores the data and uses it to build a memory. The software retains experiences that are being constantly repeated and relegates to the background those that happen only rarely. It uses this ability to fine-tune the machine instantly. The software can even predict, based on experience, when something is about to go awry so that it can correct a problem before it occurs. In effect, neural networks learn and reason in a manner that is comparable to a person's learning process.

From another perspective, information can be the basis for developing service-related knowledge for manufactured goods. For example, General Motors' Computer Aided Maintenance System (CAMS) was designed as a tutor to help novice mechanics diagnose and repair cars. However, it has evolved into an even more sophisticated system that allows expert mechanics to refine their skills. In the past, a mechanic who had absorbed 500 pages of repair manuals could fix most cars. Today, that same mechanic would need to have read about 500,000 pages of manuals. However, access to CAMS makes today's mechanics smarter without manuals. Since increased knowledge resides in the system and not in any particular person, many mechanics are smarter because they now have the experience of all the other mechanics. Because the system is continually improving by learning new techniques from the best mechanics, the net result is that there is better service for the customer.

KNOWLEDGE MANAGEMENT SYSTEMS IN MANUFACTURING

The concept that knowledge is power is an essential element of knowledge management systems in manufacturing or another functional area. In the prior section of the chapter, specific focus was on principles and important factors helpful in discovering manufacturing knowledge. This exposition of a company's collective knowledge of its manufacturing operations along with outside knowledge can help manufacturing managers to discern hidden trends and guiding rules. This, in turn, helps them to gain an understanding of important changes that may be happening in the manufacturing environment. For example, say that a company adopts improvement programs that include just-in-time lean production and TQM methods. Although these improved manufacturing methods are suited for the times, the company seems to be staying even with its competition. For the company to move ahead, it must be able to shift gears quickly based on current trends and coming changes in its industry. That is, the company may have to move from being a rapid, medium-volume manufacturer to being a large volume, low-cost producer to be profitable. Current knowledge of the upcoming changes via a KMS operating mode may assist the company to undergo a manufacturing adjustment in increments, as opposed to an abrupt change that might result in substantial financial chargeoffs in a particular time period.

Today, knowledge management systems in manufacturing need to be expanded to include the entire supply chain. In some cases, costs have risen to new levels because of adversarial relations between supply chain partners and because of poor industry practices such as overreliance on price promotions. Additionally, supply chains in some industries suffer from an excess of some products and a shortage of others because of an inability to predict demand. Although there are a number of technologies available to improve performance, companies lack the knowledge to decide which ones are best for their particular situation.

To better understand and implement manufacturing changes found in a KMS environment, it may be helpful to work with inside as well as outside consultants. There is a great deal of complexity involved in this combined area of manufacturing and supply chain operations. While supportive consulting may improve the chances for success, there can be a risk involved. Manufacturing managers and those in the supply chain might find the resulting system somewhat complex and feel a loss of complete control over their own operations. Despite the potential risks involved in development, a successful knowledge management system can have far-reaching positive effects. A successful system allows managers inside and outside the company to respond immediately to timely manufacturing issues and related problems. In addition, managers can use the knowledge of successful manufacturing and supply chain areas to examine troubled operational areas. The net result is that knowledge provided by a knowledge management system can enhance the productivity and profitability of a typical company.

Areas That Lend Themselves to Discovering Manufacturing Knowledge

Common applications related to knowledge system management include purchasing and supply chain management and production planning and execution.

Other manufacturing areas that are related to knowledge management encompass engineering, manufacturing analysis, quality control, and inventory control. Engineering efforts prior to daily manufacturing operations, for example, are a natural target for knowledge management systems since managers can analyze the ins and outs of engineering projects over time and determine appropriate knowledge (i.e., rules-of-thumb) that can be applied to future engineering projects. Similarly, a KMS operating mode can assist manufacturing managers in analyzing manufacturing operations and quality control problems, including those related to inventories, from the raw materials stage to the finished goods stage. Because in some industries, such as apparel and high technology, market demands change every quarter or two, no manufacturer wants to have a warehouse full of obsolete products. In general, knowledge management systems are useful to most manufacturing managers for overseeing and controlling factory operations. They also help manage physical distribution activities, starting with incoming materials from suppliers at the initial stage of the manufacturing process and continuing through to interactions with wholesalers and retailers after the manufacturing process is completed.

PURCHASING AND SUPPLY CHAIN MANAGEMENT

Typically, the major functions of a manufacturing-oriented company consist of buying, maintenance, and followup. In these fast-changing times, there is a need to go a step further by getting a broader perspective on these functions. This can be accomplished by having manufacturing managers oversee and review purchasing operations. In the pages that follow, consideration will be given to reengineering the purchasing process and then different purchasing issues will be investigated, including vendor and buyer evaluation as well as purchased materials and parts evaluation. In addition, product review using value analysis and knowledge discovery to develop an overall purchasing supply chain strategy will be discussed. Fundamentally, all of these areas are explored within a KMS operating mode.

A starting point for a newer direction in the purchasing process centers around reengineering in terms of the relationships between the purchasing department and its internal customers, its outside suppliers, and the IS (information system) department. Reengineering offers many companies the opportunity to create broader, more satisfying relationships with suppliers and to understand their own internal relationships better. Once they dissect their own business practices, many companies find that purchasing is not an island unto itself, but rather a complex web of interactions that takes a purchase from request to reality. This broadened perspective supports a movement toward improved productivity not only for purchasing but also for others involved in the total procurement process.

For example, Pacific Bell has created a purchasing process from scratch as part of its overall reengineering efforts, shifting the focus from processing purchase orders to managing relationships with clients. At TRW's High Reliability

Electronics Product Group, the procurement department became a reengineering project for an entire business division looking for quick success. The experience highlighted the difficulties involved in implementing new ideas through IS. In another instance, the state of Oregon used reengineering technology to put the responsibility for researching and initiating bids into the hands of the bidders and to make the process more competitive.[6]

Analysis of Vendor, Buyer, and Purchased Parts Performance

Related to a typical company's reengineering efforts is the ensurance that purchasing management has the capability to evaluate its vendors' and buyers' performance. For example, a typical monthly vendor performance report would include an evaluation of outside vendors who have supplied raw materials, supplies, and parts to a manufacturing-oriented company. A comparison between the total amount purchased last month and this month using a PPI index (as set forth earlier in the chapter) would indicate whether buyers had been shifting business to or from certain vendors. Normally, it would be expected that vendors with indices below 100 (expected PPI is 100) would currently be used less than they had been in the past.

Just as vendors can be evaluated, so can the company's buyers. From a managerial viewpoint, monthly buyer performance reports have great meaning. Purchasing managers generally have little direct control over vendors, but they exercise considerable control over their buyers. By having buyers evaluated on a comparable basis, purchasing managers can pinpoint the weaknesses of their buying staffs. Those buyers who are price-minded at the expense of quality materials and prompt delivery will be highlighted. The monthly buyer performance report can be refined for more detailed analysis. Specifically, detailed analyses on price, quality, and delivery can be made for buyers (this is also true for vendors).

In addition, both vendor and buyer performance can be evaluated by utilizing multidimensional analysis. As shown in the buyer analysis in Figure 8-2, the low value indexes for Joseph Cosgrove stand out more than those shown in a monthly buyer performance report when comparison is made to other buyers. The relatively high price index and low quality and delivery indexes indicate a buyer who is price minded at the expense of quality and delivery of incoming purchased goods. For a typical manufacturing company, the low index for quality many indicate that the company must spend some time in cleaning up the materials for production and/or spend additional time on machining before the manufacturing process can begin. Needless to say, there is the need for a meeting between the purchasing director and Joseph Cosgrove to sort out these problems and talk about how to improve the buyer's performance so that his overall PPI can meet the expected 100.

Just as vendors and buyers can be evaluated, so can purchased materials and parts. For example, a monthly purchased materials and parts performance report

Figure 8-2
Multidimensional Analysis of Buyer Performance for Three Buyers

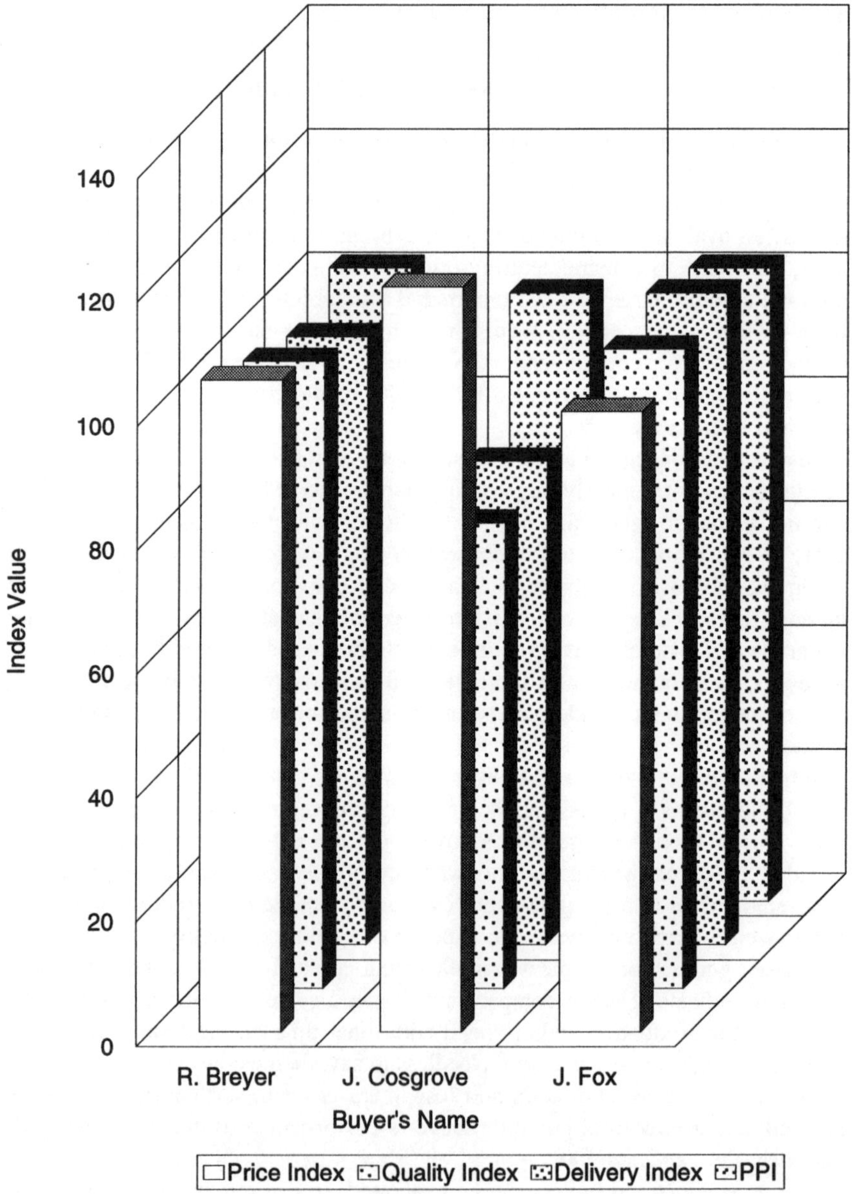

can be prepared that centers on whether or not the corporation is receiving value for parts purchased. If the *price* index is below 100, this might indicate that prices are rising, and consideration might be given to replacing this purchased raw material or part with another. The *quality* index might also be important if certain finished goods are critical for the maintenance of the company's reputation, especially if difficulty has been experienced in the past. In a similar manner, the *delivery* index might be critical in terms of meeting final customer shipment dates. The monthly purchased materials and parts performance report gives purchasing executives an overview of what buyers are procuring and how effective they are. Equally important, it provides pertinent information for the company's buyers.

An alternative way to view the purchased materials and parts information is to employ multidimensional analysis, comparable to that found in Figure 8-2. An established index of 100 or better for price, quality, delivery and PPI is a favorable condition. A value lower than 100 is indicative of problem areas that need to be addressed by purchasing management. A picture of these indexes relative to the 100 or better standard may be a signal for purchasing management to take a harder look behind the figures.

A longer-term view of purchased materials using a knowledge management system provides a means to link segments of the supply chain better. Manufacturers are coming to realize that their businesses are becoming increasingly demand-driven. They are "pulling" products to consumers rather than "pushing" a set amount of products onto a store shelf or to a dealer and then trying to sell it. However, a complex chain of communications, which includes multiple sets of data from all participants in the supply chain, must be integrated if the "pull" approach is to succeed. This new focus on demand has led manufacturers to reexamine their business processes with suppliers and customers. Manufacturers are now looking at the demand side to synchronize their operations profitably and efficiently. They have begun to view their customers and suppliers as part of a virtual enterprise. This timely and accurate movement of product based on the synchronized flow of information, which has been labeled "synchronized customer response," is also known as "quick response," Overall, manufacturers have come to the conclusion that efficiency comes from integrating distributed data and information sources in the various segments of the supply chain. This conclusion is related to a broad-based knowledge of all participants in the supply chain.

Product Review Using Value Analysis

Because expanded computer integrated manufacturing centers on a broad approach to manufacturing, it also includes final product design by engineering. To assist a manufacturer in designing products that are profitable, *value analysis* or *value engineering* is needed. This approach requires the engineer to adopt a broader point of view and consider whether the parts contained in the finished product perform their required functions both as efficiently and as inexpensively as possible. The appraisal focuses on the function that the part—or the larger assembly containing the part—performs. In an inspection-oriented plant, for example, more than half of all workers are somehow involved in finding and reworking rejects. The total investment in this process can account for 20 percent to 40 percent of production costs, and in extreme cases, 50 percent. In contrast, the Japanese inspect a product before it is made (i.e., in the design stage) and engineer the manufacturing process to be stable and reliable.

The following example illustrates a practical value analysis approach within a TQM environment: A product is dismantled and each part is mounted adjacent to its mating part on a table. The point is to demonstrate visually the functional relationships of the various parts. Each component is studied as it relates to the performance of the complete unit, rather than as an isolated element. A value analysis checklist contains literally hundreds of questions and key ideas for reducing overall costs as well as maintaining the same level of product performance.

Typical questions based on knowledge of past effective design principles include:

- Can the part be eliminated?
- If the part is not standard, can a standard part be used?
- If it is a standard part, does it complement the finished product or is it a misfit?
- Can the weight be reduced with lower-priced materials?
- Are tolerances closer than necessary?
- Is unnecessary machining performed on the item?
- Are unnecessary finishes required?
- Can the part be produced less expensively in the plant or should it be bought from a supplier?
- Is the product properly classified for shipping purposes to obtain lowest transportation costs?
- Can the cost of packaging be reduced?
- Do certain parts, such as precision motors and precision parts, exceed the expected life of the finished product?

When using value engineering to appraise overall costs, possibilities for making component part design simplifications are frequently more apparent than is possible under conventional design conditions. This in no way reflects unfavorably on the work done by the design engineer; the discovery of such potential improvements is the result of an analysis with a substantially broader orientation than that possessed by the original designer. A value analysis study undertaken by a typical company utilizes the background and skills of several people, because it is not possible to find the multiplicity of skills and experiences of that group in the person of a single designer. Resulting design changes often permit the substitution of standardized production operations for more expensive operations requiring special setup work. In other cases, an entirely different material or production process turns out to be more efficient than the one originally specified. Therefore, value analysis, operating within a TQM environment, contributes to the profitability of new products for a typical manufacturing oriented company.

Knowledge Discovery to Develop an Overall Purchasing Supply Chain Strategy

By having manufacturing managers, working with their purchasing counterparts, evaluate critical purchasing areas via multidimensional analysis within an OLAP system environment, it is possible to broaden the view of the purchasing function. Managers must assess outsourcing among multiple vendors, analyze purchasing under uncertainty, analyze availability of raw materials and parts to meet present and future growth, and examine the capability of obtaining raw materials and parts for new products being developed. In terms of day-to-day operations, critical purchasing areas that can also be evaluated using an OLAP approach include the measurement of idle machines and/or personnel resulting from a lack of purchased supplies, the measurement of the extent of successful substitutes of materials and parts, the ratio of rejected purchases to total purchases, and the savings on discounts and quantity purchases. Attention to the foregoing areas provides purchasing and manufacturing managers with the capability of having control over their operations as times change.

Although these analyses are very useful to purchasing and manufacturing management, there is a need to go a step further. A comprehensive approach that goes beyond purchasing is required. As noted previously in the chapter, this entails a supply chain approach to working with customers and suppliers. For example, Chrysler is currently concentrating less on purchasing and more on managing the supply chain and the flow of material from the chain into its plants. Most of its current savings have come from this approach, and the company expects that this is where most of its future savings will come from as well. Like Chrysler, a number of aggressive companies are concentrating on supply chain management. In essence, they are weeding out the chain to ensure that the various tiers talk to each other and communicate better. Right now, different tiers do not like to talk to one another. The first tier does not like to talk to the second tier, and the second tier does not like to talk to the third tier. Although industries have grown up this way, the chain and the work on communication between these tiers and sharing of costs is being streamlined. At Chrysler, those who will supply materials for its upcoming minivan line up through the year 2003 or 2004 are already on line. Chrysler can tell its suppliers major changes it wants to make in the supply base and set up the sourcing and presource it—without having even conceptualized the vehicle. Thus, Chrysler has a futuristic purchasing supply chain strategy in place for supplying its future manufacturing activities.

Companies can build upon this tie-in of purchasing activities with the supply chain by utilizing the Internet for making their purchases. There is a need to set standards, however, to make this a reality. In the fall of 1996, SupplyWorks, with additional funding from American Express, organized an Internet purchasing roundtable to pursue this goal. A score of *Fortune* 500 companies with large buying budgets accepted the invitation to join. The roundtable's primary goals were to help different buying systems interact seamlessly and put vendors on an equal footing. The group's first draft was called Open Buying on the Internet. Recently, the roundtable was reorganized as a nonprofit consortium open to all interested organizations. SupplyWorks handles the administrative functions.

As a general framework for busines-to-business transactions, Open Buying on the Internet offers multiple payoffs because it discourages software vendors from populating the web with proprietary systems that cannot interact. Instead, it encourages innovative vendors to jump in, since customers need not buy from a dominant vendor to ensure their software can interact with other systems. A large number of companies already have endorsed the standards, including sellers of purchasing software; large buyers and sellers of corporate supplies, such as Ford and Office Depot; and major web commerce players, such as Microsoft, General Electric, and Oracle.[7]

In the Internet environment, purchasing of goods and services is faster, more efficient, and more cost-effective in a supply chain approach for manufacturers as well as nonmanufacturers. The Internet provides organizations with complete line-item detail on each transaction, giving users real-time access to critical product information. It reduces the effort put into basic transactions by adopting simplified procedures and implementing best practices. In terms of information, the purchasing supply chain structure is linked with finance to ensure information streams easily between these functions.

In a similar manner, this Internet approach along with intranets allow companies to better analyze their operations by discovering new knowledge about themselves and their customers. Using one of the data mining tools (set forth elsewhere in the text), they can discover current trends, patterns, and relationships that lie hidden in data warehouses (extracted from the Internet and intranets) and possibly also discern upcoming trends. In addition to utilizing information from the Internet and intranets to ensure that the best opportunities in terms of products and services are achieved, the discovery of new knowledge and reinforcement of current knowledge can ensure that the best overall purchasing and supply chain strategy is being pursued. After all, a most important part of this strategy is about developing the right kind of procurement process, understanding this procurement process, and making sure it pays for itself. As times change, this combined purchasing and supply chain approach may need to be changed to account for new information and to apply its resulting knowledge to this approach.

PRODUCTION PLANNING AND EXECUTION AND QUALITY CONTROL

Since knowledge is considered to be the basis of a dynamically managed factory, it behooves manufacturing management to have a knowledge management system that not only assists in production planning and execution on the production floor but also aids in effective quality control (i.e., TQM). A manufacturing knowledge base generally consists of various elements, such as rules, heuristics, principles, strategies, standards, facts, and procedures as well as fuzzy knowledge and modeling knowledge. Within a KMS environment, a well-designed manufacturing knowledge base assists managers and their staffs in knowledge acquisition, knowledge inference, and knowledge explanation. In addition, the design should utilize a user-frientiy interface for knowledge retrieval, knowledge validation, and knowledge updating. Such is the approach taken in this section on production planning and execution and quality control. Since information is the backbone of manufacturing knowledge, the focus will be on information that is supplemented by knowledge where deemed necessary.

The production planning and execution department for a typical manufacturing oriented company is responsible for all physical movements between manufacturing departments and within their respective work centers at the plant level. This important department coordinates all activities concerning a production order from its initial recording, through inventory layup and manufacturing, to getting the finished goods ready for shipment to customers (i.e., direct shipments) or to company warehouses for shipment subsequently to customers. Production planning and execution relies heavily on the plant's database and its communications with all manufacturing work centers. Although daily manufacturing activities are the responsibility of the production planning and execution department, they need to be analyzed periodically by manufacturing managers for efficiency and effectiveness using OLAP analysis. Similarly, there may be a need to discover and track manufacturing problems. In this manner, manufacturing managers and their staffs can be assured that short-range manufacturing plans are being implemented on a current basis as mandated. Before looking at planned and actual manufacturing activities, manufacturing partnerships and their relationship with production planning and execution are examined. Determining the appropriate production planning and execution technique for current operations on a daily as well as monthly basis is also discussed. Information furnished to manufacturing management and their staffs over time can provide knowledge to discover and track quality problems.

Manufacturing Partnerships and Their Tie-In with Production Planning

Not too long ago, many large manufacturers, especially in Japan, formed *keiretsu*, or company partnerships, by grouping the subcontractors who supply them with parts. The result is a production system, distributed among many companies, that has helped manufacturers strengthen their global competitiveness. More recently, however, the subcontracting system has started changing to reflect the structural sophistication in Japanese industries. Automakers, electric machinery manufacturers, and other large Japanese firms that are suffering from sagging demand and decreasing earnings are increasingly pressuring subcontractors to cut production costs. If they do not comply, they will be excluded from the *keiretsu*.

In this new and realistic business environment, many subcontractors are looking for business partners outside their company groups. This presents a good opportunity for subcontractors to become independent. The *keiretsu* system is evolving from the existing pyramid-type coalition to horizontal or network-type coalitions. In the process, an increasing number of subcontractors are seeking to improve their technology and production to satisfy key manufacturers. Some are pursuing new business partners outside their company groups while others aim to become independent specialists in processing or manufacturing.[8] In the United States, car manufacturers (as noted previously) are heavily involved in sophisticated supply chain management systems. These systems currently include a focus on various cost-cutting programs, including reduction of work hours and model lines, extension of model-change cycles, and increased use of common parts.

Determine the Appropriate Production Planning and Execution Technique

Once appropriate manufacturing partnerships have been established, there is a need to determine the appropriate planning and execution technique for manufacturing operations. Currently, the focus is on client/server manufacturing systems. Also noted previously, a comprehensive approach to manufacturing that utilizes this system is *enterprise resource planning* (ERP). ERP is real-time manufacturing software that incorporates the entire supply chain from sales and order processing to production, inventory, and distribution. Related to the ERP approach is a *manufacturing execution system* (MES) that utilizes software to manage shop-floor activities.

Essentially, a manufacturing execution system represents the CIM concept at the lower levels of the manufacturing process. It is a set of software applications that can easily integrate into everyday legacy systems and reside on any platform, though the current trend is for PC-based client/server networks. It allows a manufacturer to produce products more effectively on the factory floor by making production visible and information accessible to factory-floor personnel. It is used by operators, setup and tool-room personnel, and supervisors. An MES can provide the following information:[9]

1. resource scheduling/allocation and status
2. operations/detailed scheduling

3. dispatch production units
4. document control
5. data collection/acquisition
6. labor management
7. quality management
8. performance analysis
9. process management
10. product tracking
11. maintenance management

Together these systems allow improved production beyond what is possible with a typical manufacturing system, like MRP-II. MRP-II systems tend to focus on accounting transactions, at best keeping score for the factory floor, but not helping to dispatch production, allocate resources, pace, and otherwise manage production.

In contrast, an MES is the data collection and dissemination of production/process information that makes it truly the new E-mail of the factory floor. It includes such functionalities as resource use, scheduling, quality management, and engineering-change notices. Typically, an MES requires a lot of data collection points that give users a real-time view of manufacturing. A recent survey of manufacturers who have used MES over the past five years confirms that the technology can be applied successfully to a broad range of shop-floor functions. Respondents cited reduced manufacturing cycle time as a very important MES benefit. The average reduction in production cycle time of surveyed respondents was 45 percent.[10]

Typically, an integral part of the production planning and execution technique is *just-in-time* (JIT) *inventory*, which is based on the elimination of wasteful or non-value-added activity within a company. Its primary goal is to reduce inventory as close to zero as possible and to reduce lead time via reduced setup and reduced lot sizes. While inventory has always been considered an asset in the past, today inventory is a liability. The more excess inventory a company has, the more the root problems that have caused a company to hold excess inventory lie hidden. Manufacturing flexibility is a key aspect of JIT, where quick response to a customer's needs means producing lot sizes when needed. Another issue addresses the reduction in the number of suppliers with which a company has to deal. Rather than having multiple product sources, one or two are now sufficient.

Daily and Periodic Production Planning and Execution

Typically, a manufacturing company's products can be produced upon receipt of customers' orders, in anticipation of demand, or in some combination of the two. If goods are being produced to order, the usual arrangement is to have the production planning and execution department initiate action on the order via its data communications network, which is then distributed on-line to stock control, shipping, and accounting departments. However, for many companies, products are produced in anticipation of demand. Then the focus is on planning manufacturing activities on a monthly basis at the corporate level, then controlling on a daily basis using one of the current MES software packages at the manufacturing plant(s).

The procedure for determining next-period's sales forecasts (one month hence) after adjusting for finished goods on order and on hand is the starting point, as shown in Figure 8-3, for on-line production planning and execution. Because finished goods production requirements for the *next month* provide the necessary input for the manufacturing function, linear programming is utilized to determine the quantity of each product that will be produced in each of the manufacturing plants. After next-period production schedules have been computed by plant, the next phase is ''exploding'' bills of materials. The materials planning-by-periods program multiplies the quantity needed of each component times the number of final products that must be manufactured. Also, it places the component requirements in the appropriate planning period, because some parts will be needed before others. In this manner, purchased parts and raw materials are placed on a just-in-time basis for production needs.

The output for the materials requirements by future-planning periods in Figure 8-3 can take two paths. The *first* one is the purchasing of raw materials and parts from outside vendors, and the *second* one is the manufacturing of parts within the plants. The outside raw materials provide the basic inputs for manufacturing specific parts used in the assembly of the finished product. Likewise, outside purchased parts are used in the assembly of the final product. Before materials are manufactured or purchased, it is necessary to determine on line if present inventories and materials on order are capable of meeting the company's needs for future planning periods. At this point, it is important to note that perpetual inventories stored on line have been adjusted to reflect physical counts in order to produce accurate output for the materials availability and EOQ (economic ordering quantity) program. In this manner, the planned requirements for purchased and manufacturing parts can reflect actual conditions.

As shown in Figure 8-3, the integrated and continuous operating mode does not stop here. Based upon established monthly production quotas that have been translated into planned daily requirements, the MES software provides the means for scheduling (i.e., executing) production orders on line through the manufacturing work centers on a *daily* basis. Additionally, other operational programs are available to record and execute daily activities (including attendance, payroll, work-in-process, etc.). The output of these programs provides operations evaluation reports on manufacturing activities. In addition, the output can be analyzed in more detail on a daily basis using OLAP analysis. In turn, these types of analyses can be extended over a longer period of time to develop knowledge about what is actually going on in the company's manufacturing operations—good, bad, or indifferent.

In order to smooth production for each working day, a daily computerized scheduler is employed at each plant. Before the start of each working day (the program is actually run at the end of the prior day shift and reviewed by the plant's management), the scheduler considers where jobs are backed up or behind schedule and where production bottlenecks are currently occurring. Based on these basic inputs, the scheduler simulates the activities of the plant for the coming day and determines what will happen as the day begins, thereby alerting the plant manager and supervisors to critical areas that need attention. Because all data affecting manufacturing activities are entered as they occur, the scheduler feeds back information in sufficient time to execute upcoming manufacturing operations. This daily computerized scheduler also allows the production planning and execution department to make adjustments, if deemed necessary, to accommodate last-minute changes that may not have been entered as yet on the plant database.

In summary, periodic (i.e., monthly) programs do not operate individually but are integrated with daily on-line operations, as shown in Figure 8-3. Sales forecasts (as discussed in the previous chapter) serve as input for finished goods product requirements which, in turn, constitute input for the next month's production schedule for each plant. In a similar manner, this monthly output is input for "exploding" bills of materials, forming the basis for materials requirements by future planning periods. This monthly information is then employed for manufacturing orders within the company's plants and for placing orders with outside suppliers on a just-in-time basis. This input-output approach using the appropriate software at the corporate level and the plant level provides a basis for day-to-day scheduling and dispatching of various manufacturing operations. The manufacturing execution system software, which is assisted by the daily scheduler, provides the means for managing the ongoing shop-floor activities of the plants on a continuous basis.

Using Knowledge to Discover and Track Quality Problems

Although the MES software and the daily scheduler are quite capable of keeping a typical company's operations under control on a daily basis, there is a need to go a step further to discover and track quality problems and resolve them. For example, knowledge sharing is one of the major keys to an effective quality partnership between General Motors and its main union, the United Automobile Workers (UAW). This jointly developed GM-UAW Quality Network has been a vital tool in transferring knowledge throughout the giant automaker's far-flung operations. Communication has been an essential tool of the network both in terms of transferring best practices from one plant to another and in building an atmosphere of trust in which collaboration and knowledge sharing can happen. For example, at the Delphi Energy and Engine Management Sys-

Figure 8-3
A Manufacturing Planning and Execution System on a Monthly Basis at the Corporate Level and a Daily Basis at the Plant Level

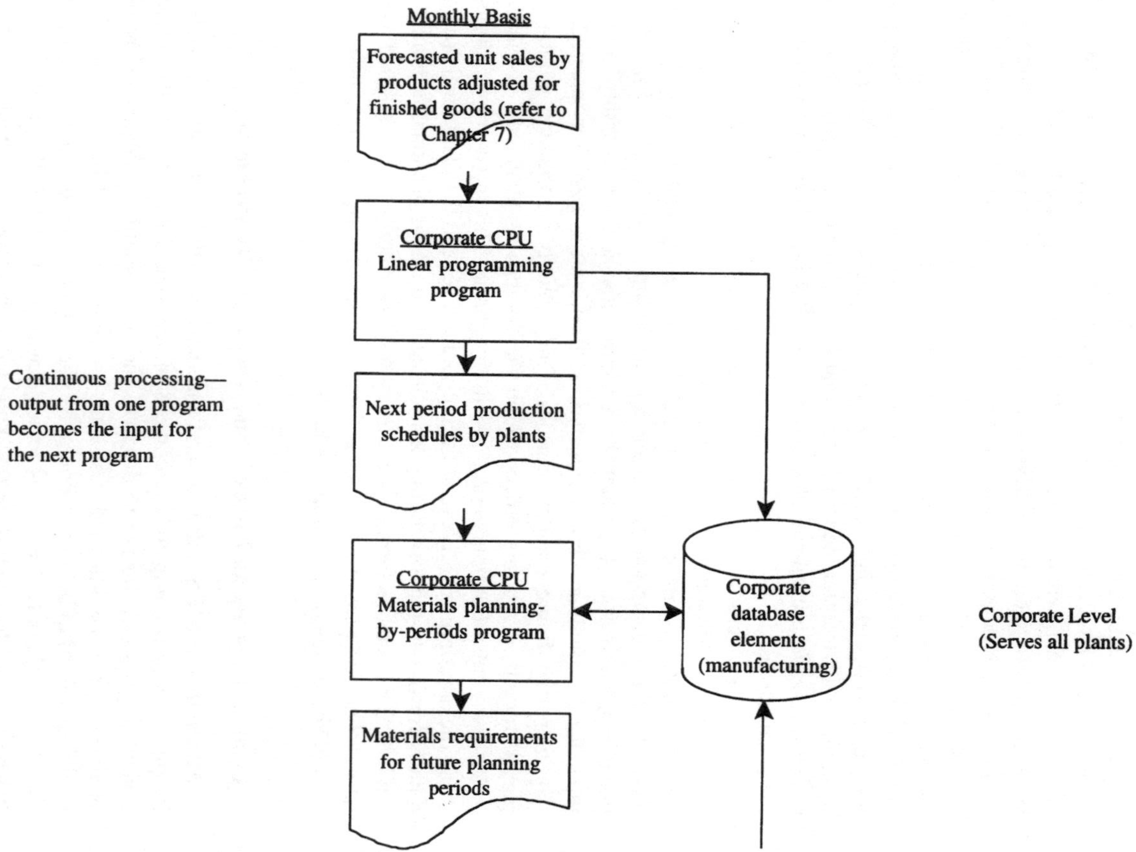

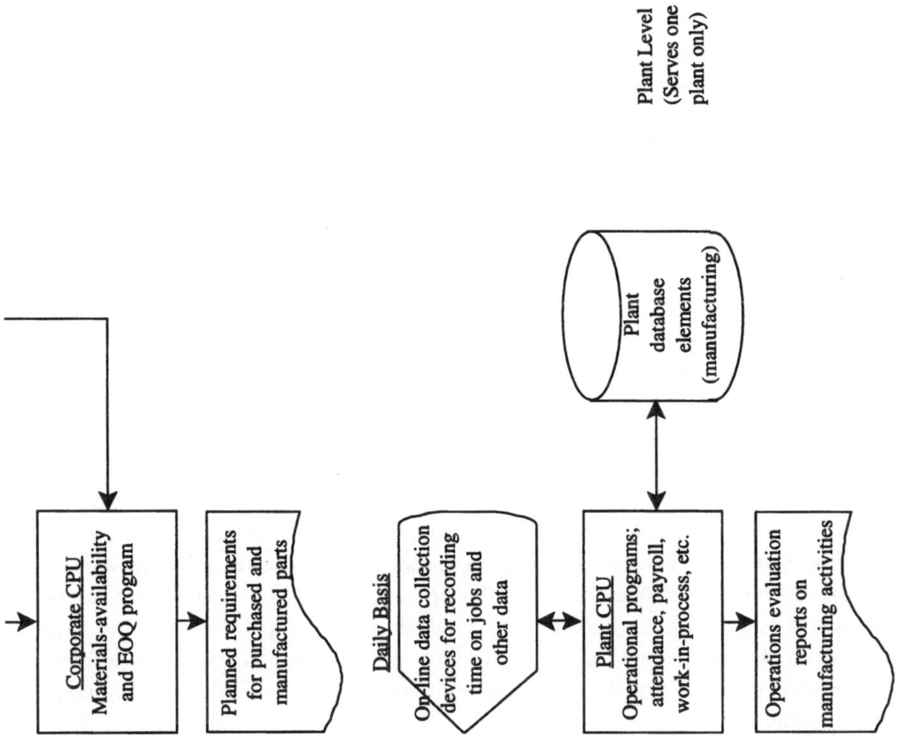
Corporate CPU
Materials-availability and EOQ program
Planned requirements for purchased and manufactured parts
Daily Basis
On-line data collection devices for recording time on jobs and other data
Plant CPU
Operational programs; attendance, payroll, work-in-process, etc.
Operations evaluation reports on manufacturing activities
Plant database elements (manufacturing)
Plant Level (Serves one plant only)

tems (a division of GM's Delphi Automotive Systems unit), the plant manager spends every Friday discussing quality concerns with members of the plant's 80-plus self-empowered work teams. The outcome of these meetings is that there is an invaluable avenue for learning and knowledge transfer across the enterprise.

A typical situation centers around quality problems for such a manufacturer. The goal of the analysis is to look through a database of assembly-line products in order to discover and track quality problems. Basically, quality problems are isolated and can be classified on the basis of two critical factors. The classification tree is then grown to a depth of three levels in order to illustrate that while a factor may not be relevant in predicting quality problems at the "general" (first level) of the tree, it becomes important when considered in the context of other factors. The example below uses a KnowledgeSEEKER analysis of engineering quality control data. In this analysis, the "exception code" field was examined. All database records were examined and edited, producing a "clean" data set of 2,001 records. Installation date and removal date were recorded and duration of service was computed.

The specific goal of the analysis was to explain an "overheating" exception code. Thus, the question was: "What characteristics in the data set tend to predict that the unit will be removed because of overheating?" If the factors that affect overheating can be identified, then potentially the production process can be improved to lower the incidence of overheating problems. Alternatively, if the circumstances that lead to overheating can be isolated, then increased quality control can be applied to the areas that characterize these circumstances. Because time is of essence in industrial processes, the sooner a problem can be fixed the less expensive the remedy. And since it is expensive to apply high levels of vigilance across all processes, any information that points to problem areas sooner, rather than later, can lead to major cost savings (for both vigilance and repair).

As shown in Figure 8-4(a), the data set exception code was mapped into two values: "Overheat" and "Other." This will allow the focus to be on overheating as a particular problem (separate from all the particular exception codes that are recorded by the manufacturing process). The first level of the decision tree shows that, overall, there were 1,037 "Overheat" exception codes in the data set. Although a number of factors turned out to be significant predictors of overheating, the field "Install duration" produced the most dramatic effect. The likelihood of an "overheat" failure increases dramatically when the length of service is more than two days. At two days only 35.6% of the units produce an "overheat" exception condition. For units that have been in service longer than 12 days, the "overheat" exceptions constitute 80.9% of the cases.

When the second level of the classification tree is grown as shown in Figure 8-4(b), "Series number" is introduced as an important classifier. This is true for both the extreme left (short install duration) node and the extreme right (long duration) node. Although different series numbers are susceptible to an over-

Figure 8-4
Analysis of Overheating Exception Code at the (a) First, (b) Second, and (c) Third Levels Using KnowledgeSEEKER

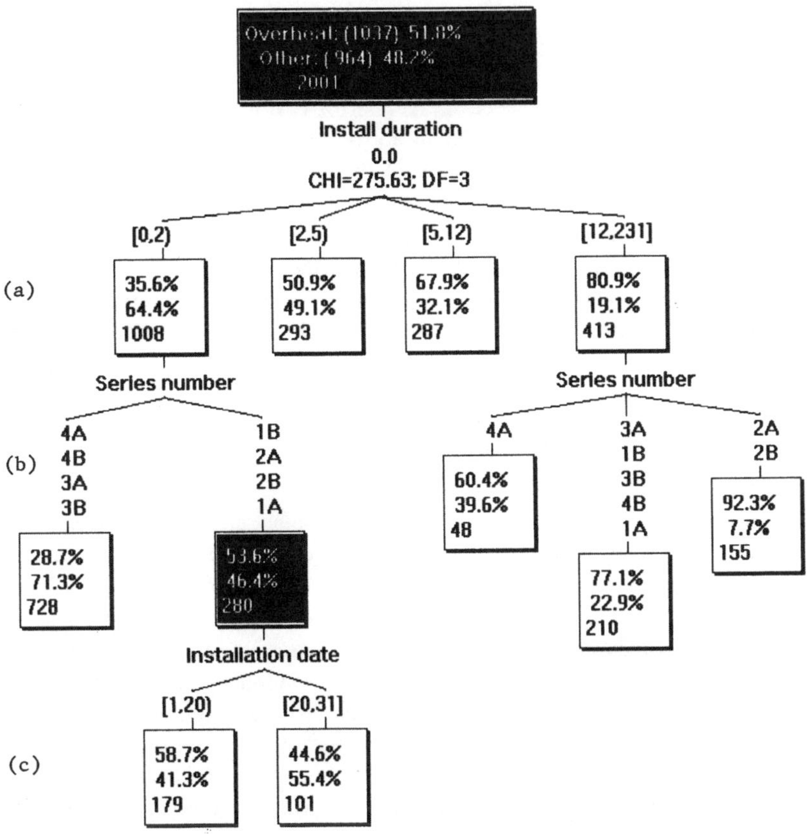

Source: Angoss Software International Limited.

heating exception in these two short and long duration extremes, it is useful to look at the "2A" and "2B" series. In the long duration installations, these two series numbers have the highest incidence of overheating exceptions, 92.3%. It should be noted that these two series numbers are also members of the node that characterize high numbers of overheating exceptions in the low duration node as well. Here codes "2A" and "2B" are grouped in with codes that produce an overheating exception rate of 53.6%.

The analysis in Figure 8-4(c) can continue to a third-level depth. As can be seen in the lower left-hand side of the classification tree, other factors in addition to service duration and series can be used to explain the presence of overheating exceptions in the data—sometimes (as shown here) in unusual ways. "Installation date'' affects the presence of overheating exceptions for the lowest service duration group (less than two days) as follows: If the unit was installed in the first 19 days of the month, then the chances of it being an overheating exception increase from 35.6% to 58.7% (first-level node results compared to the third-level node results). This applies to units with a series number of 1A, 1B, 2A, or 2B. This represents an increase of almost 25% and places these units in the same group as units that have been in service for two to five days (the second node at the first level of the tree shown above). It raises the question of why overheating exceptions should be higher in the first 19 days of the month, the exception rate for the installation dates 20th to 31st was less: 44.6%. A further examination of the procedures involved in short-duration series 1B, 2A, 2B, and 1A units would generally shed light on this question. Thus, the company has the capability to discover important causes of overheating exceptions. In turn, this knowledge is of paramount importance for suggesting appropriate remedial action.[11]

UTILIZING KNOWLEDGE TO ASSIST IN RUNNING THE VIRTUAL FACTORY

The utilization of knowledge in running real manufacturing operations can now include the virtual factory. The *virtual factory* can be defined as a number of factories linked together electronically, each focused on what it does best. Since the factories are linked by an electronic network, they can operate as one regardless of their location. This network makes it possible for companies with dissimilar information systems to exchange information about such items as inventory levels and delivery schedules. Just as it allows companies with different CAD (computer-aided design) systems to collaborate electronically on designs, it also permits potential suppliers to gain entry to the system in order to bid on jobs with minimal hassle. Finally, a virtual factory allows a small manufacturer to have the same access to information as a large partner.

Due to the complexity of virtual operations, a number of problems have arisen. A thorough investigation of these problems using knowledge obtained from a number of sources has suggested some important changes. These include the need for items, such as open computing standards, more abundant bandwidth, improved computer security, and accumulated expertise of virtual operations. For example, AeroTech (a spinoff of McDonnell Douglas Aerospace) acts as an information broker for the community by signing up new partners, tracking network memberships, overseeing security, and serving as a converter that permits partners with different formats to communicate. The network permits members to carry out a wide variety of collaborative tasks and is extremely secure.

To accommodate a broad range of tasks and users and to make the system as simple as possible to use, AeroTech employs protocols developed for the Internet, which itself is just an extra-large network that connects millions of dissimilar computers around the world. Also, AeroTech permits its members to choose from a very wide assortment of telecommunication methods and speeds. Those members with minimal or sporadic needs access the system with modems, while more permanent participants, such as customers within other large aerospace companies or in the U.S. government, use dedicated high-bandwidth links. All in all, AeroTech's approach represents a flexible, low-cost network that is a model for a new era in manufacturing.[12]

To assist in the development of knowledge to run the virtual factory, languages, such as Java, allow users to connect to a remote site and use small pieces of software, called applets, one at a time. Any computer that can run a web browser can run this kind of software. Essentially, Internet-based, Java-like languages allow customers to obtain modules for performing particular functions as they need them by downloading them across an increasingly fast and reliable Internet. Also, Java was developed with security safeguards in place to foil viruses and other threats. From this view, a manufacturer posts worksheet applets on its web pages in order to allow potential customers to simulate the function of its products before buying them. A valve manufacturer, for example, might supply an applet that allows engineers not only to see pictures and CAD drawings of its products but also to use a working spreadsheet that permits them to make key design calculations and show the results on screen.

In addition, these applets allow companies to deliver appropriate bid requests over the web. These requests include a combination of moving diagrams of the products that they would like potential suppliers to bid on. A Java-based interface for a three-dimensional CAD system not only allows companies to put catalogs on the web, it also lets potential customers examine a three-dimensional representation of products from any angle. As network-based software becomes more and more sophisticated, it will present new opportunities to extract the power of the web to help run the virtual factory. And, at the same time, the knowledge that is derived within this environment can be shared among all participants.

SUMMARY

The manufacturing function has witnessed, and is still witnessing, many exciting developments directly or indirectly related to knowledge management systems. Automated factories, industrial robots, vision systems, and new processes are typical advances useful in the area of manufacturing operations. In addition to the employment of advanced manufacturing methods and machines, newer control systems, such as MES, plus mathematical and statistical models, have helped to bring an entirely new approach to manufacturing. For these advances to be effective in discovering new knowledge about manufacturing, computer integrated manufacturing that is tied in with a purchasing and supply chain approach should be used on a daily basis. Essentially, after the products are engineered properly, purchasing must buy on an optimum basis and, at the same time, utilize value analysis to ensure good product profitability. In turn, there is a tie-in of premanufacturing activities with manufacturing operations that leads to a timely flow of raw materials and parts from outside vendors on a just-in-time basis through the company's manufacturing work centers. The end results are manufactured products for direct shipment to customers or to finished goods stockkeeping. Throughout the entire process, management can use manufacturing knowledge to get a complete overview as well as a better understanding of day-to-day operations. If problems are discovered, such as those related to quality, knowledge can be used to get a better grasp on them as a prelude to their solution.

NOTES

1. Dave Holbrook, "Stereo Viewing: Looking into Manufacturing," *Manufacturing Systems*, January 1991, pp. 30–31.
2. Frank Rose, "Now Quality Means Service Too," *Fortune*, April 22, 1991, p. 100.
3. Lura K. Romei, "Quality Becomes Integral to American Business," *Modern Office Technology*, July 1991, p. 10.
4. Michael Hammer and James Champy, "The Promise of Reengineering," *Fortune*, May 3, 1993, pp. 94–97.
5. Angoss Software, *KnowledgeSEEKER in Action: Case Studies* (Toronto: Angoss Software International Limited, 1996), pp. 3–4.
6. Meghan O'Leary, "A New Life for Purchasing," *CIO*, May 1, 1993, p. 32.
7. Mary J. Cronin, "Setting Standards for Corporate Purchasing on the Internet," *Fortune*, September 8, 1997, pp. 156–158.
8. Ikuo Umebayashi, "New Trends in the Keiretsu System," *Wall Street Journal*, November 16, 1992, p. A12.
9. John Leibert, "Manufacturing Execution Systems," *ID Systems*, October 1994, pp. 40–43.
10. Robert Knight, "MES Challenges MIS," *Software Magazine*, August 1994, p. 28.
11. Angoss Software, "Study 2: Product Assurance, Quality Control Data," *KnowledgeSEEKER in Action* (Toronto: Angoss Software International Limited, 1996).
12. David M. Upton and Andrew McAfee, "The Real Virtual Factory," *Harvard Business Review*, July–August 1996, pp. 123–133.

9

Application of Financial Knowledge

Issues Explored:

- How important is it for the typical company to integrate accounting and finance activities with strategic planning?
- What is so important about integrating a company's critical success factors with its key performance indicators and financial ratios?
- What are the important factors that are helpful in discovering financial knowledge?
- How can a typical company benefit from knowledge management in the areas of cost accounting and financial analysis?
- How can a company utilize knowledge to manage investments in order to maximize its ROI?

Outline:

Using Knowledge Management Systems in Accounting and Finance to Further a Company's Goals

Integration of Accounting and Finance with Strategic Planning

The Importance of CSFs That Tie In with KPIs and Financial Ratios

Financial Principles Based on Knowledge of a Company's Overall Operations

Important Factors That Are Helpful in Discovering Financial Knowledge

Problem Finding in Discovering Financial Knowledge

Content Analysis of Financial Statements

Using the Internet to Discover Financial Knowledge

Rethinking Cost Accounting Approaches

Software Useful in Discovering Financial Knowledge

USING KNOWLEDGE MANAGEMENT SYSTEMS IN ACCOUNTING AND FINANCE TO FURTHER A COMPANY'S GOALS

Today, as in the past, an organization's ability to manage and leverage its financial capital goes a long way toward ensuring its survival and growth. Financial markets are particularly sensitive to the financial performance of a company over time. In addition, as indicated many times, there is a need for a company and its managers to increase the value of its intellectual capital through the use of knowledge management systems to further its goals. A successful company in the 21st century and beyond will be one that does the best job of capturing, storing, and leveraging what its employees know. Intellectual property, accounting and finance databases, and other forms of knowledge management make up a large part of what is required to meet constantly changing and growing customer needs.

A company's *vision of the future* is related to the best use of financial capital and intellectual capital. In a typical company, top-level managers must want their company to be the leader in its industries, say in five years. Or they must want to achieve this goal to better serve their customers. Vision is not merely financial long-range planning intended to realize more sales. It is a fundamental change in how the company must function to become competitive or achieve a leadership role. Examples include Fred Smith's vision when he launched Federal Express. Max Hopper's vision along with that of several others created American Airlines's Sabre flight reservation system. Emil Martini's vision helped put a terminal in every drugstore for ordering inventory directly from Bergen-Brunswig. Each of these ideas—radical changes in business operations—were answers to items that solved business needs and achieved phenomenal success. In turn, visioning is linked directly to a company's critical success factors

(CSFs) and key performance indicators (KPIs). Essentially, CSFs and KPIs are tied in with a company's financial performance, which is generally captured by its accounting and finance systems. In turn, this information over time becomes essential raw material for knowledge management systems in accounting and finance to maintain and further a company's goals.

This vision of the future ties in with the materials presented in the previous chapters. Essentially, the emphasis in Chapter 6 was on the utilization of short- to long-range strategic planning by managers in order to choose objectives and goals, select strategies, develop programs, and set policies. In turn, Chapters 7 and 8 were directed toward using information and knowledge to assure effectiveness in the acquisition and use of the organization's resources by marketing and manufacturing managers, respectively. This chapter builds upon these prior chapters by centering on accounting and financial information and knowledge and their tie-in with short- and long-range strategic plans. The focus will be on discovering and utilizing knowledge to carry out a company's strategic financial plans.

INTEGRATION OF ACCOUNTING AND FINANCE WITH STRATEGIC PLANNING

To integrate accounting and finance effectively with strategic planning, top management and the corporate planning staff need to take an enlarged view of a company. Similarly, company treasurers, controllers, and their staffs must enlarge the scope of their thinking and integrate financial strategic planning via a company's critical success factors (CSFs) with key performance indicators (KPIs) and financial ratios. Basically, this means allowing them to "get the big picture" when reviewing the company's total activities so that there is optimization of resourcers for the entire company rather than for one or just a few parts of it. The success that the typical company has in attaining its general objectives and measurable short- to long-range strategic planning goals depends on the degree of integration of operations that are critical to its success. A company's critical success factors, in turn, form the basis for measurement using KPIs and financial ratios. Overall, enlargement of the scope of accounting and finance activities as well as the acceptance of responsibilities that once lay outside traditional financial areas are found within a successful KMS environment.

The Importance of CSFs That Tie In with KPIs and Financial Ratios

A logical starting point for financial strategic planning is the determination of a company's critical success factors. CSFs can be best facilitated by a company's culture where organization personnel believe what they are doing is worth doing. As noted in Chapter 6, a company's critical success factors are the limited number of areas in which results, if they are satisfactory, will help ensure successful competitive performance. Basically, they are the important areas where things must go right if the company is to flourish. If results in these key areas are not adequate, the company's efforts for the period will be less than desired. Typically, CSFs are areas of activity that should receive constant and careful attention from management. Performance in these areas needs to be measured on a continuing basis and the results should be available to higher management levels.

Due to fast-changing business times facing a typical company, CSFs need to be reviewed periodically for relevance. That is, the appropriate CSFs for today may not be appropriate for tomorrow. There is the need for higher levels of management to employ problem finding in order to relate what is known and what is not known to what needs to be known for a company to have the capability to be one step ahead of its competition. The knowledge gained from this approach, which includes the discovery of new emerging patterns and trends, provides the basis for proposing new strategies that center on improving a company's competitiveness and its return on investment. Also, such an approach provides new insights for further analysis. The bottom line is that a company's critical success factors need to be changed over time to reflect a changing world. An effective way to make the appropriate changes is to employ knowledge management resources at the proper time and place for effective results.

For a typical company, there are a number of *key performance indicators* that are useful in determining viability. Typical ones in marketing include the following:

- ability or inability to make changes to a company's marketing strategies
- increase or decrease in company sales
- increase or decrease in market share
- increase or decrease in customers' satisfaction
- market research on continuing the status quo or bringing new products to market
- acceptance or nonacceptance of new products and services by customers
- increase or decrease in quality of products and services
- improved or unacceptable delivery times
- increase or decrease in sales and operating expenses
- increase or decrease in gross profit and cash flow for a company's products and services

In a similar manner, a number of KPIs can be developed not only for a company's other functional areas but also for the company as a whole. These KPIs tend to focus on financial ratios. Overall, a company has control over KPIs. The company is able to manage the performance of these areas and make changes when necessary.

Chief among a number of *financial ratios* that are useful to financial analysts is return on investment. ROI analysis can be used to judge present performance and evaluate future investment opportunities. Analysts can also use ROI to rate managerial effectiveness and to compare potential profitability of divisions and departments. While the technique of ROI analysis is uncomplicated, the potential applications are varied and valuable. Basically, the ROI equation is earnings divided by total assets.

A problem in calculating ROI arises in identifying what is meant by earnings or total assets. Although there is no single, correct way to figure ROI, it is customary to use earnings from operations before taxes, sales after returns and allowances for bad debts, and net, year-end book value of assets. It is important that there be consistency and that the same measures of earnings, sales, and assets be used when figuring ROIs for different periods. Also, managers should be prepared for apparent surprises when comparing their company's ROI to another company's. That is, the other company may have used different measures in calculating its ROI.

Going beyond ROI, there are a number of financial ratios that can be applied to a company. Typical ones (that measure some aspect of a company) are:

- capital turnover (management efficiency)
- current ratio (liquidity status)
- investment status (measure of solvency)
- return on assets used (asset profitability)
- average collection period (receivable investment)
- return on sales (operation efficiency)
- inventory turnover (inventory utilization)
- undelivered commitments (days of sales in backlog)
- net worth debt ratio (credit strength)
- acid test ratio (immediate liquidation)
- stockholders' earnings status (percent earnings available)

These financial ratios focus on the overall aspects that assist in financial strategic thinking. They can be calculated as needed and thereby serve as the basis for management by exception where appropriate ranges are assigned to each ratio. For example, the ratio of current assets to current liabilities should be about 2 to 1. Typically, to calculate these financial ratios, there is a need to interact with a corporate database or data warehouse.

Basically, these ratios provide insight into measuring actual results against the corporate strategic plans (short-range to long-range). Management effectiveness can be measured by the capital turnover ratio, asset profitability, and ROI. In addition, the corporation's performance can be gauged through the return on sales, days of sales in backlog, inventory utilization, and receivable collections.

Financial Principles Based on Knowledge of a Company's Overall Operations

Principles that underlie efficient and effective accounting and finance activities are based on knowledge of a company's total operations. Over the years, these principles have evolved. They are subject to the fast-changing times of a global economy. Related to these financial principles is the people factor. According to a survey sponsored by Arthur Andersen and the American Productivity and Quality Center, there is a vast difference between where participants are in knowledge management and where they think they should be. Of the companies surveyed, 79 percent say managing organizational knowledge is important or essential to their strategy, but only 15 percent think they are doing a good or excellent job of it. In addition, 91 percent said that they have no way to link knowledge management to financial results or that they do so poorly. For a typical company, the essential message is that a knowledge management system needs to be implemented so that it allows a good tie-in of knowledge with financial results.[1]

A logical beginning principle for accounting and finance is that right financial policies must precede right financial tools. That is, it is essential to put the horse before the cart and not the other way around. It is necessary to complement a company's financial tools strategy with the appropriate organization and the right policies and procedures to make it all work together. Unfortunately, many companies seem to focus primarily on the tools factor (i.e., hardware and software). Eventually, they come to realize that it takes a lot more than that. An effective financial system is based on organization, governed by policies and procedures that are tied in with the financial tools that are used by organization personnel for everyday operations.

An important second principle is figuring out the best way to allocate a company's capital. Which policies should the company follow to meet its growth objectives and financial goals? This may sound simple—invest it so that the company makes more money than its capital costs and return the difference to its stockholders—but it's really not. Needless to say, choosing where to invest is an especially challenging job for a fast-growing company. Even in a stable industry, opportunities typically far outstrip a company's resources. The need to borrow seems to be on everyone's agenda, especially during expansionary times. The bottom line is a proper determination of allocating capital, whether it is generated internally or acquired externally.

Related to the preceding principle of the proper allocation of capital is one that centers on costs after the capital projects have been carried out. Essentially, the principle states that high costs in more than one area, such as marketing, capital investment, research and development, or any other area of a business can ruin any business. Too often, capital projects exceed their initial estimates by a small to a wide margin. This means that someone must make up the difference. Usually, this is where stockholders get hit if the cost overruns are substantial enough. Reading daily and weekly financial newspapers will verify this important point. This principle comes into play especially during periods of high inflation.

One principle that is often overlooked focuses on the *accountability* of the company's managers for financial performance. Accountability recognizes the significance of utilizing flexible budgeting and rethinking cost accounting approaches, among others, to improve the quality of information and knowledge provided for all management levels. Within such an approach to financial operations, finance takes on a new perspective. It goes beyond allowing managers to review current operations. It adds a new dimension by providing a means of synthesizing a myriad of information and knowledge for answering key managerial questions for one or more areas of accountability. Typically, such questions include: What happens to net profits before federal income taxes if variable costs of producing certain products are decreased by certain capital investments? What impact do interest rate changes have on net profits when funds must be borrowed from multiple sources on the outside if future economic conditions are truly uncertain? Although answering this type of question generally requires the use of mathematical and statistical modeling or the use of knowledge discovery software, an effective accountability approach can help supply answers that have far-reaching impact on the company.

A company can improve its financial operations by recognizing that the whole is worth more than the sum of its parts. The more a company can "bundle" its operations, the greater the tendency to simplify the customer's life in today's environment where time and cost savings are of the essence. Hence, this important principle makes use of bundling where customer and company costs can be kept at a minimum. As United Airlines found out, it is not enough to combine services that complement one another if the bundle does not give customers anything more than they could get by purchasing each item separately. The most successful bundles let customers replace several confusing operations with a single, simpler alternative. For example, a telecommunications company offers local, long-distance, and cellular phone service; paging; Internet access; and teleconferencing. But, unlike most of its rivals, it offers all those services in a single package, backed by a unified sales and service system, and tallied on a single monthly bill. Because customers appreciate this convenience, customer retention rates have jumped greatly. Also, its chargeoff rate on accounts has dropped correspondingly.

Another financial principle centers around making sense out a company's financial measures and applying the results to its everyday operations. In the prior discussion on critical success factors, key performance indicators, and financial ratios, these important measures were set forth and will not be repeated again. It is sufficient to say that a company's CSFs are developed by top management and appropriate financial devices are used to monitor them so that overall results are measured on a periodic basis. Going a step further, KPIs and financial ratios are the outcome of analyzing a company's balance sheet and income statement in some detail. Overall, a thorough, periodic evaluation of a company's financial operations can become the basis for corrective action where deemed appropriate.

To assist a company in meeting its growth potential, finance managers need to look outside the firm for appropriate sources of capital to fund promising new projects. Hence, a most important financial principle is one that leverages a company's funds to their fullest using creative financing. That is, to fund the project on its own, the company would have to use up its profits. Even a fifty-fifty joint venture would still require development funds. However, the company could find one or more venture capitalists willing to fund new ventures. It could well be that the company need not put up any, or at least very little, money. As such, the company is buying itself more flexibility when allocating restricted capital funds for future projects.

Related to the preceding principle on investing capital funds is a very important one that focuses on investing in people—training and improving employee skills to improve a company's *return on knowledge* (ROK). Typically, the big reason that a company spends so much on training is that it is an investment in employee retention. Because most people today have seven jobs before their careers are over, what they look for in an employer is a continuous investment in their skills. Retaining employees is good for any company; however, this is especially vital for fast-growing companies. If a fast-growing company loses one person, it ends up having to hire two more. One replaces the person lost, and the other is needed because the company is growing so fast.

In the past, the two main benefits of reengineering efforts were increased productivity and lower costs of operations. For the most part, reengineering in the past focused primarily on paring bloated organizations and eliminating unnecessary costs. This approach boosted profits in the short term but not in the long term. Hence, for short- to long-term growth in a typical company, a different financial principle must be applied which states that reengineering efforts are more successful when the focus is on improving the inflows of revenue. Without creating new revenue, reengineering efforts are not likely to produce increasing profits. Research over the years has indicated that the market value of companies that emphasized revenue growth expanded at a faster rate than the value of companies that focused on cost-cutting measures.

From a slightly different perspective, an underlying financial principle stresses the importance of employing newer computer technologies that allow a company to reduce its own costs of operations, thereby allowing it to reduce prices charged to its customers. Generally, such improvements are quite noticeable to customers, who are looking for improvements from this standpoint no matter what they are. This concern for customers goes a long way. It not only encourages them to buy more but it also makes them partial recipients of the improvements that the company has made to its own operations over time. It may well be that the company's software and, possibly hardware, can be used to effect savings for its customers. For example, this concern for customers by the McKesson Drug Company is found in their operations today. Both McKesson and its customers are benefiting from its lower costs of processing orders. This is a clear case of a "win-win" situation.

Last, but certainly not least, is the principle of building bridges from accounting and finance to a company's other functional areas. Despite the traditional view that financial systems belong only in one area unto themselves, more and more companies are turning to accounting and finance systems to bridge the gap among functional departments by providing updated information and supportive knowledge for reporting, analysis, and strategic planning. All parties from the company president to department managers to sales representatives to plant managers need to have their own view of accounting and finance. Instead of operating at cross-purposes, all functional area managers need to coordinate all of their business functions—from production management, inventory control, work scheduling, and purchasing to accounts payable, sales-order entry, and financial analysis. Building internal bridges among a company's functional areas provides the basic framework for constructing computer networks that are linked to outsiders, whether they are customers, suppliers, banks, unions, or government agencies. The bottom line is that building effective bridges from accounting and finance to others within and outside the company results in improved financial performance and productivity.

These financial principles are based on a knowledge of a company's overall operations and are summarized in Figure 9-1. As times change, there will be a need to update this listing.

IMPORTANT FACTORS THAT ARE HELPFUL IN DISCOVERING FINANCIAL KNOWLEDGE

To discover knowledge about a typical company's financial operations, treasurers, financial executives, controllers, and their staffs must enlarge the scope of their thinking. Essentially, this means allowing them to "get the big picture" when analyzing the company's total activities so that there is optimization of resources for the entire company rather than for one or just a few parts of it. The success the typical company has in attaining its mission as well as its short- to long-range objectives and goals depends on the degree of integration of its operations. Enlargements of the scope of organization activities as well as rethinking of traditional accounting and finance activities from a newer view are set forth in this chapter.

Important factors that are useful in discovering accounting and finance knowledge can focus on a wide range of topics. Among those covered below for knowledge management systems are: (1) problem finding in discovering financial knowledge, (2) content analysis of financial statements, (3) using the Internet to discover financial knowledge, (4) rethinking cost accounting approaches, and (5) software useful in discovering financial knowledge.

Figure 9-1
Financial Principles Based on Knowledge of a Company's Overall Operations

- A company needs to complement its financial tools strategy with the appropriate organization and the right policies and procedures so that they are compatible with one another.
- Figuring out the best way to allocate a company's capital is paramount in order to meet its growth objectives and financial goals.
- High costs in more than one area, such as marketing, capital investment, or research and development, can ruin any company.
- Accountability recognizes the significance of utilizing flexible budgeting and rethinking cost accounting approaches, among others, to improve the quality of information and knowledge provided for all management levels.
- The more a company can ''bundle'' or consolidate its operations from a customer's perspective, the greater the tendency to simplify a customer's life in today's environment where time and cost savings are of the essence.
- Evaluation of a company's financial operations via key performance indicators and financial ratios that tie back to a company's critical success factors forms the basis for corrective action where deemed appropriate.
- Leveraging a company's funds to their fullest using creative financing approaches allows the company more flexibility in allocating funds to its future projects.
- Investing in people, (i.e., training and improving employee skils) for a high return on knowledge (ROK) is just as important as obtainment of a high return on investment (ROI) for capital funds.
- Reengineering efforts are more successful when the focus is on improving the inflows of revenue instead of only cost-cutting measures.
- A company's computer technology should allow it to reduce its own costs of operations, thereby reducing prices charged to its customers. In turn, computer technology that is tied in with its customers can be used to reduce costs for them.
- Building effective interconnecting bridges from accounting and finance to a company's other functional areas and outsiders results in improved financial performance and productivity.

Problem Finding in Discovering Financial Knowledge

A logical starting point for demonstrating how a knowledge management system is different from previous system approaches is in the area of problem finding. Basically, problem finding is better able than traditional problem-solving approaches to diagnose more types of important financially oriented problems facing accounting and finance managers and top-level executives. To illustrate the use of problem finding within a KMS environment, consider the following example. Let's say that a measurable goal of a corporation is to increase the value of its investments by 15 percent in five years. Top-level executives and the corporate-planning staff, working in conjunction with the corporation's vice president of finance, the treasurer, and the controller, can analyze and solve the problem using different approaches. Within an OLAP operating mode, the "bottom line" for each investment approach can be evaluated thoroughly by examining ways to increase investment values. If the investment's total return does not attain the corporation's goal, the important *variables* can be examined to determine what individual profit contributor(s) is likely to fail to produce its share of gains. The net result is that these analyses are useful in identifying future potential investment problems before they happen. In turn, financial results are quickly calculated based on these problems, and the effect on the aggregrate returns is seen immediately.

From a KMS perspective, after giving consideration to a company's future return on investment, decision makers can evaluate various methods to increase ROI (return on investment) today and tomorrow by employing knowledge learned from past and current financial performance. One method focuses on the company's earning more profit without more capital through cost cutting in its manufacturing plants and warehouses by employing the KISS (keep it simple, stupid) principle. Another method centers on using less capital. For example, Coca Cola uses plastic containers for concentrate instead of costlier metal ones. Still another method focuses on the company's investing capital in higher-return projects. There is a need, however, for decision makers to make sure that these projects earn more than the total cost of the capital they require. Thus, several methods that rely on financial knowledge gained from the company's operations can be employed to increase a company's return on investment. Some of this knowledge can be tied back to the principles set forth above for a company's overall operations.

Content Analysis of Financial Statements

The purpose of reviewing a company's current financial performance via financial ratios is not only to assist in giving direction to the company's historical financial knowledge base but also to assist in giving direction to the company's top management and its corporate planning staff for furthering financial strategic thinking. By relating external environmental factors to internal ones for a typical company, its growth and profitability can be compared to that of comparable firms in the industry. This financial analysis gives an indication whether or not the company is increasing its market share and giving a fair return to its stockholders, considering the industry's current state. This overview of financial ratios needs to be supplemented by a more detailed analysis of competitors' financial statements, frequently referred to as *content analysis* of periodic financial statements and annual reports.

Basically, content analysis provides valuable clues to competitors' corporate strategic thinking. It is a source of both financial information and new directions to be taken by the competition. Content analysis of competing companies can be especially useful for getting a handle on specific issues of corporate strategy and can serve as a primary or supplementary source of information. It can be used to analyze current changes and past correlates of performance and to investigate more general questions of interest to top-level executives and their corporate planning staffs.

Graphics can be extremely helpful for conducting a thorough analysis of overall performance and variances that are tied in with financial ratios. Although financial ratios can be compared on a day-by-day, week-by-week, month-by-month, or some other time-sensitive basis, the purpose of this analysis by financial executives is to determine whether or not the company is improving its financial stature. Of equal importance is the fact that financial ratio analysis that uses graphics discloses whether or not financial managers are really managing the company effectively over the short term to the long term. Generally, ''at a glance'' graphic presentations of financial performance and knowledge allow managers to start their thinking processes quickly. A ''picture'' may tell managers immediately what they want to know about their own operations—information that might otherwise be buried in stacks of computer-generated reports. In a similar manner, information and knowledge in graphic form can be brought to bear on important comparisons to a company's competitors. Overall, computer-prepared graphics of the important content of a company's financial statements (and its competitors') are very effective for getting managers to think about new ways of running their operations and supporting decision-making efforts.

Using the Internet to Discover Financial Knowledge

Whatever service is chosen for getting on the Internet, individuals and companies can discover a vast array of financial information and knowledge that can be beneficial to meeting their needs. For example, an investor or a financial manager for a company can keep tabs on various stocks using a service called Portfolio Accounting World-Wide (Pawws). The individual can click the mouse to get the latest quotes. By clicking a second time, he or she can see a company's most recent financial statements or take a look at how its stock price has moved over the past several years. Currently, brokerage houses, investment banks, and discount brokers are offering a wide range of on-line financial services. Companies like Fidelity, Merrill Lynch, J. P. Morgan, and Charles Schwab have opened up web sites for their investors. In addition, there are a number of on-line sources, including the Microsoft Network and specialists such as the Reuters Money Network and Dow Jones News/Retrieval.

A starting place for an individual investor or company includes financial bulletin boards and investment forums. These popular gathering places are where users talk shop, exchange advice, and interact on-line with a variety of Wall Street gurus. However, take this word of warning. Investor forums are fertile ground for operators who talk up cheap, thinly traded stocks, thereby hoping to create enough buy orders to boost the price for a few days. Then they sell their holdings and leave everyone else holding issues that have little or no market. Nevertheless, if an individual has the ability to overcome this caveat, he or she operating independently or acting on behalf of a company can discover new knowledge about financial markets and services offered to best meet needs. A further step ties in with the earlier discussion in this chapter on CSFs, KPIs, financial ratios, and content analysis. Important comparisons and evaluations of the information found on the Internet coupled with upcoming economic events can allow a person to discover critical financial knowledge that was not possible in past years. From a broadened perspective, a more enlightened investment approach can prove to be highly rewarding for the individual investor or company.

Rethinking Cost Accounting Approaches

Because companies in the United States are competing in global markets, U.S. companies must get control of their production costs. The good news is that, for the most part, U.S. manufacturers have been meeting that challenge with integrated manufacturing, just-in-time inventories, factory automation, robotics, and the like (refer to the prior chapter). The bad news is that even with these manufacturing advances, costing systems have not kept pace. Generally, today's product costing data are wrong, often by extremely large margins. Without more accurate costing methods, the bottom line is a continued competitive crisis. Hence, there is a need to rethink the current cost accounting methods for the 21st century and beyond. More specifically, there is the need to take a hard look at activity-based costing, technology accounting, life-cycle accounting, and target costing.

Activity-based costing (ABC) directly relates costs to the resources used to manufacture a product. A starting point is analyzing a company in order to determine all its production and support activities. All costs are then assigned to activities. Next, activities are measured and linked with the products that consume the activities. The total cost of the finished product is an accumulation of the activities required to make the product. In addition to assigning the costs to the products that actually absorb the activities, ABC identifies cost drivers and isolate non-value-added activities. With this information, a company can establish priorities that focus on eliminating or reducing non-value-added activities.

Basically, the ABC method allows a company to identify specifically the activities that are generating costs so that management has a better idea of why budgeted numbers are being exceeded. In essence, the ABC method is a restatement of costs. If a financial analyst looks at the production department section of a profit-and-loss statement in both traditional cost accounting and ABC accounting reports, the numbers would be identical on the bottom line. However, they would be categorized differently.

Technology accounting is based on the concept that technology costs, such as plant, equipment, and information systems, should be treated as direct costs, equivalent to direct labor and materials. Today's technology costs, for the most part, are accounted for by amortization (or depreciation) and included in overhead. The problem with this method of accounting is that conventional amortization methods are time-based, not production-based. A time-based method equates time with cost and often causes amortization of idle machinery to increase overhead costs when there is little or no production. This encourages constant and ineffective production to maintain a desired cost per unit.

Product costs are further affected by the inclusion of the time-based amortization in overhead, which must then be allocated to production. By adopting a direct production-based amortization method such as units of production, costs are matched more accurately with products manufactured. When determining the number of units over which to amortize an asset, only the planned production of the asset should be considered. Simply using the asset's total lifetime production capacity does not solve the problems associated with a time-based method. Total units used to amortize an asset should be limited by planned production, product demand, and obsolescence of the asset's technology or the manufacturing process. As with activity-based costing, the choice of an overhead allocation method can significantly alter product costing. As technology costs increase as a percentage of total product costs, any misallocation will improperly influence management decisions and possibly the financial results of the company.

Life-cycle accounting accumulates the costs of activities that occur over the entire life cycle of a product, from inception to abandonment by the manufacturer and the consumer. A primary objective of life-cycle accounting is a better match between revenues and expenses. All costs are capitalized as incurred. These costs are charged to earnings as units are sold, based on the total planned number of units to be brought to market. The shortcomings of the traditional cost accounting model, then, are largely due to the changing manufacturing environment. To remain competitive in today's global marketplace, U.S. manufacturers must now adopt new cost accounting methodologies so that they know the true cost of their products and make informed cost management and pricing decisions.[2]

Although the foregoing cost accounting methodologies are quite useful to assist a company in telling the true story about costs, a more pragmatic way to get a handle on costs is to follow the Japanese. That is, it is necessary to take a look at costs before the fact rather than afterwards. More specifically, a Japanese cost-management system guides and motivates planners to design products at the lowest possible cost and gives them considerable freedom in introducing new products as well as in getting them to market quickly. Like its famed quality philosophy, Japan's cost-management system is ahead of its global counterparts.

American companies developing a new product, for example, typically design it first and then calculate the cost. If the cost is too high, the product goes back to the drawing board, or the company settles for a smaller profit. On the other hand, the Japanese start with a *target cost* based on the price the market is most likely to accept. Then they direct designers and engineers to meet this target. The system also encourages managers to worry less about a product's cost than about the role it could play in gaining market share. This strategic thinking approach is a big reason why the Japanese so often come out with winning products.

The critical feature of the Japanese cost-management system is its focus on getting costs out of the product during the planning and design stage. That is the point at which virtually all subsequent costs are determined, from manufacturing to what customers will have to spend on maintenance. This target-cost technique, used by such companies as NEC, Sharp, Nissan, and Toyota, comes in countless variations. The stripped-down version has several important features. The team in charge of bringing a new product idea to market determines the price at which the product is most likely to appeal to potential buyers. From this crucial judgment all else follows. After deducting the desired profit margin from the forecasted sales price, the planners develop estimates for each of the elements that make up a product's costs: design and engineering, manufacturing, and sales and marketing. Each of these is further subdivided to identify and estimate the cost of each component that goes into the finished product.

Overall, U.S. companies tend to build a model of the product, determine what it is going to cost, and then ask whether it can be sold at a certain price based on costs. In contrast, the Japanese turn it around, they say, ''It's got to sell for X dollars. Let's work backwards to make sure we can achieve it.'' This is not currently being done by U.S. companies with the same intensity. Western-style cost management, by basing costs on given standards, tends to maintain the status quo. The Japanese approach is dynamic and constantly pushes for improvement.[3]

Software Useful in Discovering Financial Knowledge

Today, there are a number of financial software vendors that see the merits of discovering financial knowledge. Currently, there are a number of vendors whose OLAP offerings feature the drill-down technique in their client/server applications. Their OLAP software enables users to view multidimensional data and burrow into a data warehouse to extract answers to business questions. The technology goes a long way toward helping users to realize the empowerment promised by client/server computing. Vendors such as Dun & Bradstreet Software, Hyperion Software Corporation, Oracle Corporation, SAP America Inc., SAS Institute Inc., and SQL Financials Inc. are all marketing OLAP financial software systems. Essentially, OLAP systems offered today by financial software vendors are built upon the foundation of integrated financial software. The basic data of accounting and finance that is accumulated by a typical integrated financial software package provides the input for on-line analytical processing. It does not matter where the accounting and finance data may reside (i.e., in a corporate database or a data warehouse). The important item is that the integrated financial software has data that is available for massaging, using OLAP-multidimensional analysis, which can then be reviewed by appropriate accounting and finance managers for action if deemed necessary.

Even though OLAP has improved the way managers visualize their financial operations, there is still the need to view financial results from a more enlightened perspective. The new focus is on the discovery of financial knowledge about a company's total operations using some type of computer software. Data mining software is quite capable of fulfilling this task. Banks, for example, may use data mining to identify their most profitable credit card customers or their highest risk loan applicants. They may also seek to prevent fraud by using a data mining technique called "deviation detection." Rather than finding relationships between different groups of data records, it finds events that are outside the norm that could be a sign of fraudulent activities.

A typical data mining software package that is useful in obtaining financial knowledge is Script Software International's KnowledgeMiner 2.0 (current version 2.2.3). Being a shareware tool for modeling and predicting the behavior of complex systems, this software helps users extract previously undetected patterns of knowledge from sets of data. Its uses include the modeling of economic systems, financial planning, market forecasting, medical diagnosis, and the identification and classification of visual information. In the financial area, KnowledgeMiner 2.0 can be used to find a series of formulas that describe the relationship between a company's stock price and a variety of other data, including sales figures, product pricing, the gross national product, and the Dow Jones industrial average. From this view, financial managers for a typical company can combine their own knowledge with that obtained from data mining software and leverage this combined knowledge when buying or selling a company's stock as well as other stocks.

From an enlarged view, a company can employ knowledge discovery software not only to undertake various aspects of financial planning (such as investment planning, capital planning, tax planning, and estate planning), but also to identify those customers who will give a high rate of return on a company's investment. For example, the Capital One Financial Corporation, one of the top ten credit card issuers in the United States, uses a massive data mining application that works with proprietary algorithms to let the company identify opportunities that promise the highest return at the lowest risk. This is what Capital One refers to as its Information-Based Strategy. Its payoffs are large. The company has created an infrastructure that most notably mines information on 200 million customers. The system churns terabytes of data—for example, buying behavior, payment records and other key statistics—through proprietary algorithms to tailor products down to the individual customer level. The net result of this mass customization is that Capital One can offer 3,000 credit card variations in a market where the industry norm is Gold or Regular.[4]

KNOWLEDGE MANAGEMENT SYSTEMS IN ACCOUNTING AND FINANCE

Today, accounting and finance managers are dealing with a host of disparate financial data and information that comes from many internal and external sources. They need help to consolidate all of it into financial results that have meaning for the users of this information. This is where knowledge management systems come into play and can be helpful to those in financial management. More specifically, the employment of knowledge that allows a company to reap the best return with the least risk is what a knowledge management system is all about. This ability relates back to the prior discussion about return on knowledge (ROK), which is not found in current information systems where the focus is on return on investment. In essence, knowledge management systems can make the most successful firms even more successful. This applies to companies operating locally, nationally, or globally.

Today, for example, a company engages its financial systems professionals to create business solutions based on companywide integration. Its database structure transforms the general ledger into more than just a group of accounts and balances. It is almost a repository of data for reporting on and analyzing current, budgeted, and historical business activities at any level. With one large, centralized and interrelated database, information can be accessed for financial reporting, budgeting, direct and indirect cost allocations, intercompany accounting, tax preparation and audits, and industry and trend analyses.

Although this information is necessary for managers and their staffs at all levels, the need for a companywide knowledge management system is paramount to keep one step ahead of competition. As will be seen in the second half of the chapter, new knowledge can be discovered that better serves a company's needs. Extracting financial patterns and trends transcends where the company has gone to where it should be heading. As noted in the marketing chapter, the company should lead its customers where they should be going based on coming changes. In turn, appropriate marketing plans should be based on sound financial planning within a KMS operating mode.

Areas That Lend Themselves to Discovering Financial Knowledge

Accounting and finance areas that lend themselves to discovering knowledge within a KMS environment are numerous, since there is the need for a tie-in of financial activites with other functional areas for a typical company. The integration starts with strategic planning, followed by marketing, manufacturing, and human resources. The level of integration starts with data or information.

No matter the level, the end point is improving a company's financial performance. Due to space limitations, only the areas of cost accounting and financial analysis are covered below for a knowledge management system.

A KMS environment is equally at home in the area of cash flow—not only for the short term but also over the longer term for a typical company. The management of accounts receivable is a likely candidate along with payroll which, today, is linked to human resource management systems (covered in the next chapter). In addition, the source and application of funds along with financial statements (i.e., balance sheets and income statements) lend themselves to knowledge management. Some of the important principles underlying knowledge for these areas were given previously in the chapter.

COST ACCOUNTING

Traditional, cost accounting systems have been criticized on the grounds that they do not provide useful information for internal decision making. An important reason given is that the systems were designed to provide cost data for inventory valuation in financial statements rather than for cost management. Other reasons were given in the prior discussion on the rethinking of cost accounting approaches. More recently, OLAP and knowledge management systems provide new type of costs analyses that are complementary to newer cost accounting approaches.

Enlarged View of Cost Accounting Approaches

To provide information for cost management, there must be an enlarged view of cost accounting approaches so that they can be flexible enough to analyze costs, including inventory valuation, product costing, life-cycle costing, overhead analysis, quality cost evaluation, direct and indirect labor analysis, and productivity analysis. A comprehensive accounting system for supporting cost management must include various types of data, most of which is generated internally. At the most basic level, the data consists of the activities causing the costs (i.e., the cost drivers and the costs incurred). For example, receiving department costs may be caused by the number and size of the deliveries, along with inspection and handling times of these deliveries. If the receiving department's costs are to be apportioned to the products causing the costs, the cost drivers must be identified and used to trace costs to specific products. When this is done, the cost accounting system becomes activity based (as discussed previously in the chapter) rather than volume based (like most current cost systems).

One means of developing an activity-based system is to use a database approach, which means recording events, activities, and costs in a computer database in enough detail so that they can be retrieved, analyzed, and summarized in multiple ways as the need arises. Such an approach in reality involves recording some information not required for financial reporting, such as the numbers of deliveries and purchase orders and the number and times of inspections and handling. However, the database of costed activities not only supports the cost attachment process for product costing but also provides a useful tool to support planning, coordination, and control across multiple dimensions. In addition, an OLAP approach to activity-based costing provides for an in-depth analysis of changing costs. This approach not only assists cost management in understanding costs but also helps to visualize via multidimensional analysis how costs affect a company's financial operations. An OLAP operating mode gives cost management the look and feel of an alternative world. More to the point, costs can be analyzed by cost accountants for a number of products to determine what affect the elimination of certain costs—such as costly training of machine operators or assembly operators—would have on the company. Perhaps senior personnel could act as mentors to eliminate or reduce training costs. Similarly, inspection of assembly operations may be better left to assembly personnel where production-line personnel are permitted to shut down production if there are quality problems. Changes in production activities and their resulting costs, then, are related to the company's financial statements.

From an enlarged perspective, an activity-based cost accounting approach can employ the knowledge gained from data mining over time. This knowledge can help management and cost accountants determine whether costs incurred in production or nonproduction activities really benefit the company over the long haul. From this view, a true *cost-benefit analysis* can be undertaken not only for manufactured products but also for costs related to the marketing and distribution of costs by products and product lines. Thorough analysis gives cost accountants the capability to uncover new relationships that were previously buried in cost figures. A knowledge management system that employs data mining tools, then, can be used to obtain different costs for different purposes, thereby highlighting problems and exceptions that were ignored or neglected in the past.

Accent on Target Costing to Lower Costs

Related to the above discussion about cost accounting approaches and knowledge management systems is *target costing*. It represents a powerful force that shifts from cost-led pricing to target costing. Traditionally, companies have started with costs, added a desired profit margin, and arrived at a selling price (i.e., cost-led pricing). Sears and Marks & Spencer, for example, have switched to target costing in which the price the customer is willing to pay determines allowable costs that start at the design stage. Until recently, these companies were the exceptions. Now target costing is an accepted practice. The Japanese first adopted it for their exports. Now Wal-Mart and all the discounters in the United States, Japan, and Europe are practicing this newer approach to costing.

Because target costing is a cost management technique that lets a company determine how much its customers are willing to pay for a product and then design the product within certain cost limits that allow for a predetermined profit, multidimensional analysis in an OLAP environment is quite helpful to managers throughout a company to get a handle on pricing and costing the product. For example, a marketing manager, working with a senior cost manager, could explore the relationship of pricing the product at various levels based upon making the product internally at various costs throughout the marketing and manufacturing processes. In addition, this analysis could be extended to include the outsourcing of the product that makes use of knowledge contained in its KMS. From this combined OLAP-KMS view, company managers would be able to undertake the appropriate pricing-costing analysis for a definitive answer about the product being produced internally or externally.

Although target costing has made its mark on industries in which products require a significant amount of production time, it is equally applicable to services for which the focus is the service delivery system. As in process-intensive manufacturing, process is inextricable from product. Think of the issues that are important to the delivery of health care and fast food functions. Where services and process-intensive manufacturing diverge is in their flexibility. That is, it is very costly to convert a paper machine so that it can produce a grade or weight that was not considered in its initial design. On the other hand, service delivery systems are a different matter. In customer-responsive service delivery systems, it is easy to add new services. For example, menus are easy to extend and room services can easily be added. Again a combined OLAP-KMS approach can be used that is equally at home in service-oriented industries as it is in manufacturing-oriented industries.

Using Knowledge to Determine Appropriate Costing Methods

Once the costs of a company's future products have been properly determined by a cost management technique such as target costing, the next step is accumulating costs once the products are manufactured. One approach to cost control or containment is the ABC method set forth previously, where the focus is on separating value-added costs from non-value-added costs. With this segregated cost information, company managers can determine what non-value-added activities can be reduced or possibly eliminated. Although the ABC costing method analysis will help in controlling costs, there is still a need to utilize a method to compute the real profitability of a company's products. Such a method is found in direct costing.

Essentially, direct costing segregates variable costs from fixed costs (as opposed to absorption costing which combines them). Selling price less variable costs therefore equals contribution to fixed costs and profits before federal income taxes. This value of contribution is then subtracted from fixed costs, thereby resulting in net profits before federal income taxes. Direct costing is concerned primarily with the elimination of arbitrary allocations of common or joint costs. It emphasizes the benefits of tracing costs to individual cost centers and then measuring them. To realize the benefits of direct costing, typically a cost review group is assigned the responsibility of evaluating product costs and their contributions.

Figure 9-2 relates direct costing to multidimensional analysis in an OLAP environment. This analysis depicts a comparison among a company's five principal products using direct costing. Similarly, a comparison can be made among the various products in each product line. With an accurate segregation of variable and fixed costs to determine product contribution, the company's managers are able to view important information regarding which products really contribute to overall profits and which do not. In addition, the total contribution of each of the company's product lines can be calculated. It may well be that this cost information, which is reviewed by lower-level managers, should be forwarded to a higher level of management for review. There may be a changing pattern among the products and product lines in terms of total contribution. This capability of the cost review group, who work with experienced cost accountants, allows the company to detect changing cost trends.

Although direct costing is an effective way to get at the real current and future costs of a company, there is a need to go a step further in these fast-changing times and take a comprehensive approach. American companies need to rethink how they manage costs over their operations. They need to assure their cost departments that what they are doing is worth doing. The end result is that company management will get better ideas about effective costing methods that are best suited for the company's needs. Sometimes, this means making radical changes and setting dramatic targets, whether in costs or otherwise, based on knowledge of global trends and patterns. It may be necessary to reengineer products rather than processes based on ongoing knowledge of world markets, since product design can account for as much as 80 percent of total production costs. When it comes to product design, it is not what is built into the product but what can be taken out of it that is important. The Japanese, for example, have been doing this to their cars in a big way. Basically, simplicity cuts costs and saves time. In addition, there should be a focus on giving customers less, not more, variety which can result in lower prices. Thus, accounting and finance knowledge can be used to determine appropriate costing methods that tie in with lowering a company's costs as well as improving organizational productivity.

FINANCIAL ANALYSIS

From an enlarged view, today's companies need to have the capability to focus on a thorough analysis of financial ratios that tie back to a company's critical success factors. In addition, a thorough analysis of key performance indicators and financial ratios relating to CSFs is paramount in these fast-changing times. Such an approach integrates planning or budgeting with performance reporting and is based on knowledge of cost behavior as discussed in the prior section of

Figure 9-2
A Comparison of a Company's Five Principal Products Using Direct Costing

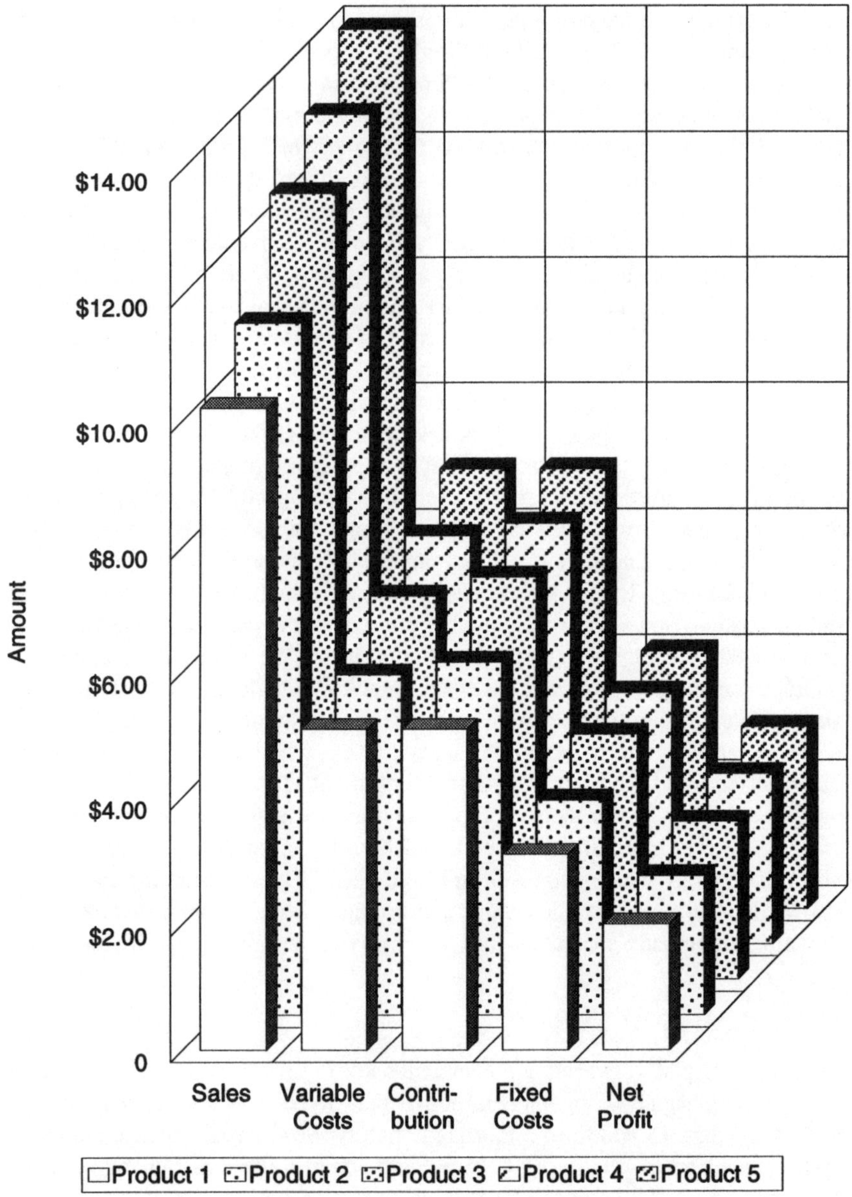

this chapter. It also recognizes the significance of flexible budgeting and costing methods to improve the quality of information and knowledge provided for all managerial levels. It is from this perspective that financial analysis is explored below.

Basically, financial performance for a typical company and its resulting evaluation in the form of critical success factors, key performance indicators, and financial ratios is related to short-range strategic planning, which forms the basis for monthly flexible department financial budgets. Actual results are compared monthly with departmental financial figures. If actual operations are within 5 percent (plus or minus) by individual expense categories, there is no need for action. However, if the amount exceeds the 5 percent limit, appropriate action is undertaken. In certain cases, it may be helpful for management to bring the knowledge of past experience to bear on the evaluation. It should be recognized that a financial planning and performance system provides for individual managers to be assigned responsibility and, in turn, to be held accountable for meeting stated budgetary finance objectives.

Also included in the discussion to follow is the use of knowledge discovery tools to assist financial managers in overseeing investments in order to maximize their return on investment. A large number of financial analysis applications employ predictive modeling techniques (i.e., statistical regression and neural networks for creating and optimizing portfolios and creating trading models). Developers and users of such applications rarely publicize their precise details and effectiveness in order to maintain a competitive advantage. However, a few examples are known and are given below.

The Fidelity Stock Selector fund has used neural network models to select investments. The output of these models is evaluated by the fund manager before the action is taken, so it is not entirely clear how to divide the credit between human and machine. LBS Capital Management, a fund management firm, uses expert systems, neural networks, and generic algorithms to manage portfolios. Carlberg & Associates developed a neural network model for predicting the Standard & Poor's 500 Index, using interest rates, earnings, dividends, the dollar index, and oil prices. The model was surprisingly successful, explaining 96 percent of the variation in the Index from 1986 to 1995. In these applications, typically predictive accuracy is paramount; the need to use the extracted knowledge to explain a recommended action is less important. Thus, the main focus is ensuring that modeling methods do not overfit the data.[5]

Analysis That Uses Knowledge to Understand Present and Future Financial Trends

To understand present and future financial trends within a KMS environment, it is helpful to start with multidimensional analysis that includes sales, costs, and profits. For example, to obtain an overview of a typical company's financial operations, reference can be made to Figure 9-3. Not only are total sales and

Figure 9-3
A Comparison of Sales to Net Profit Before Federal Income Taxes over a Five-Year Period (the Current Year versus the Past Four Years) for a Typical Company

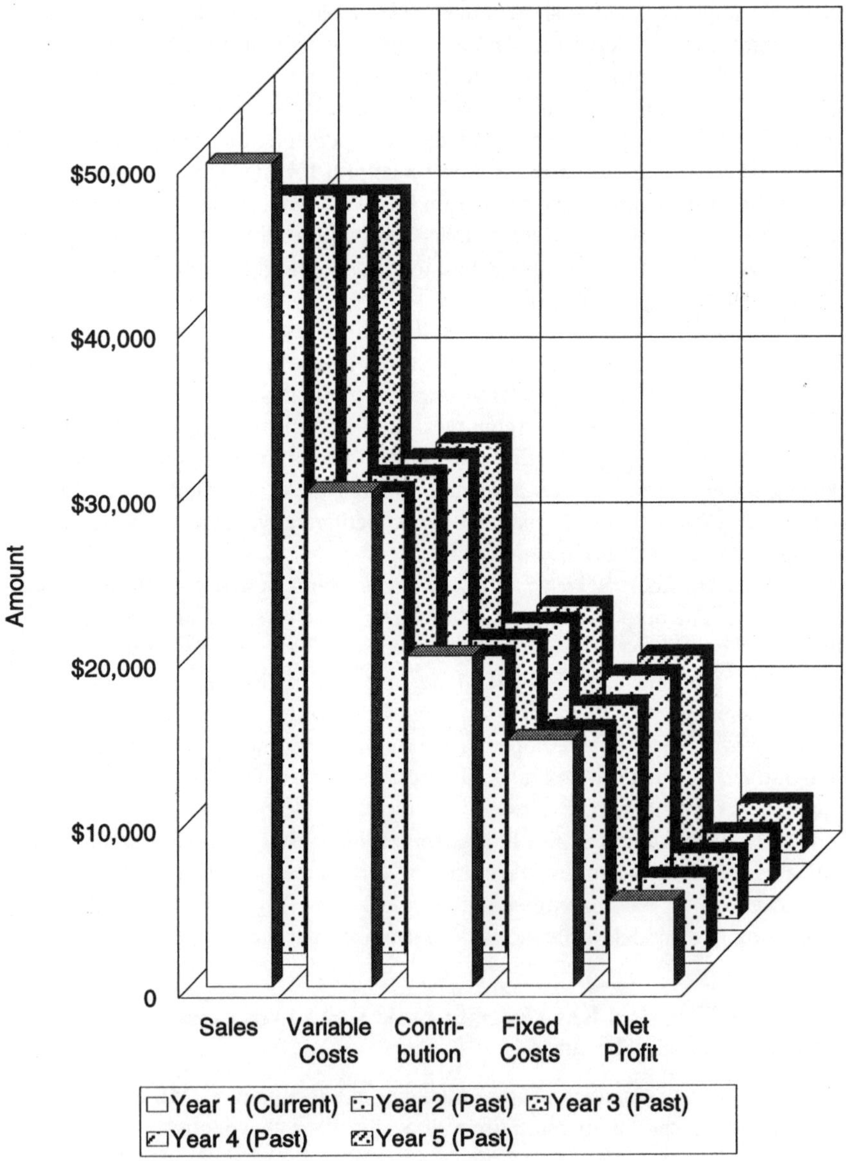

related costs and contributions illustrated over five years but the net profit before federal income taxes is also shown for the same time period. This analysis needs to be further refined over five years for rising and falling financial ratios that tell more of the story about the company's future—good, bad, or indifferent. (Refer to the information about financial ratios and ROI given earlier in the chapter.)

In terms of a shorter time frame, say this year and last year, financial information and their ratios can be compared on a day-to-day, week-by-week, month-by-month, or some other time basis. The intended purpose of this analysis by accounting and finance managers is to determine whether or not the company is improving its financial stature. Of equal importance is the fact that financial information and analyses disclose whether or not company managers are really managing effectively over the shorter term. Generally, this type of "at a glance" multidimensional analysis allows managers to start their thinking processes quickly. A "picture" may tell managers immediately what they want to know compared to information that might otherwise be buried in stacks of computer-generated reports. From another viewpoint, managers may view a printout of multidimensional analysis to ponder later.

Even though the foregoing analysis helps accounting and finance managers meet their decision-making responsibilities, there is still a need to get a grasp on the longer term by using knowledge. Key performance indicators and financial ratios over a longer time frame may indicate changing patterns and emerging trends that need to be explored by top management and the corporate planning staff. The analysis may indicate the need for problem finding to get the company back on track. In addition, the analysis may send an urgent signal to company managers warning that they must change their financial knowledge base as now constituted to a more global perspective that includes the emerging nations of the world. From this view of changing world knowledge, it may be necessary for a company's top management and its staff to go back and ask questions about the company's critical success factors. Although current CSFs are the guiding force for top management, this may not be the case for tomorrow. Hence, financial results that are produced by a knowledge management system may indicate a change is necessary in the overall direction taken by a company, including changing its CSFs.

Using Knowledge of Competitors to Enhance a Company's Performance

A most important reason for reviewing a company's financial performance via key performance indicators and financial ratios, as just noted, is to give direction to the company's top management and its corporate planning staff. By evaluating external environmental factors as related to internal ones, a typical company can compare its growth and profitability to comparable firms in its industry using multidimensional analysis as a starting point and then further refining the analysis by using knowledge of the competition. For example, one competitor's current financial position can be compared to the company's own financial picture along with those of other competitors. This financial analysis gives an indication of whether or not this one competitor is giving a fair return to its stockholders when considering the industry's current status. This overview of financial ratios needs to be supplemented by a more detailed analysis of competitors' financial statements, frequently referred to as *content analysis* of periodic financial statements and annual reports. Also, knowledge of competing products and services that includes their marketing philosophy is very important in the analysis.

Basically, content analysis provides valuable clues to competitors' corporate strategies. Content analysis of competing companies along with their marketing policies and their future marketing directions can be really useful for understanding specific issues of corporate strategy and can serve as a primary or supplementary source of information and knowledge. It can be used to analyze current changes and past correlates of performance as well as for more general investigations of potential future directions that are of interest to top-level executives and their corporate planning staffs.

For example, content analysis may disclose that one of the company's competitors is showing improved cost performance—that is, its costs are declining. The appropriate corporate response for a typical company is to get involved in a cost-analysis technique called *benchmarking*, which focuses on what the competitor does and how much it costs to do it. In the company's lab, analysts tear apart the competitor's products and estimate the cost of designing and producing each part. The analysis extends beyond product costs. To pin down distribution and handling costs, company executives need to order some of its competitor's products, then trace where they were shipped from and examine how they were packed. Typically, cost savings for a particular product start at the earliest stage, when engineering determines the product design. The challenge is to find ways to make engineering more cost effective without stifling its creative efforts.

Taking another perspective on benchmarking, using the activity-based costing method, a decision maker can transform dollar amounts and priorities assigned to projects into colorful, interactive virtual worlds that can be explored. As the individual works with one budgeted item or changes an assignment priority, a ripple takes place in real time. That is, the decision maker can explore how money is spent at all levels of the company and can make better decisions about how funds are spent. In such cases, virtual reality (VR) software is useful for creating a walk-through scenario of how a company spends its money. Particular attention is given to flagging low-priority activities that were overfunded. Activities are assigned tall or short bars by their spending levels and color-coded from green to red to show priority. Exploring this 3-D landscape, managers are able to determine which activities to view, touch, and manipulate. For example, they can focus on tall red bars, indicating low-priority activities with high costs. Touching these bars activates detailed information about the resources consumed. At any point, they can step back to see how resources are consumed for each high-level business process and for the entire company. Hence, VR can be a very effective means for assisting in benchmarking, because it uses size, shape, and color in a 3-D landscape to convey useful knowledge that has been highlighted from extensive analysis. Similarly, VR has the potential to turn a company's knowledge about its customers into a giant simulated structure of itself and its competitors that is much easier for managers and their staffs to understand.

Using Knowledge to Manage Investments and Maximize ROI

The application of KnowledgeSEEKER to financial analysis and forecasting problems has as its goal the capability to extract a multiple cause-and-effect model that allows the user to understand trends in the marketplace and make trading decisions based on its predictive model. Although the following example represents a small but nevertheless sophisticated trading system, the task is to manage the profitability of six portfolios.[6] In this example, each portfolio contains investments that are classified as either "cash cows," "stars," "dogs," or "question marks." This portfolio classification is based on common marketing practices of grouping products into one of these four categories. In addition, there are also "mixed" portfolios—quadrant I–IV (combining investments that are classed as either group I and IV) and quadrant II–III (combining a mixture of investments from groups II and III). Because the task is to manage the distribution of investments in each of these six portfolios in order to maximize return on investment, the investment philosophy is straightforward. When situations are observed that predict an overall increase in profitability, investments are sold according to the specific rules that point to this increase. The outcome that one wants to predict in this example—consolidated profit and loss—is calculated by computing the difference between the current selling price of the portfolio (at the time the measurements were taken) and the original buying price. A large number of alternative investment philosophies and trading and measurement practices can be handled in a similar fashion. With a large investment portfolio—as seen here, where prices fluctuate across a large number of investments in response to a multiplicity of factors—it is absolutely essential to automate the trading system in order to handle the resulting complexity and trade optimally.

In order to construct a predictive model for trading decisions, the average prices for each of the six portfolios have been chosen. Although these measurements (i.e., average price for the day) are used as predictors, it was decided to construct a variety of derivative measurements for each of these averages in order to capture some of the subtleties of price changes and their impact on market behavior. By deriving measurements that capture movements in prices through time as well as movements resulting from dynamic swings in the market, it is possible to develop a rich predictive structure that will also provide

Figure 9-4
Tree Diagram That Shows the Results of "Cash Cow" Investments Using KnowledgeSEEKER

(a)

(b)

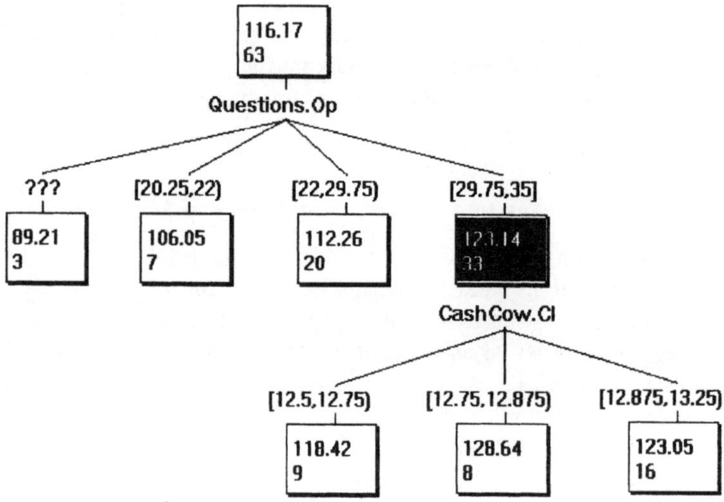

Source: Angoss Software International Limited.

strong signals—even timing signals—to trigger an appropriate trading decision. For each of the six collections of investments, the opening price, the closing price, daily high, daily low, volume traded during the day, and the difference between the daily high and the daily low, are calculated. Thus, for each portfolio in the analysis, there are seven predictors—that is, across the entire data set there are 42 (7 predictors × 6 portfolios) predictors of the average consolidated profit and loss.

Since this information is contained in a database that is updated constantly during the day in order to reflect the most recent transactions, one day's activity will be used in the financial analysis. When patterns are seen among the predictors that show an increase in consolidated profit and loss, a trading rule is uncovered that can be invoked to maximize return. Once many of these rules have been developed, then a number of alternative rules can be invoked to maximize profit at various points in the trading day, depending on the circumstances that characterize the trades. To better understand this financial analysis, a small example is used, starting with a price/profit database. During import, consolidated profit and loss is defined as a dependent variable (this is the field that was calculated as reflecting the difference between buying price and selling price—calculated at the time that the six predictor prices are calculated). This produces the results that are summarized in the node in Figure 9-4(a). This node shows that there are 63 records in the data set. These are records from the previous day's trading activities. The average consolidated profit and loss from the trades is $116,170. The goal is to use KnowledgeSEEKER to increase the amount of average gains. By growing the first branch of a decision tree using KnowledgeSEEKER, the results are also shown in Figure 9-4(a).

This tree shows that of 42 predictors in the data set ''Questions Op''—the average opening price for the ''Questions'' portfolio—is the best predictor. The average consolidated profit and loss increases steadily as the average opening price of ''Questions'' type of investments in the data set increases. According to the KnowledgeSEEKER classification tree, the best single predictor of profits is the opening price of ''Questions.'' Moreover, once the average opening price of ''Questions'' increases beyond $29.75, there is no significant effect on the return in consolidated profit and loss. So $29.75 can be taken as the bottom threshold opening price to trigger sales across the collection of six investment portfolios. In the display, it should be noted that there are three records in the database where information is missing for the opening price. These three records are indicated as [???] in the display. As shown, missing data were grouped separately, This means that missing value cases were statistically different from the other nodes at that level of the tree. If the missing values are similar, they are grouped in with one of the other categories at that level of the tree. This process is done automatically by KnowledgeSEEKER.

One of the major advantages of KnowledgeSEEKER is its ability to identify multiple predictive factors that influence a given field in a data set. To illustrate this capability in the context of this example, it is necessary to look inside the highest average consolidated profit-and-loss node at the extreme right of the first branch where the average consolidated profit and loss is $123,140. In order to determine if there are any factors in the data set that can be used to increase this average return further, it is necessary to view the results. The results of looking within this node are displayed in Figure 9-4(b). There are a number of alternative predictors that can be used to predict an increase in consolidated profit and loss. ''Cash Cow'' prices were selected as the predictor since it complements the trades that one wants to make with ''Questions.'' It should be noted that the closing price of ''Cash Cow'' investments have a different relationship with consolidated profit and loss from ''Questions''—the relationship is shaped like an umbrella where the left and right nodes are lower than the central node. This indicates that for those trades where the opening price of the investments is high (at least $29.75), consolidated profit and loss is maximized when the closing price of ''Cash Cow'' investments is in the mid-range (between $12.75 and $12.875 in this example).

Overall, these are the basic elements of the design of the trading confirmation system constructed here to serve as an example of how KnowledgeSEEKER can be used in financial analysis and forecasting. The current model indicates that the average consolidated profit and loss in the portfolio is increased when investments are sold when the opening price of the investments is high and the closing price of the ''Cash Cow'' investments is in the mid range. In the absence of any other information, then investments would be bought that matched these attributes with the expectation that the pattern would persist. A full example would continue to grow the tree that was illustrated. In the end, a full tree would yield a handful of nodes where consolidated profit and loss was highest. The branches that form these nodes represent market conditions that tend to maximize returns. The final system would incorporate a market monitor that tells the trader when any one of the profit maximization conditions was reached (i.e., this is the time to sell). One of the advantages of this system is that it can be observed and tested over time. Rules that tend to work over time can be given "seniority," while rules that do not work can be demoted or eliminated altogether. Currently, a number of KnowledgeSEEKER users are using this kind of approach to trade successfully on the market. With KnowledgeSEEKER, it is possible to construct a sophisticated trading system that would have cost many thousands of dollars in the not-too-distant past.

In addition to knowledge discovery software, virtual reality can also be used to manage investments better. Today, money managers analyze thousands of companies using a number of criteria, such as low-price earnings ratio, to come up with undervalued stocks to buy. The problem is that too many investment institutions have the same ideas about the kinds of stocks they want to purchase. The net result is that these stocks are now overvalued because the institutions have bid up their prices. To assist market analysts in their never ending search for stocks to buy and sell under varying market conditions, VR technology provides the capability to represent vast amounts of stock market information in an interactive, real-time mode. This capability allows stock market analysts to organize information in new ways and find new relationships that were not apparent before. Typically, the major stocks in one specific industry can be evaluated by the analyst. Or several selected stocks in different industries can be evaluated against one another. Essentially, the analyst can fly over the stocks where the volume of the stock for the day is shown along with the price range of the day. The shape, position, and color of the stocks are dependent on the stock market variations. The stock analyst can assess the behavior of the stocks to help determine whether or not a specific stock would be a candidate for a buy or a sell. From this perspective, virtual reality offers an effective way to condense and streamline financial information for stock market analysts. In turn, the analyst will acquire knowledge not found with prior computer technology which can be encapsulated into a KMS environment. The interplay of VR technology with knowledge management will enhance the financial savvy of the analyst over time.

REAPING THE BENEFITS OF CPAs AS KNOWLEDGE MANAGEMENT PROFESSIONALS

In the prior exposition on applying financial knowledge, an underlying assumption was that accounting and finance personnel at all levels can benefit from this knowledge. However, before this can happen, there is a need for a change in mind set of these professionals. For example, certified public accountants (CPAs) should think of themselves not so much as accountants—those who balance the books and prepare financial statements—but as knowledge professionals. They need to discover where the knowledge is and how to mine it as a resource. They must also learn who needs the knowledge and in what form so that they can build a computer infrastructure that is readily available throughout the organization via the company's intranet. They should recognize that while knowledge has always been power, in today's fast-paced and highly competitive business world, speedily delivered knowledge often can mean keeping one step ahead of competition at best. CPAs need to determine the departments in the company that need what can be supplied, thereby thinking of themselves as partners of these departments. Their job is to knit together the basic elements of decision making: strategic planning, forecasting, budgeting, benchmarking, etc. In other words, by integrating these functions, CPAs become principal drivers in the decision-making process.

Based on their job as agents of change whose goal it is to make better use of financial knowledge, CPAs are in an excellent position to develop the appropriate metrics for a company's knowledge assets. New approaches will be needed to measure the "knowledge flow" and return on knowledge (ROK, mentioned earlier in the chapter). These approaches will be somewhat comparable to the way traditional accounting methods determine a company's cash flow and return on investment. Several firms have made attempts at knowledge by numbers but there are no set formulas at this time.[7] These new approaches go beyond the old adage, "If it ain't broke, don't fix it." A more contemporary focus is, "If it's too old and not keeping with the current times, fix it whether it's broken or not." Thus certified public accountants have a great opportunity at their doorsteps. If they undertake this opportunity as knowledge managers in a professional manner, a typical company can reap many benefits today and tomorrow.

SUMMARY

The main focus of this chapter has been on the application of knowledge management to the areas of accounting and finance. However, this exposition was preceded by important principles and factors that are useful in discovering financial knowledge. The need for these newer directions is driven by an environment that can be characterized as highly dynamic, complicated, and knowledge intense. Investment banks, commercial institutions, regulatory institutions, and brokerage houses find their staffs increasingly strained in financial times—good and bad. To help streamline operations and keep up with the times, it is necessary to provide the most intelligent, timely, and focused information and knowledge for these decision makers by augmenting the traditional with KMS capabilities. As a result, accountants and financial analysts can view information and knowledge from a multidimensional, longtime framework as a whole or in detail. They can see elements in association with one another or individually and can link those elements together in a logical manner. Hence, judgments based on knowledge can be made not only on a sounder basis but also on a basis more in tune with changing times.

NOTES

1. Steve Alexander, "Is It Knowledge Yet?" *Computerworld*, January 8, 1996, p. 73.
2. Dennis Peavey and Jim DePalma, "Do You Know the Cost of Your Products?" (New York: Coopers & Lybrand Executive Briefing, May 1990), pp. 7–9.
3. Ford S. Worthy, "Japan's Smart Secret Weapon," *Fortune*, August 12, 1991, pp. 72–75.
4. Jane Morrisey, "Mining for Gold," *PC Week*, May 19, 1997, p. 137.
5. Ronald J. Brachman, Tom Khabaza, Willi Kloesgen, Geogory Piatetsky-Shapiro, and Evangelos Simoudis, "Mining Business Databases," *Communications of the ACM*, November 1996, p. 45.
6. Angoss Software, "Study 4: Financial Analysis and Forecasting," *Knowledge-SEEKER in Action* (Toronto: Angoss Software International Limited, 1996).
7. Walter A. Kleinschrod, "In Business, Knowledge Is Power," *Beyond Computing*, March–April 1995, p. 38.

10

Application of Human Resource Knowledge

Issues Explored:

- What is the importance of taking a broad perspective of the human resources function in a KMS environment?
- What are the important principles and factors related to discovering human resource knowledge?
- How can a human resource management system be an integral part of a KMS operating mode?
- How can knowledge discovery help HR management in the areas of personnel selection and development plans, and wage and salary administration?
- What role can knowledge play in resolving work force issues and confronting coming changes in human resources?

Outline:

USING KNOWLEDGE MANAGEMENT SYSTEMS TO LEVERAGE PROFESSIONAL KNOWLEDGE

A recurring theme throughout this text is the concept that knowledge is power. How companies can use this important valuable asset has also been discussed. To be successful, a company must collect and share its knowledge more effectively than the competition. Managing knowledge requires new techniques that reward innovation and risk taking and promote knowledge sharing among employees. It also means that companies must be able to collect, retrieve, and analyze accurate information easily to develop essential knowledge, not only for survival but also for continued growth. It is from this perspective that knowledge management systems can be used to leverage professional knowledge of employees. Data warehousing is useful in creating corporate memory from a company's collective knowledge so that corporate decision makers can uncover hidden trends and predict changes.

The human resource (HR) function underlies the information given in previous chapters on a company's other functional areas. More specifically, successful companies focus their attention on integrating their short- to long-range strategic plans directly with the plans of the HR department. There is a great accent on human resource planning and execution, centering on three important activities that help leverage the professional knowledge of company employees.

They are: (1) identifying and acquiring the right number of people with the proper skills, (2) motivating company personnel to achieve high performance, and (3) creating interactive links between overall organizational objectives and HR planning activities. For the human resource function to be effective in terms of planning and execution, it must be capable of providing a good fit among the employee, the task, and the organization unit. If there is a poor fit, the employee will not be as productive as possible, not to mention the cost to management of motivating the individual to at least perform at a satisfactory level. The underlying thrust of the HR function for a typical company is to provide a good fit for personnel throughout the organization. This is accomplished more easily by allowing human resource managers to apply knowledge of personnel to their everyday activities.

With this in mind, the chapter initially looks at a broad-based integration of human resources with other functional areas so that professional knowledge can be leveraged for the company's benefit. Important factors that are helpful in discovering human resource knowledge and its application are then presented, followed by sample applications of knowledge management systems for personnel selection and placement as well as wage and salary administration. The use of knowledge to resolve work force and future company issues is set forth at the end of the chapter.

A BROAD-BASED INTEGRATION OF HUMAN RESOURCES THROUGHOUT AN ORGANIZATION

Within a typical KMS environment, a company's HR managers are concerned with spotting adverse trends in turnover and absenteeism. This responsibility does not end with problem identification. The goal is to determine the causes of these problems and what is actually needed to help the company solve them. HR managers have to be more creative (i.e., proactive) in these areas of responsibility, and their staffs need to become involved in providing them with advice that is workable and useful. In addition, HR managers have to become increasingly oriented toward company growth and efficiency instead of merely administering traditional human resource activities. This means greater emphasis on planning the structure of the future organization and its HR requirements, identifying and selecting the right people to meet those expected needs, developing and utilizing the company's current human resources, and assessing and rewarding performance. All of these activities require HR knowledge of a company's past and current operations. The purpose of these activities is to ensure growth of both the company and the individual employee.

From this broad-based view, there is a need to think in terms of the total company and not the HR department by itself. For a comprehensive approach to this important function, HR activities must be integrated into the company's overall strategic planning process as well as be related to basic marketing, manufacturing, and finance activities. Instead of a melange of diverse activities, the HR department must represent a broad-based integration of these activities in order for a company's human resources to be used effectively. It must be sensitive to the organization's requirements and be committed to making the company more efficient and effective. As will be seen in the material to follow, this means centering initially on developing a new position—namely, a chief knowledge officer (CKO) to take an enlarged view of the total company.

Need for a New Position of Chief Knowledge Officer (CKO)

The position of CKO was touched upon earlier in the text. Essentially, the raw data that people wade through and crunch in their workaday worlds need to be maintained and distributed by an organization's technical staff. However, helping everyone to work smarter is increasingly becoming the responsibility of an emerging corps of top executives known as *chief knowledge officiers*. For professionals with the people skills and the thinking power to match their technical skills, the pay scale is quite high. Chief information officers (CIOs) in large organizations make between $250,000 and $400,000, while CKOs salaries start at the high end of that spectrum and climb to $1 million. Some of the large companies and consulting firms who have CKOs include Egon Zehnder International Inc., Coca-Cola, Burson Marsteller, and Coopers & Lybrand.

Currently, there is no model applicant for the CKO position, also titled chief learning officer. Generally, the person holding this position fits into one of three molds: (1) a strategist who uses knowledge for strategic advantage, (2) an information technologist primarily interested in architecture and how information and its consequent knowledge is collected and dispersed, or (3) a human resource expert who capitalizes on collective experience as a corporate asset.[1] Ideally, a CKO candidate should have an excellent grasp of the technical infrastructure; be capable of determining what information and consequent knowledge is critical to the company's success; have the respect of the CEO, chair, and board members; be able to work independently, sometimes without budget or benchmarks; and have a background in consulting, academia, or technology. This individual should also have the full backing of the full board of directors. The ideal candidate knows how to use technology economically and has a sense of what the future holds from human, capital, and knowledge viewpoints. The bottom line is that these visionaries can determine what is important and how to distribute it to the appropriate parties when deemed necessary.

For example, Ellen Knapp of Coopers & Lybrand (now merged with Price Waterhouse) knows strategy. Prior to her promotion to the post of CKO, Knapp was vice chairman for technology—a role in which she sets strategy for internal technology at the worldwide consultancy. In the past, Knapp managed the deployment of Lotus Notes to 170,000 staffers in 142 countries. For the past year and a half, C & L has been building an intranet and Internet web site as well. Knapp's new role as keeper of content is a natural extension of her work on that infrastructure. For a professional services firm, the primary driver for technology investment is to leverage people assets.

As chief knowledge officer, Knapp retains responsibility for technology strategy and adds responsibility for education, market research, and analysis. One of her direct reports is to the company's CIO, who has operational responsibility for technology. She also oversees a director of education, a director of market research, and several partners in the organization from various lines of business, all of whom are key contributors to the content that will comprise C & L's knowledge network. Her new role focuses on utilizing that network to share knowledge internally among employees and to make money on it externally. Two initiatives demonstrate C & L's market orientation. The Tax News Network which is on its World Wide Web is both a repository of tax-related news and a discussion forum. Tax specialists in C & L's client organizations can access the site for news and commentary—not just for information but for knowledge about information. The second effort involves dismantling all the physical libraries within C & L and building a ''cyberlyb'' that clients can access via the web for a fee. In summary, a company's CKO must have a good foundation in technology; but it is also important to understand the business and its client base.

Pat Fortune, CIO at Monsanto Corporation, does not officially wear the CKO hat, but he does perform the duties of one. In addition to managing Monsanto's technical infrastructure, he oversees a knowledge management architecture that includes an internal news and information network. In addition, he chairs a knowledge management working group that focuses not only on technical details and implementation but also on issues and opportunities with respect to knowledge management across the company. Since Monsanto takes an architectural approach to knowledge management, one project involves making the information in the company's data warehouses more meaningful across business lines. Monsanto is working with data visualization (i.e., graphical representation of numbers and text is intended to help employees more easily interpret data). Another project involves departmental trials to assess whether workers are using knowledge to gain advantage. For example, is the sales force leveraging account knowledge to greater effect? For the most part, the toughest project Fortune has encountered is understanding the organization's knowledge and processes. At the simple end this involves data visualization; at the complex end, a rethinking of the role of middle management over the next 10 to 20 years.

Typically, the base of experience and connection of CKOs to the business is stronger than in the traditional CIO role. The average chief knowledge officer tends to fit more naturally in the boardroom than does the traditional CIO. The rationale is that CEOs increasingly understand that intellectual capital is the basis for competition in these fast-changing times. CEOs have the necessary confidence in their CKOs, who bring new insight to their business. Today, there is no better candidate than the CKOs who understand the business and its ever-widening infrastructure.[2]

Human Resource Principles Based on Knowledge of Organization Personnel

Over the years, many human resource principles based on information about organization personnel have come into being. In turn, this information over a long time span has produced knowledge of the HR element in a typical company. Newer HR principles take into account the evolving role of the human resource department amid massive structural and cultural changes that have impacted the business world. In an era of reengineering, restructuring, reorganizing, downsizing, rightsizing, and the like, some of the traditional ideas about work and its relationship to the HR department are quite different from the past. Hence, many of the principles set forth below have evolved recently, specifically in the past decade.

As proof of this statement, consider the first principle, which states the value of a company's "knowledge capital" is related primarily to its employees. From this view, companies today realize that the true value of their operations lie in their knowledge capital, which is hidden in employees' minds and needs to be developed over time. Today, HR has become a strategic function rather than a cost of doing business. Many older HR applications have been replaced by integrated HR packages from companies such as SAP and PeopleSoft. Such packages create large databases of employee information that save money and can help the entire company operate more effectively. In turn, this information can be turned into knowledge to assist in making the HR department a real strategic unit of a typical company.

Currently, a most important human resource principle is related to *empowering* company personnel in their everyday activities. This enlightened approach to human resources is an integral part of the TQM (total quality management) concept (refer to Chapter 8). Because people demand more from their jobs than just their paychecks, companies have found that empowering employees with broad jurisdictional powers pays large dividends to a company. Employees enjoy greater job satisfaction since they have a greater, or even a final, say so over their activities. From this enlightened view, companies have finally recognized that people are their most important asset. Typically, companies have always talked about their core business, but people were not discussed as part of that core business. Now, the empowerment of people is considered to be a strategic part of a successful company.

An integral part of empowering employees involves a related principle that fosters employee creativity on the job. The proverbial "If it ain't broke, don't fix it" attitude of managers needs to be replaced with a more positive and proactive one that encourages employees to provide ideas and suggestions without risking their jobs. Creativity need not and should not be confined to the corporate planning, marketing, and product development departments. Rather, company personnel in inventory and operations need to be creative as well. For a company to live up to its potential, it needs to tap into every employee's creativity. Typically, current employees already have the knowledge they need to act on new ideas. In addition, they understand which procedures work and which do not, and they know how to blend in creative new approaches.

Another important HR principle relates to upgrading employee service to bolster a company's overall productivity. Clearly, the need is great for the HR deparment to provide a measurable, quality employee service product that creates and enhances value for the company over time. In this way, employees feel that they are a most important part of a company. Organizational value is at the core of a company's effort. Companies are aligning with corporate goals, taking the long-term view, lowering costs, improving service, and raising employee morale. Yet they are also building in a level of flexibility that allows them to change whenever and however necessary. They are delivering value to the company's employees that is perceived by employees as focusing on them rather than on just the company.

To enhance a quality employee program, consideration should be given to training needs. In the past, computer-based training (CBT) centered on delivering training to employees on their PCs via floppy disks or CD-ROM. Today, this approach has been broadened to include web-based training (WBT), also called on-line training. In large, highly dispersed companies, such as General Motors, WBT—specifically, educational applications that integrate hyperlinked text and graphics with interactive testing, feedback forums, and other functions—promises to make training accessible to employees who have not previously had access to company courses or who have had to travel long distances just to participate. In addition, web-based training utilizes updates from a central location that are immediately available to everyone on the intranet. Most important, WBT is flexible. Employees can access it from their desktops or by dialing into the company's intranet. They may want to undergo intensive training or spend an hour refreshing particular skills or track down an immediate answer to questions that arise throughout the business day.

To assist in assessing HR activities in terms of the value received for cost incurred, HR managers are benchmarking their activities against other companies in similiar and dissimilar businesses to determine HR's effectiveness. In the past, a lot of the human resource work that was performed had been undertaken from a defensive or a reactive standpoint. When there was a HR problem, it was somehow rectified. But the whole area has changed, and the HR department is now being required to add value. Problems are being handled before they arise from a proactive viewpoint. Effective benchmarking is an ongoing process, since change is a way of life in American industry today. The more a company learns about change and the more it is willing to listen to others, the better equipped the company will be to make moves that will enable its HR department to excel in its everyday operations.

Another important HR principle which also applies to any functional area of a company is that knowledge is not constant and does change over time. Basically, knowledge makes itself obsolete over time. Today's so-called advanced knowledge may prove to be worthless tomorrow. Knowledge that is subjected to abrupt technological shifts tends to change within a short time frame. In the computer industry, the abrupt shift from PC-based internal computer networks to external ones based on the Internet and the World Wide Web is a good example of changing knowledge. What an effective manager needs to know about the utilization of computers seems to change overnight due to the increasing capabilities of computer networks.

Related to this principle is the growing realization by business that an important advantage of developed countries like the United States and Japan is the vast number of knowledge workers. Knowledge workers, unlike their blue-collar counterparts, carry their knowledge in their heads and, consequently, can take it with them. As a result, an increasing number of these people identify themselves by their own knowledge rather than by the organization for whom they work. From this viewpoint, knowledge workers are not being managed in the traditional sense. In fact, in many cases, they will not be employees of the organizations for which they work but rather contractors, experts, consultants, joint-venture partners, and the like.

In terms of the last HR principle set forth, HR managers must be adaptable to the ever-increasing international issues confronting them. Basically, competition and technology are causing businesses to think globally and to act locally. Companies that recruit on a global basis are cultivating a work force that is better prepared to deal with globalization requirements. In this era of going global, HR departments must make certain that employees are prepared to handle the demands of globalization. Globalization places numerous demands on HR departments. HR managers need to be flexible, to anticipate change, and to be able to evaluate different employees and practices that span organizations, cultures, languages, and countries. For example, an HR policy on annual reviews of employee performance in the United States may not be acceptable in another country because of cultural or legal differences. All in all, a "one size fits all" HR approach does not work well in today's world.

The above HR principles are summarized in Figure 10-1. Essentially, they are based on recent knowledge of organization personnel.

IMPORTANT FACTORS THAT ARE HELPFUL IN DISCOVERING HUMAN RESOURCE KNOWLEDGE

Important factors relevant to the HR function within an effective KMS environment go beyond its own basic structure. For example, production planning and execution require the proper placement of factory personnel to effect the desired level of output. Shipment of finished goods inventory considers the number of warehouse personnel handling customer orders. Also, payroll master data provides a starting point in terms of present personnel cost. An effective HR system, then, must relate to other functional areas in order to provide the necessary human resources for accomplishing organizational objectives.

Because the HR function is all-encompassing, companies need to expand their managerial decision-making processes. Not only is it necessary to develop short- to long-range plans in this area but it is also extremely important to mesh these plans with other systems encompassing marketing, manufacturing, finance, and other related operations. Competition and technical innovations portend far more

Figure 10-1
Human Resource Principles Based on Knowledge of Organization Personnel

- The true value of a typical company lies in its "knowledge capital." From an enlightened view, the HR function is now seen as a strategic unit of a typical company rather than just a cost of doing business.
- Companies have found that empowering their employees with broad jurisdictional powers over their work and the environment in which they operate makes the company more successful.
- The need to encourage employee creativity that centers on developing ideas and suggestions for furthering a company's objectives is paramount if a company is to live up to its full potential.
- The need is great for the company's HR department to provide a measurable, quality employee service program that creates and enhances the value of its employees. A well served employee will help to bolster a company's overall productivity.
- Web-based training provides a flexible means for employees to undergo intensive training in a specialized area or to engage in some type of refresher course to maintain current skills.
- The use of benchmarking helps an HR department to measure its effectiveness. The more a company learns about change and the more it is willing to listen to others, the better equipped the company will be to make appropriate changes in its HR function.
- Knowledge about personnel or other areas in a company is not constant and does change over time. Knowledge that is subject to abrupt technological shifts tends to change within a short time frame.
- Because knowledge workers carry their knowledge in their heads, they can take it with them if they leave an organization. They tend to identify more with their profession than the organization for which they work.
- Today, HR managers must think globally and act locally to be effective. They need be to be flexible and anticipate change as well as be able to evaluate different employees and practices that span the globe.

than new packaging, engineering, or merchandising programs. The "people element" is indispensable to the typical company. Personnel executives and their staffs must display a high level of analytical ability based on relevant information and knowledge to provide useful solutions for a wide range of people problems confronting them. To assist in the development of knowledge management systems and the discovery of knowledge underlying them, the following important factors are explored: (1) problem finding in discovering human resource knowledge, (2) finding human resources on the Internet, (3) the role of human resources in reengineering, (4) utilization of human resource management systems and other models, and (5) software useful in discovering human resource knowledge.

Problem Finding in Discovering Human Resource Knowledge

The human resource function in a typical organization is called upon to assist senior management and its corporate planning staff in ways that result in more effective use of both human resources and the capabilities of the personnel system. This enlarged perspective means that the personnel decision process must change from problem solving to problem finding. Hence, there is a need to expand on this approach to provide for the impact of human factors on organizational success and productivity. This realization leads to bringing human resource specialists into corporate planning. Once admitted, these specialists begin to shift administration's orientation from *reactive* administration to *proactive* management and planning. The organization and its human resources department begin to think in terms of projected labor needs, five-year hiring plans, anticipatory talent development, employee recycling, productive task distribution, and cost accountability.

Since these issues have for the most part not been seriously contemplated before, the typical organization finds that it has neither the collected data nor the analytical capability to tackle them and so has turned, in many cases, to outside consultants for assistance. The consultants, in turn, have developed tools to create the forecasts and models that clients are requesting. Only recently have some of these tools begun to appear as software for human resource management systems (HRMSs).

The message should be clear. The real value of a human resource planning system is not after-the-fact analysis but anticipatory capability. The critical need is to solve problems before they arise. The human resources system within a KMS environment, then, must be increasingly aware of the signficance of the organization's human resources today and tomorrow. It must review the efficient use of existing personnel at present and future levels of development, assess the level of present and anticipated performance of company employees, and concern itself with the enhancement of the individual's skills and talents currently and in the future in order to improve productivity and overall contribution of the work force.

From this perspective, top management must change its thinking about the company and its employees. Too often, seeking short-term gains is the accepted practice in American business as well as politics. Typically, these short-term gains result in reduced head count. What happens to jobs that have been simplified, automated, and eliminated? The layoffs in the automotive and computer industries are examples of job functions that have been lost. In prior recessions, when the business climate improved, laid-off employees were brought back. This is certainly not true today. Their job functions have been automated (i.e., eliminated). These previous company employees are structurally unemployed. Those who have reaped the benefits of automation are responsible for those who suffer as a result of automation. This structural unemployment is the hidden cost of automation that business and politics must face. What should have been done?

Companies should have had in place an educational plan for the year 2000 and beyond. Top management needs to define what job skills will be required in five to 10 years, then train and educate the work force to fill those jobs as needed. Future job skill needs require long-range HR strategic planning. Failing to manage change today means that the typical company will not be able to react to change at the appropriate times tomorrow.

Finding Human Resources on the Internet

The Internet is the latest means by which job applicants and notices for jobs can find each other. Several software providers are using the Internet to offer this type of service to corporate HR departments. Essentially, companies, academic institutions, government entities, professional associations, or individuals use an outward-bound access to services and servers run by these software providers. For example, IntelliMatch provides a worldwide multiple-listing service for jobs and job seekers. It also enables individuals to file résumés in a set format on a World Wide Web site that employers can download for a fee. The prescribed format helps prescreen applicant qualifications. Currently, IntelliMatch offers software for employers to access its database via the Internet and use the company's search engine to find candidates with certain skills. Employers pay only for contacts with the skills that match their needs.

Additionally, this new direction in hiring employees involves HR's participation in intracompany on-line initiatives. More and more companies recognize not only the potential of providing a web presence to the outside world via their home pages that post job openings but also the usefulness of implementing an internal web for posting information, handling routine and administrative transactions, and facilitating companywide communication. When an organization decides to become involved in the Internet and the World Wide Web, it takes a proactive stance in furnishing information to an external or internal audience.

The Role of Human Resources in Reengineering

Historically, human resources has been an unlikely place to invest significant time and dollars. Although the HR function has been relegated to the bottom of most IT projects, more companies are reengineering their personnel processes. Instead of simply counting heads and administering personnel rules, HR professionals are intimately involved in the strategic side of their businesses. Companies recognize that their biggest asset is people, and they are finding ways to best manage and utilize this asset. This means that many companies are replacing first- or second-generation HR packages. From an overall perspective, reengineering of human resouces centers on improvements in hiring, training, placement, and tracking of employees. The end result should be better employees in the right jobs, reduced turnover, and greater efficiency of a company's operations.

In a typical HR reengineering undertaking, two things tend to happen. First, reengineering changes jobs that incumbents are not ready to have changed, either because they are not trained to handle the new job requirements or simply because the old familiar ways are more comfortable. Backsliding into old processes is a common pitfall of reengineering. This necessitates continuing communications and training to prevent this from happening. Second, a changed process turns out to be no improvement at all, but rather a focus on automation by itself at the expense of quality or other desired company values. A system that takes the human element out of service-providing functions, such as an automated telephone system that asks callers to push 1 for this, push 2 for that, and so forth, can backfire in many companies.

To help overcome these barriers to successful reengineering, there is a need for HR professionals to plan for technological change that will remake jobs far beyond the work of job redesign and systems implementation. Not only must the new requirements of a changed job be clearly defined and spelled out, but the HR professionals must also take this planning several steps further. More specifically, which current employees have the skills and talents needed to perform successfully in these redesigned jobs? What training will they need? What are their new measures of successful performance? Are the existing compensation plans adequate? How can these employees be motivated in these changed jobs and kept motivated to use the new technology? And just as important, is this change really an improvement or just a way to do things faster and with less human intervention?

Advanced planning for new technology must consider the appropriateness of any given technology for the tasks to be performed. The major issue of the right system goes beyond technical considerations. The technical issues can be addressed by client/server, enterprise applications and networked systems that place the various types of computer operations on the appropriate hardware and in the right hands. Currently, it is technically feasible to put data administration on the host server, applications on middleware or PCs, and user presentation and local processing on desktop PCs.

Going beyond these technical considerations are questions of functional appropriateness that are crucial to the success of the new technology. From this perspective, an effective approach to HR system implementation is one that focuses on the ''vision'' of the new technology to achieve specific bottom line results. Technology planners who begin from the CEO's perspective—that is, what will be the total cost of the new technology and what benefits can be expected from its implementation—are in the best position to make the right choices when selecting new technology and are most likely to succeed in keeping the implementation project right on track. Thus, proper HR technology planning begins with a business-based mission that is sharply focused on identifiable returns to corporate profitability rather than high-tech solutions to problems of lower magnitude.

Utilization of Human Resource Management Systems and Other Models

A starting point for software useful in discovering HR knowledge is a human resource management system (HRMS). HRMS software fits the needs of most companies and operates on a variety of hardware and networking environments. It is somewhat inexpensive, relatively easy to install, and pays for itself in terms of time saved and penalties avoided. These systems have staked out a vital claim in the structure of strategic planning. Human resource management systems can be used in a variety of ways to meet internal and external needs. They can track such information as skills, prior employment, and training courses to aid in career path planning. They can be used for recruiting, training, and educating employees. They can track and administer employee benefits and monitor absences.

A most important element related to human resource management systems is the planning for human resources, commonly referred to as manpower planning. Human resources planning is greatly needed because of the decreasing supply of high-talent personnel. The Research Institute of America has stated that managers will be the most urgent personnel need for the future but will also be the most critically scarce resource. As a result, planning must be aimed toward management development. Not only will managers be in short supply but so will personnel with high levels of technical knowledge. This latter shortage is due to rapid technological change. It is difficult for even a qualified professional to keep abreast of any field, a fact that may cause obsolescence of technical manpower. The increasing shortage of management and technical personnel, together with their high cost, has also forced companies to recognize that manpower itself must be considered a resource as important as other corporate resources. To assist in the forecasting process, personnel models are useful for manipulating available human resource data by using mathematical and statistical models and are related to data mining software. They provide a simplified and logical view of the levels and flows of personnel throughout an organization. They focus on variables considered by managers to be significant and examine assumptions or parameters underlying system behavior.

The role of the HRMS has expanded to include the full range of human resource functions. One way to justify the investment in HRMS software is to identify the benefits and the costs in each of the areas set forth as follows: human resources planning, salary planning, pension planning, benefits administration, career planning, management development, training, equal employment opportunities, applicant tracking, recruitment, skills inventories, time and attendance, and employee directory. Other important areas are: payroll, productivity programs, employee communications, job postings, labor relations, performance evaluation, flexible benefits, and postemployment services. Another way to justify the cost of this software is to focus on its role in performing key functions of greatest concern to top management, such as planning and implementing strategic changes as well as employee benefits administration. A cost-benefit analysis will indicate typically that investing in HRMS software is a wise move for a company where HRMS implementations have been on client/server platforms. Client/server systems are less procedure bound and help companies migrate to process-oriented approaches.

The data and information supplied by a human resource management system can be used for a number of mathematical and statistical models. These include the utilization of mathematical models such as linear programming (LP) and simulation for manpower management. The LP model can be used to analyze personnel policy combinations in terms of their appropriateness for maintaining a steady flow of people into, through, and out of an organization. Simulation is useful in problem solving. It can simulate a manpower planning process that sets up a predictive model of internal manpower supply, utilizes forecasts of external supply of manpower and external demand for a company's services, and, most importantly, evaluates two different policies of the manpower management process—internal promotion or possible demotion and external recruiting. In addition, Markov chains can be used to predict the flow of personnel into and out of a company over a number of years to determine how many people should be hired at what levels over that time period.

Another approach to HR management centers around the employment of expert systems to manage legal compliance in human resource matters. The use of automated expert system tools can increase HR's management productivity and bring a measure of control and predictability to the organization as a whole by implementing consistent and repeatable processes to assure legal compliance. These processes meet the objectives of better managing legal administrative tasks, reducing financial exposure, and keeping costs in check. Most important, they enable executives to run their HR organizations more effectively and take a more strategic role in managing the company business as a whole.

As discussed throughout the text, on-line analytical processing is a useful tool for managers at all levels. An OLAP approach is a natural tie-in with a human resource management system due to the vast amount of data and information stored therein. An OLAP system supports modeling business problems and analyzing business data and information along multiple dimensions. An example in the HR area is the analysis of EEO (Equal Employment Opportunity) data according to employee attributes. The capability of HR managers to utilize multidimensional analysis with OLAP technology is related to part of their need for ad hoc reporting.

Software Useful in Discovering Human Resource Knowledge

Due to the vast capabilities of a human resource management system to store HR data and information, it is a logical candidate for the utilization of data mining software. This type of software can get at the underlying issues confronting HR personnel today. In fact, discovering HR knowledge can be helpful in setting a strategic direction for handling important personnel issues of the day. For example, uncovering present-day knowledge about personnel productivity can go a long way toward reducing union-management conflicts. The ability to lay bare the essential facts using data mining software can help both sides in an objective evaluation as opposed to the present mode of a subjective evaluation. Similarly, knowledge about advanced computer technology in pruning management layers, cutting costs, decentralizing decision making, encouraging a team environment, and even improving internal communications can be beneficial to both management and union members.

A typical data mining tool that has been applied to human resources is the DataMind Professional Edition. As part of an effort to provide a more customer centric attitude, the customer support organization of ADP decided to analyze support call data. This analysis helps them identify ways to improve their service and better understand their customers. Using the DataMind software, ADP found some interesting and useful information buried within the database. An important finding was that personnel seniority was not a significant indicator in determining a successful call. This finding plus others will help ADP build an organization that delivers on the corporate objective of putting the customer first. Prior to the DataMind Professional Edition, ADP was using statistical techniques to determine metrics within the customer support organization. By design, these tools were cumbersome when analyzing support data and information. Instead of providing an intuitive means to build the model and deploy prediction, many of these packages had techniques that were not integrated. The user, therefore, had to perform several analyzes and then analyze the collective results. On the other hand, DataMind Professional Edition provides one package that makes model building and prediction seamless and intuitive. In a later section of this chapter, a more detailed application of another software package, namely, KnowledgeSEEKER, will demonstrate its use in the human resource area.

Knowledge about human resources, including other areas, can also be provided for a typical company by outside consultants. For example, by leveraging its professional knowledge, KPMG Peat Marwick LLP (now merged with Ernst and Young) has captured a leadership position by providing services that focus on four key functional areas—human resources, financial administration, tax compliance, and internal audit. The firm's Business Process Solution provides a broad menu of process management services, ranging from strategic counseling on how a company can get the most out of its people and processes to day-to-day management and performance of those people and processes. In certain cases, outsourcing certain business processes to an external provider like KPMG, which has world-class strength in these areas, allows customers to focus their resources, capital, and talent on their core competencies. The consulting firm's research indicates that corporate executives increasingly view business process outsourcing as a strategic tool that will allow them to run their businesses more competitively, efficiently, and cost effectively.

KNOWLEDGE MANAGEMENT SYSTEMS IN HUMAN RESOURCES

As in other functional areas of a typical company, a broad-based view of human resources is necessary if this functional area is to reach its full potential. Similarly, this expanded view must take into account the preceding HR principles and important factors for discovering knowledge before the proper management of knowledge can take place. As discussed previously, HR departments are rapidly being transformed into centers for creating and delivering enterprise-wide value. Global requirements, process redesign, and new technology are blending together in a way that is driving this new direction. Companies are realizing the value of knowledge capital and using HR as a *strategic* function rather than looking upon HR departments as an added cost of doing business. This strategic HR philosophy that is found in a KMS environment can be disseminated to company personnel and refined over time by utilizing company intranets and the Internet.

To assist managers in acting in a more strategic manner, knowledge management systems can provide specific knowledge about employee-related issues. For example, because managers must control labor costs and motivate employees to improve customer service and, at the same time, search out new and better ways of doing both, these strategic objectives may necessitate going outside the firm for a conclusive answer (i.e., benchmarking). These objectives must take into account a shrinking head count and a global environment in which employees are more culturally diverse and located throughout the world. This level of complexity demands more sophisticated solutions that go beyond simply improving the management of routine employee activities. Essentially, company managers need to exploit appropriate strategies based on current knowledge from within and outside organization to better manage their human resources. Such an approach will be found in this second half of the chapter, which focuses on the application of human resource knowledge within a KMS operating mode.

Areas That Lend Themselves to Discovering Human Resource Knowledge

Essentially, the knowledge management systems and the discovery of knowledge contained in these systems that have been demonstrated in previous chapters are complementary to those presented in this chapter for human resources. Typical issues explored in this chapter that lend themselves to knowledge management include personnel selection and development and wage and salary administration. Additionally, the training of new managers for a company's various functional areas could include the utilization of specific knowledge for their use on the job. Other natural applications for knowledge management revolve around long-range human resource planning, where the focus is on getting a grasp on the company's changing work force. A typical company could, for example, be moving in the direction of more specialized technical products and services that require a higher level of basic skills. A thorough analysis of the company's future human resource requirements would be helpful in deciding whether the present work force can be retrained or whether it will be necessary to go outside to recruit a different type of technically qualified personnel. Overall, there are a number of human resource areas that lend themselves to knowledge management and the discovery of this knowledge which, in the final analysis, can assist a typical manager in better understanding the interworkings of the human element.

PERSONNEL SELECTION AND DEVELOPMENT

The personnel selection and development system for either a typical manufacturing-oriented or service-oriented company centers around the recruitment, screening, and selection of employees before and throughout their employment. In turn, these employees need to undergo periodic training in order to ensure that a company's changing needs are met. The discussion below focuses initially on forecasting human resources, followed by solving human resource problems before they arise, using an HRMS to discover human resource knowledge and using a company's intranet to distribute HR knowledge. It should be noted that appropriate human resources information and knowledge can be passed on to the corporate planning staff for short- to long-range strategic planning. Although multidimensional analysis can be used to measure personnel cost savings, productivity, analysis of lower turnover and complaints within an OLAP operating mode, a knowledge management system goes a step further by getting a handle on important HR knowledge to further management objectives and goals.

Forecasting Human Resources

An integral part of a personnel selection and development system is forecasting future personnel needs. A work force simulator, for example, can be employed to determine personnel information under varying future conditions. The work force simulator is a broad-based planning model that takes into account the interaction of different work force factors. As a starting point, data about the current plant-level work force—age, work classification, experience, education level, and comparable data—are accessed from the corporate database. A decision concerning a mandatory retirement age is normally included. Also, an estimate of attrition due to reasons other than retirement is set forth. Factors for recruiting new personnel for growth are added and provisions are made for internal transfers of employees because of promotion or retraining. The work force simulation model therefore considers increasing and/or decreasing job levels over time, such as a one-year on up to a five-year span. Based on these factors—which can be simulated for one plant, several plants, or the entire company—the results can be graphed and reviewed for comparison over varying time periods.

In the example shown in Figure 10-2, a company is contemplating a fourth factory in the second year, with an increase in employees over the first year (for three plants) of approximately 20 percent. Additionally, net increases in employment are expected to be over 10 percent in the third, fourth, and fifth years. The job classifications used in the illustration are: (1) senior engineers, (2) junior engineers, (3) production planning and control personnel, (4) department foremen, (5) engineering assistants, (6) tool and die makers, (7) machinists, and (8) assembly workers. Over the five-year period, increases in the eight engineering and manufacturing job types are shown in this multidimensional analysis. Hence, the current or base year can be compared to succeeding years, indicating the need for additional personnel in the coming years. Although not shown in Figure 10–2, answers to ad hoc questions based upon different personnel policies of hiring can be answered. For example, the actual number of trained employees would be lower than that required for untrained employees. The net effect of this work force simulator model is that it allows a hypothetical test of different personnel policies for review. This approach to human resource forecasting in an OLAP environment provides human resource managers with short- to long-range personnel information. In turn, this information provides the necessary raw material for developing a broader knowledge base to determine appropriate HR levels.

In a manufacturing plant, for example, there is a need for a system that assists manufacturing plant managers and supervisors in matching current employees to job openings. An intracompany approach using a company's intranet could be employed. Or if one or more job openings go unfilled for two weeks or more, then plant management could interrogate the plant database in order to screen possible applicants. If none are available within the requesting plant, the databases at other plants can be interrogated. In either case, an on-line computer comparison can be made on the prospective applicants. The output—the job applicant review profile—becomes the basis for discussion by plant management of a possible transfer of one or more employees. On the other hand, if no one is available internally, or if the available personnel are not interested, it is generally necessary to go outside to recruit the appropriate factory personnel. As discussed previously, the Internet could also be used to recruit the desired personnel. This access capability can be extremely helpful to plant management for high-skill jobs.

The foregoing procedures for matching employees (current and prospective) to job openings is very responsive to the task of meeting the newer skills required in a changing manufacturing environment. Throughout the process, plant management brings certain personal parameters (intuition, past experience, and judgment) to the process of matching employees to jobs. They have the total freedom and flexibility to accept or reject the employees under consideration.

Figure 10-2
Forecasted Personnel Needs for a Typical Company over a Five-Year Period

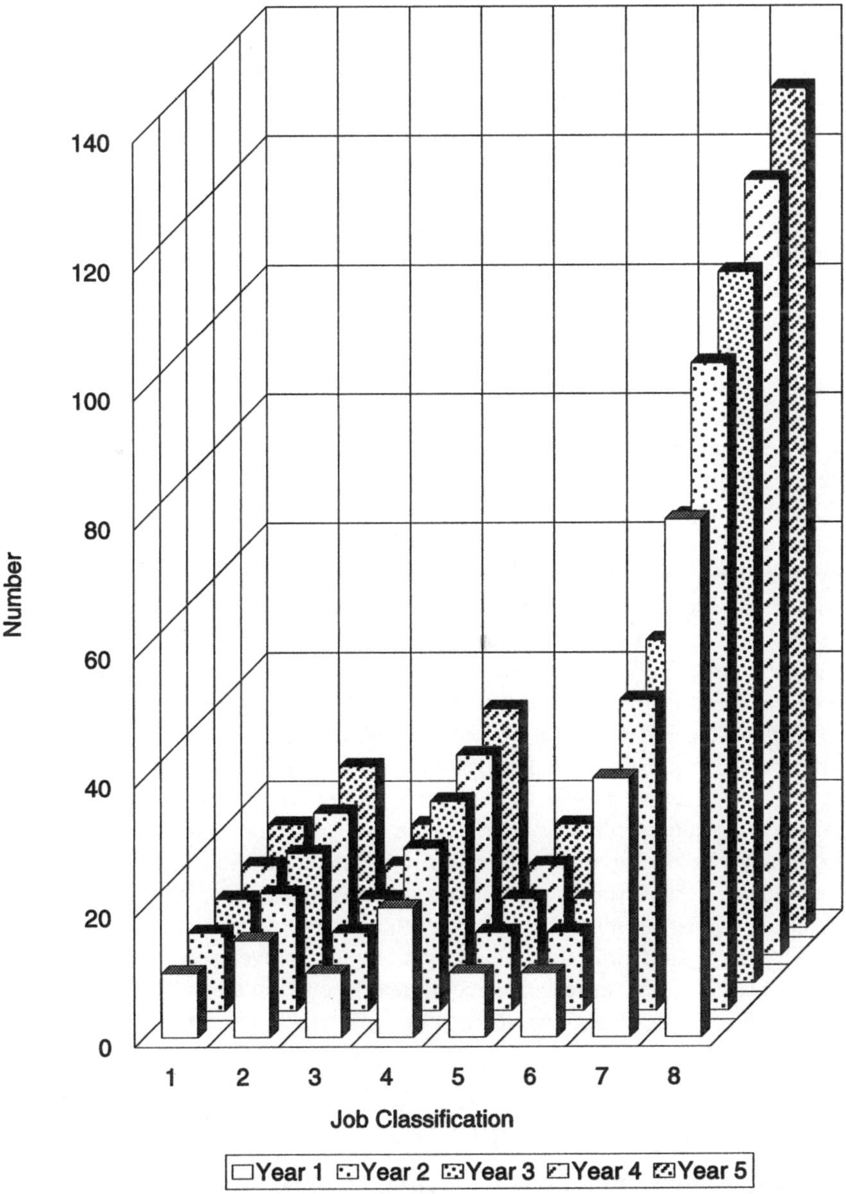

With this view, the individual's subjective feelings are integrated with the objective findings via the job search program.

Solving Human Resource Problems Before They Arise

An integral part of the human resource function is determining employee problems before they arise. These problems can take many forms. For example, they can center on downsizing. This restructing in most companies has left human resources with a smaller work force and yet with equal or greater responsibilities and new demands. Time has become as crucial a resource as talent and money. Human resources management, then, must review its own work so that problems are anticipated before they arise. Typically, areas to be investigated now revolve around the following: What work must continue to be done? Of that work, which can be done better by searching out efficiencies and economies of scale? Which can be done better by delegating and collaborating with line managers and employees or other functional staffs? Which would most benefit from creative time, talent, and resources? In essence, how can the problems of working harder, smarter, or with more vision be resolved now? Needless to say, training is a major player in solving these problems.

When searching out efficiences and economies of scale, company managers, assisted by those in human resource management, could advocate streamlining the processing of employee records, payroll, and benefits by standardizing and eliminating unnecessary paper handling and reporting. This can be accomplished by utilizing a human resource management system. In this manner, an HRMS could allow a company to be a low-cost provider for critical administrative work as well as a more accurate and timely provider of HR information. To improve delegating and collaborating with line managers and employees, human resources can collaborate with line managers or others to become more responsive to their needs. For example, HR could replace a merit pay process requiring product line managers to follow an imposed standard set of guidelines with a system encouraging human resource and line managers to customize pay increase plans jointly for their units. While HR contributes the incentive design expertise, line managers contribute their hands-on understanding of customer demands and the rewards that would best motivate employees to achieve those demands. Under an innovation strategy, human resources could allocate 10 to 15 percent of staff time to exploratory work to discover new HR knowledge. From this view, human resources could reach new customers by providing expertise to other organizations, thereby making human resources a profit center for its KMS activities.

Using a HRMS to Discover Human Resource Knowledge

The human resource system of a typical company must be able to answer pertinent management questions as they arise. By using an HRMS in an OLAP operating mode, such questions are answerable with the assistance of three-dimensional analysis, if applicable. For example, What is the cost of laying off a shift in a particular plant? The HRMS system is able to provide an answer on the basis of the labor contract. The other parts of the HRMS answer questions that relate to the rules—that is, the policies, contracts, and federal regulations that govern the way people within the company can do things. When these rules are incorporated into the system, appropriate questions posed by managers to make personnel more effective can be answered and decisions administered properly. If the company has a policy of hiring only people with a particular background at a certain level, for example, management needs to have its HRMS system enforce this. From this perspective, the HRMS serves top-level managers as well as the HR department. Additionally, the HRMS should allow company managers to produce ad hoc or special reports. The HRMS should be able to provide top-level managers with an answer to a question such as this: If a 5 percent increase were given to all salaried personnel employed by the company for over five years, a 7 percent increase given to all employees with over eight years of service, and a 4 percent increase to nonsalaried personnel, what do salaries look like for the coming year and the following two years (i.e., over three years)?

Today, however, there is a need to go one step further by using the data and information contained in a human resource management system to discover general and in-depth knowledge about the ins and outs of a company's human resources. From a general view, knowledge that is helpful in assisting a company find a good fit among the employee, the task, and the organizational unit will go a long way toward motivating an employee who is on a certain career path. On the other hand, in-depth HR knowledge could assist managers in improving employee productivity throughout the organization. In-depth HR knowledge derived from a company's own HRMS and that found in its industry (and possibly related industries) is helpful in developing complete fringe benefits options so that desirable employees can be retained. By contrast, managers tend to miss important relationships that lie buried in the mounds of detail found in a typical human resource management system.

Using a Company's Intranet to Distribute HR Knowledge

Currently, some company training departments, venturing onto the corporate web (i.e., the company's intranet), are finding compelling financial reasons for doing so. Silicon Graphics, Inc., for example, is reducing the cost of training its sales staff on workstation products by an estimated $150 per person. Sun Microsystem, Inc. anticipates saving over $2,000 each time it can refer a salesperson or system engineer to an intranet-based training course rather than flying them to headquarters for live instruction. In a similar manner, the consulting organization, Ernst & Young LLP uses an intranet-based training model and, in the process, has empowered its users with the ability to craft the learning experience themselves. The training department has created an interactive continuous learning site where people from a particular community of practice can share their insights on what is happening in their industry. The training group helps shape the discussions, asks questions to get the conversations going, and adds collateral material to the site. The end result is that people are given a much better feeling for the issues companies are facing in the industries they serve.[3]

Underlying this training department approach using a company's intranet is the acquisition of new knowledge by managers and their staffs. Learning is at the heart of a company's ability to utilize this knowledge in order to adapt to a rapidly changing environment. It is the key to being able to identify opportunities that others might not see and to exploit those opportunities rapidly and fully. To be more effective, a company has to learn better than its competition and apply that knowledge throughout its businesses faster and more widely than competitors do. In essence, managers who are accountable for making a profit should also be involved in creating and distributing HR knowledge that the company can use to make a profit.

To illustrate, British Petroleum (BP), which is a flat and lean corporation, has some 90 business units that span the globe. There is nobody between the general managers of the business units and the group of nine operating executives who oversee the businesses with John Browne, BP's chief executive. The way Browne sees it, the people in the business units—those closest to BP's assets and customers—should run their businesses. From this view, the value that can be derived from sharing knowledge, not geographical location, should drive the interactions among the business units, which is why Browne deems BP's virtual team network to be so important. The aim of this computer network is to allow people to work cooperatively and share knowledge quickly and easily regardless of time, distance, and organizational boundaries. In effect, no matter where knowledge comes from, the key to reaping a large return is to leverage that knowledge by replicating it throughout the organization so that each unit is not learning in isolation.[4]

WAGE AND SALARY ADMINISTRATION

Typically, wage and salary administration can take several directions since it involves working with selected information and ratios. In many companies, it centers primarily on utilizing various types of wage and salary analyses to answer "what if" questions. In other companies, it includes these analyses and delves into other human resource issues by evaluating output on the effectiveness of human resource management in controlling departmental budgets, the backup of key positions in the office and in the manufacturing plants, the amounts paid to factory production workers, the promotability of office and factory employees, the company's progress toward affirmative action, and, in general, human resource department goals and progress toward realizing them. The focus below will be on wage and salary administration issues.

Wage and Salary Analysis to Resolve a Company's Human Resource Issues

An annual wage and salary survey can be useful in making appropriate comparisons. To gain a better understanding of an annual wage and salary survey, consider the case of a typical manufacturing-oriented company. The company's HR managers could make comparisons of the industry average with its own wages and salaries paid in the various manufacturing plants for the current year. For example, using three manufacturing plants, the current yearly data could be graphed in three dimensions for the various categories of highly technical, technical, and semitechnical personnel. The resulting graph might indicate that the company is underpaying or overpaying some of its engineering and manufacturing personnel for the current year. In addition, comparable analyses could be performed over the last five years to see whether or not these patterns hold true over time. If so, action may be necessary to bring the company's engineering and manufacturing wages and salaries in line with the industry average as well as its own manufacturing plants.

Going beyond the above wage and salary analysis, many questions can be asked and answered using the same type of multidimensional analysis. For example, HR management could evaluate over a five-year period how wages and salaries in a company's plants and warehouses compare to budget, how the cost of wages and salaries compare to sales, and how one plant or warehouse ranks against other plants and/or warehouses and against the company average. Similarly, HR management may want to go a step further and utilize current knowledge from its knowledge management system to focus on present and future HR issues. The company may want to determine the impact, if any, of wage imbalances because of different costs of living for each of the plants and warehouses and to determine, given the economic conditions, the impact on employees of adjusting salaries. In addition, other personnel issues related to wage and salary administration that can be resolved center on evaluating human resources departmental goals and progress toward realizing them, plant goals and progress toward realizing them, the backup of key position in the office and the plants, and the promotability of employees. To assist in evaluating these issues, HR management needs knowledge about current wage and salary information, comparable positions and skills for plants and warehouses in different geographical areas, the current and future estimated cost of living and consumer price indices for each plant and warehouse, and the optimal wage and salary package that the company should offer its workers for certain skills and positions. Thus, a KMS operating mode can help management understand today what wage and salary administration issues they might face tomorrow and how to address them.

Wage and Salary Analysis of Pay Differentials between Males and Females

To assist in wage and salary analysis, KnowledgeSEEKER was used for Canada's Employment and Immigration Commission.[5] Drawing from information contained in the administrative records of various people across the country who had recently found jobs, the commission had information on previous job, age, educational background, gender, previous rate of pay, and the rate of pay that was eventually obtained in the position that the job applicant ultimately secured. They also had information on the type of training assistance that the job applicant obtained prior to finding the new job—for example, job-specific training, career skills training, general skills training, or no skills training at all. Commission officials were interested in learning more about the people who received training assistance and wanted to know if they got the jobs. If so, how much were they paid and did training have any obvious influence on the job search and final placement? One important issue was the pay rate of females, which was generally thought to be lower than males.

Previous analyses using standard socioeconomic analysis approaches (primarily multiple linear regression) had produced poor results. Many of the fields contained incomplete or missing information. The explanatory regression equations described only partially the effect of such factors as region of the country from which the job applicants came. On the other hand, the results of the KnowledgeSEEKER analysis were both strong and helpful to commission officials. One example is displayed in Figure 10–3(a)—the rate of pay that the job applicants received in their new employment. Overall, the 1,394 people drawn from the administrative files received an average rate of pay of $8.20 per hour. In reviewing all possible fields in the administrative database that could explain or characterize rate of pay, KnowledgeSEEKER determined that gender was the best descriptive factor. Whereas males earned on average $9.13 per hour, females earned considerably less—$6.53 on average. This provided rapid confirmation of the informal opinion about pay differentials between males and females in the organization.

By employing KnowledgeSEEKER's preview facility to examine alternative partitions, it was determined that education level was also a strong factor in explaining rate of pay. However, there was a desire to stick with the gender field in the descriptive analysis of the employment records. Given two equally strong potential classifications at any step during the construction of a decision tree, the best results are normally obtained by selecting the factor that has the strongest theoretical relationship with the criterion that is being classified. In this case, both gender and education have a strong theoretical relationship with rate of pay, but the relationship of gender is stronger theoretically since it can affect both educational level and pay level. KnowledgeSEEKER was used to carry on with the analysis of the descendent nodes that were created when it partitioned the data set on the gender field: there were 896 male records and

Figure 10-3
(a) Tree Diagram About the Hourly Rate of Pay for Females and Males Using KnowledgeSEEKER and (b) Tree Diagram About Hourly Pay in Terms of Education for Females and by Region for Males Using KnowledgeSEEKER

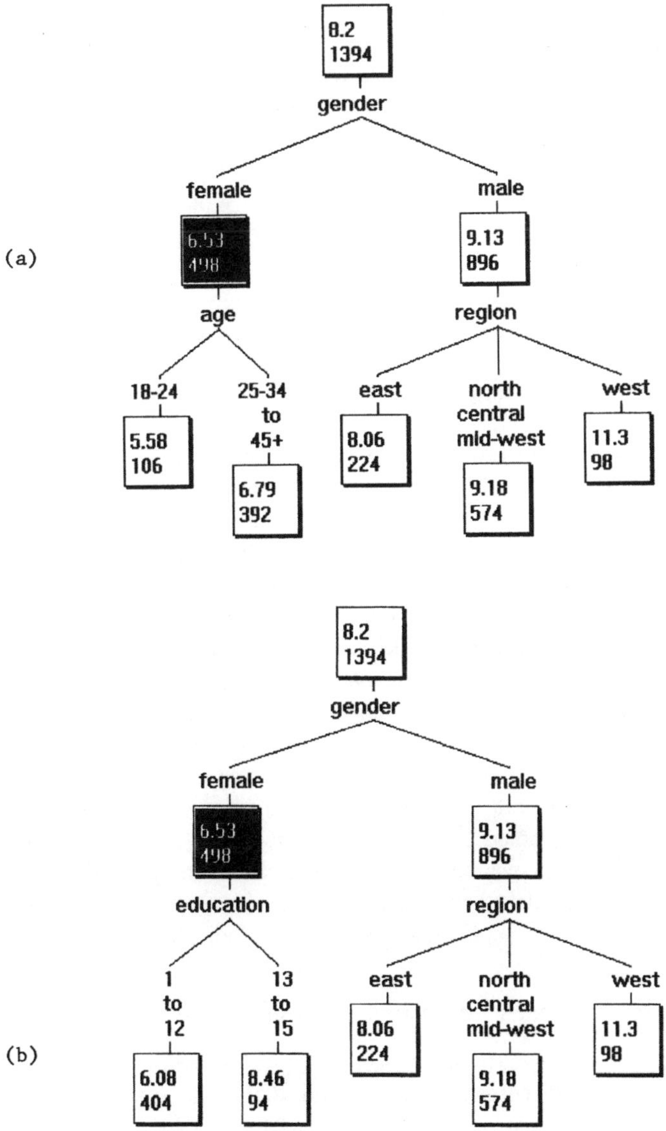

Source: Angoss Software International Limited.

498 female records. As shown in Figure 10-3(b), it turned out that region was the best way of describing variations in the rate of pay received by males. Males from the East received less on average than the other males in the file, $8.06 per hour. Those in the North Central and Midwest earned $9.18 per hour, and those from the West earned $11.30 per hour. KnowledgeSEEKER combined the Northern, Central, and Midwestern category nodes since it determined that they had essentially the same effect on male rate of pay. This determination is made on the basis of a statistical test of significance. This feature of Knowledge-SEEKER is always employed by default when the software is attempting to find the best way of characterizing variations in a parent node.

On the female side of the KnowledgeSEEKER classification tree, age turned out to be the strongest predictor of rate of pay: females in the younger (18 to 24 years of age) group earned just under $6.00 per hour. Women over 25 years of age earned more, $6.79 per hour. Clearly, however, there is a ceiling on pay rate for women, regardless of age. Could this be a sign of missing skills-upgrading opportunities for women as they get increasingly older in the work force? Most highly educated females (i.e., those with 13 to 15 years of education) have an average rate of pay of $8.46 per hour. This is well above average for the other women on the file and is about the same rate of pay as males from the eastern region.

In summary, KnowledgeSEEKER has identified an effect between sex and education: while females generally earn less than males, this is not true for highly educated females. Highly educated females earn about the same as males from the East. It is the discovery of these effects in subpopulations of the database that makes KnowledgeSEEKER so useful. In terms of personnel policy, findings such as these could lead to an organization-wide program to ensure that females have the same access to training and skills-upgrading programs as males and, if pay equity continues to be a major concern, to pursue remedial skills upgrades for particularly poorly educated and underskilled females. Of course, a complementary policy—to address pay differentials among males, particularly those in the east—would go a long way toward introducing the kind of balance in the policy program that would continue to justify employee counseling and training efforts. It should be noted that personnel policies and pay performance of the employees will change over time. The system can be run periodically to reflect the actual changes in data values and can help management to evaluate the success of organizational personnel policies on a periodic basis.

Problem-Centered Approach for Analyzing Future Wage and Salary Issues

Related to the foregoing discussion on wages and salaries is the need to bring together top managers to address important future problems that should be dealt with today. For example, the top management of a service-oriented company must make sure that the current work force is being paid appropriate wages and salaries plus fringe benefits. To facilitate this evaluation, management needs recurring reports, such as current wage and salary information for comparable positions and skills within each sales-geographical area, the estimated future cost-of-living and consumer-price indices for each sales area, and the optimal wage and salary package the company should offer its employees by certain skills or positions. In addition, ad hoc reports are needed to determine if the company paid its employees fair wages and salaries over the past several years; to determine the impact, if any, of wage imbalances because of different costs of living in each of the sales-geographical areas; and to determine, given an economic condition, what will be the impact of adjusting salaries for the employees. Ad hoc wage and salary reports tend to stop here for the short run. Typically, however, they need to be related to future labor costs over the next five years, especially if a company plans to increase its sales significantly. Under these circumstances, although an OLAP operating mode can help top management to understand and solve wage and salary problems of a short-term nature, a knowledge management system approach goes a step further by taking a longer-term view that allows the creation of longer-term intelligence and ultimately ''instinctive behavior'' about how to handle wage and salary problems and solve them. With this in mind, the discussion that follows focuses on a problem-centered approach to labor costs over the next five years by a typical top management group.

In the *generation* phase (first step of the problem-centered approach), the top management group examines the potential labor cost problems that might arise in the next five years. First, wages and salaries will undoubtedly rise due to the cost of living. Second, the sales growth of the company will affect changes in the wage and salary structure. Third, the prior item will affect the company's relations with its unions—that is, the unions will be demanding more with robust sales growth. Fourth, the impact of paying wages and salaries to new employees must be assessed. Additionally, a number of related problems need to be addressed currently by the top management group. All of the foregoing problems need to undergo a thorough *evaluation* (second step) today by the top management group to determine what future impact these problems have on maintaining profitable operations.

In the *validation* stage (third step), the top management group focuses on the company's relationship with its unions. Top management concludes that its future relationship with its various unions is the key factor in meeting its significant increase in sales goals over the next five years as well as in meeting its profitability goals. The *establishment of boundaries* (fourth step) is related to maintaining operations in this country only, since the company is not contemplating any foreign operations in the years to come.

The *solution* to this wage and salary administration problem centers on utilizing the modeling capabilities of current software but, more importantly, on knowledge discovery software. Questions can be answered for each economic situation (good, average, and bad). Typical questions center on the following:

What will be the impact of paying salaries to current employees as well as new employees entering the company? How much will the company have to pay by position and skill? What will be the wage and salary structure at each sales office as a result of new hires as well as layoffs? Answers using appropriate information and knowledge software can be obtained based on certain input parameters and assumptions that can be adjusted to accommodate changing economic conditions.

Even though *implementation* is sometime off, the top management group needs to convey the results to the corporate planning staff so that this knowledge can be an integral part of the company's strategic long-range plans. Overall, a problem-centered approach can help top management better understand future wage and salary problems that are related to the company's rapid expansion plans and its desire to improve profitability over the next five years.

UTILIZING KNOWLEDGE TO RESOLVE WORK FORCE AND FUTURE COMPANY ISSUES

Inasmuch as a company's work force today comprises a diverse group of people, it is the job of HR managers to bring together employee skills and needs within a changing organizational structure, accommodate flexible work schedules, and administer a host of programs for compensation, benefits, and training. In addition, HR has to keep track of a wide range of legislation and regulations, including EEO rules, ADA, FMLA, ERISA, COBRA, and OSHA regulations, not to mention HMOs, PPOs, and 401(k)s. At the same time, the HR department needs to move beyond personnel's administrative legacy and take on a much more strategic role in the company. In many organizations, human resource managers and information system managers are collaborating to provide information and essential knowledge about work force issues.

For example, newer HR technology has helped Holiday Inns Worldwide, whose reputation hinges on the level of service provided by its employees. Managing human resources for the Atlanta-based chain with almost 2,000 hotels in 60 countries has always been a critical task. Just recently, HR's involvement in establishing strategic direction has expanded with the growing importance of computer technology. In the past, whenever Holiday Inn looked into a new business venture, financial implications would be the first consideration. Viability from an HR perspective would not be considered until much later in the process. By that time, finance may have spent considerable time and resources looking at deals that had no chance of getting off the ground due to the lack of required personnel skills. However, that has changed. Now HR can track executives' experience and skills using newer PC-based software—HRSoft Inc. (Morristown, New Jersey). In adition, newer HR technology is also helping Holiday Inn enhance career development for its top 125 corporate executives and key operational personnel at each hotel. The HRSoft application allows the company to store a detailed resume for each executive, including work history, education, and special skills, in a customized format. A manager can query the database and get a report of all qualified candidates.[6]

Although newer computer software is and will continue to help HR managers, knowledge management, as emphasized throughout the text, has the capability to provide basic learning and the compounding of learning for HR managers. This learning process provides a basis for HR managers to create long-term intelligence and knowledge about their HR departments. It is from this view that HR management can provide new directions that link people to knowledge for improved results. For example, Parsons Brinckerhoff, which is a leading transportation engineering enterprise employing 5,000 people, provides multidisciplinary services centering on a primary market of "infrastructure." The collective expertise and technical knowledge of its professional staff is its most valuable asset. To ensure that Parsons Brinckerhoff fully leverages this asset, it has deployed knowledge management software from Fulcrum. Included in the solution are a Business Information System devoted to managing business development activities and Practice Area Networks (PANs), which provide forums for the exchange of technical information among engineers in different disciplines and geographic regions.

Parsons Brinckerhoff is an example of an organization moving away from simply collecting information relevant to its business processes in disparate "information silos." This organization is bridging these silos and exchanging information with the use of knowledge management software. For its Business Information System, Parsons Brinckerhoff uses Fulcrum's Knowledge Network to connect an Oracle database and Microsoft Exchange public folders in a single application. Marketing staff use the application to pinpoint resumes and project experience for proposals, a crucial aspect of developing the company's consulting engineering business.

In addition, the company is using knowledge management software to facilitate information exchange with its PANs. With advanced information retrieval, engineers can pinpoint relevant project information within a large knowledge base. Since the PANs use Microsoft Exchange, engineers can also take advantage of its messaging infrastructure to discuss strategies and solutions to design problems and then manage the information collected during these discussions with advanced information retrieval. Overall, the company's approach to knowledge management ensures that its customers are best served through the greater use of superior knowledge by its own employees.[7]

SUMMARY

Human resource systems for a typical company are related directly to other systems because all functional areas depend on the human element to accomplish a company's objectives and goals. For example, human resources rely heavily on the payroll function of the accounting system and information available from the manufacturing system, such as technical skills required for specific jobs and the apprenticeship requirements for a certain job level. However, despite this important level of integration, many HR activities originate from the function itself. As illustrated in this chapter, the development of an effective HRMS system needs to be integrated with knowledge discovery and storage from within and outside the human resource department so that consideration is given to changing conditions. The integration of an HRMS with a knowledge management system extends the capabilities of both systems. It should be noted that all of the newer information and knowledge technology in the human resource area and other functional areas of a typical company cannot replace a sharp person who understands how to use the technology and is good at problem finding and problem solving. This probing and proactive approach to knowledge discovery, complemented by knowledge management systems, is an important way for a company to beat or, at least, meet the competition today and tomorrow.

NOTES

1. Laura B. Smith, ''The Thinkers,'' *PC Week Executive*, August 5, 1996, pp. E1 and E4.

2. Ibid.

3. Beth Shultz, ''Brain Power,'' *Intranet*, December 1996, pp. 42–45.

4. Steven E. Prokesch, ''Understanding the Power of Learning: An Interview with British Petroleum's John Browne,'' *Harvard Business Review*, September–October 1997, pp. 152–153.

5. Angoss Software, ''Study 3: Human Resource Policy,'' *KnowledgeSEEKER in Action* (Toronto: Angoss Software International Limited, 1996).

6. Megan Santosus, ''Human Resources Systems: Personnel Matters,'' *CIO*, May 1, 1995, pp. 46 and 48.

7. Eric Goodwin, ''The Journey Toward Knowledge Management,'' *Special Supplement to Imaging World*, October 6, 1997, pp. S4–S5.

Selected Bibliography

Angoss Software. *KnowledgeSEEKER in Action: Case Studies*. Toronto: Angoss Software International Limited, 1996.

Applehans, W., A. Globe, and G. Laugero. *Managing Knowledge: A Practical Web-Based Approach*. Reading, MA: Addison-Wesley, 1999.

Aubrey, A., and P. M. Cohen. *Working Wisdom: Timeless Skills and Vanguard Strategies for Learning Organizations*. San Francisco: Jossey-Bass, 1996.

Badaracco, J. I., Jr. *The Knowledge Link: How Firms Compete Through Strategic Alliances*. Boston: Harvard Business School Press, 1991.

Collins, J. C., and J. I. Porras. *Built to Last: Successful Habits of Visionary Companies*. New York: HarperBusiness, 1994.

Davenport, T. H., and L. Prusak. *Information Ecology: Mastering the Information and Knowledge Environment*. New York: Oxford University Press, 1997.

———. *Working Knowledge: How Organizations Manage What They Know*. Boston: Harvard Business School Press, 1998.

Denning, P., and R. Metcalfe, eds. *Beyond Calculation: The Next Fifty Years of Computing*. New York: Copernicus, 1997.

Drucker, P. F. *Managing in a Time of Great Change*. New York: Truman Talley Books/Dutton, 1995.

Gray, P., and H. Watson. *Decision Support in the Data Warehouse*. Upper Saddle River, NJ: Prentice-Hall, 1998.

Hamit, F. *Virtual Reality and the Exploration of Cyberspace*. Carmel, IN: Sams Publishing, 1993.

Helsel, S. K., and J. P. Roth, eds. *Virtual Reality: Theory, Practice, and Promise*. Westport, CT: Meckler Publishing, 1991.

Kline, P., and B. Sanders. *Ten Steps to a Learning Organization*. Arlington, VA: Great Ocean Publishing, 1994.

Koulopoulos, T. M. *Corporate Instinct*. New York: John Wiley & Sons, 1997.

———. *Creating Corporate Instinct: Building a Knowledge Enterprise for the 21st Century*. New York: Van Nostrand Reinhold, 1997.

Leonard, D. *Wellsprings of Knowledge: Building and Sustaining the Sources of Information*. Boston: Harvard Business School Press, 1998.

Martin, J. *Cybercorp*. New York: AMACOM, 1996.

Maynard, H. B., Jr., and S. E. Mehrtens. *The Fourth Wave: Business in the 21st Century*. San Francisco: Berrett-Koehler Publishers, 1993.

Nonaka, I., and H. Takeuchi. *The Knowledge-Creating Company: How Japanese Companies Foster Creativity and Innovation for Competitive Advantage*. New York: Oxford University Press, 1995.

Nuernberger, P. *Increasing Executive Productivity: A Unique Program for Developing the Inner Skills of Vision, Leadership, and Performance*. Englewood Cliffs, NJ: Prentice-Hall, 1992.

Pimentel, K., and K. Teixeira. *Virtual Reality: Through the New Looking Glass*. New York: McGraw-Hill, 1993.

Rheingold, H. *The Virtual Community: Finding Connections in a Computerized World*. Reading, MA: Addison-Wesley, 1993.

Richardson, J. W., Jr. *Knowledge-Based Systems for General Reference Work: Applications, Problems, and Progress*. San Diego, CA: Academic Press, 1995.

Sandler, B-Z. *Computer-Aided Creativity: A Guide for Engineers, Managers, and Inventors*. New York: Van Nostrand Reinhold, 1994.

Simon, A. *Workgroup Computing: Workflow, Groupware, and Messaging*. New York: McGraw-Hill, 1996.

Thierauf, R. J. *Creative Computer Software for Strategic Thinking and Decision Making: A Guide for Senior Management and MIS Professionals*. Westport, CT: Quorum Books, 1993.

———. *Virtual Reality Systems for Business*. Westport, CT: Quorum Books, 1995.

———. *On-Line Analytical Processing Systems for Business*. Wesport, CT: Quorum Books, 1997.

Torsun, I. S. *Foundations of Intelligent Knowledge-Based Systems*. San Diego, CA: Academic Press, 1995.

Index

About the Author

ROBERT J. THIERAUF is Professor of Information Systems, Xavier University, Cincinnati, Ohio. He was formerly a staff accountant (CPA) and consultant at Coopers & Lybrand. This is his thirty-first book and thirteenth for Quorum, all on various facets of information systems and their management.

ISBN 1-56720-218-7
90000>
EAN
9 781567 202182
HARDCOVER BAR CODE